BIBLICAL
IN AFRICAN PERSPECTIVE

BIBLICAL CHRISTIANITY IN AFRICAN PERSPECTIVE

Wilbur O'Donovan Jr.

paternoster press

© Wilbur O'Donovan 1992, 1996

First published 1992 as *Introduction to Biblical Christianity from an African Perspective* by Nigeria Evangelical Fellowship, Ilorin, Kwara State, Nigeria

Second edition 1995 published by The Paternoster Press, P.O. Box 300, Carlisle, CA3 0QS, U.K.

02 01 00 99 98 97 96   7 6 5 4 3 2 1

The right of Wilbur O'Donovan to be identified as the Author of this Work has been asserted by him in accordance with the Copyright, Designs and Patents Act 1988.

All rights reserved. No part of this publication may be reproduced, stored in a retrieval system, or transmitted in any form or by any means, electronic, mechanical, photocopying, recording or otherwise, without the prior permission of the publisher or a licence permitting restricted copying.

British Library Cataloguing in Publication Data
O'Donovan, Wilbur
   Biblical Christianity in African
   Perspective. – 2Rev.ed
   I. Title
   276

      ISBN 0-85364-711-9

All scripture quotations unless otherwise indicated, are taken from the HOLY BIBLE: NEW INTERNATIONAL VERSION. Copyright 1973, 1978, 1984, International Bible Society. Used by permission of Zondervan Publishing House. All rights reserved.

Typeset by Photoprint, Torquay, Devon, U.K.
Printed by R.R. Donnelley & Sons Co., U.S.A.
for Paternoster Press

Abbreviations for Books of the Bible

Unless written out in full, books of the Bible are abbreviated as follows.

Old Testament		New Testament	
Gen.	Genesis	Matt.	Matthew
Ex.	Exodus	Rom.	Romans
Lev.	Leviticus	Cor.	Corinthians
Num.	Numbers	Gal.	Galatians
Deut.	Deuteronomy	Eph.	Ephesians
Sam.	Samuel	Phil.	Philippians
Chr.	Chronicles	Col.	Colossians
Neh.	Nehemiah	Thess.	Thessalonians
Prov.	Proverbs	Tim.	Timothy
Eccl.	Ecclesiastes	Heb.	Hebrews
Isa.	Isaiah	Pet.	Peter
Jer.	Jeremiah	Rev.	Revelation
Ezek.	Ezekiel		
Hab.	Habakkuk		
Mal.	Malachi		
Zech.	Zechariah		
Zeph.	Zephaniah		

Contents

Biblical Christianity in African Perspective

C.   The problem of syncretism: In which rituals,
ceremonies and other cultural practices may a
Christian participate?   254
D.   Who can be a mediator between God and
mankind?   258
E.   What is a Christian's responsibility to his country's
government?   259
Summary   261

15   THE CHURCH AND CULTURAL PREJUDICE   265

A.   What does the Bible say about a Christian's cultural
origin (clan, tribe, race and language)?   266
B.   What are some of the problems in the church
caused by multi-cultural membership?   268
C.   How may problems of cultural prejudice in the
church be solved?   270
D.   What is God's plan for the church in relation to
different cultures, races, and languages?   272
Summary   273

16   MARRIAGE, SEX, AND FAMILY ACCORDING
TO THE BIBLE   276

A.   What is God's plan for marriage?   277
Marriage was God's idea   277
Marriage, the first institution in human society   277
God's design for marriage   278
God's plan for unity in marriage   279
B.   What is God's plan for husbands and wives?   281
God's plan for the husband   281
God's plan for the wife   282
God's plan for the husband and wife as parents   283
C.   What is God's plan concerning sex?   283
The problem of lust   285
Love or lust?   285
D.   What is God's plan concerning the family life of
Christians?   287
E.   What is the Bible's perspective on polygamy?   288
F.   What does God say about divorce?   291
Problems in marriage   292
G.   What are some biblical guidelines for choosing a
marriage partner?   293
H.   How should a Christian couple deal with the
problem of childlessness?   294
Summary   296

Acknowledgments

There are many books on theology to be found in the libraries of Bible colleges and seminaries in Europe and North America. However, among those involved in theological education in Africa, a great need has been felt for many years for a theology textbook written in everyday English, from an African perspective. This need has been expressed by many African theologians over the past twenty years. In 1988, Dr. Yusufi Turaki, then General Secretary of the Evangelical Churches of West Africa (ECWA), expressed this need to the author. The author had been involved in theological education for many years in Nigeria. Dr. Turaki requested that the author draft a basic survey of Christian doctrine in readable English, written from an African perspective, in cooperation with African pastors and theologians. The present book is the result of that request.

The author is very grateful to Dr. Turaki for his encouragement and his patient analysis of the trial edition of this book. He is also grateful to other theologians and church leaders in Africa who are concerned about the need for contextualized theological materials. The author would like to express special thanks to Dr. Tite Tienou, Dr. Titus Kivunzi, Dr Julius Muthengi, Dr. Richard Gehman, Dr. Paul Bowers, Dr. John Gration, Dr. James Pleuddemann, Dr. Philip Steyne, Dr. Haruun Ruun, Dr. Lois Fuller, Rev. Stephen Akangbe and the late Rev. William G. Crouch, who assisted him in reviewing various parts of the present manuscript or who have offered wise counsel from their years of ministry in Africa.

A very special word of thanks is offered to Pastor Jeremiah Gado of the ECWA church, Nigeria, and to Pastor Kibii arap Maiyo of the A.I.C. Kenya, for their patient critique of the original manuscript of the trial edition of this book and for their valuable suggestions and counsel. Pastor Gado, who is currently working on his doctorate, was the former principal of the Billiri Bible College in Nigeria. Pastor Maiyo, who holds the Th.M. degree from Western Theological Seminary in Holland, Michigan, is the Academic Dean of the A.I.C. Missionary College, Eldoret, Kenya. The fellowship and encouragement of these two servants of God has been a great blessing to the author. Without their help, this book would not have been possible.

The author is also indebted to the many students and friends who shared with him the true stories and experiences related in this book. The author especially would like to thank missionary-teacher Dorothy Clark for her helpful critique of the English grammar and Michael Battermann for his practical assistance in many ways. The author deeply thanks his dedicated wife, Esther, whose constant prayers and loving support were the greatest human factor in enabling this book to be written. Above all, the author gives thanks and praise to the God of all creation, about whom the book is written and whose strength and guidance alone have enabled him to complete this work.

Wilbur O'Donovan, Jr.

Introduction

Caleb, a missionary with an indigenous African mission agency, had been assigned to church planting among traditional people in a rural village in his country. There were no Christians in the village and the village elders were not interested in the gospel. They were strong in their traditional beliefs. Some months of preaching had produced no results. Caleb prayed for a breakthrough.

That year, there was not enough rain. Crops had been planted but they were drying up with little hope of a harvest. Rain was desperately needed. Caleb saw an opportunity for the gospel and approached the village elders. He asked them if they would like him to pray to the God of the Bible for rain They were more than willing for him to pray. But Caleb put conditions on his prayer.

Would they agree that if the God of the Bible answered with rain, his word (the Bible) was the truth? Would they believe that Jesus was the one through whom prayers are answered and the only one through whom people can find forgiveness of sins, as he had been telling them? The elders agreed to Caleb's conditions.

Caleb went back to his house and began to pray. The truth of God's word and the souls of these people were at stake. Caleb spent 28 hours on his knees in prayer. Finally the Lord sent a long, heavy rain. Caleb trekked through the mud to the compound where the village elders were gathered. They were ready to listen and they were ready to believe. Very soon the believers were meeting in Caleb's house for prayer and the reading of God's word. A church was planted and it is still growing today.

This true story introduces the subject of this book and the God of the Bible. Whoever this God is, he is greater than all. To find him is to find the greatest treasure in life.

Do you know what God is really like? Perhaps you have questioned how God could be three persons and still be one God? Could you explain to someone where the Bible came from? Have you ever wondered how Christ could be tempted by sin if he was God? Where do evil spirits come from? Do you know what a Christian can do if someone places a curse on him? How would you counsel a Christian couple who are unable to bear children? What is a Christian's responsibility to his ancestors? What is the biblical way for the church to deal with polygamy? This book will address these questions and many other issues which relate to Christianity in Africa.

This book is an introduction. It provides a survey of Christian theology from a traditional African perspective in a readable and relevant form. With this goal in mind the book will discuss the basic truths of Christianity as they relate to the context of traditional African life. There will be some issues raised in these pages which will require a more thorough treatment by other theologians. It is the prayer of the author that the book may be a means of stimulating African authors to present the results of their own study in written form. There is also a need to address other important issues which are not addressed in these pages.

Although this book does not deal with every question it does make an effort to address some of the more important and more difficult issues of theology. Books are suggested at the end of each chapter for further reading. These books were especially chosen because they are easy to read or cover the subject area very well, or because they give special attention to the African context. The reader is encouraged to read one or more of these suggested books if they are available from a nearby Bible college library.

At the end of each chapter there is also a list of questions, group exercises and projects. These assignments are intended to fix the truth of that chapter in the reader's mind. They are not only a review of the chapter but a means of applying the truth to real life situations. It will be very helpful for the reader to do these exercises together with other Christians.

The church is growing rapidly in Africa. Some people think it will be the most Christian continent in the world by the year 2000 AD. Although that may be true, many African Christians still struggle with cultural questions and problems to which they have not found answers. That does not mean there are no answers. It does mean that many churches, church leaders and missionaries have failed to relate the teaching of the Bible to the special needs of those in their churches. It is the purpose of this book to answer some of those questions from the Bible.

The truth of the Bible was not intended for just one group of people because the Bible is a revelation from God to all mankind. God says, 'Turn to me and be saved, all the ends of the earth, for I am God and there is no other' (Isa. 45:22). This means that the message of the Bible is for all people of all times. But to each group of people the truth of the Bible will also seem somewhat foreign because it is a revelation from God and not from man. Since God wants all people to understand the message of his word, it is very important that the Bible makes sense to each group of people in the world.

This book is an attempt to express the truth of the Bible in terms of the African situation. It is an effort to build a Christian theology from an African perspective. In order to do this it is necessary to answer a few questions:

A. What is the meaning of world-view?
B. Is there really a traditional African world-view?
C. How do we build a theology that is biblical?
D. What problems have been encountered in the past in trying to build a theology which is both biblical and also African?
E. How can we overcome the problems of the past and build a theology which is truly biblical and also truly African?

A. WHAT IS THE MEANING OF WORLD-VIEW?

World-view means just what the word says. It is the view which a person has of his world. It is the way he understands and interprets the things which happen to him and to other people. It is a person's way of understanding life and the world in which he lives. It is a person's belief about what is real and what is not real.

Different groups of people in the world have different world-views. The way they understand and explain life would make them foreigners to each other even if they spoke the same language. The world-view that a person has depends on the group of people to which he or she belongs. It will depend on the community where he grew up and on what he learned from his family and his teachers. The world-view of a people is one key to understanding why a particular group of people act the way they do.

The Bible also has a world-view. Since the Bible is a revelation from God, the world-view of the Bible is the correct view of reality. For a person to really understand the truth of God, he must believe the world-view presented in the Bible even if that world-view has some elements contrary to his own world-view. In this book the world-view of the Bible will be presented in relation to different aspects of human experience.

B. IS THERE REALLY A TRADITIONAL AFRICAN WORLD-VIEW?

Every group of people in the world has their own world-view. This will depend on the culture that was passed down to them. From the study of different groups of people it is clear that there are some strong similarities among many traditional African groups. For many people there is a stronger sense of being African than of belonging to one country or another. What are some of these similarities?

The first common element is the emphasis on life in community with others of the same extended family and clan. Africans tend to find their identity and meaning in life through being part of their extended family, clan and tribe. There is a strong feeling of common participation in life, a common history, and a common destiny. The reality in Africa may be described with the statement: 'I am because the community is'. The feeling may be stronger in some groups than in others but it is very important throughout Africa.

A second related element has to do with the relationship between the living and those who have died. Part of belonging to the community is a person's relationship to those who have gone before. Almost all groups of traditional African people have very important beliefs about their relationships to the spirits of their ancestors.

A third common element is the viewpoint that is taken toward the spirit world and the relationship between the spirit world and the physical world. In his heart every African knows there is a God. He also believes there is a world of spirits around him. The sense of relationship between the physical world and the spirit world is strong in traditional Africa.

A fourth common element has to do with priorities in life. Africans tend to place a higher priority on people and human relationships than on technology and material things.

A fifth element common to many African people is the history of colonial rule and the later experience of independence.

A sixth common element is a holistic view of life. This means that all the parts of life fit together into one piece like the woven design of a piece of cloth. Life is not divided into separate and unrelated parts. All the parts together form a beautiful picture called life.

A seventh common element is an emphasis on the events of life more than an emphasis on schedules and time as found in Europe and North America.

There are other elements common to the African situation but these seven elements are sufficient to justify the writing of a Christian theology from a traditional African perspective.

C. HOW DO WE BUILD A THEOLOGY THAT IS BIBLICAL?

A theology that is biblical is a statement of what the Bible teaches on a particular subject as one encounters that subject in various books of the Bible. There are three steps needed to establish what the Bible teaches on a particular subject:

First, we must carefully observe all that the Bible says on that subject in all the places where the subject is mentioned in the Bible.

Second, we must determine what all these statements mean concerning that subject. This is done by analyzing each statement according to the proper rules of grammatical analysis. We must then analyze each statement in view of the historical situation in which the statement was made. Following this, we must compare the various statements in the Bible on the subject with each other, in order to understand the Bible's complete teaching on that subject. Many mistakes are made by lifting a single verse out of its context or by failing to consider how that verse relates to other verses on the same subject.

Third, we must apply the Bible's teaching on the subject to life today. If a person carefully follows these three steps he will discover the true teaching of the Bible and how God wants him to use it in his life. We will follow these three steps in this book.

D. WHAT PROBLEMS HAVE BEEN ENCOUNTERED IN THE PAST IN TRYING TO BUILD A THEOLOGY WHICH IS BOTH BIBLICAL AND ALSO AFRICAN?

A major problem in the period before 1960 was that very few efforts were made to relate Christian theology to the African context. Many Africans found that the presentation of Western issues in theology did not answer their inmost questions or solve some of the spiritual problems related to African culture. Western methods of thinking and learning were often unsuited to African ways.

As a result Christian theology was thought by many Africans to be something Western, instead of universal to all mankind, as it really is. The historical fact is that Christianity came to Africa before it came to Europe and North America. This can be seen in the story of the Ethiopian official in Acts 8:27–39. In reaction to a Western theology another problem has developed in recent years.

To counteract the failure of a Western theology, various statements have been made in the past 25 years about how to create a genuinely African Christian theology. In an effort to give serious consideration to the traditional life of Africa, some of these statements have attempted to join the elements of African traditional religions to the teachings of the Bible. This process has resulted in a mixture called syncretism. Syncretism does not result in a theology that is biblical. The word of God should not be mixed with other religious beliefs in order to arrive at the truth.

The need is not to mix the truth of the Bible with the teachings of other religions, but to state the biblical truth in ways that are true to African life and experience. In other words, theology must be truly Christian but also truly African in expression. An example of where this is already taking place would be the indigenous Christian music created by various church groups.

E. HOW CAN WE OVERCOME THE PROBLEM OF THE PAST AND BUILD A THEOLOGY WHICH IS TRULY BIBLICAL AND ALSO TRULY AFRICAN?

To overcome the problem of a Western theology and to avoid the problem of syncretism, a three-step process is suggested:

(a) First we should ask what the Bible does say on the subject.
(b) Second we should ask how African culture relates to what the Bible says on the subject. In other words, what are the actual African beliefs and practices related to this subject?
(c) Third we should ask how we can express the truth of the Bible on the subject in a way that is clearly related to African culture.

In this book we will follow the guidelines of these three questions.

To change lives, theology must be more than stated in a culturally relevant way. It must also be applied to daily life. Applying the truth of God to a local culture is called contextualization. Contextualization is badly needed in Africa today. To be most effective, the process of contextualization should include these steps:

(a) Define the cultural problem or issue which needs to be resolved.
(b) Determine what the Bible says concerning this issue.
(c) Identify what the culture says about the issue and why.
(d) Determine what cultural similarities or differences exist on the issue between the biblical situation and the local situation.
(e) Decide how you would apply what the Bible says on the issue to your culture.
(f) Determine how your people will have to change their world-view and their beliefs in order to adopt the viewpoint of God on the issue.
(g) Determine how your people will have to change their practices in order to do the will of God in the matter.
(h) Decide what you must do to help your people make the necessary changes.
(i) Decide what strategy your local church could adopt to help your people make the necessary changes to deal with the problem.

If pastors and Christian leaders would adopt these steps in their local churches, the members could experience new spiritual vitality, strength and renewal in their walk with the Lord.

1

Who and What Are We To Believe?

Awoje and Mbwani had become good friends since they came to Teachers' College. They had grown up in different parts of the country. They both grew up in families which practiced traditional religion. They had been attending a church since they came to college because some of their friends at college attended church. Today their conversation concerned some of the new ideas they had learned from their Christian friends.

Awoje: 'I have noticed that our Christian friends talk much about their faith. They seem to think that what you believe is very important.'

Mbwani: 'I have noticed that and I am confused by some of the things they say. Does it really matter what you believe? I think that what you do is more important than what you believe.'

Awoje: 'I agree with that. But why do people do what they do? Is it not because of what they believe? Take my father and my uncle. When my father gets sick he always goes to the witch-doctor and never goes to the hospital. Is it not because of my father's belief about who is causing his sickness that he goes to the witch-doctor? My uncle took medical training. When he gets sick he always goes to a hospital or a chemist. His belief about what causes his sickness and how he can be cured comes from his training.'

Mbwani: 'Perhaps you are right. I have been wondering why the Christians pay no attention to the rituals which must be performed at death. Last year when my relative died my father performed the sacrifices of goat and chickens which must be performed at the death of a relative. He also made the three day ceremonial journey to the hills to perform them even though it was the right time for planting corn. The Christians said he was wasting his time. They said he should have continued planting

7

corn. It seems to be true that what a person believes will affect his actions. But what is a person to believe if he is to be sure he is right?'

In this chapter we will seek to answer the following questions:

A. What does it mean to believe in something or someone?
B. What is truth?
C. Where can we find the truth?
D. How does what we believe affect our actions?
E. What will happen when you believe the truth and what will happen when you believe what is false?
F. Who are we to believe?

A. WHAT DOES IT MEAN TO BELIEVE IN SOMETHING OR SOMEONE?

In the conversation above, Awoje's father believed in the witch-doctor and his ability to cure his sickness. By contrast, his uncle believed in the ability of trained medical doctors and the power of their medicines. In both cases their belief was a form of trust. One trusted in the witch-doctor and the other in the medical doctor to be able to help them in their time of need. In both cases what they believed came from what they had learned from others. In both cases their belief led to certain actions.

Their actions showed that they had confidence in the ability or power of the person they trusted. When we believe in someone we have confidence in that person to help us. Sitting in a chair is a simple illustration of trusting in something. A person will not sit in a chair unless he believes that the chair will support him. Some people have been disappointed when they put their faith in a broken chair! How much worse is it when you put your trust in the wrong person to help you in your time of need and that person cannot help you?

If you are wise you will only put your trust in someone who has given evidence of being worthy of your trust. Consider flying in a plane: Before you enter a plane you must have confidence in both the plane and the pilot. You must believe that the plane will fly. You must also believe in the ability of the pilot to fly the plane. Your trust is probably based on the safety record of the pilot and the airline which owns the plane. Whether the plane and pilot are trustworthy or not can be a matter of life and death.

How important it is whom you can trust to help you in your times of personal crisis! How important it is whom you can trust to forgive your sins before God!

Who can really help people in their time of need? Who has the power to answer their prayers? Who can forgive people's sins and give them eternal life? In whom can people believe and not be bitterly disappointed? Everyone has a system of belief. The question is, what will be the outcome of your beliefs? Will your belief result in eternal salvation or eternal death?

The proof of a person's belief comes in the time of need. The person or thing someone turns to for help in his or her time of great need is the person he or she really believes in.

Everyone believes in something or someone. For most people their belief is the result of what they have heard from others. Many times those who spoke to them were deceived themselves and did not know the truth. It is very important to believe the truth but what is the truth? What is the ultimate reality?

B. WHAT IS TRUTH?

Truth is a statement of what is real or what is right as compared with what is false or what is wrong. Truth is a statement about the ultimate realities of life. Because truth has to do with ultimate reality, truth will affect a person's destiny.

Many people think that if something is spoken by a teacher in school or written in a book it must be the truth. Unfortunately that is not always the case. Sometimes the teacher himself has been taught what is wrong and so he teaches others what is wrong. Sometimes books print things which are not true because the writer did not know the truth. Sometimes people purposely try to deceive others.

Here is an example of something that is not true and how it has affected many people who believe it. Among a great many educated Europeans and Americans there is a belief that there are no absolute standards of right and wrong given by God, as the Bible teaches. These people do not believe that God holds them responsible for their behaviour. They have no standard to measure right and wrong beyond their own opinions. They make up their own rules of what is right and what is wrong.

The rules they make up are based on what they personally want to do. One popular saying in North America today goes like this: 'If it feels good, do it.' Following this foolish idea has resulted in terrible sexual sin in Europe and America. It has caused the breakdown of the family in Western society. Families are being torn apart by adultery and divorce because people don't believe that God holds people responsible for their behaviour. They believe in their own ideas instead of the truth of God. The Bible says, 'He who trusts in himself is a fool' (Prov. 28:26). This verse is being proven true today in many parts of the world.

C. WHERE CAN WE FIND THE TRUTH?

How is one to be sure of believing the truth? In the past, Africans usually looked to the traditions of their people to determine what they would believe. In many traditional African societies the idea of truth is related to the stories and myths about life and human experience which are passed down from one generation to another by the elders or grandparents of the clan. In modern Africa there are many new voices, especially political voices, insisting that we believe this or that. There are many appeals being made to Africans today.

In addition, many religions have their sacred writings. Many people claim to be prophets of God. Who is really right? Is there any way we can be sure of finding the truth?

Jesus said, 'For this reason I came into the world, to testify to the truth' (John 18:37). When Jesus said this, the Roman governor Pontius Pilate asked him, 'What is truth?' (John 18:38). Pilate was asking about ultimate reality. As a politician Pilate knew that most people were liars just like he himself was, and so he found it hard to believe that Jesus or anyone else spoke only the truth.

Jesus said he came to bear witness to the truth. He said, 'I am the way, the truth and the life' (John 14:6). He went on to say, 'No one comes to the Father except through me.' Can Jesus prove such a claim?

If Jesus was right, then other religious teachers and even many clan elders must be wrong, for Jesus left no place for them. In John 10:8 Jesus said, 'All who ever came before me were thieves and robbers . . . I am the gate. Whoever enters through me will be saved.' Is Jesus Christ the way to God the Father? Is he the source of truth? Is he really the one who gives life? How can we know? In what way can we test the claims of Christ?

What about a test of character and a test of power to do good? Character is very important and the power to do good is very important. Who in history was really perfect in his character? Who in history only used his power to help others? Who has the power to help me in my time of need? Who has the power to answer my prayers?

Power is important in Africa. Power can also deceive people. There are people who have power to use magic or to pronounce spells and curses. Some even have power to cure sicknesses. Such people have power but how do they use their power? Do they use it only for the good of others? Or do they use it for their own gain or to make money? That is the test of both character and power.

Everyone knows that God's power is greater than all other power. But God uses his power for man's good. If someone claims to have the truth from God, then we should find that he uses his power for the good of others and not for his own benefit. Has there ever been such a person? To discover who has the truth let us briefly compare Jesus

Christ with others who claimed to teach the truth. Let us see who used his power only for the good of others. Let us see who has the power to answer prayer.

JESUS COMPARED TO OTHER RELIGIOUS TEACHERS

What other man in history was born of a virgin woman? What other man ever lived a sinless and perfect life, for the good of others, as Jesus did? When did Krishna of Hinduism ever calm the storm and waves for his followers? When did Gautama of Buddhism ever cleanse the leper or give sight to those born blind? When did the teacher Confucius feed more than 5000 men and women who listened to his teaching? When did Mao Tse Tung of China ever heal an epileptic child? When did Marx or Lenin ever raise a widow's only son from the dead?

What other man in history besides Jesus has ever answered the desperate prayers of hurting people who cried out to him for help? Which prophet cast a multitude of demons out of a madman and restored his health and sanity? Which teacher or religious leader ever made 180 gallons of water into wine for the joy of a newly married couple at their wedding feast? When did Mohammed die for the sins of mankind? When did Mohammed rise from the dead to give people eternal life?

The answers to these questions tell us that Jesus Christ was different from every other man who ever lived. No one except Jesus ever did such things. Jesus alone has power over sickness, tragedy and death. Jesus alone has power over demons and the forces of nature. Jesus used his power to answer the prayers of needy people. Jesus alone has power over life and death. By his miracles Jesus showed that he had power over heaven and earth (Matt. 28:18). But Jesus only used his power for the good of mankind. What other religious teacher can be compared to Jesus?

By his acts of love and power Jesus proved himself to be the one he claimed to be. His virgin birth, his sinless life, his miracles of love and mercy, his forgiveness of our sins, his compassion for people, his healing of their diseases, his answers to their prayers, his ability to restore joy to the brokenhearted, his power over nature, his power over demons, his death for our sins, and his resurrection from the dead: All these things prove that Jesus alone is the way, the truth and the life. These things prove he is the only Saviour of mankind. He is the only one in whom men can put their trust and not be disappointed.

Believing in Christ is much like trusting a plane and its pilot as in the illustration given earlier. It means we trust him to know what to do when a problem or a crisis arises. It means that we trust him to help us when we are in trouble. It means we believe that Christ is the man who is God. It means we believe that he is the one who died in our place on the cross. It means that we believe that he rose from the dead and has overcome death. It means that we trust him to forgive our sins. It means we trust him instead of trusting in charms, or rituals, or the spirits of ancestors, or witch-doctors. Believing in Christ means that we trust him for what happens to us in this life and for what happens after we die.

Jesus was different from all other great religious teachers of history in that others taught the word of God, but Jesus is the Word of God (John 1:1,14, Rev 19:13). Even the Qu'ran speaks of Jesus as the Word of God (Sura 4:171). Others preached about the truth, but Jesus is the truth (John 14:6, John 18:37). Others told men how to live, but Jesus lived a sinless and perfect life as no other man has ever lived. Other prophets taught people about God, but Jesus revealed God to men because he is God (John 1:1, Colossians 2:9).

THE PROOF OF JESUS' MIRACLES

One way to test the truth of a person's words is to see what that person's enemies say about him. We see this happening in politics all the time. A politician will make many claims for himself or his party but it will not be long before his enemies will expose the unpleasant facts which the politician would rather hide!

The Scribes and Pharisees strongly opposed Jesus. They were jealous of his popularity with the common people of Israel. They hated him bitterly because he exposed their religious hypocrisy and pride. If any persons wanted to disprove the miracles of Christ, it were the Scribes and Pharisees. Let us see what these enemies of Christ had to say about his miracles and good works. Did they deny that he did miracles? Did they say he never did good works?

Notice what Jesus' enemies said in response to Christ's challenge in John 10:32, 'I have shown you many great miracles from the Father. For which of these do you stone me?' To this question the enemies of Jesus replied, 'We are not stoning you for any of these. . .but for blasphemy, because you, a mere man, claim to be God' (John 10:33). By their reply they admitted that Jesus had indeed performed great miracles! But they refused to accept the reason why he was able to do such miracles. The amazing fact is this: The statements of Christ's enemies are some of the strongest proofs in history that Jesus really did perform great miracles of love and power to help people.

Christ's enemies could not find fault with his sinless life. In John 8:46 Jesus asked, 'Can any of you prove me guilty of sin?' Once again the enemies of Christ could not find fault by bringing evidence of any sin in his life. Instead they simply refused his claim to be God and took up stones to kill him for claiming to be God (John 8:59). Thus his worst enemies admitted that he was sinless. Again, even the Qu'ran teaches that Jesus was 'faultless' (Sura 19:19).

Try to imagine the same situation with any other person in history. If anyone dared to claim that he was sinless that person's enemies would immediately bring evidence of his faults. Even the Qu'ran admits that Mohammed was an ordinary man (Sura 47:19, 48:1–2). But Jesus was sinless and no charges could be made against him. When we consider all of these facts together we realize that Jesus is the very person he claimed to be. He is the God of heaven and earth and the Saviour of the world.

D. HOW DOES WHAT WE BELIEVE AFFECT OUR ACTIONS?

As we saw earlier, what we believe will determine how we act and the kind of persons we are. Why do people behave the way they do? It is because of what they believe in their hearts to be true. A tragic example of this took place at the creation of man. In the garden of Eden, Eve believed the lie of Satan instead of the truth of God when Satan said, 'You will not surely die' (Gen. 3:4). Because she believed this lie, she disobeyed God, and ate the fruit from the tree which God had forbidden (Gen. 3:6). As a result death came upon all mankind (Rom. 5:12) just as God said it would (Gen. 2:17).

This book will try to make clear the relationship between Christian belief and Christian behaviour. Theology is not just a study of ideas about God. It is also a practical study of how people act when they have a personal relationship with the living and true God.

What do you believe about God? What do you believe about man? What do you believe about life and where it came from? What do you believe about sin, sickness, tragedy and death? What do you believe about spirits and the spirit world? This book will address these and other important questions because what you believe about these things will determine how you live your life and where you will spend eternity after you die.

E. WHAT WILL HAPPEN WHEN YOU BELIEVE THE TRUTH AND WHAT WILL HAPPEN WHEN YOU BELIEVE WHAT IS FALSE?

What you believe is a matter of life and death. Many years ago medical doctors believed sickness was caused by something in the blood. Although this is true, doctors in those days did not understand how to cure what was wrong in the blood. Because of this they believed that when a person got sick, enough blood should be removed from the person to take away the sickness! This was actually done by a medical doctor to George Washington, the first president of the United States.

Washington had a sickness in his old age. The doctor who treated Washington wanted to save his life but he actually killed him by bleeding him to death because what he believed was wrong!

This can also happen in spiritual matters. It is possible to be very sincere but to be sincerely wrong, resulting in eternal death. In John 8:24 Jesus said, 'If you do not believe that I am the one I claim to be, you will indeed die in your sins.'

F. WHO ARE WE TO BELIEVE?

Who has the truth and whom may we trust? The word of God says, 'There is no other name under heaven given to men by which we must be saved' (Acts 4:12). That name is not Buddha. That name is not Marx. That name is not Mohammed. That name, above every name, is Jesus Christ (Philippians 2:9). Jesus said, 'I am the gate; whoever enters through me will be saved' (John 10:9).

Jesus is Lord of heaven and earth. The day will come when every tongue in heaven and on earth will confess that Jesus is the Lord (Philippians 2:9–10). Unfortunately, although many will confess that he is the Lord, they will not be able to say that he is their Lord. Jesus said, 'Many will say to me on that day, Lord, Lord . . . then I will tell them plainly, I never knew you' (Matt. 7:22–23).

However, for those who have humbled themselves before him now, confessing their sins and their need for his forgiveness, and have received him as their Lord and Saviour, he will indeed be their Lord and they will have eternal life (John 1:12, 3:16).

SUMMARY

In the world today there are many who claim to have the truth. Who should we believe? Where can we find the truth? What is truth? Truth is a statement of what is real or what is right. Although many religious teachers and prophets in history have claimed to teach the truth, only Jesus Christ has demonstrated by his life of perfect love, perfect holiness and perfect power that he is the way, the truth and the life, as he claimed to be (John 14:6). When we compare Jesus to other persons in history, we find that there has never been a person like him.

What we believe to be true is very important. Our actions result from what we believe to be true. It is most important that we believe what is true, or we may lose our souls forever. If we believe in Jesus Christ, we will find the truth, God's forgiveness of our sins and eternal life with God forever.

DISCUSSION QUESTIONS AND PROJECTS BASED ON CHAPTER ONE

1. How would you answer a person in your school who said, 'All roads lead to God since he created the world and all that is in it. It doesn't matter which religion you follow as long as you are sincere.'

2. A professor at a certain university says, 'Modern science has proved the Bible to be wrong. The solution to mankind's problems lies in more research and better education.' Make a statement before the group to challenge the statement of this professor.

3. A Muslim student says, 'We believe that Jesus was a prophet but that Mohammed was the last and greatest of the prophets.' How would you answer this person's statement?

4. A teacher of religious knowledge in a certain school says, 'African traditional religion is a preparation for Christianity for Africans, much as the Old Testament was a preparation for Christianity for the Jews.' Let groups of four students each study 1 Kings 18:17–39 in class to find out how the Bible would respond to such a statement.

5. Make a list of practical problems in African life which need answers from the Bible. Divide into groups of three persons each to find out what the Bible has to say about the problems listed.

6. Divide into small groups of three each and let each group make a list of false beliefs held by people they know. Show how these beliefs determine their actions.

7. What is considered true in Africa? How do you arrive at a knowledge of the truth?

8. In what ways is Jesus different from spirits, ancestors and divinities?

SUGGESTED FOR FURTHER READING

Kato, Byang. *Theological Pitfalls In Africa*. Kisumu, Kenya: Evangel Publishing House, 1975.

McDowell, Josh. *Evidence That Demands A Verdict*. Amersham: Scripture Press, 1990.

McGrath, Alistair. *Explaining Your Faith*. Leicester: InterVarsity Press, 1995.

Parrinder, Edward G. *Africa's Three Religions*. London: Sheldon Press, 1976.

2

The Bible – The Basis Of What We Believe

Magaji: 'Why do the Muslims say that the country can only be run on the basis of Muslim law?'

Nyanzet: 'My friend Sanusi says that the Qu'ran was a divine revelation from God to the prophet Mohammed. He says it contains the law of God and the will of God for mankind. If we do not obey his will and live by his laws as revealed in the Qu'ran, we shall all be punished by God.'

Magaji: 'But my friend Peter says that the Bible is the divine revelation from God and that we must believe the Bible if we are to know God and find his salvation. I have been reading parts of both books and they both sound very inspired. How is one to know which book is from God?'

Nyanzet: 'I don't know the answer to that. In my village we follow the oral tradition of our elders.'

Most of the great religions of the world have their oral traditions and their sacred writings. Their followers claim that their traditions and books were inspired by God. How is a person to know which, if any, of these books really did come from God? This is a very important question if we are to find the truth. In this chapter, therefore, we will consider the following questions:

A. How can we know if the Bible is the word of God and not just the words of men?
B. Is the Bible the only revelation from God or are there other books which are also revelations from God?
C. What did Jesus teach about the authority and accuracy of the Bible?
D. What about contradictions in the Bible?
E. What may we say about things we don't understand in the Bible?

F. What is the relationship between the Old Testament and the New Testament?

G. What is meant by the inspiration of Scripture?

A. HOW CAN WE KNOW THAT THE BIBLE IS THE WORD OF GOD AND NOT JUST THE WORDS OF MEN?

Everyone has some basis for what he believes. It may be a book, or the teaching of his parents, or the ideas of other people. We all believe something about the real issues of life and we all have a basis for those beliefs. Many people base their beliefs on a book which they claim was revealed by God. Is there any book which can support the claim that it is the word of God?

People sometimes observe that the things Christians say about Christ are found only in the Bible. Can we believe the Bible? How do we know whether the Bible is the word of God, as Christians claim, or if it is just another book written by human beings? Obviously our faith in Christ and his words depends upon whether or not the Bible is really from God.

To answer this question we need to examine the evidence which God himself presents to us in the Bible. We will then be in a position to compare the Bible with all other religious books which claim to be revelations from God.

EVIDENCE FROM APOSTOLIC TESTIMONY

The Bible was written by men who were recognized as the prophets and apostles of God. An example in the Old Testament would be Moses. Jews, Muslims and Christians all recognize that Moses was a prophet of God. An example in the New Testament would be the Apostle John, who wrote the gospel of John. In some cases books were written by other men who were authorized by the apostles to write down the word of God, as in the case of the gospel of Luke.

EVIDENCE FROM PROPHECY

No one in the world can completely know the future except God. A book which can correctly predict the future 100 percent of the time, must be a revelation from God. The only book which does that is the Bible.

God challenges men to a contest of ability to predict the future. In the book of Isaiah he says, 'Who then is like me? Let him proclaim it. Let him declare and lay out before me . . . what is yet to come? Yes, let him foretell what will come' (Isa. 44:7). With this challenge, every sacred book in the world except the Bible will be found lacking because no other book correctly predicts the future at all times.

In Deuteronomy 18:21 God suggests a question which many people have: 'How can we know when a message has not been spoken by the Lord?' God's answer in verse 22 is very simple. 'If what a prophet proclaims in the name of the Lord does not take place or come true, that is a message the Lord has not spoken.'

In other words, the test of whether or not revelation is from God, is fulfilled prophecy. Predictive prophecy which is from God always comes true. It is here that most prophets prove they are not from God. Africa has many self-styled prophets today. If a prophet is right nine times out of ten, he is not speaking from God. The prophecies of God are right ten times out of ten. God is never wrong and he never makes a mistake.

Among all the books which claim to be revelations from God, the Bible stands alone as the only book whose prophecies always come to pass. All other books fail this test or they avoid the issue by not making any predictions. The fulfilled prophecies of the Bible are nothing less than miraculous. They prove that the Bible is the word of God.

SOME EXAMPLES OF FULFILLED PROPHECY

In Psalm 22, written about 1000 BC by King David, there is a very detailed description of the crucifixion of a man. The details of this description fit one person, and that person is Jesus Christ. Psalm 22:16–18 says, 'Dogs have surrounded me; a band of evil men has encircled me, they have pierced my hands and my feet. I can count all my bones; people stare and gloat over me. They divide my garments among them and cast lots for my clothing.' How could anyone write such a description as this without having seen the event? But this description was written 1000 years before the event took place! And that is not all.

Crucifixion had never been seen by any human being before the Romans invented it as a way of killing criminals in about 250 BC. In other words, the Psalm was written 750 years before anyone had ever seen a person crucified. There is no satisfactory explanation for how this psalm could have been written apart from a revelation by God. This prophecy proves that it was God who revealed this event to the human author.

The prophet Isaiah also described how the Messiah would be crucified for the sins of his people and how he would suffer in their place. Isaiah 53:5 says, 'he was pierced for our transgressions, he was crushed for our iniquities; the punishment that brought us peace was upon him, and by his wounds we are healed.'

Seven hundred years before Christ, Isaiah also revealed two other surprising details about Jesus' death. 'his grave was assigned to be with wicked men, yet with a rich man in his death' (Isa. 53:9 NASB). The details were that Christ's death would be with wicked men, yet his death would be associated with a rich man. In the actual event, he was crucified between two thieves (Matt. 27:38,44). After that he was buried by the rich man Joseph of Arimathea (Matt. 27:57–60).

There are no mistakes in the prophecies of the Bible. The Jewish leaders of Christ's time knew that the Old Testament was the word of God. When the wise men came to King Herod to enquire about where the Messiah would be born, the rabbis were able to give King Herod an exact answer from Old Testament prophecy. 'But you, Bethlehem Ephrathah, though you are small among the clans of Judah, out of you will come for me one who will be ruler over Israel, whose origins are from of old, from days of eternity' (Micah 5:2, Matt 2:1–6). Their answer that the Messiah would be born in Bethlehem was correct. Jesus the Messiah was born in Bethlehem (Luke 2:4–7).

There are also many prophecies about other matters in the Bible. Who in Africa can correctly predict what will take place in their country 200 years, or 500 years from now and never make a mistake? Yet the Bible makes such predictions again and again. For example, God prophesied through Isaiah (Isaiah 44:28), that Cyrus, King of Persia, would order the rebuilding of the Jewish temple in Jerusalem after it had been destroyed by King Nebuchadnezzar. This prediction was made 200 years before Cyrus was born and was fulfilled just as God had stated (Ezra 1:1–3).

OTHER EVIDENCE THAT THE BIBLE IS THE WORD OF GOD

There is also other evidence which shows us that only the Bible is the inspired word of God. Here are some examples of this evidence. We will discuss three of the points listed below in more detail.

1. The Bible was probably written by more than 40 different human authors. It was written in different times of history and in different places by men who often did not know each other personally. Yet it reads as if it is one book written by one author. The reason is that the real author is God, who spoke through the human authors.

2. Although the Bible is not a book about science, it speaks correctly about many discoveries of science long before those discoveries were made by men.

3. Jesus Christ, who died and rose from the dead, testifies about the Old Testament that it is the word of God.

4. Those who read the Bible and believe its message about salvation in Christ are consistently changed in their character from sinners to godly persons even when they have been very evil people.

5. The study of ancient civilizations in the Bible lands (the study of archaeology) has confirmed many historical details found in the Bible.

6. God makes many promises in the Bible to Christians. God keeps these promises when Christians meet the conditions given in the Bible. The most frequently fulfilled promises relate to prayer. No other sacred book in the world can offer this evidence.

7. The writers of the Bible knew they were given the word of God and they said so (e.g. 1 Thess. 2:13).

8. The Bible has been translated into more languages than any other book in human history. It has also sold more copies than any other book in the world.

9. The Bible promises that there will be miracles in the lives of those who put their trust in Christ. The history of the church is full of such miracles.

10. There is a consistent testimony from Christians of all cultures in the world that the Bible is the word of God. This comes from the inner witness of the Holy Spirit as God's people read the Bible.

THE UNITY OF THE BIBLE

Consider the unity of the Bible. The Bible is really not one book, but 66 different books, written by about 40 different people at different times and in different places. In Bible times there was not the freedom of communication and travel that we enjoy today. Many of these writers did not know what others were writing or what would be written in the future. They only knew what God was telling them to write.

Yet the miraculous fact is this: After all these scrolls were gradually collected over many years and put together in one book, it became clear that it was really just one continuous story! How could that have happened unless God was the real author who guided the human authors? When we read it now the Bible reads as if it were one single book written by one person. Who planned this unity in the Bible if not God?

THE POWER OF THE BIBLE TO CHANGE HUMAN LIVES

What about the life-changing moral effect of the Bible on those who were converted to faith in Christ through reading the Bible? What other book in history has so consistently changed sinners and evil men into saints and holy men as the Bible has done? An example would be John Newton, the writer of the hymn, *Amazing Grace*. John Newton was among the most evil men of his generation. He was a slave-trader. Yet, when this man came to Christ and repented of his sins he became a godly man.

The same story could be told about many other sinful men. There have been many in Africa who were in bondage to witchcraft, immorality and violence who have been changed by Christ into good and godly people. What other book besides the Bible has consistently changed people in this way? The answer is none because only the Bible is truly from God. This is the God who says in the Bible that his purpose is to change men from sinners to saints. Eph. 2:10 says, 'For we are God's workmanship, created in Christ Jesus to do good works, which God prepared in advance for us to do.'

ANSWERS TO PRAYER

Consider the answers to prayer experienced by those who have put their faith in Christ. Men of every race and culture pray at some time in their lives. However, only Christians can testify to regular, specific answers to their prayers.

This is because God has promised in the Bible to answer the prayers of those who come to him on the basis of faith in Jesus Christ (John 16:24). In his kindness God sometimes answers the prayers of non-Christians also, because he is merciful, but these are unusual cases. It is the Bible which leads men to faith in Christ. It is faith in Christ which leads to answered prayer. This also shows us that the Bible is the word of God.

B. IS THE BIBLE THE ONLY REVELATION FROM GOD OR ARE THERE OTHER BOOKS WHICH ARE ALSO REVELATIONS FROM GOD?

It is certainly a fair challenge to compare the Bible with all other books which claim to be a revelation from God. We have just considered several important facts about the Bible which show us that it is the word of God.

If any other supposedly sacred book is really from God, then the above listed facts about the Bible should be just as true about the other book as it is about the Bible. A careful consideration of each of the other religious books which claim to be from God shows us that every one of them fails to match the Bible in the ways listed above. We must conclude that the Bible is the only book which is actually God's word. It is the only true revelation from God.

This leads to another important question: How accurate is the Bible? To answer this question let us consider what Jesus said about the accuracy of the Bible.

C. WHAT DID JESUS TEACH ABOUT THE AUTHORITY AND ACCURACY OF THE BIBLE?

1. Jesus said that the word of God is the truth. In John 17:17 he said, 'your word is truth.'

2. Jesus claimed that the Old Testament was historically accurate. In Matthew 12:40,41 Jesus indicated that the story of Jonah in the belly of the fish really took place and that there will be a judgment.

3. Jesus said that it would be easier for heaven and earth to pass away than for even the smallest part of the Law of God to be changed (Matt 5:18). In other words, the word of God is fixed and unchangeable forever (Psalm 119:89).

4. Jesus said that even though heaven and earth will pass away, God's words will not pass away (Matt. 24:35).

5. Jesus said that Psalm 110 (and by implication all of the Old Testament) was inspired by the Holy Spirit (Mark 12:36). He also suggested that there would be further revelation by the Holy Spirit (the New Testament) after he was gone (John 16:13).

6. Jesus called the written Old Testament the word of God (Mark 7:13).

7. Jesus taught that even the individual words of Scripture, including the tenses of verbs (i.e. past, present or future), are exactly as God intended them to be (Mark 12:26–27). This was true in spite of the fact that each human author expressed himself in his own style of writing.

8. Jesus said that all the promises and prophecies of the Bible must be fulfilled (John 10:35b, Matt 5:18).

From these statements by Christ we can come to a correct understanding of the accuracy and authority of the Bible. The Old Testament prophets and the writers of the New Testament also explained other things about the accuracy and inspiration of the Bible. These statements add to our understanding of Jesus' teaching. For example Paul said, 'All Scripture is God-breathed, and is useful for teaching, rebuking, correcting and training in righteousness' (2 Tim 3:16). The apostle Peter said, 'For prophecy never had its origin in the will of man, but men spoke from God as they were carried along by the Holy Spirit' (2 Pet. 1:21).

From these and other statements in the Bible we can form a summary statement about the inspiration, authority and accuracy of the Bible. This statement about the accuracy of the Bible is a summary of Jesus' statements and the statements of other writers of Scripture. Here is such a statement:

The entire Bible in the Old and New Testament as it was first given to those who wrote those words, is the accurate and complete word of God. It was inspired by the Holy Spirit and given through each human author in the words and style of that author. These writings were without error and contain the full revelation of God to man. All that man needs to know for his salvation and his relationship to God is found in the Old and New Testament.

Due to extensive discoveries in manuscript evidence in recent years, it has become clear that the modern versions of the Bible we use today are probably very close to those original documents written by the writers of Scripture.

D. WHAT ABOUT CONTRADICTIONS IN THE BIBLE?

Some people insist that the Bible is full of contradictions and mistakes. It is true that where the same stories are told in different books of the Bible, the details sometimes appear to contradict each other. An example of this would be the four stories of the resurrection of Christ in the four gospels. Each story is somewhat different concerning the details of what took place but the main story is the same. The authors reported that Jesus rose from the dead and was seen by his followers. How should we deal with such problems?

The solution to apparent contradictions in the Bible sometimes comes from a very careful study of the passage and sometimes from a careful study of the historical conditions surrounding the event. For example in the case of the four resurrection stories, a close examination reveals that the stories have the character of being written by uneducated eyewitnesses or by those who listened to the testimony of such eyewitnesses.

If several students were to describe a riot which took place in their school, their stories would not all be the same. The general account of the riot might be the same but each student would describe different details which he personally saw. Each description would be somewhat different. This is just the way the resurrection stories read in the four gospels.

In some cases of apparent contradiction it would require very detailed knowledge of the actual historical situation to discover why the stories seem to disagree. Sometimes that detailed information has been lost in history so it is not possible to discover the reason for the apparent contradiction. The discovery of the Dead Sea scrolls in 1947 was an important addition to our knowledge about life in the first century. These scrolls also confirmed the accuracy of the more recent Old Testament manuscripts which scholars have used for many years. Above all, Christ taught the complete accuracy of Scripture as we have seen. For these reasons we can trust the Bible even if all our questions about apparent contradictions are not fully answered.

E. WHAT MAY WE SAY ABOUT THE THINGS WE DON'T UNDERSTAND IN THE BIBLE?

There are passages in the Bible about whose meaning even the most educated Bible scholars are uncertain. For most of us there are many such places in the Bible. In Luke 10:21 Jesus said, 'I praise you, Father, Lord of heaven and earth, because you have hidden these things from the wise and learned, and revealed them to little children.' This statement suggests that God the Father may have purposely hidden some of the answers to life's questions from proud and educated men. Perhaps he did this so that all people would have to humble themselves and come to God with the faith of small children. Finding God's wisdom does not depend on the extent of someone's education. If it were so, only educated people would have God's wisdom and find his salvation. As it is, all people may find God's salvation and God's wisdom regardless of their education. The psalm writer says, 'I have more insight than all my teachers, for I meditate on your statutes' (Psalm 119:99).

We can safely base our belief in the accuracy and authority of the Bible on Jesus' words concerning the Bible even if we cannot explain every problem. Sometimes God gives people light to understand these problems and sometimes he does not. Sometimes Bible commentaries and Bible encyclopedias can answer our questions.

F. WHAT IS THE RELATIONSHIP BETWEEN THE OLD TESTAMENT AND THE NEW TESTAMENT?

An important question deals with the relationship between the Old and New Testament. What is that relationship? What is the purpose of the Old Testament? What sort of things does God want a Christian to learn from the Old Testament?

Since the Holy Spirit inspired all the writers of the Bible, the best way to understand the Bible is to let the Bible explain itself. Comparing one place in Scripture with another will help us to understand the teachings of the Bible. The New Testament is God's inspired commentary on the Old Testament.

The book of Hebrews explains the relationship between the Old and New Testament in detail. Other passages in the New Testament give us further light. The book of Hebrews tells us that the institutions, ceremonies and rituals of the Old Testament were given by God in order to provide a visual picture or shadow of the spiritual realities of salvation in the New Testament. Hebrews 10:1 says, 'The law is only a shadow of the good things that are coming, not the realities themselves. For this reason it can never, by the same sacrifices repeated endlessly year after year, make perfect those who draw near to worship.'

Because life in many parts of Africa is similar to life in the Old Testament, many people feel close to the stories found in the Old Testament. For this reason it is especially important to understand the progressive nature of God's revelation to man in the Bible.

In order to understand this progressive revelation we must understand the difference between the moral laws of God, the ceremonial (ritual) laws and civil laws of God. The moral laws of God do not change from one period of history to another. The ceremonial and civil laws of God were different at different times in history. Today God wants us to live by the full revelation of the New Testament rather than following the partial revelation of the Old Testament.

It is not necessary for Christians today to perform the ritual sacrifices of the Old Testament. Jesus Christ has fulfilled these rituals by his death and resurrection (Heb. 10:1–10). Today we are not restricted to the food and civil laws of the Old Testament (Mark 7:18–19, Col. 2:16–17).

The entire Old Testament ceremonial law, such as that found in Exodus, Leviticus and Numbers, was a series of illustrations planned by God to explain many aspects of salvation in Christ. Colossians 2:16–17 says, 'Therefore, do not let anyone judge you by what you eat or drink, or with regard to a religious festival, a New Moon celebration or a Sabbath day. These are a shadow of the things that were to come; the reality, however, is found in Christ.' Jesus said, 'Do not think that I have come to abolish the Law or the Prophets. I have not come to abolish them, but to fulfill them' (Matt. 5:17).

After his resurrection Jesus began to explain the meaning of the Old Testament to his disciples. Luke records the following conversation of Christ with two of his disciples on the road to Emmaus: 'Beginning with Moses and all the Prophets, he (Jesus) explained to them what was said in all the Scriptures concerning himself' (Luke 24:27).

Up to the time of Jesus' resurrection the events in the life and death of Christ were not clearly understood by his disciples (Matt. 16:21–22, Luke 24:19–21). With the teaching given by Christ to his disciples during the 40 days following his resurrection (Acts 1:3) and with the illumination given by the Holy Spirit at Pentecost (Acts 2:1–4), the disciples began to correctly understand the meaning of the many sacrifices and rituals of the Old Testament.

Many spiritual truths presented in the New Testament were illustrated by God through the historical events of the Old Testament. Speaking about some of these events in Israel's history, Paul said, 'These things happened to them as examples, and were written down

as warnings for us, on whom the fulfilment of the ages has come'
(1 Cor. 10:11).

Thus the Old Testament is very important for the Christian to read
and correctly understand. It is rich in prophecy, ceremony, history and
stories from real life. From these passages a Christian can learn of
God's ways, his salvation, and his will concerning man.

G. WHAT IS MEANT BY THE INSPIRATION OF SCRIPTURE?

It is important to note the means by which God gave his word. The
Bible says, 'Men spoke from God as they were carried along by the
Holy Spirit' (2 Peter 1:21). In other words, the Holy Spirit inspired
the writers of the Bible. This means that he moved in their minds in
such a way that they wrote down exactly what he wanted them to say.
Yet they did it in their own words and in their own style. The Bible
teaches that 'all Scripture' (the whole Bible) is inspired in this way
(2 Tim 3:16).

God did not dictate the individual words to his servants. If that were
true, each book of the Bible would be exactly alike and there would be
no difference in style or vocabulary between them. But the fact is that
each book is different. Each book reflects the language, culture and
personality of the particular author. God allowed each writer to use his
own words. He did it in such a way that what the authors wrote were
the very words God wanted to be written. This is because the writers
were 'carried along' by his Holy Spirit (2 Peter 1:21).

Jesus Christ is also called 'the Word of God' in John 1:1–2,14 and in
Revelation 19:13. Just as the Bible is God's word in man's language, so
Christ was God's Word in man's flesh. There are many interesting
similarities between the Bible as God's word and Christ as God's
Word.

Christ was without sin and the Bible is without error. Christ's holy
life exposed men's sins and the Bible's pure teaching exposes men's
sins. Evil men hated and crucified Christ. Evil men have hated the
Bible throughout history and have tried to destroy it. In spite of the
efforts to destroy him, Christ rose from the dead proving himself to be
God. In spite of the efforts to destroy the Bible, the Bible has
overcome its critics and has proved itself to be the book from God.
Christ came to bring men salvation from sin and the Bible was given to
reveal that salvation to men. Christ came to save men of all races and
cultures and the Bible has been brought to more races and cultures
than any other book in the world.

Inspiration, Revelation and Illumination
It is important to understand three words which are used to describe
the work of the Holy Spirit in giving us the Bible. These words are
inspiration, revelation, and illumination.

Inspiration was the process by which God moved upon the minds of those who wrote the Bible to write down his words. He has finished doing this. Because the Bible is now complete (Rev 22: 18–19), Proverbs 30:6 warns us, 'Do not add to his words, or he will rebuke you and prove you a liar.' No one today can claim the same kind of inspiration from God which the writers had who wrote Scripture.

Revelation was the act of God in making known to the writers of the Bible what they could not have known for themselves. An example of this would be God's revelation about what happened at creation (Genesis 1–4). Another example of revelation is the knowledge of what God is like (the Trinity), which man could not have imagined. Because the writing of the Bible is finished, God's inspired revelations for all men are also finished. In other words, nothing can now be added to the Bible (Deut. 4:2, Psalm 119:89). For this reason Christians cannot accept the Book of Mormon and other such books which are claimed to be later revelations from God.

This does not mean that God will never reveal anything to his people again. In the gift of knowledge given to Peter in the case of Ananias and Sapphira, God revealed certain facts to Peter about their deception (Acts 5:1–10). God sometimes gives similar gifts of knowledge today in his church. This, however, is a different kind of revelation from the revelations in the Bible, which are for all men of all cultures.

Illumination is the process by which the Holy Spirit gives understanding of God's word to those who read it and study it. He does this for his people in every generation. We can pray for the Holy Spirit to illuminate our minds today to understand God's word and he will faithfully answer this prayer. The psalmist prayed for such illumination in Psalm 119:18 when he prayed, 'Open my eyes, that I may see wonderful things in your law.'

SUMMARY

The books of the Old and New Testament as given to those who wrote them, are the complete, authoritative, final and accurate word of God. This is what was believed and taught by Jesus Christ. The Bible proves itself to be God's word when compared with all other religious books which make that claim. The Bible does what none of them can do. It correctly predicts the future and it is never wrong.

It is also proved to be the word of God by many other tests. God himself inspired the writing of the Bible and gave it to men by divine revelation. We come to understand its truth by the illumination of the Holy Spirit.

DISCUSSION QUESTIONS AND PROJECTS BASED ON
CHAPTER TWO

1. A professor of religion in a certain University states that the Bible
   is just one of many books in the world on religion, and that it is of
   no greater or lesser value than other books. Let each person in the
   group prepare a verbal response to this professor. Then let three
   people deliver their responses before the others.

2. Assign each person in the group to spend time with a friend from
   another religion. He is to ask his friend to share the three most
   important things he understands from his religious tradition or
   from his sacred book. After this the Christian will share his three
   most important verses from the Bible.

3. Let each student in the group list five answers to prayer which he
   has experienced. Each person should then explain why these
   answers to prayer help to show how the Bible is the word of God.

4. Divide into groups of three. Let each small group locate five
   prophecies about the first coming of Christ from the Old Testament and then find their fulfilment in the New Testament.

5. Let each person carefully read Psalm 22 and make a list of every
   specific detail about the crucifixion of Christ found in this psalm.

6. Ask each person to prepare a verbal testimony about his own life
   experience emphasizing how God changed his behaviour from sin
   to righteousness as a result of believing in Christ.

7. Divide into groups of three. Read Mark 12:26–27 carefully. Let
   each small group explain the way in which Christ used this passage
   (a) to demonstrate that there is a resurrection, and (b) to demonstrate that Scripture is precisely accurate even down to the
   individual words.

8. Let each person record four or more experiences within one
   month, when the Holy Spirit illuminated a verse in the Bible to
   him.

9. How would you answer someone who said that the Old Testament
   does not apply to Christians today?

10. How would you answer someone who said that Christians ought to
    do what people did in Old Testament times (such as observing the
    Old Testament food laws), since the Old Testament is as much the
    word of God as the New Testament? Give Scripture verses to
    support your answer.

11. Let the group discuss whether it is right or wrong to consult oracles or diviners to learn about the future. Scripture verses should be given to support the answers given.

12. Discuss the value of African oral traditions and legends in comparison with the Bible.

SUGGESTED FOR FURTHER READING

Bruce, F.F. *The Books and the Parchments*. London: Marshall Pickering, reissued 1988.

Bruce, F.F. *The New Testament Documents*. Leicester: InterVarsity Press, 1960.

Goldsworthy, G. *According to Plan: The Unfolding Revelation of God in the Bible*. Leicester: InterVarsity Press, 1991.

Lindsell, Harold. *The Battle For The Bible*. Grand Rapids, Michigan: Zondervan, 1976.

MacArthur, John F. *Focus On Fact: Why You Can Trust The Bible*. Old Tappan, New Jersey: Fleming Revell, 1977.

Packer, J.I. *God Has Spoken*. London: Hodder, 2nd edn 1979.

3

How the Bible Came To Us

Chindo: 'Where did the Bible come from?'

Yaliyet: 'I would like to know that myself. I have heard some stories but I don't know for sure. My non-Christian friends often ask me the same question.'

Chindo: 'My religion teacher in school says he thinks the Bible has been changed a lot since it was first written. I wonder if there is any way we can know if that is true or not?'

Yaliyet: 'My Catholic friend John says we must trust the church to answer such questions. But you know something? I looked at his Bible today and discovered that it was different from my Bible! His Bible has more books in it than ours does! Why is that? And whose Bible is the right one?'

It is important to review how we got the Bible in the first place. When did different versions and translations appear? We saw in the last chapter that the Bible was accurate and inspired as it was given to those who first wrote it down. Has it been changed as it was passed down from early times until now or is it still basically the same? Why does the Catholic Bible have more books in it than the one used by non-Catholics? We will consider the following questions in this chapter:

A. How did we get the Bible?
B. Has the Bible been changed as a result of being translated and passed down over many centuries?
C. What are the major English translations of the Bible?
D. Why is the Roman Catholic Bible different?
E. Which version of the English language Bible is the most accurate?

A. HOW DID WE GET THE BIBLE?

The Bible is a collection of 66 books which came to us over a writing period of about 1500 years. It is important for us to understand how we got the Bible. Here is a brief summary of the events which led to the Bible as we have it today.

THERE WAS A SPOKEN TRADITION IN THE BEGINNING

In the beginning (Gen. 2; 3) the Lord spoke face to face with Adam and Eve in the garden of Eden. The things which God said and the knowledge of other events were passed from one generation to another by word of mouth (oral tradition). Perhaps it took place in much the same way that stories are passed from one generation to another around the fire at night in African villages. There were no written scrolls or books at that time.

THE BEGINNING OF A WRITTEN TRADITION

Later God revealed to Moses what had taken place at the creation and in the early history of mankind (Numbers 12:7,8, Deut. 29:29). Moses wrote down on a scroll the things he heard from God (Ex. 24:4).

Picture writing began early in man's history, probably after the flood of Noah. By the time of Abraham and Job (about 2000 BC) cuneiform writing was common in Mesopotamia. Cuneiform writing was made by pressing a stylus into a piece of soft clay. A stylus was a small stick with a wedge shape on the end. Words were formed by making different combinations and patterns of wedges.

Moses wrote the first five books of the Bible called the Pentateuch. Moses may have used Egyptian picture writing called hieroglyphics to write down these early records since he had been educated at Pharaoh's palace in Egypt. The records were handwritten on long rolls of special paper called scrolls. These scrolls were made from papyrus, a material made from a reed that grew near the Nile river. Other types of scrolls were made from dried goatskin. These scrolls were up to 30 feet long and nine to ten inches high. Some of them contained more than one book of the Bible on the same scroll.

From time to time God moved others to write down his word (2 Peter 1:21). These men wrote down what God intended them to write, probably beginning with the book of Job.

The original scrolls were read to different groups. As the original scrolls became worn there arose the need for people to copy the original scrolls. Thus the work of scribes began. The scribes carefully copied these scrolls letter by letter.

Copies of the originals were made very carefully by hand. The scribes often counted the total number of letters in the entire scroll and compared this with the original. They would sometimes even find the middle letter of the scroll to ensure that no mistake was made in copying. By putting such a concern for accuracy into the hearts of these scribes we can see that the Holy Spirit was protecting the transmission of the Bible text from changes and mistakes. The copies of the Old Testament manuscripts were written in Hebrew.

WHAT IS THE CANON OF SCRIPTURE?

The meaning of the word canon is standard or guideline. A question which people often ask is how people knew which books were inspired by God and which were ordinary books. In other words, how did they know which books belonged in the Bible? The books which belong in the Bible are called the canon of Scripture, that is, the standard or approved books.

In Old Testament times the means of accepting or rejecting books as the word of God was a process of general acceptance by God's people. God's people, especially the priests who were trained in the Law of God, recognized the books that were from God. Ezra was an example of such a priest (Ezra 7:10). Perhaps this recognition took place in much the same way as a son would recognize a letter from his father even if the father's name was not on the letter.

An example of an occasion where the people of God recognized and honoured God's word in the Old Testament can be seen when Ezra the priest read the Old Testament in Nehemiah 8:1–8. The people stood and then bowed and worshipped, showing that they recognized and honoured the word of God (Neh. 8:5–6).

The process of recognizing the word of God in New Testament times was somewhat more formalized. In the years just after the writing of the New Testament scrolls, certain tests were applied to each book to decide which documents were actually the word of God. The most important test was whether the book or letter was written by one of the apostles of Christ, or whether its writing was approved by an apostle. Another test was whether all the churches agreed that the book or document was the word of God?

In some cases where Christians did not know for sure who wrote the book, as with the book of Hebrews, it took a long time for the churches to decide whether or not the book should be included in the canon. By the time of the Council of Carthage (in North Africa) in 397 AD all the books of our present New Testament were included as part of the canon of Scripture.

THE SEPTUAGINT

Between the time of the Old Testament and New Testament, Greek became the trade language of the Roman World. The Old Testament was translated into Greek by a group of 72 Jewish scholars in about 250 BC. This version of the Old Testament is known as the Septuagint. Later when the New Testament books were written they were also written in Greek.

THE VULGATE

One of the most important translations of the Bible in the history of the church was done in 388 AD by a Catholic scholar named Jerome. His translation, which is called the Vulgate, was a translation of the Bible into Latin. It was made from the Septuagint along with the New Testament Greek manuscripts. This translation contained the same 66 books of the Bible which we use today.

THE CODICES

By the third century AD copies of the Bible were kept in a form called a codex. Two or more were called codices. A codex consisted of hand copied pages that were held together like a book in a form something like a notebook. Because they were hand copied there were very few codices. The average church member never saw one. The copies that existed were kept in monasteries and studied by monks and priests of the Catholic Church. It was not until the invention of printing 1000 years later that an ordinary church member could have a Bible for his own use.

WHAT WAS THE ORIGIN OF THE ENGLISH LANGUAGE BIBLE?

The gospel of John was translated from the Latin Vulgate into a very old form of English called Anglo-Saxon by a monk named Beda in 735 AD in England just before Beda died. In 1384 AD an Englishman named John Wycliffe, together with some friends, completed the first translation of the Bible into the English language. At that time there was no way to print and distribute his translation.

The most important invention in history for the widespread use of the Bible was printing. Printing was invented in Germany by Johann Gutenberg in 1456 AD. The first book he printed was a portion of the Bible. Printing made it possible for many people to have a Bible. The first German Bible was printed in 1467. The first French Bible was printed in 1487.

In 1526 William Tyndale produced an English language New Testament for printing for the ordinary church member. The Catholic Church was unhappy about Tyndale's translation because it reduced their influence over church members. Now the common man could read the Bible for himself to see if what the Church was teaching agreed with the word of God. For his blessed service to all English speaking people, William Tyndale was strangled and burned to death in 1536, a martyr for the word of God.

The printing and distribution of Bibles was an important change which led to many Christians breaking away from the Roman Catholic Church. This led to the Protestant Reformation in which Martin Luther and John Calvin were leading figures.

Luther was a Catholic priest. He did not want to divide the Catholic Church because of his ideas but he refused to conform to the ideas of the Catholic Church when the Church's ideas plainly opposed the teaching of the Bible. One issue where Luther disagreed with the Catholic Church was in how a person can be saved. The Bible says, 'For it is by grace you have been saved, through faith – and this not from yourselves, it is the gift of God – not by works, so that no one can boast' (Eph. 2:8–9). The Catholic Church taught that salvation resulted from a combination of faith and good works. Protestants still disagree with Catholics on this issue.

B. HAS THE BIBLE BEEN CHANGED AS A RESULT OF BEING TRANSLATED AND PASSED DOWN OVER MANY CENTURIES?

A criticism which is often made about the Bible is that it has been changed in the process of being passed down over many centuries. Christians have always believed that the Holy Spirit guarded the transmission of the Bible just as he inspired the writing of the Bible. Up until 1947 there was really no way to prove this. Until 1947 the oldest complete copies of the Hebrew Bible only dated back to the Middle Ages. These were the Masoretic Hebrew texts, which had been copied and preserved by the Masoretes, an order of monks. Since there were no earlier manuscripts with which to compare these documents no one knew for sure if the Bible had been changed as it was copied and passed down.

THE DEAD SEA SCROLLS

In 1947 an Arab shepherd boy discovered some very ancient scrolls which he found in pottery jars in some caves near the Dead Sea in Israel. The scrolls had been hidden in the caves by Essene scribes in the first century. Among these scrolls fragments have been found from every book of the Old Testament except Esther. These scrolls have become the most important Bible discovery in modern times.

The discovery of the Dead Sea scrolls has confirmed the accuracy of the transmission of the Bible. Critics had said that the Bible we have today must be quite different from the original manuscripts. The Dead Sea scrolls revealed that the Masoretic text of the Old Testament was much the same as earlier manuscripts. The Dead Sea scrolls enabled scholars to compare their later manuscripts with these early ones. When they compared them they discovered that they were essentially the same.

Among the Dead Sea scrolls a complete manuscript of the book of Isaiah was found which dated back to the time of Christ. Scholars carefully compared the Isaiah scroll with the Masoretic text verse by verse. It was found that the text was essentially the same, although the Isaiah scroll was over 1000 years older than the Masoretic document. This discovery revealed how careful the scribes and monks had been in copying the scrolls of the Bible by hand. It also showed that the Holy Spirit had indeed protected the transmission of the Bible.

WHAT ARE THE MOST IMPORTANT MANUSCRIPTS OF THE BIBLE?

The most important manuscripts of the Bible are listed here. The reader may see these names in other books about the history of the Bible.

(a) The Codex Sinaiticus – 75 percent of the Old Testament and New Testament in Greek.
(b) The Codex Vaticanus – 90 percent of the Old Testament and New Testament in Greek.
(c) The Codex Alexandrinus – 90 percent of the Old Testament and New Testament in Greek.
(d) The Vulgate Latin translation
(e) The Masoretic Hebrew scrolls of the Old Testament.
(f) The Dead Sea scrolls.

C. WHAT ARE THE MAJOR ENGLISH TRANSLATIONS OF THE BIBLE?

(a) The Coverdale Bible – 1535 AD. This was the first complete printed Bible in English.
(b) The King James Version – (KJV) 1611. The King James translators did not have the early manuscripts to work with that scholars have today. However, they were godly men and prayed each day before they began their work.
(c) The English Revised Version – 1881.
(d) The American Standard Version – 1901.
(e) The Revised Standard Version (RSV) – 1952.
(f) The New American Standard Bible (NASB) – 1960.
(g) The Good News Bible (GNB) – The Bible Society 1976.
(h) The New International Version (NIV) – 1978. This version is scholarly but easy to read.

In producing the RSV, NASB and NIV, scholars had earlier manuscripts and more recent archaeological material to work with than the translators had for the versions produced before 1930.

What are the Differences Between Various Translations and Versions of the Bible?

Some translations of the Bible were done by one person while others were done by a committee of scholars. Committees had the advantage of the cooperation and knowledge of many scholars. As a result, the versions produced by such translation committees were of better historical quality and accuracy than the translations done by one person.

The RSV, NASB and NIV are English language versions done by committees of very capable scholars. The Weymouth, Moffatt, Goodspeed and Phillips versions are examples of translations done by one person. The Living Bible is a paraphrase rather than a translation. It was done by one man. Although the Living Bible is helpful in being very easy to read, it is not intended to be an accurate study Bible. For careful study of the Bible a person should choose one of the modern versions done by a committee of scholars. Some of these modern versions are published with marginal cross-references so that one verse of Scripture can be compared with other verses on the same subject. This kind of study Bible is very helpful for the serious Bible student.

D. WHY IS THE ROMAN CATHOLIC BIBLE DIFFERENT?

If you have ever used a Catholic Bible you would have discovered that there are some additional books and parts of books in the Catholic Bible which are not found in the Bible used by non-Catholics. These additional books are called the Apocrypha. Why are they there and what is the Apocrypha? Which Bible is correct?

The Apocrypha

Between the time of the Old Testament and the New Testament a number of books were written. Some of these books were based on the history of this period and some were legends. As a group these books are known as the Apocrypha.

The church began using these books along with the Bible from the first century onward but there was no general conviction that they were the word of God along with the other canonical books of the Old Testament. Jerome, the Catholic scholar who produced the Vulgate in 388 AD, did not consider these books to be the word of God. For this reason the Vulgate included only the 66 books found in the Protestant Bible of today.

At the time of the Protestant Reformation, Martin Luther, another Catholic scholar, also insisted that the apocryphal books were not part of the word of God. Partly in reaction against Luther, the Apocrypha was officially added to the Bible by the Roman Catholic Church at the Council of Trent in 1546 AD after a bitter argument over Martin Luther and the Protestant Reformation. At this council it was decided by a very close vote to include the books of the Apocrypha in the Bible. That is why the Roman Catholic Bible is different from the Protestant Bible.

Although evangelicals today, like Luther, do not accept the Apocrypha as part of the word of God, it should be understood that the books of the Apocrypha do have historical and spiritual value. They are now commonly available in a special RSV translation. Here are the names of the seventeen books of the Apocrypha. The third and fourth books of Maccabees are included only by the Eastern Orthodox Church. These books do not appear separately in the Catholic Bible by these names:

First Esdras	Tobit
Second Esdras	Judith
The Wisdom of Solomon	The rest of the book of Esther
Ecclesiasticus	Baruch the Prophet
The letter of Jeremiah	The Song of the Three Children
The Story of Suzanna	Bel and the Dragon
The Prayer of Manasseh	Third Book of Maccabees
First Book of Maccabees	Fourth Book of Maccabees
Second Book of Maccabees	

E. WHICH VERSION OF THE ENGLISH LANGUAGE BIBLE IS THE MOST ACCURATE?

From 1611 to 1945 the most widely read version of the English language Bible was the King James Version. The men who produced the King James Version were dedicated and godly men. God honoured their devotion to his word. Unfortunately the English language of the King James Version is somewhat different from our present use of English. The King James Version also lacks the benefit of many recent discoveries in Bible scholarship. As a result it is not the most accurate version available today for careful study of the Scripture although it is still beloved by many Christians.

In 1952 the complete edition of the Revised Standard Version (RSV) of the Bible was published. It had the benefit of much modern scholarship and research. The RSV is a very scholarly translation of the Bible. It was an important step in relation to the modern use of English and also in relation to recent manuscript discoveries.

Probably the most precisely literal translation of the Bible ever made into the English language was the New American Standard Bible (NASB) in 1960. This version attempts to express in English the exact tense of each Greek verb. The translators of the NASB were excellent scholars who made use of the most recent manuscript and archeological discoveries.

A more recent version which has become very popular throughout the English speaking world is the New International Version (NIV).

This version is also very scholarly. It has the advantage of being easier to read than the NASB and the RSV.

Still another recent version, translated especially for modern readability is The Bible in Today's English Version (BTEV) commonly called the Good News Bible. This version is useful for people for whom English is a second or third language.

SUMMARY

The Bible is a collection of 66 books, written by 40 or more authors, which came into being over a period of about 1500 years. In the beginning there was an oral tradition about the events of ancient history which was passed down for many centuries. Later these stories were written down, beginning perhaps with Job and the books of Moses. As God continued to reveal his truth to his prophets, more and more books were added to the written word of God. God's people came to recognize which books were from God (the canon) among the many books which claimed to be written by prophets or apostles.

The Old Testament was written in Hebrew, the language of the Israelites. The New Testament was written in Greek and Aramaic, the languages of Palestine during the Roman Empire. In 388 AD the 66 canonical books of the Old and New Testament were translated into Latin by a scholar named Jerome. This translation, called the Vulgate, contained the same 66 books found in the Protestant Bible of today. The Roman Catholic Bible contains 15 additional books, called the Apocrypha, which were added in 1546 AD by a decision of a Roman Catholic Church Council.

The first translation of the Bible into English was done by John Wycliffe in 1384 AD. However, the Bible did not find wide circulation until the invention of printing in Germany in 1456 AD. Until recent times, the most widely used English language translation of the Bible was the King James Version, which was completed in 1611 AD. Modern discoveries in archeology have enabled scholars to translate several very accurate versions of the Bible into English in the past 50 years. The discovery of the Dead Sea scrolls in 1947 confirmed to scholars that the books of the Bible had been very carefully copied by scribes from one generation to the next. We can be confident that the Bible we have today is very close to the original written manuscripts.

DISCUSSION QUESTIONS AND PROJECTS BASED ON
CHAPTER THREE

1. Make an outline teaching plan on the history of the Bible. The plan should be made to teach either 12 year olds or adults.

2. Divide the class into language groups. Let each group write down the story of how the Bible was first translated into their language. It may require some weeks for each group to contact the right people in order to find out this information.

3. Assign 15 people to read a different book of the Apocrypha each and give a book report and summary of it. The report should include the spiritual benefit of reading the book.

4. Let two people give a report on how the Septuagint translation was done and some of the ways in which it is different from the other Old Testament manuscripts.

5. Form groups of three to ten members each who speak the same language. Let each group sing several Scripture choruses in their language. They should first write the English translation and Bible reference for the choruses on the chalkboard. If they have no Scripture choruses in their language, let the group create one such chorus.

6. Form several translation groups of two to six members each to represent different language groups in the class. Let each group work together to translate Psalm 23 and Psalm 34 from English into their language.

7. Make a report on the present progress of Bible translation in the world including how many translations have been done, and how many remain to be done. List those translations which still remain to be done in your country. This information is available from Wycliffe Bible Translators, 730 Mercury Avenue, Duncanville, Texas 75137.

8. Have a discussion with the group on the ways in which Muslims today seek to discredit the Bible.

SUGGESTED FOR FURTHER READING

Bruce, F. F. *The History Of The Bible In English*. Cambridge: Lutterworth, 1986.

Duthie, A. *How To Choose Your Bible Wisely*. Carlisle: Paternoster Press, 1995.

Renwich, A.M. and Harman, A.M. *The Story of the Church*. Leicester: InterVarsity Press, 2nd edn, 1985.

Schaaf, Ype *On Their Way Rejoicing*. Carlisle: Paternoster Press, 1995.

4

The God We Cannot Understand

Hassan: 'Last night Bitrus was telling me that Christians believe God is three persons. How can they believe such things? If there is a God, he obviously can only be one person!'

Magaji: 'It is just as I have been telling you, Hassan. These Christians are confused. They believe in three gods. They claim that Jesus Christ is God as well as someone they call the Father and someone else they call the Holy Spirit. But I read in their Bible where Christ prays to God. I saw it myself in Matthew 27:46, where he says, "My God, my God, why have you forsaken me?" How can he be God if he prays to God?'

Hassan: 'A Muslim teacher told me that Jesus was a prophet. He also showed me a place in John 20:17 where Christ said, "I am returning to my Father and your Father, to my God and your God". How can he be God if he says he is returning to God?'

Magaji: 'I think you are right, Hassan. But I am still puzzled by these stories of miracles performed by Christ. How can anyone restore sight to the blind, or calm the storm, or walk on water, or raise the dead if he is only a prophet? There is something very different about this man Jesus. And what about the story about him rising from the dead? I do not know what to think of it.'

Hassan and Magaji are not the first people to struggle with the strange truths about God revealed in the Bible. People have been puzzled by these matters ever since they were first written by the prophets and apostles of God. Men have probably made no more progress in understanding God than when he first revealed himself to them. He is the God we cannot understand. In this chapter we will seek to answer the following questions:

A. What can we learn about God from African traditional religions and from nature?
B. What additional revelation about God is given to us in the Bible?

C. How can one God be three persons?
D. What happened when God became a human being?
E. How can God be present everywhere at the same time?

A. WHAT CAN WE LEARN ABOUT GOD FROM AFRICAN TRADITIONAL RELIGIONS AND FROM NATURE?

African life is rich with an awareness of the supreme Being. Someone has observed that there is probably no native-born African who is not aware of the existence of God. In some countries lorries and taxis display a motto on the front of the vehicle which not only mentions God but also reflects some basic truth about God. In some cultures the personal names of people include a name for God or a reference to God. If there is any continent in the world where God is known and acknowledged, it is Africa.

It should not come as a surprise that God is so well-known in Africa. A large proportion of people, even in modern Africa, still make their living from farming. Most farmers are directly dependent on God for rain to make their crops grow and only God can give rain. Some people speak of rain as 'God's spittle'. In some cultures, such as the Daasenach, this image is used to pronounce a blessing from God by gently spraying water from the mouth on those who are being blessed. The question is, how accurate is the traditional African idea of God?

God is known to be the creator and the sustainer of life. He is respected and honoured as the exalted One, high above all his creation, and high above all other divinities, all spirits and all men. It is partly because God is known to be the highly exalted One that he seems to be removed and separated from the everyday lives of many people. He must be approached through intermediaries. What common person would ever think of approaching a great king directly, without going through the appropriate intermediaries? Even in his or her own village or town a person does not just walk into the presence of a king or chief without permission granted from the chief and without going through the appropriate intermediaries. How much less can one approach the King of heaven directly, according to most traditional beliefs?

God is regarded as the all-powerful (omnipotent) One. The Gikuyu speak of him as, 'The One who makes mountains quake and rivers overflow.' He is the all-knowing (omniscient) One, 'The One who sees both the inside and outside of men', according to the Yoruba. He is the final judge and the One who is present everywhere (omnipresent). It is evident that the traditional view of God in Africa is very close to the biblical revelation of Almighty God. It is also evident that many traditional views of God require a system of intermediaries who can approach the exalted One on man's behalf. Belief in the mediatorial work of divinities and ancestral spirits makes very good sense in the African concept of God and his relationship to his creation although it is contrary to what the Bible reveals.

Prayers are sometimes made directly to God by ordinary people in times of crisis and desperation, especially when spirit intermediaries seem powerless to change the situation. So there is a sense in which God is felt to be close at hand as well as far removed from ordinary life. For the ordinary business of life, however, God must not be troubled with the petty requests of people. The elders and the ancestral spirits are in charge of handling the regular affairs of everyday life, according to the traditional view.

What does the Bible have to say about these ideas of God and about man's relationship to God? The Bible tells us that God has left clear evidence of his existence and of his activity in the world. Romans 1:19–20 says, ' what may be known about God is plain to them, because God has made it plain to them. For since the creation of the world God's invisible qualities – his eternal power and divine nature – have been clearly seen, being understood from what has been made, so that men are without excuse.' It is not surprising, therefore, that there is a strong awareness of God throughout Africa.

Unfortunately, it is just at this point that people go astray in their understanding of God and their relationship to him. Romans goes on to say, 'although they knew God, they neither glorified him as God nor gave thanks to him, but their thinking became futile and their foolish hearts were darkened' (Rom. 1:21). The systems of traditional religions, relying as they do on the work of divinities and ancestral spirits ('other gods') is the very thing God does not want! The very first commandment given to Moses concerned this issue. God said, 'You shall have no other gods before me' (Ex. 20:3). He went on to say, 'You shall not bow down to them or worship them; for I, the LORD your God, am a jealous God' (Ex. 20:5).

It is clear in the Bible that God wants to have a personal, direct relationship with human beings. He and he alone is Lord and God. He does not want people to honour, venerate, worship, submit to, or seek help from, any other gods or spirits. Here lies a deadly error of traditional religions all over the world. There is no one whom God will accept as a mediator between God and human beings except Jesus Christ (1 Tim. 2:5).

The physical creation does indeed reveal the existence of God and African traditional religions confirm this. However, based on what we can see or hear or touch, we can know very little about what God is like. We know that he exists because we can see the evidence of his great power and wisdom in the world around us. We also see the evidence of his care for the things he has made, so we have an idea of his character. It is like finding the tracks of an animal in the bush. We may never see the animal, but from its tracks we know it had passed that way. From the size and shape of the tracks we may even get an idea about the size of the animal.

Who is responsible for the miracle of life, if not God? People have been studying living things for hundreds of years but they still cannot copy what God has done by making a living thing. Who created the balance and harmony of nature, if not God? Who makes the rain or withholds the rain, if not God? People have been trying for many years to make rain, but they are no more successful now than when they first tried.

Who is this invisible God and what is he like? We can get a limited idea of what God is like by looking at nature. From the world around us we see that he has very great power and intelligence. From the care he shows for his creation, such as providing rain, crops and food, and by providing each kind of animal with a mate, we can see that God has a will, and emotions, and that he cares for the creatures he has made. What we can see in the world around us is called the natural revelation of God. All people on the earth are given this natural revelation.

B. WHAT ADDITIONAL REVELATION ABOUT GOD IS GIVEN TO US IN THE BIBLE?

The Bible reveals the nature and character of God in a way that we cannot discover from nature. God reveals to us who he is and what he is like in the Bible. The most amazing part of this revelation is that God revealed himself to mankind in the man, Jesus of Nazareth. We can understand many of God's attributes (characteristics) by studying Jesus Christ. We will study the attributes of God which were revealed in Christ in chapter five.

What else does the Bible reveal about God? Some of the things which the Bible reveals about God are beyond the ability of our minds to understand. Because of this, many people reject the truth which God has revealed in the Bible. However, the truth about God is not the only kind of truth which is hard to explain. For example, people can produce electricity very easily and use it for many purposes. But when they try to explain electricity in science textbooks they use difficult words because electricity is hard to explain.

Long ago people were limited in the number of stars they could count by what they could see with their eyes on a clear night. With the invention of the telescope men discovered there were more stars in the sky than they could count or imagine. So it is with God. The whole truth about God is more than the human mind can imagine.

C. HOW CAN ONE GOD BE THREE PERSONS?

The Bible reveals a truth about God which no person in the world could have imagined. The Bible reveals that God is one being (Deut.

6:4) and that there is no other God except him (Isa. 45:5). At the same time the Bible reveals that God is not one, but three distinct persons: God the Father, God the Son, and God the Holy Spirit. For example, in Isaiah 9:6 the Bible says, 'For to us a child is born, to us a son is given, and . . . he will be called, Wonderful Counsellor, Mighty God, Everlasting Father, Prince of Peace.' In this passage, the name Counsellor (a name of the Holy Spirit in John 14:26), God, Father and Prince of Peace, are all applied to the child who would be born. The son to be born was Jesus, the Saviour (Matt.1:21). Jesus was also given the name Immanuel, a name which means, 'God with us' (Matt. 1:23).

In another mention of the Trinity, Jesus commands that men be baptized in the name (not names) of the Father, the Son, and the Holy Spirit (Matt. 28:19). Here there is but one name, yet three persons are mentioned. 1 Corinthians 8:4 says, 'there is no God but one.' James 2:19 says that even the demons know there is but one God. How can God be three persons and still be one being?

We have great difficulty accepting the truth of the Trinity. To us, if there is only one being, there can only be one person. That is because we are human and that is the way we ourselves are made. Each of us is one being and each of us is also one person. It is not so with God. He is indeed one being, but the Bible reveals that he is three persons. As a fly is unable to understand a human being, so the human mind is unable to fully understand God.

The three persons of God speak to each other and relate to each other. This can be seen in Genesis 1:26; 3:22, and in other places in the Bible. At the baptism of Jesus all three persons of God were present and related to each other. The Father spoke and said, 'You are my Son, whom I love; with you I am well pleased.' At the same moment the Holy Spirit descended on Christ in the form of a dove (Mark 1:9–11).

The Bible teaches that the Father is God (Rom. 1:7). The Bible teaches that the Son is God (Heb. 1:8). The Bible teaches that the Holy Spirit is God (Acts 5:3–4). Yet the Bible makes it very clear that there is only one God (Deut. 4:35) and that there is no one like him. In Isaiah 44:6–7 God says, 'I am the first and I am the last; apart from me there is no God. Who then is like me?' This revelation about the nature of God is so difficult that all men struggle with it, including Christians. He is the God we cannot understand.

Each person of God does a different work. God the Father rules the universe. He makes the final decisions about all things (Acts 1:7; 17:24–26). The motto on an African lorry correctly says, 'When God says yes, who will say no?' God the Son is the one through whom the universe was made and the one who holds all things together by his word (Heb. 1:2–3). He is the commander-in-chief of the angels of God (Rev. 19:11–14). It is he who humbled himself and came to earth to accomplish man's salvation through his death on the cross (Col. 1:19–

20). God the Holy Spirit is the active person of God at work in the world today (John 16:7–14), especially in the church (1 Cor. 12:1–13).

Muslims often say that Christians believe in three Gods. Jehovah's Witnesses say that Christ is the highest angel created by God. Unitarians say that Christ was just a great man. The problem is that each of these groups of people tries to understand God from a human viewpoint. The truth is that God is far too great for any human mind to understand. The only accurate knowledge we can have about God is what he reveals to us about himself in the Bible.

A careful study of the Hebrew word used to describe the unity of God in the Old Testament will increase our understanding. The word is *echad*. It is used in Deut. 6:4: 'Hear, O Israel: the Lord our God, the Lord is one (*echad*).' This word describes a compound unity, such as the unity God planned for marriage ('they shall be one' – Gen. 2:24). It is used to describe the people at the Tower of Babel as being 'one' people (Gen. 11:6). There is a different Hebrew word, *yacheed*, which means one in the absolute sense. This word is not used to describe God.

Sometimes illustrations are given to help us understand the truth of the Trinity. Some people suggest that God can be thought of as one thinks of water. Water is one substance, but it can exist as steam, liquid and ice at the same time. Each of these three forms is the same substance, but each one has different characteristics. This illustration has value only in showing us that even a common thing in life can be three and be one at the same time.

We must be careful with illustrations. God is not like an egg, water or like anything else our human minds can imagine. Indeed, all human illustrations fail to correctly portray the nature of the triune God as he is revealed in the Bible. We must simply believe what the Bible reveals to us about God. There is only one God and he is three persons. There is no one like him (Isa. 44:6–7).

Why then does Christ speak of returning to his Father and his God (John 20:17)? Why does he pray to the Father as his God (John 17:1, Matt. 27:46)? Why does he say that the Father is greater than he is (John 14:28), if Jesus himself is God (John 1:1)? Such questions are often raised by Jehovah's Witnesses and by others who refuse to accept the revealed truth of the Bible. We shall now seek to answer these questions.

D. WHAT HAPPENED WHEN GOD BECAME A HUMAN BEING?

In Philippians 2:5–8, we are given a key which opens the door to understanding these difficult questions. The key is the Greek word *ekenosen*, which means 'emptied'. Philippians 2:5–8 (NASB) says, 'Have this attitude in yourselves which was also in Christ Jesus, who although he existed in the form of God, did not regard equality with God a thing to be grasped, but emptied (*ekenosen*) himself, taking the form of a bondservant, and being made in the likeness of men . . . he humbled himself by becoming obedient to the point of death, even death on a cross.'

In becoming a man of flesh and blood, Jesus laid aside his equality with God the Father (Phil. 2:6). He emptied himself of his divine glory in order to totally identify himself with the human race. It is not that he did not possess the attributes of God. Rather, the attributes of God were hidden most of the time by his humanity. He purposely chose not to use these attributes in his earthly life except when the Father wanted him to use them. He laid aside his glory and equality with the Father in much the same way we might take off a robe we are wearing. It is still our robe, but we choose not to wear it.

In addition to laying aside his equality with God the Father during his 33 years on earth, Jesus also took upon himself the limitations caused by dwelling in a human body of flesh and blood (Heb. 2:14). This is the meaning of the word incarnation. He became confined to the conditions of flesh and blood existence in the same way we are confined to our bodies. His body could feel hunger, fatigue and pain just as much as our bodies (Heb. 4:15). As he grew up, he had to learn to walk and to read and write, just as any other child would do (Luke 2:52). During his earthly life, the glory and the attributes of God were hidden by the humanity of Jesus.

Many times in Jesus' earthly life he displayed his equality with God the Father by his miracles (John 10:37–38). He demonstrated that he was God when he did things that only God can do, such as raising people from the dead (John 11:43–44). His divine glory was also seen by Peter, James and John on the Mount of Transfiguration (Matt. 17:2–7). Although it was a brief experience, Jesus' transfiguration was so awesome that the disciples never forgot this brief glimpse of his deity and glory (2 Peter 1:16–18).

During his earthly life as a man of flesh and blood, there were times when Jesus did not use his omniscience. In Matthew 24:36, he said that only the Father knew the time of his return. There were times when he did not use his omnipotence, as in Matthew 4:3–4, when he refused to turn stones into bread. In order to become our high priest (Heb. 2:17–18; 4:14–15), and in order to accomplish our salvation (Heb. 2:9–10), he limited himself to being fully human.

By becoming a human being Christ made himself depend on God the Father for every need just as we must do. He would not turn the stones into bread in the wilderness to satisfy his hunger (Matt. 4:3–4). Instead he depended on God to provide his food just as we must do. He made himself depend on God the Father through prayer to meet his earthly needs just as we must depend on God through prayer to meet our earthly needs (Luke 6:12). As our high priest he prayed to the Father as his God on our behalf (John 17:1–26). For this reason it was altogether correct for Jesus to say that the Father was greater than he himself was during his earthly life (John 14:28).

Because Jesus was fully human, he struggled with life just as we do (Heb. 4:15). As a result of his complete humanity he is able to sympathize with our weaknesses and temptations. He can help us in our struggles (Heb. 2:18; 4:16). Because he suffered as we do, he is fully qualified to represent us before God the Father as our great high priest (Heb. 4:14–16). Even now he prays for us in heaven with compassion and pity, because he has personally experienced our suffering and weakness (Rom. 8:34, Heb. 7:25).

E. HOW CAN GOD BE PRESENT EVERYWHERE AT THE SAME TIME?

The Bible teaches that God is present everywhere in the universe at the same time. This attribute is called his omnipresence. African traditional religions also believe in the omnipresence of God. The Langi say, 'He is like the air.' The Ngombe speak of God as, 'The One who fills everything.' The Barundi speak of him as, 'He who is met everywhere.' In the traditional African idea of God, he is usually associated with the sky in some way.

King Solomon declared, 'The heavens, even the highest heavens cannot contain you. How much less this temple I have built' (2 Chron. 6:18). King David said, 'Where can I go from your Spirit? Where can I flee from your presence? If I go up to the heavens, you are there; if I make my bed in the depths, you are there' (Psalm 139:7–8). In the book of Jeremiah, God said, ' "Can anyone hide in secret places so that I cannot see him?" declares the Lord. "Do not I fill heaven and earth?" declares the Lord' (Jer. 23:24).

From these verses we understand that God is present everywhere in the universe at the same moment. He is omnipresent. This idea is really more than our human minds can understand. How can God be here in this place and there in that place at the same time? How can he be hearing and answering our prayers while at the same moment he is hearing and answering the prayers of everyone else all over the world? The reason is not hard to understand. God is spirit (John 4:21–24) and a spirit is not necessarily restricted by space.

The problem for us is the limitation of our bodies and our minds. We can only be in one place at one time. We can only listen to one person at a time. We find it difficult to understand how it can be otherwise.

Our children sometimes ask how God can hear the prayers of all the people who are praying in the world at the same time and manage to answer them all. Even as adults we find it difficult to answer this. But the truth is, God is not a man. He is God and there is no one like him (Isa. 40:18). He is present everywhere at the same time (Jer. 23:24). The Bible says, 'The eyes of the LORD are in every place, watching the evil and the good' (Prov. 15:3 NASB).

Because God is spirit we are warned not to make any image in the likeness of him (Ex. 20:4, Deut. 4:15–19). To worship an image or form of God would be idolatry, and we are warned to avoid idolatry (1 John 5:21). Concerning the earthly body of Jesus, Paul says, 'From now on we regard no one from a worldly point of view. Though we once regarded Christ in this way, we do so no longer' (2 Cor. 5:16). It is important for us to learn to worship God in spirit and in truth because God is spirit (John 4:24).

SUMMARY

From the revelation of nature we know there is a God. We can easily see that he has infinite power and wisdom. In special revelation the Bible reveals truth about God that no person on earth could have imagined. He is one being but he exists in three persons called the Father, the Son, and the Holy Spirit. All three persons are equally God. The three persons together are the one supreme Being. He is the creator and sustainer of all things. In his earthly life Jesus rightly said that the Father was greater than he was (John 14:28). He said this because in becoming a man of flesh and blood, Jesus laid aside his equality with God the Father and became dependent on the Father as ordinary people are dependent on God (Phil. 2:6–7). He accepted the limitation and weakness of a human body in order to accomplish our salvation. As a spirit, God is present everywhere in the universe at the same time. Although we cannot understand this truth, it is a source of comfort to know that God is with us wherever we may be.

DISCUSSION QUESTIONS AND PROJECTS BASED ON CHAPTER FOUR

1. How would you explain the truth of the Trinity to a Muslim who strongly insists that there is only one God?

2. Divide into small groups of three or four each. Make a list of the needs and fears people have to which the omnipresence of God might be a comfort or an encouragement.

3. Divide into working groups of five each. Let each group make an outline listing the kind of works done by each person of God, the Father, the Son, and the Holy Spirit.

4. Prepare a written defense for the truth of the Trinity by finding verses which show that:
   (a) The Father is God
   (b) The Son is God
   (c) The Holy Spirit is God
   (d) There is only one God

5. How would you answer the question of Magaji at the beginning of this chapter, where he asks how Christ can be God while he himself prays to God?

6. Have the group discuss the difference between knowing God in the way that all Africans know God and knowing God in the way Jesus meant in John 17:3.

7. Divide into small groups of four each. Find verses or passages in the Bible which clearly teach that Jesus is God and that the Holy Spirit is God. Each person should write down these references in his or her own Bible for times of opportunity to speak with a Muslim or a Jehovah's Witness. Each group may use a concordance and a cross-reference Bible.

SUGGESTED FOR FURTHER READING

McGrath, A. *Understanding the Trinity*. Michigan: Zondervan, 1990.

Milne, B. *Know the Truth*. Leicester: InverVarsity Press, reprinted 1991.

Packer, J.I. *Knowing God*. London: 2nd edn 1993.

Shelly, Bruce L. *Christian Theology In Plain Language*. Waco, Texas: Word Books, 1985.

Smail, T. *The Forgotten Father*. London: Hodder, 1980.

5

Jesus Christ – The Man Who Revealed God

'Soon afterwards, Jesus went to a town called Nain, and his disciples and a large crowd went along with him. As he approached the town gate, a dead person was being carried out – the only son of his mother, and she was a widow. And a large crowd from the town was with her. When the Lord saw her, his heart went out to her, and he said, "Don't cry." Then he went up and touched the coffin, and those carrying it stood still. He said, "Young man, I say to you, get up!" The dead man sat up and began to talk, and Jesus gave him back to his mother' (Luke 7:11–15).

What is God like? That is a question people have asked throughout history. Listen to the request of Philip, one of Jesus' followers: 'Lord, show us the Father and that will be enough for us' (John 14:8). Like all of us, Philip wanted to see God. He wanted to know what God is like. Almost all people are curious about God. They would like to see him and to know what he is really like. In answer to Philip's question Jesus said, 'Don't you know me, Philip, even after I have been among you such a long time? Anyone who has seen me has seen the Father' (John 14:9). Jesus was telling Philip that he (Jesus) had the attributes (characteristics) of God. The writer of the epistle to the Hebrews said, 'The son is the radiance of God's glory and the exact representation of his being' (Heb. 1:3). In other words, Jesus Christ reveals the character and the attributes of God exactly as they are.

If we could promise people that God would appear at 2:00 p.m. next Tuesday in the local football stadium, the whole city would come out to see God and to hear what he has to say. Yet, God did come to our world 2000 years ago in the person of Jesus Christ. Unfortunately many people did not believe in him then and many people still do not believe in him today.

We have seen that in order to believe what the Bible teaches about Christ, we must be able to believe the Bible. We must be sure that it is true and that it is the word of God. Therefore we have presented evidence in chapter two to prove that the Bible is true and that it is the word of God. We can believe what the Bible teaches about Christ. In this chapter we will consider what it teaches about who he is, what he did and what God is like.

A. What does the Bible tell us about Jesus Christ? Who is he?
B. What are the attributes of God as revealed in Jesus Christ?
C. What can we learn about God from the names of God?

A. WHAT DOES THE BIBLE TELL US ABOUT JESUS CHRIST? WHO IS HE?

'When Jesus saw the crowd around him, he gave orders to cross to the other side of the lake . . . Then he got into the boat, and his disciples followed him. Without warning, a furious storm came up on the lake, so that the waves swept over the boat. But Jesus was sleeping. The disciples went and woke him, saying, "Lord, save us! We're going to drown!" He replied, "You of little faith, why are you so afraid?" Then he got up and rebuked the winds and the waves, and it was completely calm. The men were amazed and asked, "What kind of man is this? Even the winds and the waves obey him!" ' (Matt. 8:18–27)

What kind of a man is Jesus Christ? A few people say he was not really a man. They suggest that he just looked like a man, but that he was really a spirit. This would be an acceptable explanation in Africa where many people have seen spirits. However, Jesus was not just a spirit. He was not just like a man. He was a real man of flesh and blood like us. He was born of a woman and grew up like any other Jewish child (Luke 2:51–52). He was a carpenter in a small town and was well known by his neighbours. He grew up in a family of four brothers and had two or more sisters (Mark 6:3). He became tired (John 4:6) and thirsty (John 4:7). He became hungry (Matt. 4:2) and he slept (Matt. 8:24) like any other man.

Jesus was a real man in history. He lived a simple life. He never travelled very far from his home area. He did not have many years of formal education. He was never a political or military leader. But there is something about this man that is different from every other man who ever lived.

No one can be compared to Jesus Christ. He stands alone in history. He is different from all men of all times. His virgin birth, his sinless life, his holy character, his incomparable love, his proven miracles, his power over all things, his sacrificial death, his victorious resurrection from the dead, and his bodily ascension into heaven all tell us one thing: There has never been a man like this. Jesus is the man who is God. He is God who became a man.

John's gospel begins: 'In the beginning was the Word, and the Word was with God, and the Word was God' (John 1:1). Then in John 1:14 the writer says, 'The Word (Jesus) became flesh and lived for a while among us.' In other words, God took on a human body.

A little further John writes, 'No one has ever seen God, but God the One and Only who is at the Father's side, has made him known' (John 1:18). Jesus said, 'Anyone who has seen me has seen the Father' (John 14:9). Paul writes, 'For in Christ all the fulness of the deity lives in bodily form' (Col. 2:9). The writer of Hebrews states, 'But about the son he says, "Your throne, O God, will last for ever and ever" ' (Heb. 1:8). These verses all plainly teach that Jesus Christ is God. God revealed himself to mankind in the person of the man, Jesus of Nazareth.

What we know about God does not depend on what we can imagine. We can know about God because God has chosen to reveal the truth to us in the Bible. The fact that God became a man may not be so difficult to understand. In some African traditions, one or more of their great ancestral kings or warriors was thought to be a god in human form. The Bible reveals that the supreme Being himself, not a divinity or an ancestral spirit, took on an earthly body in the person of Jesus of Nazareth.

The Arians were people who lived in the early years of the Christian church. They followed the wrong teaching of a misguided elder from Alexandria, named Arius. Arius taught that Jesus was not really God, but a person created by God and higher than men. Many people, like the Arians of long ago and the Jehovah's Witnesses of today (who teach a similar wrong idea), refuse to believe that Jesus is God as the Bible plainly tells us. They cannot understand this truth with their minds so they reject the truth. As we saw in chapter four, the complete truth about God is more than our human minds can fully understand. The English author C.S. Lewis spoke about this limitation of our human understanding when he said, 'If I could understand God, he would not be God.' Lewis was saying that a God which we could easily understand would not be the true supreme Being who is revealed in the Bible.

The Bible reveals that Jesus Christ is fully man and fully God. He is not half man and half God. He is the God-man. There is no one like him. With their eyes, ears and other senses, people cannot know what God is like. Jesus reveals who God is and what he is like. Therefore, if we want to know who God is and what he is like, we must study the man, Jesus of Nazareth.

B. WHAT ARE THE ATTRIBUTES OF GOD AS REVEALED IN JESUS CHRIST?

THE OMNIPOTENCE AND PROVIDENCE OF GOD

How did Jesus reveal God? What is God like?

He is the man who walked on water (Mark 6:45–51).

He is the man who instantly dried up a fig tree (Matt. 21:19–20).

He is the man who spoke to the wind and the waves and they obeyed him (Luke 8:22–25).

He is the man who cast a legion of demons out of one man (Mark 5:1–16).

He is the man who changed a greedy and corrupt tax collector into an honest and generous man (Luke 19::1–9).

He is the man who brought a man to life who had been dead four days (John 11:38–44).

He is the man who changed water into wine to keep a marriage celebration from ending (John 2:1–11).

He is the man who fed more than 5000 hungry men and women from five small loaves of bread and two fish and ended with 12 baskets of fish and bread left over (Matt. 14:15–21).

He is the man who gave an enormous catch of fish to fishermen who had worked all night and had caught nothing (John 21:3–6).

The Omnipotence of God
Just about everyone realizes that God is all-powerful (omnipotent). People in Africa have understood this truth for countless centuries as they daily observe the natural creation of God around them. The Zulu people say that God is, 'He who roars so that all nations be struck with terror.'

What do we learn about the power of God as we look at the life of Jesus? More importantly, what do we learn about how God uses his power?

When Jesus calmed the storm by speaking to the wind and waves, his disciples were amazed. What kind of a man could control the violent forces of nature with a spoken word? Somehow healing the sick may have seemed reasonable to them. Perhaps they thought God was answering Jesus' prayers for the sick. But how could any person speak to the wind and waves and have them obey him? What kind of a man was this?

On another occasion Jesus walked on the water. How could anyone walk on water? Jesus seemed to be able to change or suspend the very laws of nature. How could he do such things? Something similar happened on the land. He simply spoke to a fig tree and the tree instantly dried up and died (Matt. 21:19–21)! How could anyone remove life from a tree just by a spoken word?

The extent of Jesus' power was more than the disciples could understand. He had shown power over diseases and deformities (Matt. 12:10–13). He had revealed power over demons (Matt. 8:28–32). He had demonstrated the power to change water into wine (John 2:1–11). He had displayed power to create enough bread and fish to feed a huge crowd from a few small pieces of bread and fish (Matt. 14:15–21). He had demonstrated power over both the physical world and the spirit world. He had even shown that he had the power to change corrupt human beings into honest people, as he did in the case of the greedy and corrupt tax collector named Zacchaeus (Luke 19:1–8). What kind of a man was this?

Then Jesus performed the ultimate miracle. He did what no one but God could possibly do. He raised a man from the dead – a man who had been dead for four days (John 11:38–44)! The truth slowly became clear to his followers. This man not only had power, he seemed to have all power in heaven and on earth. He had to be more than a prophet. Who was he? God?

Jesus performed every miracle with a purpose. In most cases one of those purposes was to reveal who he was. Jesus said, 'even though you do not believe me, believe the miracles, that you may learn and understand that the Father is in me, and I in the Father' (John 10:38). His miracles showed that he had power that belongs only to God. He did what only God can do. He demonstrated power over everything in heaven and on earth. He revealed that he had power over things and people and the forces of nature and even over the spirit world.

The unusual thing about Jesus was the way he used his power. In just about every situation, he used his power for the benefit of others or to help those who were suffering, discouraged or beaten down by life. Unlike so many medicine men and witch-doctors in Africa, he did not take payment or gifts from people for healing or helping them. He simply told the people he helped to go and tell others about the great things God had done for them (Mark 5:18–19).

There is only one correct explanation for the life and miracles of Jesus Christ. He was not just a great moral teacher, as many people insist. He is not the highest angel, as the Jehovah's Witnesses claim. He was not just one of the prophets, as the Muslims teach. No, Jesus Christ is God himself. This was demonstrated by his life and miracles. There has never lived a man like this man. The Bible says in Colossians 2:9: 'For in Christ all the fulness of the deity lives in bodily form.'

The Providence of God

Africans are consciously aware of the fact that God is the provider of life and the one who sustains it. This attribute is called the providence of God. An Ovimbundu name for God has the meaning, 'He who supplies the needs of his creatures.' It is clearly understood that God is the one who makes it possible for man to grow crops for food, especially by providing rain. He is often referred to as the 'giver of rain'. He is also known as the giver of the greatest gift of all, the gift of human life from the womb.

These ideas are in agreement with the word of God. When he spoke to Job, God challenged Job with questions such as, 'Can you raise your voice to the clouds and cover yourself with a flood of water? Do you send the lightning bolts on their way? Do they report to you, "Here we are" ' (Job 38:34–35)? God spoke through the psalmist and said, 'Behold, children are a gift of the LORD' (Psalm 127:3–NASB).

The miracle of the feeding of the 5000 and the miraculous catch of fish show us the providence of God in the life of Christ. The Lord was not willing to send the crowd away hungry, so he created a great quantity of bread and fish to feed them (Matt. 14:15–21). God knows our need for food and he supplies us with food by providing rain, sunlight, soil and seed for crops to grow, and animal life (Matt. 5:45, Acts 14:17). In feeding the more than 5000 people, the Lord simply bypassed the usual gradual process by which he provides food for mankind, and produced the food instantly. On another occasion he showed his concern for the disciples' need to catch fish for their income, and he provided them with a large catch of fish (John 21:3–6). In providing the fish, Jesus also showed them that without God's help their labours were useless (John 21:5–6).

Usually God supplies our needs naturally by giving men strength to farm the land (Gen. 2:15) and by making the earth produce crops (Isa. 55:10). He is just as able to provide supernaturally. So he provided manna for two million Israelites in the desert for 40 years. However, we need to have the right perspective on the miracles of God. The normal way God provides for our needs is through the laws and regular seasons of nature and not by supernatural miracles. Thus while God provided manna for the Israelites during their wandering in the desert where they could not grow food, this provision ceased when they entered the land of Canaan where they could get food and farm the land (Joshua 5:12). In whatever way he does it, it is still God who provides what people need. Psalm 145:16 says, 'You open your hand, and satisfy the desires of every living thing.'

Life is a gracious gift from God. According to the Bible, the birth of children in marriage is a gift from the Lord (Psalm 127:3). It must not be assumed, however, that if a couple is unable to have children, they are therefore cursed by God, as many traditional people believe. We will look at the problem of childlessness more closely in the chapter on marriage.

God also decides how many days each of us will be given to live on the earth (Hebrews 9:27). The psalmist said, 'All the days ordained for me were written in your book before one of them came to be' (Psalm 139:16). In his providence Jesus Christ gives life, he sustains life, and he takes away life. He also holds the world together by his word (Heb. 1:3). The most dramatic evidence that Jesus Christ is the giver of life took place in those cases where he brought the dead back to life, as in the story at the beginning of this chapter (Luke 7:11–15).

God provides for people in many different ways. Because he knows people's deepest emotional needs, he has made a general provision to meet those needs through marriage and family. Every human being in the world wants to be loved and appreciated by someone else. Marriage meets this deep need of men and women. God is love (1 John 4:8) and he has given people the gift of love, companionship and emotional security in marriage. Since not all people have the opportunity to be married, God is also able to provide other ways to meet these needs. One way this can happen is through the fellowship of the local church.

The miracle at the wedding feast in Cana of Galilee (John 2:1–11), shows us that Jesus has power to change things. He can take the ordinary things of life (like water) and turn them into unusual things (like wine). On this occasion Jesus revealed that he has power over the quality of things, and over the quality of life itself. On this occasion he also revealed that he personally cared about the happiness of the young bride and groom. When Jesus enters a person's life, the quality of that person's life is changed. Just like the water became wine, a selfish and greedy person (like Zacchaeus in the New Testament) became an unselfish and generous person (Luke 19:8).

THE SOVEREIGNTY AND OMNISCIENCE OF GOD

How did Jesus reveal God? What is God like?

He is the man through whom the universe was made and who sustains it by his word (Heb. 1:2–3).

He is the man who has been given all authority in heaven and on earth (Matt. 28:18).

He is the man who chose us to be his holy people, even before the world was created (John 15:16, Eph. 1:4).

He is the man who knows the future before it happens (Luke 21:1–28).

He is the man who sometimes revealed to his disciples the details of what was about to take place (Mark 14:12–16).

He is the man who knew exactly how much the poor widow had given, and why she had given it. (Mark 12:42–43).

He is the man who knew the secret sins of the woman of Samaria (John 4:17–18).

The Sovereignty of God
Sovereignty means absolute rule or authority over a kingdom, a geographical area, or an empire. A person who is a sovereign is an

absolute ruler. A simple but profound statement about the sovereignty of God as the highest ruler in the universe, is expressed by the motto on the front of an African lorry: 'No king is God.'

And so it is. God rules over all. God caused Nebuchadnezzar, the arrogant and boastful king of Babylon, to lose his mind (Dan. 4:28–33). After seven years of insanity, Nebuchadnezzar was thoroughly humbled before God. In an open letter to his entire kingdom he testified, 'I praised the Most High; I honoured and glorified him who lives for ever. His dominion is an eternal dominion; his kingdom endures from generation to generation. All the peoples of the earth are regarded as nothing. He does as he pleases with the powers of heaven and the peoples of the earth. No one can hold back his hand or say to him: "What have you done?" . . . Now I, Nebuchadnezzar, praise and exalt and glorify the King of heaven, because everything he does is right and all his ways are just. And those who walk in pride he is able to humble' (Dan. 4:34–37). What an amazing testimony from the king who once defiantly said to Daniel's three friends, 'What god will be able to rescue you from my hand?' (Dan. 3:15).

Indeed God is the supreme and ultimate King, and he rules over all (Psalm 103:19).

In the book of Job we read that the fallen angel Satan had to come before God to get permission before he could trouble poor Job (Job 1:6–12). Later Job himself testified of God's sovereignty when he said, 'I know that you can do all things; no plan of yours can be thwarted' (Job 42:2). What a great comfort it is to understand that even the terrible afflictions which Satan is allowed to bring upon people must pass the holy gate of God's permission. God alone rules.

Who is this God with ultimate authority over all things and all persons in the universe? What is his name? Jesus said, 'All authority in heaven and on earth has been given to me' (Matt. 28:18). In the last book of the Bible, Jesus Christ is seen leading the armies of heaven. On his robe is written his eternal title: 'King of Kings and Lord of Lords' (Rev. 19:16). In the book of Philippians, Paul reveals that one day, 'at the name of Jesus every knee should bow, in heaven and on earth and under the earth, and every tongue confess that Jesus Christ is Lord, to the glory of God the Father' (Phil. 2:10–11). There can be no question. Jesus Christ is King of the universe.

God is sovereign. God decides and does not consult anyone. When speaking to his disciples who thought they had chosen to follow him, Jesus surprised them when he said, 'You did not choose me, but I chose you and appointed you to go and bear fruit – fruit that will last' (John 15:16).

One very practical application of the truth of the sovereignty of Jesus Christ over all things is found in the book of Revelation. Jesus spoke to the Christians in the church at Philadelphia and said, 'See, I have placed before you an open door that no one can shut' (Rev. 3:8).

He had just revealed himself to this church as, 'him who is holy and true, who holds the key of David. What he opens no one can shut, and what he shuts, no one can open' (Rev. 3:7). What an encouragement this is to Christians who give their lives to serve the Lord. They serve the one who is sovereign over all things. When he opens a door of ministry, no power in the world can shut it!

This is exactly what the whole world has seen in the former Soviet Union during the early 1990s. The former atheist leaders determined during the communist revolution of 1918 that they would forever shut the door on the truth of God. But God's people prayed fervently that God would bring down communism and open the door again to the gospel. In answer to their prayers, Jesus Christ forced that door wide open and brought down communism, so that the Russian government has even sought Christian teachers for their schools and requested that the *Jesus* film be shown in all primary schools! Jesus will not allow the doors he has opened to be shut when he has determined to keep them open. And when he shuts a door, no power in the world can open it. It is just as the motto says on one African lorry: 'When God says yes, who will say no?' God is sovereign.

The Omniscience of God

God knows everything. This attribute is called omniscience. God knows everything there is to know about our lives. He knows what we hide from others and even what we try to hide from ourselves! He knows things about us that even we ourselves don't know, such as the number of hairs on our heads (Luke 12:7). He knows our every movement and our every thought. The psalmist says, 'You know when I sit and when I rise; you perceive my thoughts from afar . . . you are familiar with all my ways. Before a word is on my tongue, you know it completely, O Lord' (Psalm 139:2–4). He knows everything there is to know about the past, the present and the future. In short, he knows everything. This attribute is called omniscience and it has great importance for our lives.

Because God knows the future, nothing can take him by surprise. He cannot be deceived, or frightened, or defeated. Nothing can be done by anyone, anywhere, that he does not already know about beforehand. He also knows the result of every action that will take place. Therefore no one, including Satan, can successfully oppose God. No one can frustrate his plans (Job 42:2, Eph. 1:11)

Jesus revealed the omniscience of God when he spoke to the woman at the well of Sychar in Samaria and told her about the secret sins of her life (John 4:17–18).

We must understand that nothing can happen to one of God's children that God has not already known about. He has also decided in advance what he will do about it according to his perfect love and wisdom. The psalmist declares, 'All the days ordained for me were written in your book before one of them came to be' (Psalm 139:16). Because of his infinite knowledge and infinite power, God is able to cause all things to work together for good for those who love him (Rom. 8:28). This is one of the most amazing and most encouraging truths found in the entire Bible.

Imagine a believer who is overtaken by a terrible situation (like Job). To that person it may seem like the end of everything. But God already knew about the situation before it happened. He also knew how he would make that situation work out for good because he has promised to do that (Rom. 8:28). Because Jesus has all authority in heaven and on earth, he can make good come from even the most wicked plans of men or of fallen angels.

It is very unlikely that we will understand how God is working for good in our lives when difficulties come upon us. Perhaps we will only understand it in heaven when we look back on our lives. But God says it is so and God does not lie to us. For our part, we must learn to trust God in difficult situations, and to believe his promises about using it for good.

The book of Job teaches this truth. God gave Satan permission to torment Job with many severe trials. God knew what he would do for Job in the end, although Job did not understand what was going on, or why. In the end, God worked out these trials for the good of Job, who loved God, just as Romans 8:28 teaches.

It is impossible for evil people or fallen angels to defeat God. For this reason Christians are taught to, 'give thanks in all circumstances' (1 Thess. 5:18). This kind of faith delivers us from the fear of man's evil plans against us (Psalm 27:1–3). This kind of faith destroys Satan's power over our lives (Rev. 12:11).

Consider what God did about Satan's plan for man's destruction in the garden of Eden. Before it ever happened, God planned how he would handle the situation. Before the foundation of the world he planned how he would accomplish our salvation through Jesus Christ (Eph. 1:4, 1 Pet. 1:20). From this we can see that God is able to make good come from the most terrible circumstances.

The Bible says, 'He who did not spare his own Son, but gave him up for us all, how will he not also, along with him, graciously give us all things?' (Rom. 8:32). God can do that because he knows the future and because he has all power in heaven and on earth to change the circumstances that affect our lives. He knows everything. He is in control of all things. He is omniscient and he is sovereign.

As another example, recall how Joseph was bitterly mistreated by his brothers and later by others in Egypt (Gen. 37–40). For all the good Joseph did, he ended up forgotten in an Egyptian prison (Gen. 40:23). But God not only changed Joseph's situation, he made good come out of it to such an extent that even his sinful brothers were blessed (Gen. 41–50). Joseph realized it was God who had done this miracle. Joseph said to his brothers, 'You intended to harm me, but God intended it for good to accomplish what is now being done, the saving of many lives' (Gen. 50:20).

Recall also how Mary and Martha sent urgent word to Jesus about their brother Lazarus' sickness (John 11:3). Yet Jesus allowed Lazarus to die and allowed the sisters' hearts to be broken (John 11:4–19). Thus it often happens to us. Our hearts are broken and we think the Lord has forgotten us. Jesus had not forgotten Mary and Martha. In the end he brought far greater good from the situation by raising Lazarus from the dead than if he had only healed Lazarus.

God chose David to be king of Israel even though he knew that David would commit great sins. He chose him because he knew that David was a man after God's heart (1 Sam. 13:14). He knew David would repent of his sin and grow through the experience. The other sons of Jesse looked more promising (1 Sam. 16:5–7) but they did not have the love for God that David had. God knew that. God is omniscient and God is sovereign.

THE LOVE OF GOD

How did Jesus reveal God? What is God like?

He is the man who healed ten outcast lepers who had no hope of wholeness and no hope of any normal relationships with other people (Luke 17:11–19).

He is the man who was willing to forgive a prostitute who washed his feet with her tears (Luke 7:36–48).

He is the man who felt pity for the widow of Nain whose only son had died. He is the man who raised her son from the dead and gave him back to her (Luke 7:11–15).

He is the man who forgave those who tortured and murdered him even as they were doing it (Luke 23:34).

He is the man who paid for our sin with his own life while we were still sinful and rebellious (Isa. 53:5, Rom. 5:8, 1 Pet. 2:24).

For many people the most important attribute of God is his love for mankind. Although Africans do not traditionally speak about the love of God, they are aware of his goodness in providing rain, crops, children, and their physical needs. God's goodness and his love are closely related in the African world-view.

Real love is always seen much more by actions than by words. Love is usually expressed in some specific action which is for the good of the one who is loved. God's love is revealed in his actions for the good of his creatures. God's love is seen most clearly in the life and works of Jesus Christ. By his actions Jesus revealed that love is a primary part of the character of God. Jesus did things which revealed a depth of love beyond human understanding. He forgave the very men who were murdering him even while they were doing it. From his agony on the cross, Jesus cried out to God the Father and said, 'Father, forgive them, for they do not know what they are doing' (Luke 23:34).

The entire period of his public life, Jesus acted in kindness, love, and mercy. He healed the sick, restored the blind, cleansed the lepers, cast out demons, raised the dead, and ministered to people's pain and need in countless ways.

The opening story of this chapter reveals the love and compassion of Jesus Christ in a powerful and touching way. The only son of a widow had died. She had lost her husband and had but one son. He was very likely her only source of material support as well as the only source of emotional comfort and encouragement since the death of her husband. Now this one source of comfort and help was gone. The son was dead. Jesus saw this poor woman, and by his omniscience he knew the anguish and despair in her heart. In a single moment of time, with one brief spoken sentence of omnipotent power and compassionate love, Jesus totally changed this poor woman's life from hopeless despair to overwhelming joy. There are no words to describe the emotions she must have felt in her heart.

Isaiah spoke about this wonderful love of God to mankind, revealed in Jesus Christ. He said the Messiah would, 'bestow on them a crown of beauty instead of ashes, the oil of gladness instead of mourning, and a garment of praise instead of a spirit of despair' (Isa. 61:3). How true this was for the poor widow, and how true it has been for millions of people since then! For many of us, it was the love of Christ which first brought us to repentance and to faith in him. No one in all of human history has ever loved others as this man has loved us. This is the heart of God. This is what the exalted One is really like. The Bible says, 'Whoever does not love does not know God, because God is love' (1 John 4:8).

A parent might give his life to save his child from fire or drowning, but no person in his right mind would willingly give up his life for a stranger, and certainly not for an enemy! That is just what Jesus did. He gave his life for us when we were enemies of God because of our rebellion. Paul wrote, 'Very rarely will anyone die for a righteous man, though for a good man someone might possibly dare to die. But God demonstrates his own love for us in this: While we were still sinners, Christ died for us' (Rom 5:7,8).

Because of his love, Jesus prayed on the cross asking the Father to forgive those who were killing him (Luke 23:34). Because of his love for men, the King of the universe laid aside his royal majesty in heaven and became the servant of men in the person of Jesus Christ (Mark 10:45, Phil. 2:6–7).

How could God become a servant to men? The very idea is unthinkable! But it happened. And Jesus did more than become a humble servant of men. He permitted himself to be tortured and killed by evil men (Phil. 2:8). Why? Because he loved us even before the world existed and because he determined to secure our forgiveness and our salvation (Eph. 1:4, Rev. 13:8). How can it be that God loved us before we were even born? It is because God is love (1 John 4:8). It is his essential nature. Love exists because God exists. And we have seen the love of God through the man, Jesus.

THE COMPASSION AND GOODNESS OF GOD

How did Jesus reveal God? What is God like?

He is the man who saw the emptiness and emotional scars of the woman of Samaria, and gave her something to live for (John 4:4–29).

He is the man who cured the deaf-mute and made him able both to hear and to speak (Mark 7:31–37).

He is the man who took the children in his arms and blessed them, in spite of the complaints of his irritated disciples (Mark 10:13–16).

He is the man who instantly restored a cripple's arm (Mark 3:1–6).

He is the man who wept for the bitter grief of his friends over the death of their brother, and who then changed their sorrow to joy by bringing the dead brother back to life (John 11:33–44).

He is the man who answers the pitiful cries for help from hurting and suffering people and gives them a reason to praise and thank God (Luke 18:37–42).

The Compassion of God

Jesus is the man who has compassion on those who are hurting and suffering. Compassion is an attitude of caring about someone's need to the point of doing something about it. Jesus is the man who cares when we are sick, or disabled or discouraged. He is the one who hears the cries and prayers of the suffering, the hurting, and the outcasts of society.

He is the one who has power to heal, to help, to cure, and to restore. He is the one who is willing to use his power to help those who have lost hope, and to restore to them the joy of being alive (Luke 18:42–43). In Isaiah 61:1 Christ spoke through the prophet and said, 'The Spirit of the Sovereign LORD is on me, because the LORD has anointed me to preach good news to the poor. He has sent me to bind up the brokenhearted.' Jesus revealed the God who loves, who cares and who helps us in our time of need. He revealed the God who answers prayer.

What is God like? From our study of Jesus so far, we have learned that God is omnipotent, sovereign and omniscient. There is nothing that he cannot do if he chooses to do it. Yet he uses his power not for himself, but for man's good. We have seen that God is caring and compassionate, and has a heart of love for his creation. He knows and cares about our suffering and pain. Unlike us, he also has the power to do something about suffering. He is able to heal the sick, to cleanse the leper and to restore the sinner. He is able to lift up the fallen and to heal the broken-hearted. He is able to change our sorrow into joy and our depression into praise and thanksgiving.

The Goodness of God

We also learn from these examples that God is good. He used his power to help those in need and to relieve suffering. He used his power to do good because he is good by nature. The fact is, there is no one truly good, except God. Jesus said to the rich young ruler, 'No one is good – except God alone' (Luke 18:19).

Why then do Christians suffer, if God is good and compassionate? The truth about God's goodness and compassion presents a great problem to Christians. Why does God allow godly people to suffer? Why does God choose to heal some and not to heal others? Why does he allow some devoted Christians to live their lives in great pain and suffering while some clearly evil people escape suffering?

Some people think that all suffering comes from witches and evil spirits. It is true that witches and demons do have evil powers. We will examine this subject more closely in a later chapter. But the vast majority of human suffering cannot be explained by witches and demons. Others think that suffering is the result of some hidden sin in a person's life, or because they lack faith in God. Sometimes hidden sin or lack of faith may be the problem, but this does not explain all suffering. In the case of the man born blind, Jesus rejected the idea that his sin was the reason for his blindness (John 9:2–3). Consider the suffering of Job. The Lord himself said that Job was blameless (Job 1:8)! Furthermore, the gospels relate how Jesus helped some who had little or no faith (Mark 9:24–27). No, there is a mystery about much of our suffering. Only the Lord will be able to explain it all to us in heaven.

We live in a world that is evil because of sin and its effects in people's lives. The world is sick unto death, like a person whose body is being destroyed by a terrible disease. Some of our suffering is the result of our own sins and foolish decisions. However, much of the suffering which takes place in our world is a result of other people's sin and the effects of their sin on society. An example of this would be the bitter suffering and death of thousands of Christians in Rwanda in 1994. Most of these Christians suffered and died not because of some sin in their own lives, but because of the horrible effects of the sin of tribalism and tribal revenge between members of the two main ethnic groups in that country.

Because of the effects of sin, many people suffer from emotional and mental problems more painful to bear than physical problems. Consider, for example, the emotional suffering of children who have watched their parents' love turn to hatred and divorce. In this case, the children become victims of the sinful attitudes and anger of their parents. Much additional suffering in the world is also caused by the activity of Satan. Jesus said that Satan was a murderer from the beginning (John 8:44).

We know that Jesus healed the sick and restored sinners. We know he has the power to do the same today. Jesus is able to heal mental and emotional problems as well as physical problems. Because the spirit of a person will exist forever, the healing of the mind and heart is even more important than the healing of the body.

Jesus still performs miracles in his church today where and when he chooses to do so. At other times he does not. He did not heal all the sick people in Galilee or Judea either. Why did he choose to heal some and not others? No answer is given in the Bible. Since he is God he does what is best. No one can question him. There is a mystery in his mercy.

We are taught to pray, 'Your kingdom come, Your will be done on earth as it is done in heaven' (Matt. 6:10). We know there is no sickness, blindness, pain, or death in heaven (Rev. 21:4). But this prayer has two parts. We are first told to pray, 'Your kingdom come'. It is not likely that we will see the complete answer to the prayer, 'Your will be done on earth as it is done in heaven' until the kingdom of God has fully come on earth. The last chapter of this book describes what it will be like when Christ's kingdom finally comes. This will happen when he returns to this world. Only then will God's will be fully done on earth as it is in heaven.

There are many questions in life to which we are given no answers. Moses wrote that the things which are revealed are for us and for our children, but the things which are not revealed belong to the Lord (Deut. 29:29). We are wise to leave the unanswered questions with God and to trust the Lord for those things he chooses not to explain to us. We know that God is good. We know that he is compassionate. That is what we need to know.

THE HOLINESS AND WRATH OF GOD

How did Jesus reveal God? What is God like?

He is the man who was holy, blameless and pure (Heb. 7:26).

He is the man who committed no sin and told no lies (1 Pet. 2:22).

He is the accused man whose judge declared him innocent of wrongdoing (Luke 23:4).

He is the man in whom his worst enemies could find no fault (John 8:46, John 10:32–33).

He is the man whom even the demons called, 'the Holy One of God' (Mark 1:24, Luke 4:34).

He is the man who publicly exposed the sin and hypocrisy of the Pharisees before everyone (Matt. 23:1–33).

He is the man who drove the greedy money changers from the temple with a whip (John 2:14–16).

He is the man before whom demons were terrified of being destroyed (Mark 1:24).

The Holiness of God

In traditional African beliefs there is usually an unspoken awareness of the sinless perfection of God. This is demonstrated by the strict rules which must be followed during rituals having to do with God. Yoruba people speak of God as, 'the pure King who is without blemish.' However, even though God is understood to be pure and without fault, sin is not generally understood among African peoples to be an offense against God's holiness. Instead, sin is thought to be behaviour which brings shame or defilement to the community. More will be said about this in chapter seven.

The word holiness in the Old Testament had to do with being set apart from common use, for God's use. When the physical objects and clothes used for worship in the tabernacle were made holy (sanctified), it meant that they were set apart from common use, and consecrated or dedicated to God (Lev. 8:10). Thus holiness came to mean dedicated or consecrated to God and hence pure from defilement.

Referring to God, holiness has to do with his character. He is perfect, faultless, pure, and free from all defilement by sin. The prophet Habakkuk said about God, 'Your eyes are too pure to look on evil; you cannot tolerate wrong' (Hab. 1:13). Job said, 'even the. . .stars are not pure in his eyes' (Job 25:5). There is absolutely no sin, defilement or corruption with God. He is not like man. He is altogether righteous. Everything he does is right and perfect. He never does what is evil. He only does what is good.

In one sense God's holiness is his most basic attribute. Most, if not all, of his other moral attributes are related to his holiness. Because God is holy, he is good. Because he is holy, he is compassionate. Because he is holy, he is kind and loving. Because he is holy, he is just. Because he is holy, he has great wrath against sin. Because he is holy, he is faithful to his people.

Because God is holy, he utterly hates sin (Hebrews 7:26, 1 Peter 1:15–16). He also hates sin because sin has spoiled his perfect creation (Gen. 1:31). Therefore he has condemned sin with the death penalty (Gen. 2:17, Rom. 6:23). His hatred for sin reveals his wrath (anger) against sin.

How did Jesus reveal the holiness of God? The statements made about Christ by the apostles clearly teach that he was without sin of any kind (Heb. 7:26, 1 Pet. 2:22). Jesus challenged the Jewish leaders who hated him and eventually murdered him with the question: 'Can any of you prove me guilty of sin?' (John 8:46). Incredibly, the very men who were looking for a way to discredit Christ were unable to name even one sin or fault in his life! This is truly amazing. If Jesus' question had been asked by any other human being, that person's enemies would be quick to list his or her sins and faults.

At Jesus' trial before Pontius Pilate, Pilate insisted several times to the Jews that Jesus was innocent of any wrongdoing (Luke 23:4,14,22). Pilate's wife sent a message to Pilate and referred to Jesus as, 'that righteous man' (Matt. 27:19–NASB). At the announcement of Jesus' birth to Mary by the angel Gabriel, the angel referred to Jesus as 'the holy one' (Luke 1:35). Even the Muslim Qu'ran testifies that Jesus was 'faultless' (Sura 19:19).

Perhaps the most powerful testimony about the holiness of Jesus came from a very unusual source. When Jesus confronted the demons, they called him 'the Holy One of God' (Mark 1:24, Luke 4:34)! Christ's encounters with the Pharisees and the anger with which he drove the money changers out of the temple also reveal the sinless purity of Christ and his hatred for sin.

The temptations of Christ raise two important questions concerning God's holiness which puzzle many believers. First, how could Christ be tempted to sin if he is God? The Bible says, 'God cannot be tempted by evil' (James 1:13). Second, even if he was tempted, how could it mean anything, since God is holy, and cannot sin? The answers to these two questions give us a deeper understanding of the earthly life of Christ.

To answer the first question we must remember that Christ had two natures combined in one person. We have only one nature, a human nature. We are simply people. Christ had two natures. Christ was fully man, as we are, but at the same time he was also fully God. He was not partly man and partly God, but completely man and completely God. In the temptations of Christ it was his human nature, not his divine nature, that was tempted. Since he was completely human as we are, his human nature could feel the trials, struggles, pain and discouragements of life just as much as we can. His human mind and body could also feel the temptation to sin, even though his divine nature could not be tempted and could not sin. We must remember that temptation itself is not sin. It is just an appeal to sin.

The fact that Jesus had a complete human nature also answers the second question. Jesus' human body and mind could feel the appeal to sin (temptation) just as much as our bodies can feel such an appeal. We learn, for example, how deeply Jesus felt the anguish of his trials when we observe his words and behaviour in the garden of Gethsemane. In the anguish which Jesus felt, his sweat became like drops of blood and he cried out to the Father to remove the cup of suffering if that was possible (Luke 22:42–44). Jesus' human nature was being severely tempted to avoid the horror of the cross and the separation from God the Father which the cross would mean (Matt. 27:46). This is an amazing fact because Jesus knew and told others that he had come into the world for the very purpose of going to the cross (John 10:17–18)! Yet when the time came for him to go to the cross, his human nature struggled bitterly with that terrifying reality.

Because of his human mind and human body, Jesus' suffering, trials, and temptations were altogether real. The Bible says he learned obedience through the things which he suffered (Heb. 5:8). That is why he qualifies to be our sympathetic great high priest before the Father (Heb. 4:14–15).

The Wrath of God

Wrath means great anger. In addition to revealing God's love for his creation, Jesus also revealed the wrath of God against sin. Jesus openly exposed the hypocrisy of the Pharisees (Matt. 23:1–33). How did he know they were hypocrites? He obviously saw into their hearts and knew their real thoughts rather than what they pretended to be before others. The Pharisees pretended to be holy but they were not. Their religious practices were only external. The Lord knew their hearts and he was angry with the proud, greedy and selfish thoughts he saw in their hearts. He promised the Pharisees that they would be punished in hell for their sin (Matt. 23:33)! From the way Christ condemned the Pharisees, we learn that God sees what is in the heart. He is an impartial and just judge who cannot be deceived. Jesus' condemnation of the Pharisees reveals God's wrath against hypocrisy and other sins.

We also learn from Jesus' condemnation of the Pharisees that no religious formalities can save us from the just judgments of God, or the wrath of God against sin. Many people are greatly deceived in their practice of religion, just as the Pharisees were. They think that by doing certain rituals or religious practices like baptism, formal prayers, or giving gifts to the poor, they will be acceptable to God. They forget that 'Man looks at the outward appearance, but the Lord looks at the heart' (1 Sam. 16:7).

We see God's wrath against sin when Jesus drove the money changers out of the temple with a whip. Even though he was just one person and they were many, they fled when faced with his wrath. The wrath of God against sin is serious. He will punish every sin (Heb. 2:2). He has prepared eternal punishment for the devil and his angels because of their sin (Matt. 25:41). People whose sins are not forgiven will be cast into the same place of punishment (Matt. 25:41).

The wages of sin is death (Rom. 6:23). No one will escape the death penalty just by doing good works, or by going to church, or by going on pilgrimages, or by saying ritual prayers, or by giving gifts to the poor, or by any other religious practice. There is only one way we can escape the wrath of God against our sin. We must accept the sacrifice which Jesus made for us on the cross (2 Cor. 5:21). Jesus was sacrificed on the cross in our place as a sin offering to God (Rom. 8:3). If we do not accept his sacrifice in our place, we will each pay the death penalty for our own sin. There is no other sacrifice, or ritual or religious duty which God will accept. As the writer to the Hebrews warns us, 'How shall we escape, if we ignore such a great salvation?' (Heb. 2:3).

What can we learn from the encounters which Jesus had with evil spirits? We see his holiness and wrath against sin in a somewhat different way. We also see his sovereign authority over all creatures in the universe. From these encounters we can see that Jesus is Lord of all the spirits.

Evil spirits then and now, are terrified of Jesus Christ because of his holiness and because he is God. The demons correctly referred to him as the Holy One of God (Mark 1:24, Luke 4:34). In the Old Testament, God revealed himself as the Holy One many times (as in Psalm 71:22, Psalm 89:18, Isa. 1:4, 5:19, 10:20, Hos. 11:9). An important application of this fact for today is that a person no longer needs to fear the hatred of Satan or the anger of ancestral spirits. Jesus Christ made all things, including angels and spirit beings (Col. 1:16). He is Lord over them all. He is very willing and very able to deliver his people from the attacks of Satan and evil spirits in answer to prayer (Psalm 50:15, 2 Thess. 3:3). It is important to remember that all evil spirits are subject to Jesus Christ (Luke 4:34). He is their God and he will be their final judge.

Jesus said, 'All authority in heaven and on earth has been given to me' (Matt. 28:18). All spirits in the universe are under his power. The good ones serve him with awe and reverence (Psalm 103:20–21). The bad ones fear him and tremble at his presence, because they know he is going to judge them and punish them for their sin and rebellion (Matt. 8:29, James 2:19). When Jesus is your Lord, you never again need to fear the power of other spirits. God requires that we must serve no one but him (Matt. 4:10, Deut. 6:13). The bondage of living in fear of ancestral spirits is not only unnecessary, it is wrong. When we belong to Jesus Christ, he together with the Father and the Holy Spirit is our Lord and our God.

THE JUSTICE AND MERCY OF GOD

How did Jesus reveal God? What is God like?

He is the man who said that if a man looks on a woman lustfully, he has already committed adultery with her in his heart (Matt. 5:28).

He is the man who allowed a prostitute to wash his feet with her tears and wipe them with her hair, and who told her he had forgiven her sins (Luke 7:36–48).

The Justice of God
God is just. All of his judgments are totally right, fair and impartial. He is never wrong. He is never unfair. He is never corrupt. He does

not excuse sin. In Numbers 14:18 we read, 'The LORD is slow to anger, abounding in love and forgiving sin and rebellion. Yet he does not leave the guilty unpunished.' The epistle to the Hebrews tells us, 'For if the message spoken by angels was binding, and every violation and disobedience received its just punishment, how shall we escape if we ignore such a great salvation' (Heb. 2:2–3)?

God clearly defines good and evil in the Bible. He tells us what is evil and he condemns it. He also tells us what is good and he encourages it. Every culture in the world has its own idea of what is evil and what is good. Cultural ideas of good and evil seem important to us because they determine our acceptance by the community. However, what really matters is how God defines good and evil. If we do what is accepted by the community but is condemned by God, we are in very, very serious trouble. If we do what God condemns as evil, then there will be a just punishment waiting for us, and perhaps even for our children, since our sins will also affect our children (Ex. 34:7). In some cultures, killing for revenge is considered a good and even heroic thing to do. However, God has condemned all forms of murder in his word (Deut. 5:17). In fact, God requires the death sentence for the murderer (Gen. 9:6).

Jesus revealed the justice of God when he interpreted the Old Testament Law of Moses to his listeners. We are surprised and defensive about Jesus' statement concerning lustful desire and adultery. To us adultery is an act. To God it is the secret desire of the heart. Jesus said that if a man looks on a woman lustfully, he has already committed adultery with her in his heart (Matt. 5:28). We bitterly complain that this is an unfair judgment. We resent this judgment because we know we are guilty of this sin. The truth is, it is a totally just judgment. Actions are the result of the hidden desires of the heart. God knows that we deceive our own hearts. He knows what really goes on in our hearts because he knows everything.

God doesn't just examine the actions of a person as an earthly judge must do. He looks right into our hearts and he knows the reason for our behaviour. Thus his judgment is based on the all-important matter of motives. Why do we act as we do? Only God knows the true answer to that question. Only God can make a correct judgment because only he knows what happens in people's hearts. He is the one and only just judge in the universe. Abraham said, 'Will not the Judge of all the earth do right?' (Gen. 18:25).

The Mercy of God
There is good news. Although God is just and omniscient and knows that we are sinners, he is also merciful. Because he is merciful, we do not get the full punishment we deserve. David wrote, 'He does not treat us as our sins deserve, or repay us according to our iniquities' (Psalm 103:10).

Jesus knew all about the sinful life of the prostitute who came to him at the house of Simon the Pharisee (Luke 7:39). He also knew what Simon did not know. In her heart the woman was truly sorry for her sins. Hence he revealed his great mercy. He explained to Simon, 'her many sins have been forgiven' (Luke 7:47). God looks into the heart of a person, and knows whether there is hardened pride or repentant humility. When he sees genuine repentance, he shows his great mercy. He did this for King David when David truly repented of his sins (Psalm 51:1–4). In Psalm 51:17 David said, 'The sacrifices of God are a broken spirit; a broken and a contrite heart, O God, you will not despise.'

The story of King David's sin, repentance and forgiveness gives us some additional understanding of God's justice. David was forgiven for his sin when he truly repented of his sin, because God is merciful (2 Sam. 12:13, Psalm 32:5). However, even though David was forgiven by God, God said there would be earthly consequences in David's life and in his family because of what he had done. Receiving forgiveness of sin from God does not mean there will be no consequences for the wrong we have done. When a person kills another person, forgiveness from God will not bring the dead person back to life. When a person has contracted the disease of AIDS through sexual immorality, finding forgiveness from God for the sin will not kill the AIDS virus. The prophet Nathan explained this fact of earthly consequences to King David when he confronted David about his sins (2 Sam. 12:9–11).

THE ETERNAL EXISTENCE AND IMMUTABILITY OF GOD

How did Jesus reveal God? What is God like?

He is the one who spoke with Abraham (Gen. 18:1–33) and walked on the earth 2000 years before he argued with the Jewish leaders about Abraham (John 8:56–59).

He is the one who spoke to Moses out of the burning bush (Exodus 3:3–14) 1400 years before he spoke to Moses on the Mount of Transfiguration (John 8:57–59, Matt. 17:2).

He is the one whom King David knew as his shepherd and his Lord (Psalm 23:1) 1000 years before his birth as the good shepherd in David's home town of Bethlehem (John 10:14, Luke 20:41–44).

The Eternal Existence of God
Traditional African beliefs about God consistently speak of his eternal existence. The Yoruba call him, 'The mighty immovable Rock that never dies.' The Ngombe speak of him as, 'The Everlasting One of the forest.' The African view of God as the Eternal One, without beginning or end, is in full agreement with the revelation given to us about God in the Bible.

Jesus Christ reveals the eternal existence of God in a way which surprises some people. John's gospel begins, 'In the beginning was the Word . . . and the Word was God' (John 1:1). According to John 1:14, 'the Word' refers to Christ. Even though he came into the world as a man of flesh and blood, the son of Mary, Jesus Christ had always existed. He has no beginning and he has no end. In speaking to the Jewish leaders Jesus said, 'I tell you the truth . . . before Abraham was born, I am' (John 8:58). If we do not understand the full significance of Jesus' words, the Jews to whom he was speaking understood him fully! They immediately picked up stones to stone him because they realized that he was identifying himself as the God who spoke to Moses from the burning bush (Ex. 3:13–14)! In another argument with Jesus some time later, the Jews said to him, 'We are not stoning you for any of these, . . . but for blasphemy, because you, a mere man, claim to be God' (John 10:33).

In the book of Revelation, Jesus said to the apostle John, 'Do not be afraid. I am the First and the Last. I am the Living One; I was dead, and behold I am alive for ever and ever' (Rev. 1:17–18). In speaking of Christ in the book of Hebrews, it is stated, 'about the son he says, your throne, O God, will last for ever and ever' (Heb. 1:8). Later the writer of Hebrews says, 'Jesus Christ is the same yesterday and today and for ever' (Heb. 13:8). Since Jesus Christ is God and has always existed, it should not come as a surprise that he appeared in the Old Testament to Abraham and to Moses.

In a discussion with the Jews, Jesus referred to a time when he appeared to Abraham (John 8:56–57). The story of his appearance to Abraham is recorded in Genesis 18:1–33. He also appeared to other people in the Old Testament such as Adam and Eve (Gen. 3:8–21), Cain (Gen. 4:4–15), Joshua (Joshua 5:13–15), Manoah (Judges 13:17–22) and many others. In the New Testament, before men recognized who Jesus was, the demons knew very well who he was (Mark 1:24).

The appearances of Christ in the Old Testament are referred to as theophanies. A theophany was a visual appearance of God to men before the time of Christ's earthly life as the son of Mary. The appearances of Christ to people in the Old Testament reveal to us the eternal existence of God. When we understand these Old Testament appearances of Christ, we are likely to ask what the difference was between his appearances in the Old Testament and in the New Testament.

The difference between Christ's earthly presence in the Old and New Testament is important. In the Old Testament he simply appeared to people at different times much as an angel might do. In fact, in some cases his earthly appearance in the Old Testament is described as, 'the angel of the Lord' (as in Judges 2:1–5). He appeared as the angel of the Lord to Manoah, the father of Samson, in Judges 13:1–22.

In the New Testament, Christ did not just occasionally appear to men in a human form. Instead, he was born of a human mother and lived in body of flesh and blood among the people of Galilee. He did this to accomplish our salvation, because in order to accomplish our salvation he had to die physically. The Bible says, 'the wages of sin is death' (Rom. 6:23). In his Old Testament appearances he was not a man of flesh and blood. In the Old Testament Jesus appeared in a human form of heavenly origin.

During his earthly life recorded in the New Testament, Jesus was a man of flesh and blood with every human limitation, except sin. He had to learn to read and write just as we do. He became tired and had to sleep. He became hungry and had to eat. He suffered and was tempted as we are (Mark 1:13, Heb. 4:15). He died on the cross as a physical man (John 19:30–33) for our sins.

As a heavenly being, Jesus could not suffer and be tempted as we are and thus qualify to be our great high priest (Heb. 8:1). As a heavenly being, he could not physically die and pay the death penalty for sin (Gen. 2:17, Rom. 6:23). As a heavenly being, he could not qualify to be our Saviour.

In a similar way, no angel could have accomplished man's salvation because angels are heavenly and cannot die physically (Luke 20:36). Jesus had to be born of a woman, and live as a human being of flesh and blood so that he could suffer and die in our place (Heb. 2:9,14). By doing this Jesus paid the death penalty which our sin had brought upon us (Heb. 10:10,12, 1 Peter 2:24, Romans 8:3).

The best news that man can ever hear is this: Jesus suffered the awful wrath of God against sin, in our place, on the cross. As a result, we can be spared that wrath, and can have the hope of eternal life, if we put our trust in Christ and are joined to him by faith (Rom. 5:1, 1 Thess. 1:10).

The Immutability of God
As he appeared from time to time in the Old Testament and again in the New Testament, Jesus revealed another important attribute of God. God does not change (Mal. 3:6, Heb. 13:8). This attribute is called immutability. He is the same forever. God was the same in his character and actions toward Abraham 4000 years ago as he is with us today. He was the same in his character and actions toward King David 3000 years ago as he is with us today. Indeed David knew him as his shepherd just as Christians do today (Psalm 23:1, John 10:14). We can therefore be sure he will be the same in his character and actions towards us in the future. His love, his compassion, his goodness, his justice and his hatred for sin will never change. The Bible says that Jesus Christ is the same yesterday, today and forever (Heb. 13:8).

We may not always be able to depend on one another or our family but we can always depend on Jesus. He can be trusted completely. He is the friend 'who sticks closer than a brother' (Prov. 18:24). He is worthy of our obedience and our worship. He will never fail us or forsake us because he does not change (Heb. 13:5–6). He is the good shepherd who gave his life for the sheep (John 10:14–15).

C. WHAT CAN WE LEARN ABOUT GOD FROM THE NAMES OF GOD?

In African culture names are very important. Names are meaningful, often describing the person's character, the circumstances of his or her birth, and the person's family lineage. A person's name usually reveals his or her family, clan or tribal attachments. In many cases the name given to a child reflects the character of a respected ancestor. Often a person will also have a secret personal name (which the person considers to be his or her real name) which no one else knows. Some people feel that if they reveal this secret name to another person they will somehow come under the influence or control of that person. It is interesting that Jesus Christ also has a secret name which no one knows except he himself (Rev. 19:12).

The Bible gives many names for God. These names reveal different things about the character and characteristics of God. An example of this is the name YHWH (often pronounced Yahweh) by which he was known to the Israelites. This name is translated as the LORD in the New International Version and the New American Standard Bible. The Hebrews considered this name too holy to speak. The name YHWH is related to the Hebrew verb 'to be' and carries the idea, 'to be actively present'. One interpretation of the name YHWH is that God revealed himself as 'He who causes to be' (that is, 'He who creates'). Another interpretation would be, 'He who is.'

In a very similar revelation, God revealed himself to Moses at the burning bush with the name, 'I am' (Ex. 3:14), where he was revealing himself as the one who is. As stated earlier, Christ identified himself by this name to the Jewish leaders in John 8:58 when he said, 'before Abraham was born, I am!' In Exodus 3:1–15 the Hebrew text says that it was YHWH (the LORD) who called to Moses and spoke with him from the burning bush (Ex. 3:4,7,15). Exodus 3:1–15 is also an example of a passage where 'the angel of the Lord' (Ex. 3:2) is clearly identified as the Lord himself.

In the name, 'I am,' in Exodus 3:14, God as the second person of the Trinity is revealed as the self-existent and everlasting One for whom there is no past, present or future. The revelation of the name of God as, 'I am,' can also be related to the revelation Jesus gave to the Apostle John in the book of Revelation, where Christ revealed himself as the, 'Alpha and the Omega (the first and last letters of the Greek alphabet) . . . who is, and who was and who is to come, the Almighty'

(Rev. 1:8). Later in the same chapter Jesus expands this revelation of himself by saying to John, 'Do not be afraid. I am the First and the Last. I am the Living One; I was dead, and behold I am alive for ever and ever!' (Rev. 1:17–18).

Paul applies the name YHWH to Christ when he quotes Joel 2:32 in Rom. 10:13. In Romans 10:12–14 Paul applies Joel 2:32 to those who call on Christ for salvation. Joel wrote, 'everyone who calls on the name of the LORD (YHWH) will be saved' (Joel 2:32).

God's biblical names reveal some of his attributes, some of his works and his relationship to mankind. There are many kinds of names and titles given to God in the Bible. Some are individual names and some are compound names. In this book we can only summarize some of the more familiar names of God.

Individual Names

Saviour: The one who saves. Some political leaders in Africa have claimed to be the saviour of their nation. There is only one Saviour, and that person is Jesus Christ. Concerning Jesus, an angel said to Joseph, Mary's husband; 'He will save his people from their sins' (Matt. 1:21). The main reason why Jesus came into this world was to save sinners (1 Tim. 1:15).

Son of God: This title of Christ defines his special relationship to God the Father as the second person of the Trinity, equal with the Father (Col. 2:9). Jesus called himself the Son of God (John 5:25, 10:36, 11:4). Most Muslims and even some Christians misunderstand this name of Christ. Muslims strongly (and correctly) insist that, 'God has no wife and God has no child!' They refer to the fact that God has no child as in human reproduction.

Even some Christians are confused by this title of Christ, in some cases because of the English wording of the Nicene Creed. The Creed speaks of Christ as being, 'begotten of the Father before all worlds.' The word 'begotten' is taken from the Greek word *monogenes* in John 1:18 and John 3:16. The word *monogenes* really means 'unique', or 'one of a kind' in these two verses. It is probably best expressed in the New International Version of the Bible, where it is translated as, 'one and only.' In other words, Jesus is the one and only person in the universe who has the unique position of being, 'the exact representation of his (God's) being' (Heb. 1:3). The Jews of Jesus' time understood what he meant by this title: that the Son of God was the one having the characteristics of God, even as a human son has the characteristics of his father. The Jews therefore sought to kill him, because, 'He was even calling God his own Father, making himself equal with God' (John 5:18).

Son of Man: This is the Old Testament title of the one presented to the Ancient of Days (God the Father) to be worshipped by all creation and to rule over all peoples, languages and nations (Dan. 7:9–14). Jesus used this title more than any other for himself in the gospels. In John 5:27, Jesus said that all judgment would be given into his hand because he was the Son of Man, which is probably a reference to the passage in Daniel.

Holy One: This is a name by which God identified himself to Israel to reveal his holy character, as in Isaiah 10:17. It is significant that even the demons called him by this name (Luke 4:34).

The Almighty: In both the Old and New Testament, God reveals himself as the one of infinite strength, the one who is omnipotent (the Almighty) (Gen. 17:1, Rev. 1:8).

Word of God: Jesus not only spoke the words of God as a prophet would do, he is called the Word of God (John 1:1,14; Rev. 19:13). He is even known in the Muslim Qu'ran by this name (Sura 4:171).

King of Kings: Jesus is seen in a vision by the Apostle John as the one who rules all the rulers of this world. He is King of Kings and Lord of Lords (Rev. 19:16). According to what the Bible says in Eph. 1:20–22 and Col. 1:16, this includes not just human kings and rulers but also angels and rulers in the spirit world. Jesus is Lord of all (Acts 10:36).

Immanuel: This is an Old Testament name which means, 'God with us' (Isa. 7:14). It testifies to the incarnation of God in Jesus Christ. In Christ, God came and lived among men (John 1:1,14,18).

Judge of all the earth: This was a name ascribed to God by Abraham in Gen. 18:25. This office is confirmed by Christ in John 5:22,27 and by Paul in Acts 17:31.

Lamb of God: This is a name John the Baptist ascribed to Jesus at his baptism (John 1:29,36). It describes Christ's work in becoming the sacrificial lamb, provided by God to propitiate (turn away) the wrath of God against sin. It was prefigured in the blood of the passover lamb which protected the Israelites from God's judgment against Egypt (Ex. 12:3–13 and 1 Cor. 5:7).

Lion of the tribe of Judah: This is a symbolic title given to Christ concerning the kingly power he will display at his return to this world as the conquering King (Rev. 5:5). It is therefore associated with his title as the Son of Man (Dan. 7:13) as seen in Matt. 24:30. The title reflects his human lineage through the tribe of Judah. In his first coming, Christ came as the Lamb of God, a symbol of innocence, weakness and sacrifice. In his second coming, Christ will come as the Lion of Judah, a symbol of sovereign authority and unchallenged power. The lion is often called the 'king of the beasts'.

Wonderful Counselor: This title is given and described in the Old Testament (Isa. 9:6, Prov. 8:13–19). The ministry of giving counsel, encouragement, and wisdom to believers is performed by the Holy Spirit (John 14:26, John 16:13,14, James 1:5).

The merciful (compassionate) One: The Lord revealed this title to Moses when he gave Moses the ten commandments (Ex. 34:6–7). It reveals the great compassion of God for mankind, so perfectly revealed in Jesus. Psalm 145:8–9 says, 'The LORD is gracious and compassionate, slow to anger and rich in love. The LORD is good to all; he has compassion on all he has made'.

I am: This name was given to Moses to identify God as the Eternal One who sent Moses to deliver the Israelites from Egyptian slavery (Ex. 3:14). This name reflects God's eternal existence and immutability.

Alpha and Omega: These are the first and last letters of the Greek alphabet. Jesus revealed himself to the apostle John with these words in Revelation 1:8; 22:13, showing his eternal existence. In the same passage, Jesus revealed himself as the Almighty and as the Lord God.

Messiah: This is a title meaning 'Anointed One'. In the Septuagint this title is given as *Christos*, that is 'the Christ'. Christ is thus not a name but a title. The title Christ means 'the Messiah'. The name Jesus Christ means 'Jesus the Christ', or, 'Jesus the Messiah'. The Messiah was the one the Jews were looking for to come and deliver them from their political bondage and oppression. Thinking that Jesus would be this political Messiah, the crowd proclaimed Jesus their king on Palm Sunday (John 12:13–14) but turned against him later in the same week when he did not fulfil their political desires (Mark 15:13–15).

Prince of Peace: This title reveals God as the one who gives peace. It was revealed to Isaiah in a passage where the three persons of the Trinity are mentioned together (Isa. 9:6), and where the future peaceful rule of Christ on earth is prophesied (Isa. 9:7).

Good Shepherd: This name is one of the most beloved by God's people. King David knew Christ as his shepherd (Psalm 23:1) just as Christians today know him as their good shepherd (John 10:14). He is the one who not only cares for his sheep but who laid down his life for his sheep (John 10:2–11).

King of Glory: The awesome, glorious, omnipotent, returning Messiah is called the King of Glory (Psalm 24:7). He will once again enter the gates of Jerusalem in triumph (Psalm 24:8–10).

Compound Names
There are many occasions in the Old Testament where God's name YHWH is joined with another word to form a compound name. These compound names also reveal his character and attributes.

YHWH-**Elohim**: 'The Lord (is my) God' (Gen. 2:7).

YHWH-**Jireh**: 'The Lord (is my) provider' (Gen. 22:13–14).

YHWH-**Tsidkenu**: 'The Lord (is my) righteousness' (Jer. 23:6).

YHWH-**Ra'ah**: 'The Lord (is my) shepherd' (Psalm 23:1).

ʏʜᴡʜ-**Rapha**: 'The Lord (is my) healer' (Exodus 15:26).

ʏʜᴡʜ-**Shalom**: 'The Lord (is my) peace' (Judges 6:24).

ʏʜᴡʜ-**Nissi**: 'The Lord (is my) banner' (Exodus 17:15).

Other compound names combine the word for God (El) with another word.

El-Shaddai: God Almighty (Gen. 17:1).

El-Elyon: God Most High (Gen. 14:18).

El-Roi: God who sees (Gen. 16:13).

El-Olam: God everlasting (Gen. 21:33).

SUMMARY

Jesus Christ is the man who revealed what God is like. Jesus is the God-man. He is fully God and fully man. If we want to understand the attributes of God, we can see them plainly displayed in the life and works of Christ. Jesus revealed the omnipotence of God by doing miracles of omnipotent power, such as healing the blind, walking on water and raising the dead. He showed the providence of God as he changed water into wine for a wedding feast, created bread and fish for a multitude, and provided a huge catch of fish for his disciples. He demonstrated the sovereignty of God by his control over people, nature, and even the spirit world. He showed the omniscience of God when he revealed the details of the secret life of the woman of Samaria and the exact amount of money a poor widow had put into the temple treasury.

He revealed the compassion and goodness of God by his countless acts of mercy and healing for the poor, the sick and the needy, such as cleansing the lepers, restoring the crippled and deformed and raising from the dead a poor widow's only son. He showed us that God is holy by living the only perfect and sinless life ever lived on the earth. He revealed the justice of God when he exposed the greedy motives of the temple money changers. He exposed the wrath of God against sin when he confronted the religious hypocrites of his day with their sins and drove the money changers from the temple. He displayed the mercy of God when he forgave the prostitute who washed his feet with her tears of repentance. He demonstrated that God is love by his self-denying ministry to others, and by finally giving his life on the cross for the sins of the world. He manifested the eternal existence and unchanging nature of God as he appeared to Abraham 2000 years before his birth in Bethlehem, as he ministered to people for 33 years on earth, as he talked with his disciples after his resurrection, and as he now lives forever to intercede for his people and to answer their prayers.

There has never been a person like Jesus Christ. He is the man who is God and the God who became a man. He is the man who reveals the invisible, eternal God to all people of all cultures on earth.

DISCUSSION QUESTIONS AND PROJECTS BASED ON
CHAPTER FIVE

1. Which attribute of God enables him to be totally just in his judgment of mankind, in a way that no human judge can be?

2. To what kind of person will God show his mercy and forgiveness?

3. Describe which attributes of God are revealed through the following events in Jesus' life:
   (a) Telling the Samaritan woman at the well about her past sinful life (John 4:18).
   (b) Raising Lazarus from the dead (John 11:43–44).
   (c) Healing the blind (Matt. 9:27–30) and lepers (Luke 17:12–14).
   (d) Condemning the Pharisees for their hypocrisy (Matt. 23:1–33).
   (e) Driving the money changers out of the temple (John 2:14–16).
   (f) Forgiving a prostitute of her sins (Luke 7:47–48).
   (g) Mentioning the occasion when he talked with Abraham 2000 years earlier (John 8:56–57).

4. Divide into groups of three or four. Be sure each group has at least one married person. Discuss how you would counsel a Christian couple who were unable to have children. As part of the counseling process each group should refer to one or more of the attributes of God and provide Bible references.

5. What evidence would you give to a Muslim who believes that Jesus was only a prophet to show that Jesus Christ is God?

6. Using Psalm 84:11 as a starting point, explain how you would counsel a single woman who longs to be married.

7. Using Scripture verses on the omniscience and sovereignty of God, describe how you would counsel someone who had just lost a beloved child in an accident. List the verses of Scripture you would use.

8. After you have presented the story of Jesus and his salvation to an old pagan man, he tells you that he would like to follow Christ, but he is afraid that the spirits will be angry and will punish his family with sickness. What would you tell this man and which Scripture passages would you use to counsel him?

9. Let the group discuss why Jesus is greater than the ancestors.

10. In what ways are the omnipotence and the providence of God seen in Jesus?

11. How is the sovereignty of God seen in the life of Christ?

12. Divide into groups of four each to discuss in what ways the sovereignty of God as revealed in Christ should be a help to those who fear sickness, evil spirits, witches and other problems.

SUGGESTED FOR FURTHER READING

Green, Michael. *Who is this Jesus?* London: Hodder, 1991.
McGrath, Alister. *Understanding Jesus*. Michigan: Zondervan, 1990.
McDowell, J. *More than a Carpenter*. Eastbourne: Kingsway, 1979.
Morris, Leon. *The Lord from Heaven*. Leicester: InterVarsity Press, 1995.
Packer, J.I. *Knowing God*. London: Hodder, 2nd edn 1993.

6

Mankind – Ruler and Rebel

'God, the giver of all things, made the world with everything in it. He made heaven as his own dwelling place. To prevent heaven from falling in he supported it all around with pillars just as the roof of a round hut is propped up by pillars. After God created the sun and the moon he made clouds and put them in the sky. He then created a big rooster from which lightning originates. The rooster is of reddish colour and lives among the clouds. Whenever it shakes its wings there is lightning, and whenever it crows there is thunder.

Having created the sun, God asked himself, 'For whom will the sun shine?' This led to God's decision to create the first man. Because the man could talk and see, he needed someone to whom he could talk. God therefore created the first woman to be his partner. There was then a wonderful 'golden age' with no separation between human beings and God. But then something terrible happened. The human beings God made, repeatedly refused to share their food with a chameleon who asked them for some of their food. To punish them, the chameleon cursed the human beings and they became mortal and subject to sickness and death.'

So goes the story of man's creation and the explanation for his present painful circumstances according to one traditional African legend. What is the truth about man's creation? What is the real reason why man struggles with sickness, sorrow and death? Why is the world in such a great mess?

The questions of where we came from, why we are here, and why life is such a hard struggle, have puzzled people as long as they have lived on the earth. God has revealed the answers to these all-important questions in the Bible. In this chapter we will compare the answers given by non-Christians and the answers given by God in his word to the following questions:

A. Who are we and where did we come from?
B. Why do we exist?
C. How are people made in the image of God?

D. Is mankind really different from the animals?
E. What is the result of man's disobedience to God?
F. What is the result of God's curse on man and on the earth?
G. How did sin spread to all mankind?
H. Why are we born as sinners?

A. WHO ARE WE AND WHERE DID WE COME FROM?

Chindo: 'Garba, where do you think we came from? Both my Muslim and Christian friends say that long ago God created man from the dust of the earth. But the books we use in school teach that people came from lower animals by a process called evolution. On the other hand, the elders in my village say that human souls exist before people are born, and simply enter into the wombs of different women.

Garba: 'My science teacher, Mr. Ibrahim, said he does not believe the Bible because it says that the world was created in six days. He said that scientists claim that it took millions of years to form the earth.

'One day my friend, Peter, asked Mr. Ibrahim a question that made me think. He asked if Mr. Ibrahim thought people had developed from other animals as our science textbook says. Mr. Ibrahim answered that scientists have proved that people came from lower animals. Then Peter asked him to give the class an example where scientists in a laboratory had changed one kind of animal into another. Mr. Ibrahim could not give him an example.'

Chindo: 'I think the elders in my village have the right answer. Some of my people have seen relatives after they have died or have been visited by these relatives in a dream, so their spirits are still around. If they can appear to their children, why shouldn't they be able to enter the baby forming in a mother's womb? The elders say that God created all human souls long ago and that they are born into the same family from one generation to another. When the person with that soul dies, his soul goes back to the spirit world for a time until he enters another child growing in the womb. The soul then lives another life in that child, so that the same soul is re-born into the same family many times over many generations. However, part of the soul stays in the spirit world and acts as a guardian spirit for the living person. Usually the person doesn't remember his former lives. Deformed or abnormal children or twins may be born when an evil spirit takes the place of the human soul.'

Garba: How can we know who is right?

The question of where people come from and who they are is very important in Africa. Most traditional beliefs in Africa are centered around people and the communities in which they live. We can generalize and say that life in Africa is people-centered. As a result, traditional beliefs are also people-centered. The community of the living and all those who have died in the past is of very great importance. Hence the question of the origin of man is very important.

In some parts of Africa the belief described by the elders of Chindo's village is held very firmly. Evidence of the presence of the former person's spirit is found in the similarity of character and appearance of a child to that of the ancestor who is believed to live in the child. Sometimes the parents have been told by the very ancestor himself, in a dream, that they must give the child about to be born, the name of that ancestor.

What does the Bible say about the possibility of the existence of human souls before they are born? Is there any additional light on this subject from modern science? We will examine these two questions in some detail.

The idea that human souls have an existence before the conception of a human life in the womb is not found in the Bible and it is not supported by modern science. Both the Bible and modern science indicate that the human personality and soul is formed at the moment of conception in the womb. Modern science also explains the reason for some of the evidence given in support of human pre-existence.

To understand the Bible's teaching on the subject of human souls we must understand how God created man in the beginning. The Bible tells us that God created man out of the dust of the earth (Gen. 2:7). By this act he created man's physical body. Then God breathed the 'breath of life' into the physical body he had made and man became a 'living being' (Gen. 2:7).

When God breathed life into Adam's body, he created Adam's soul. After the creation of Adam, God made a woman from the man (Gen. 2:21–22). From this point on it was God's plan that all future human beings would be created and enter the world through the sexual union of a man and woman in marriage (Gen. 1:27–28, Gen. 2:24, Gen. 4:1). It has only been in the twentieth century that scientists have fully seen the microscopic details of what takes place when the seed of the man (the sperm) joins the seed of the woman (the egg). When we understand that process, we will understand the origin of the human soul.

After Adam and Eve were created, they sinned against God by eating the fruit God had forbidden them to eat (Gen. 3:6,11). Adam's sin brought spiritual death (separation between man and God, Gen. 3:10) and physical death (separation of the soul from the body and the subsequent destruction of the body, Gen. 3:19). Both of these separations were contrary to the original purpose of God. God wanted human beings to be spiritually joined to himself in fellowship, and he created the human body and soul to be joined together.

At death the soul separates from the body and the body returns to dust (Gen. 3:19). In the Bible we learn that at death human souls are taken from their bodies and separated into two groups. Souls are separated according to the relationship they had to Christ in this life (Luke 23:40–43). The souls of those who belong to Christ are taken into Christ's presence (Psalm 49:15, Luke 23:43, 2 Cor. 5:8). They will remain in Christ's presence until Jesus brings them with him at his return (1 Thess. 4:14). At the time of Christ's return, the souls of those who belong to Christ are given resurrection bodies (1 Thess. 4:14–16). After these souls receive their resurrection bodies they will remain joined to their resurrection bodies forever (1 Thess. 4:16–17). This is the completion of God's plan of salvation for his redeemed people (Rom. 8:23).

All other souls are imprisoned in a place called Hades in the New Testament (Luke 16:23,26) and Sheol in the Old Testament (Psalm 49:14). They are conscious in Hades and they await the final judgement of God in that place (Heb. 9:27, Rev. 20:11–13). Hades will be discussed in more detail in chapter thirteen. In the story of the rich man and Lazarus in Luke 16:19–31, Jesus clearly stated that although the rich man (in Hades) wanted very much to have Lazarus sent back to warn his brothers about Hades, neither his soul nor the soul of Lazarus was permitted to return (Luke 16:27–31). There may be biblical exceptions to this. These exceptions will be discussed in chapter thirteen.

The story of the rich man and Lazarus makes it very clear that the souls of the dead are not permitted to return to the living. Human souls are allowed to live in only one human body. The Bible says, 'it is appointed for men to die once and after this comes judgment' (Heb. 9:27–NASB). If souls could live in more than one human body they would be able to die more than once. This statement makes it clear that human souls have only one existence in this life. It also makes clear that after death the next thing which will happen is the judgment of God.

Scripture offers other evidence that human souls do not exist before the conception of a child in the womb. The Bible's statement concerning Esau and Jacob before they were born reveals that human souls do not have an existence before they are conceived. Paul tells us that before Jacob and Esau were born, they had not done anything, either good or bad (Rom. 9:11). This indicates that human souls begin responsible action only after they are born. The Bible states that it is God who gives life and breath to all men (Eccl. 12:7, Acts 17:25). In Zechariah 12:1 it is plainly stated that it is the Lord 'who forms the spirit of man within him'. These statements rule out the pre-existence of human souls. With the exception of the first man and woman, the formation of the human soul begins at the time of conception in the mother's womb.

At the end of history Christ will unite every human soul with his or her own resurrection body (John 5:28–29). The resurrection bodies of Christians will be formed in the glorious resurrection image of Christ himself (Phil. 3:20–21). The resurrection bodies of all others will be subject to shame and everlasting contempt (Dan. 12:2, John 5:29). Thus every human soul has a destiny which is linked to his or her own body. In this life, it is linked to his or her body of flesh and blood, and in the age to come, it is linked to his or her resurrection body. There is just one specific body for every human soul.

This raises many questions in Africa where the dead have been seen and even spoken to. It is important to understand the biblical explanation for these appearances of the dead. The Bible makes it clear that other spirits (demons, not human spirits) can occupy human bodies and can greatly change the personalities and even the appearances of the people they occupy (Mark 5:2–9). More important in understanding appearances of the dead, it is possible for demons to present visionary appearances to human eyes (Rev. 16:13–14). Visionary appearances of the dead explain a great many situations experienced in Africa.

Once human souls have separated from their bodies at death, the Bible says they are restricted to specific places by God. We must therefore conclude that a human soul cannot occupy more than one human body, in God's sovereign plan.

WHAT DOES MODERN SCIENCE TELL US ABOUT THE ORIGIN
OF HUMAN SOULS?

Modern science gives us considerable light on the subject of the origin of the human soul and personality. Biological science accurately explains the similarity of appearance and character which is often observed between children and their parents or their more distant ancestors. Scientists have discovered that the physical, mental and emotional characteristics of every person are contained in a set of chemical instructions which are located in the nucleus of the living cells of that person.

These chemical instructions are found in things that look, under a powerful microscope, like extremely tiny threads. These threads are called chromosomes. Each thread, or chromosome, consists of a complex pattern of chemical pairs which look something like the steps of a twisted ladder. Groups of these chemical pairs are called genes. It is these genes which are the specific chemical instructions which determine many of the physical, mental, and emotional characteristics of each person at the moment they are conceived in the womb. In other words, a unique human being starts at the moment of conception.

Since these chromosomes are passed from one generation to the next through the combination of the male and female cells (sperm and egg) in the process of reproduction, it is to be expected that children will show a strong resemblance to those who lived before them in their family line. Indeed, they must show such resemblance because their cells are made of the same chemical instructions (genes) that were in the cells of their parents. One set of genes is passed on by the mother and one set of genes is passed on by the father. The child will reveal a combination of characteristics resulting from the two parents, who, in turn, got their genes from their parents before them, and so forth.

A good summary of the opinion of many scientists is found in the *National Geographic Magazine*, in the November 1985 issue, in an article entitled, 'The Search For Early Man'. There is a fold-out colour drawing (pp. 574–577), showing the stages of development as these writers imagine that we changed from a kind of ape into the modern people of today. This chart summarizes the opinion of many of the best educated scientists in Europe and North America today. It summarizes part of the theory of evolution.

Evolution teaches that life began on earth by the chance combination of chemicals in the sea long ago. Many scientists believe that after this happened, simple forms of life slowly developed over millions of years. Then after many more millions of years, these life forms gradually changed and became more and more complex. According to this theory, one kind of animal gradually changed into another kind of animal over a very, very long period of time. Eventually animals such as baboons and gorillas appeared. Human beings gradually emerged from these higher animals. We must remember that the chart is made of picture drawings, not photographs. It is only the opinion of the scientists. No scientist has ever seen this process actually happen. More significantly, no scientist has ever been able to produce such changes in the laboratory, although experiments to try to do this very thing have been performed for more than 70 years.

If there is not laboratory evidence to support the theory of evolution, why do so many scientists believe this is the means by which we came to exist? There is a reasonable answer to this question. The answer has to do with the great similarity between living things. Baboons and gorillas are very similar to human beings in the way their bodies are made, so scientists assume that men developed from animals similar to gorillas. There is also a great similarity in the life processes of all living things. For example, all animals take in food and eliminate waste material.

In addition to this, there are many laboratory experiments which show that animals and plants can indeed adapt to a limited extent through controlled breeding. The problem is, scientists cannot change one kind of animal or plant into another kind of animal or plant. God has apparently placed biological limits on living things. For example, dogs cannot be changed into horses. This barrier is found with the mule. When a male donkey is bred with a female horse, the result is a mule. This kind of a combination is called a hybrid. A mule combines the size of a horse with the strength, endurance and stubbornness of a donkey. But mules are sterile and cannot reproduce. The same is true for hybrid experiments with plants. There seems to be a biological limit placed by God on each kind of animal and plant.

An application of this limit as applied to human beings is given in the Old Testament. God specifically commanded that a human being must not have sexual relations with an animal (Lev. 18:23). If this happened, God required that both the person and the animal must be killed (Lev. 20:15–16).

How do we know if the ideas of evolution are true or not? What does the evidence in nature tell us? First, the record of the bones of animals found in the earth (called fossils) indicates that there is a distinct break in the fossil record between different kinds of animals. If evolution were true, these bones should show very gradual changes from one kind of animal to another, with all the steps of change. Such a fossil record of very gradual transitions is not found in the earth. Second, if evolution were true, scientists should be able to repeat the process of changing one kind of animal or plant into another in their laboratories, at least in some cases. They are not able to do this. There are also other problems with evolution for which there is no answer.

It is very difficult to scientifically support the theory of evolution except to show small changes that have taken place within the same kind of animal or plant. Thus there are different kinds of dogs, but they are all still dogs. There are many, many kinds of birds but they are still birds, and birds are very different from all other creatures. According to Genesis, God created each of these different kinds of creatures separately (Gen. 1:24–25).

There are some Christians who believe in a form of evolution which was guided by God. This is called theistic evolution. People with this view would say that evolution did, in fact, take place, but that evolution was the process God purposely followed in order to create us. Thus they say that we were not the result of chance, but the result of the creative purpose and plan of God. Those who believe in theistic evolution would interpret the biblical record of man's creation in Genesis as poetry or mythology rather than as a literal event.

In answer to the question why we exist, the secular evolutionist would say we exist because of the accidental changes of nature. We exist because of random biological changes which took place over millions of years. He or she sees no reason to believe in the creation of man by God.

In most places in Europe and North America today, evolution is the only theory of origins taught in government schools. We have discussed this theory here because so many Africans are being trained in Europe and America today. Many African teachers trained in the West are now passing on the ideas of evolution to their students. It is important to understand these ideas.

WHAT DOES THE BIBLE SAY ABOUT THE ORIGIN OF MAN
AND WOMAN?

The Bible describes the creation of man as a special act of God, after all the other animals had been created. In both the Old and New Testament, the events recorded in the Genesis account of man's creation are interpreted to be literal events. The Bible describes man's origin in the following way: 'God said, let us make man in our image, in our likeness . . . So God created man in his own image . . . male and female he created them' (Gen. 1:26–27). In Genesis chapter two there is a more detailed account of exactly how God made Adam, the first man. The record says, 'The Lord God formed the man from the dust of the ground and breathed into his nostrils the breath of life, and he became a living being' (Gen. 1:26–27, Gen. 2:7).

The creation of the first woman (Eve) is described as follows: 'The LORD God said, "It is not good for the man to be alone. I will make a helper suitable for him" . . . So the LORD God caused the man to fall into a deep sleep; and while he was sleeping he took one of the man's ribs and closed up the place with flesh. Then the LORD God made a woman from the rib he had taken out of the man, and he brought her to the man' (Gen. 2:18–22).

The Bible reveals that God created man in a special act, as a special creature, different from all other creatures on earth. Man's existence was God's idea and God's decision. It was not the result of chance. God had a reason and a purpose for our existence.

Most groups of traditional people have a story about the creation of man such as the story at the beginning of this chapter. Sometimes these stories are similar to the Bible and sometimes they are different. It is generally understood by all people in Africa that God created man, but the correct details of man's creation are only found in the Bible.

B. WHY DO WE EXIST?

The Bible says God made man in his own image and likeness (Gen. 1:26–27). This is not said of any animal. Human beings are thereby different from all the animals. The fact that people are made in the image of God helps us to understand why God created us.

In Gen. 2:18, the Lord said, 'It is not good for the man to be alone. I will make a helper suitable for him.' As a person and as a social creature, man needed a companion. Evidently God also wanted the fellowship of man (Gen. 3:8–9). Since man was made in the image of God, we can assume that God also wanted the fellowship of personal human beings. This explains the activity of Satan in the garden of Eden. As a rebel against God, Satan wanted to hurt God by tempting man into a rebellion against God, similar to his own rebellion. Such a rebellion would destroy the close relationship God could have with man and woman. Unfortunately, that is just what happened (Gen. 3:8–9). In the cross of Christ, we see God's plan to restore this broken relationship between mankind and himself (Col. 1:20).

God planned for man to rule over his creation on earth (Gen. 1:26) just as God rules over all the universe (Psalm 103:19). Since people were made in the image of God, God intended for them to reflect the holiness and goodness of God. But Adam and Eve fell into disobedience and sin. As a result, all human beings became corrupt. In some ways they became morally lower than the very animals over which they were to rule. Animals do not torture and harm other animals just to see them suffer, or to eliminate a group of them from the earth. Some twisted human beings do. Animals fight when they are trying to get food, to defend their offspring, to secure a mate, or to carry out some other natural instinct. But people carefully and wickedly plan evil against others because of pride, tribalism, selfishness and greed. The Bible says, 'the heart is deceitful above all things, and beyond cure. Who can understand it?' (Jer. 17:9).

Animals do not have a consciousness of good and evil as human beings have. God therefore expects responsible behaviour from human beings which he does not require from animals. God holds people responsible for their decisions and their behaviour. People have wills to choose what they will do just as God has a will to choose what he will do. The actions of animals are based on their instincts and nature. The actions of people are based on their thinking and their decisions.

C. HOW ARE PEOPLE MADE IN THE IMAGE OF GOD?

The Bible says God made man in his own image and likeness (Gen. 1:26–27). In what sense is man made in the image of God?

Since God is a spirit (John 4:24) and not a physical creature, the image of God is not a physical likeness to God. The image of God has to do with the non-physical part of man. A mirror reflects the image or likeness of what shines on the mirror. So also we are created to reflect the character and characteristics of God. What is the character of God, and what are his characteristics which God wanted us to reflect?

THE IMAGE OF GOD AS REFLECTING THE CHARACTER OF GOD

God's character is perfect holiness, righteousness and goodness. We can assume that the first people were holy, righteous, and good when God created them, and the Bible confirms this (Eph. 4:24). God created them to reflect his holiness and goodness. Because of the sin of the first man and woman, the holy image of God was defiled and distorted just as the image of a person's face might appear distorted in a broken mirror. Because the first man and woman fell into sin, human character is now corrupt instead of holy. That is why people steal, cheat, tell lies, commit adultery and sexual immorality, despise and murder others, and start wars.

One of God's greatest purposes in mankind's salvation is to restore the holy image of God which was ruined by sin (Eph. 4:24). This is one of the central themes in the Bible. Leviticus 20:7 says, 'Consecrate yourselves and be holy, because I am the LORD your God.' The context of this statement has an important application in Africa. In the preceding verse, God says, 'I will set my face against the person who turns to mediums and spiritists to prostitute himself by following them' (Lev. 20:6). Many African Christians are tempted to turn to diviners, mediums, wizards and other traditional specialists when they face a crisis or problem. God calls us to forsake these practices and to turn to him instead. Isaiah warns us, 'when they say to you, "Consult the mediums and the spiritists who whisper and mutter", should not a people consult their God?' (Isa. 8:17–NASB). According to Leviticus 20:7, drawing near to God in a time of need instead of consulting traditional specialists is part of what it means to be holy.

In the New Testament the Apostle Peter says, 'But just as he who calls you is holy, so be holy in all you do, for it is written, "Be holy because I am holy" '. (1 Pet. 1:15–16). An application of New Testament holiness is found in Ephesians 2:10, 'For we are God's workmanship, created in Christ Jesus to do good works, which God prepared in advance for us to do.' Doing good to others is another very important part of personal holiness.

The glory of God is seen in his holy character of goodness and good works. Jesus said, 'I have brought you glory on earth' (John 17:4). In other words, Jesus perfectly reflected and revealed the holy character of God by his goodness and good works. God wants us to do the same thing. He created us to demonstrate his character of goodness and good works. He made man in his own image. For this reason the Westminster Confession of Faith says, 'The chief end (purpose) of man is to glorify God.' Man was created to glorify God by reflecting the holy character of God. This is the most important reason for man's existence. The greatest thing any one can do with life, is to reflect the holy character of God.

THE IMAGE OF GOD AS REFLECTING THE CHARACTERISTICS OF GOD

The image of God in man is also seen in the characteristics of God as a person. Like God, man is personal, with intellect, emotions, and a will. Because people are created in the image of God, they are accountable to God for their character and for their behaviour.

A person has an intellect and therefore is able to think. It is true that the thoughts of God are incomparably higher than our thoughts (Isa. 55:8–9). Nevertheless, people are like God in that they think and plan. Like God, they are able to communicate thoughts in words. They write down thoughts on paper. They design and plan things. By means of words and pictures they pass on the information learnt from one to another and from one generation to the next. Animals cannot do this but act on instinct. God has passed on the thoughts of his mind to human beings in words which are written for us in the Bible.

D. IS MANKIND REALLY DIFFERENT FROM THE ANIMALS?

Because people can think and plan, they can design and make things that did not exist before, such as cars and computers. This is because people are made in the image of the creator of all things. People have knowledge through talking to others, reading, thinking, observing, and remembering. They do not have all knowledge (omniscience) as God does, but they can add to their knowledge by studying, experience, and learning from the knowledge of others. By acquired knowledge alone mankind differs greatly from all other creatures. In contrast, animals live by their inborn instincts. Although animals do learn, their form of learning is very basic in comparison with the learning which is possible for human beings.

Although people have certain instincts like animals, they do not live only by their instincts as animals do. Human beings are able to control their instincts by what they decide. Because they are able to make decisions on the basis of their knowledge, people are able to change things in their environment. Like God, they can make things that didn't exist before. There are many examples.

Birds instinctively build nests from leaves and branches. Each kind of bird builds a certain kind of nest as its instinct determines. Each kind of bird always builds the same kind of nest. Because people are able to think and learn from others, they are not limited to build one kind of building or house. People build many kinds of houses and buildings using their ideas and knowledge, not their instincts. The same person may build many different kinds of buildings.

Birds can fly because of the way they are made but people were not made to fly with their bodies. However, by observing birds, and by studying the laws of nature, they discovered the principles of flight and eventually made planes to fly even faster and higher than birds. People made something which did not exist before (planes) because they are made in the image of God, who is the Creator. Mankind's capacity to make new things is so great that God said at the Tower of Babel, 'Nothing they plan to do will be impossible for them' (Gen. 11:6). That is an awesome statement concerning mankind's knowledge and power. People are not God, but are definitely made in the image of God.

As made in God's image, people are different from everything around them. They have wills with which to make decisions. They are free to choose what they will do. This ability to think and decide what to do is a great gift from God to mankind.

The freedom to choose also makes people responsible to God for their behaviour. In the garden of Eden, God gave Adam the freedom to enjoy the garden (Gen. 2:16). He also gave him the freedom to choose to obey the command not to eat the fruit of the tree of the knowledge of good and evil (Gen. 2:17). With the freedom to obey or disobey, God warned Adam that there would be a serious result (death) if he disobeyed God (Gen. 2:17).

God held Adam responsible for his decision. It was in choosing to disobey God that Adam committed sin. Sin is disobedience to the will of God. God pronounced a curse on mankind and a curse on the world we live in (Gen. 3:17–19) because of Adam's disobedience. Human beings are fully responsible for the condition of this world and for the misery in which they live, including sickness, death, unhappiness, hatred, tribalism, wars, immorality, crime, violence, and even the calamities of nature (Rom. 8:20–22).

E. WHAT IS THE RESULT OF MAN'S DISOBEDIENCE TO GOD?

God told man that the result of disobedience would be death (Gen. 2:17). Little did Adam realize how terrible death would be! Physical death of the human body is only part of the terrible death penalty. Death touches everything in a person's existence. It touches a person's body, mind, emotions, relationships, marriage, family life, society, government, and even the physical earth itself. The Bible says, 'sin entered the world through one man, and death through sin, and in this way death came to all men, because all sinned' (Rom. 5:12).

The first part of the death sentence for Adam's sin was that the close relationship between God and mankind was broken. Adam and Eve became like guilty criminals, trying to hide from God (Gen. 3:8). People have been running away from God ever since.

There is no one whom we need more than God. Yet because of sin we feel guilty and afraid of God, so we try to hide from him. People desperately need to pray and have God answer their prayers, but their sin and rebellion separates them from God so that he will not answer their prayers (Isa. 59:1–3).

God knew what Adam had done. He gave him an opportunity to confess his sin and to ask for forgiveness when he asked Adam, 'Have you eaten from the tree that I commanded you not to eat from?' (Gen. 3:11). Because of his pride, instead of admitting his sin, Adam began to blame the woman and even to blame God himself (Gen. 3:12). People are like that today. They still blame others and blame God for the problems that come from their own sinful rebellion and pride. They would rather fight with others and suffer than to admit their sin and to humble themselves before God. Truly, mankind is fallen and sinful. We have turned the world in which we live into a miserable mess.

F. WHAT IS THE RESULT OF GOD'S CURSE ON MAN AND ON THE EARTH?

Because Adam chose to disobey God (Gen. 3:6) and because he refused to repent of his sin when given a chance (Gen. 3:12), God pronounced a curse on mankind and a curse on the earth itself. He also cursed the serpent who tempted them (Gen. 3:14–19). It is important to understand the nature of this curse in order to understand why life is the way it is today.

God made women to bear children (Gen. 1:28). The curse greatly multiplied the pain of women in childbirth (Gen. 3:16). God made men to farm and work with their hands (Gen. 2:15). The curse took the pleasure out of work and added toil and sweat to men's labour. In other words, the normal work of men and women remained the same but their work became hard and painful rather than enjoyable. God made the earth to bear fruit abundantly and easily (Gen. 1:11–12). The curse made the earth much more difficult to cultivate for food (Gen. 3:17). Sin took the joy out of life for men and women. Life became a burden instead of a blessing.

People often struggle with questions about why there are natural calamities such as earthquakes, hurricanes, tornadoes, floods, droughts, and other disasters which take human lives and cause great suffering. Although the Bible does not explain these things in detail, there is a strong suggestion in Scripture that the whole natural creation has been severely disrupted because of the presence of sin in the world. Immediately after the fall of mankind in Genesis, God announced that the earth would be changed to produce painful things like thorns and thistles (Gen. 4:18). Surely this must include other painful things as well, such as the sting of scorpions and poisonous snakes, which Jesus identified with Satan's activity (Luke 10:19).

In Luke 10:19 Jesus indicated even more results of sin in the natural world when he said that the apostles' authority would extend, 'over all the power of the enemy.' In the book of Job, when God gave Satan permission to bring harm on Job, Satan brought about the death of Job's sheep and his shepherds through lightning (Job 1:16) and the death of his children through a violent storm, which was probably a tornado (Job 1:19). He also brought pain to Job through physical sickness (Job 2:7). As a general summary of the effects of sin on the natural creation, Paul wrote, 'We know that the whole creation has been groaning as in the pains of childbirth right up to the present time' (Rom. 8:22).

The sad fact is that mankind has participated in a rebellion against God in which Satan was the original rebel. As a result, mankind along with the rest of the physical creation has been suffering the terrible effects of that evil rebellion ever since. Sickness, crime, corrupt and oppressive government, broken homes, human cruelty, tribalism, wars and even the disasters of nature, are all part of our lives because of sin against God. The terrible reality is this: 'The wages of sin is death' (Rom. 6:23).

As part of his salvation, Jesus came to put back into life the joy and blessing of God which sin has taken away (John 10:10B). Even though the creation will continue to groan under the effects of sin until Christ returns (Rom. 8:21), it is now possible for people to be forgiven for their sins (Eph. 1:7) and to be reconciled to God (Col. 1:21–22) by Christ's death. Isaiah 61:3 says God has given us 'the oil of gladness instead of mourning, and a garment of praise instead of a spirit of despair.'

G. HOW DID SIN SPREAD TO ALL MANKIND?

Adam chose to disobey the command of God by eating the forbidden fruit of the tree of the knowledge of good and evil (Gen. 3:6). Because of this disobedience he deserved punishment from God, who is a holy and just judge. What may not be clear to us, is how Adam's sin spread to the rest of the human race. The Bible says all mankind is now included in the guilt and condemnation of Adam (Rom. 5:18–19). Some believers may feel that it is unjust of God to include all mankind in the guilt and punishment of Adam since it was Adam, and not us, who disobeyed. How is it that all mankind has been included in Adam's sin?

To understand this we must understand whether we are sinners because we commit sin, or whether we commit sin because we are already sinners from birth. The Bible's answer is clear. We commit sin because we are born as sinners. Psalm 51:5 says, 'Surely I was sinful at birth, sinful from the time my mother conceived me.'

Many people think we are sinners only because we commit sin. They think that if we would just not commit sin, we would not be sinners. But who does not commit sin? What child ever has to be taught to tell lies? The truth is that all people are born sinners. We are inclined to sin from the time we can speak or walk. In Ecclesiastes 7:20 King Solomon said, 'There is not a righteous man on earth who does what is right and never sins.'

H. WHY ARE WE BORN AS SINNERS?

We are born sinners because we have inherited a sinful nature from Adam and Eve, the parents of all mankind. The genetic information which determines a person's characteristics is passed from one generation to another through reproduction. So we have all inherited from Adam and Eve every characteristic of being human. All men and women have Adam and Eve's human nature in their bodies.

The fall of Adam and Eve affected their very nature as human beings. This sinful nature has been passed on to all other generations of mankind. Since Adam and Eve were the parents of all mankind, each of us was 'in' Adam and Eve in their reproductive seed and in their human nature. In this sense, God sees all mankind as one family coming from one couple. All mankind is thus included with Adam and Eve in their sin against God. Because Adam was the father of the human race, all of us were physically 'in' Adam when he sinned and so we shared in his sinful rebellion.

Sin is also passed on from one generation to another by way of the bad example parents set for their children. Children grow up copying their parents' behaviour which, from the time of Adam, has been affected by Adam's sinful nature.

Sin affected the very first baby ever born in the world. Cain grew up to be a murderer, killing his own brother (Gen. 4:8). Sin has also spoiled God's plan for harmony and faithfulness in marriage. In his wisdom and goodness God made one woman for the man he created and brought the woman to the man (Gen. 2:22). Because of their sinful nature inherited from Adam, men soon decided to take more than one wife (Gen. 4:19), thus causing jealousy between the wives and conflict in the home. Later on men began to divorce the wives they had taken, causing still more bitterness, pain and suffering in the family (Deut. 24:1–3). Is it any wonder that God says he hates divorce (Mal. 2:15–16)?

Disease, tribalism, pride, hatred, bitterness, divorce, revenge, crime, war, and most kinds of suffering in the world today can be traced back to mankind's sin. The result of sin is death (Rom. 6:23). Physical death is just one part of the death penalty for sin. Death can be seen in mankind's social life (pride, greed, selfishness, lies, hatred, betrayal, tribalism, crime), married life (conflict, unfaithfulness, divorce), political life (corruption, oppression, wars), and in every other part of human existence. As it says in Romans 5:12, death has spread to all, because all sinned. We are all children of Adam and Eve and we all share their sinful nature (Rom. 5:19a, 1 Cor. 15:49a).

There is a third way we are included in the sin of Adam. Some people may feel that it was unfair that God allowed Adam to be tempted instead of them. Why did God allow Adam to be tempted and not one of us? An illustration from the Olympic Games may help us understand. For the Olympic Games every four years, a country chooses its very best athletes to represent the nation. If an athlete wins a competition, the whole country rejoices and shares in the victory. 'We won!' they shout, when in fact it was that athlete who won.

In the same way our father Adam represented mankind before God because he was the first man and the father of us all. He was also the most righteous and perfect man of the human race because he was created perfect by God. If anyone had the possibility of being victorious for mankind, it was Adam. He was the champion. None of us could have done as well. The race is lost because the champion fell.

But God had a greater champion. The 'last Adam' would not fall. Jesus was the last Adam. He became the true champion who would save the human race. The Bible says, 'The last Adam (Christ) became a life-giving spirit' (1 Cor. 15:45). Paul wrote, 'For as in Adam, all die, even so in Christ, shall all be made alive' (1 Cor. 15:22 – KJV). The bad news is that 'the wages of sin is death.' The good news is that 'the gift of God is eternal life in Christ Jesus our Lord' (Rom. 6:23).

SUMMARY

There are different theories about the origin of man, both in Africa and in the Western world. We must look to the revelation of God in the Bible to find the truth about man's origin.

The truth is that God created man in his own image as a unique and glorious being, with a brilliant mind and a free will like God. He was created to rule the earth and to glorify God by displaying the righteousness of God. Instead of fulfilling God's plan, man rebelled against God and by his rebellion brought terrible suffering upon the human race and upon the rest of creation. By his sin, Adam brought death upon himself and all mankind and a curse on the human race and on the earth itself. Since Adam and Eve were the physical parents of the human race, all mankind has inherited their sinful nature. Ever since, every child is born into the world as a sinner. God was just to allow Adam to be tested on behalf of the human race since God created Adam as a perfect man. The human race was lost because

Adam sinned. Through Christ, the last Adam, the human race can be saved, because Christ took the death penalty for mankind's sin.

DISCUSSION QUESTIONS AND PROJECTS BASED ON CHAPTER SIX

1. How was mankind 'in' Adam when he sinned?

2. Explain how the Bible shows that human souls cannot re-enter foetuses growing in the womb and be born many times over.

3. Divide into groups of four each. Let each group make a list of all the ways in which sin has ruined the world. Combine the lists of the groups to make a complete list of the ways in which sin has ruined the world.

4. Using the lists from the previous question, let each of the same groups determine how the salvation of Christ can overcome the specific results of sin which they had listed.

5. Explain three reasons why the sin of Adam was passed on to the rest of mankind.

6. Prepare a Sunday School lesson for 10–16 year olds to explain how man is created in the image of God. Include stories or illustrations.

7. Divide into tribal groups. Discuss and list those aspects of tribalism which are the result of man's sinful nature.

8. In the same groups as for the previous question, determine from the Bible what God would have each ethnic group and individual do about the problem of tribalism.

9. Compare the traditional African perspective with the biblical perspective on why man exists.

10. Divide into a group of single people and a group of married people. Let the single students list all the ways they can think of in which their sinful nature has affected the way they relate to the opposite sex and in courtship. Let the married students list all the ways they can think of in which their sinful nature has affected their marriages and their relationship to their spouses and children.

11. When the previous exercise is finished, let the two groups search the Bible, using concordances, to find out how God would have them replace each of the wrong practices they listed.

12. Let the group discuss the African concept of a curse, and its result. How does this compare with the curse God pronounced, and its result?

13. What is sin according to African understanding? How does this compare with the biblical understanding of sin?

14. Let members of the group share some of the African legends of man's origin.

15. In what ways are Africans tempted to try to manipulate God?

SUGGESTED FOR FURTHER READING

Hoekema, Anthony A. *Created In The Image Of God.* Carlisle: Paternoster Press, 1994.

Houston, J.M. *I Believe in God the Creator.* London: Hodder, 1979.

McDonald, H.D. *The Christian View of Man.* London: Marshall Pickering, 1981.

Roberts, Linleigh J. *Let Us Make Man.* Edinburgh: Banner of Truth Trust, 1988.

7

Jesus Christ – The Source of Our Salvation

Kpaga and Gunati are from families which practise traditional African religions. Since they came to college, they have been listening seriously to their Christian and Muslim friends speaking about their religious beliefs. Kpaga and Gunati are sincere young men who want to know the truth about God. The more they talk with their friends, the more questions they have.

Kpaga: 'The Christians say that Christ is the only way by which men can find God.'

Gunati: 'I wonder why they say that? We all know there is a God and we all believe in him. In fact, we all have a name for God in our own languages. If a man is sincere, he should be able to find God in his own way.'

Kpaga: 'The Christians also say that people can only find forgiveness of sin through Christ.'

Gunati: 'Why is God's forgiveness so important? I am more concerned about what the elders of my people say is right to do. If I do not follow our traditions, I will be considered a rebel and will be punished by them. I think God has put the responsibility for our behaviour into the hands of our elders.

I am concerned about the witchcraft in my village. Recently my uncle died because he was eaten by witches. The medicine man in our village told me this.'

Kpaga: 'I am confused by what my Christian friends tell me. They say that God loves us but they also say that God will punish sinners in hell. Why would a God who loves people send anyone to hell?'

Gunati: 'That is a good question. If God loves people as they say, why will he not forgive everyone? My Muslim friends say that God will forgive those who ask him for mercy on the day of judgment.'

Kpaga: 'What I don't understand is, what does the death of Christ have to do with us today? How can the death of one man such a long time ago be of any value to us now?'

These are probably some of the most important questions a person could ask. If God loves people, why will he not forgive everyone? Why is God's forgiveness so important? What does the death of Jesus have to do with us today? How could the death of one man almost 2000 years ago change the whole history of mankind?

Gunati has expressed what is probably true for many people in Africa, including some Christians. They are more concerned about acceptance by their people then they are about acceptance by God. In many African creation stories, God withdrew from mankind for one of several reasons. In one story, it was because a woman kept bumping him with her grain pestle while she was pounding the grain. In another story, there was a rope between heaven and earth. The rope was broken by a hyena, and ever since then, there has been no relationship between God and men. For whatever reason, God now seems far away, and therefore the words of the village elders and the will of the tribal ancestors seem to be much more important for daily living than the knowledge of God.

Also, the matter of finding forgiveness with God does not seem to be nearly as important as finding protection from the threat of witchcraft. Many experiences of sickness and death are blamed on witchcraft. Many people, including Christians, live in fear of witch-craft.

Since human life is so important in the African world-view, it is a matter of great importance that people possess life force, be able to live strong lives and have many children. If there is a traditional view of salvation, the most important elements of that traditional view would include acceptance by the clan, protection from evil powers and the possession of life force. How does this compare with the world-view of the Bible? What elements in the gospel of Jesus Christ correspond to the needs felt in Africa for acceptance by the commun-ity, for protection from evil powers and for the possession of life force? What other realities should Christians consider in salvation? How does the death and resurrection of Christ meet all the needs of an African heart?

The Importance of the Death and Resurrection of Christ
About one third of the four gospels is devoted to the last few days of Christ's life and the details of his death and resurrection. By contrast, only one short passage (Luke 2:41–52) gives us any detail about the first 30 years of his life, apart from the story of his birth. When the apostles spoke about Christ, they primarily spoke about his death and resurrection (Acts 2:22–36, 1 Cor. 15:1–4). Why is this?

It is because the death and resurrection of Christ are the foundations of God's plan of salvation for mankind. In the Bible, the Holy Spirit emphasizes matters of great importance such as the death of Christ, by devoting long passages of Scripture to it.

From this we learn that the gospels are not really a biography of Jesus. They are a selection of those events in the life of Christ which are related to man's salvation. It is also clear that the most important events in the coming of Christ were his death and resurrection. There is something so important about these two events that God did not want us to miss the truth.

The death and resurrection of Christ are the most important events in the history of mankind. Without Christ's death there is no way God could allow a sinful human being into his holy presence. Through Christ's death on the cross, a way was made possible for human beings to be released from the punishment due to sin. Through Christ's death on the cross, we can be reconciled to God.

Through the resurrection of Christ, death has been abolished for those who believe in him (2 Tim. 1:10). Jesus said, 'Because I live, you also will live' (John 14:19). Without Christ's resurrection, there would be no hope of eternal life. The resurrection of Christ gives every Christian a living hope of being in heaven with Christ forever (1 Pet. 1:3–4). The resurrection also makes possible a life free from the bondage and control of sin. Paul wrote, 'just as Christ was raised from the dead through the glory of the Father, we too may live a new life' (Rom. 6:4).

In this chapter we will focus on the purpose of the death and resurrection of Jesus Christ and on the importance of his ascension into heaven. We will seek to answer the following questions:

A. How great is the love and forgiveness of God?
B. How was mankind's salvation accomplished?
C. What is the meaning of salvation?
D. What are the results of salvation?
E. What are some ways in which salvation applies to the needs felt in Africa?
F. What is sanctification?
G. How do we know if Christ really rose from the dead?
H. What does the resurrection of Christ mean for the Christian today?
I. What was the purpose of the ascension of Christ and what is he doing now?
J. Who will be saved?

A. HOW GREAT IS THE LOVE AND FORGIVENESS OF GOD?

'This is how we know what love is: Jesus Christ laid down his life for us' (1 John 3:16).

The most important reason for the coming of Jesus was to die as a sacrifice for mankind's sin. His death made a way for people to be forgiven and brought back into fellowship with God (2 Cor. 5:18–19). Mankind's close relationship with God had been broken by man's sin in the garden of Eden (Gen. 3:8–24).

Mankind was dead in sin (Eph. 2:1–2). People had earned God's just punishment for their sins (Rom. 1:18). There was no escape from that punishment (Heb. 2:2–3a) because God is a holy and just judge (Psalm 143:2). He punishes sin, and all people are guilty before him (Eccl. 7:20, Rom. 2:11–12; 3:23).

Many groups of people in Africa think that wrongdoing is a matter of doing the things which bring shame to the family or the clan. Unfortunately, things which certain groups of people consider acceptable behaviour, are unacceptable to God. For example, some groups permit unmarried people to engage in sexual intercourse before marriage. God says this is sin, and that he will punish it (1 Cor. 6:18, 1 Thess. 4:3–6, Rev. 2:20–22).

Wrongdoing is not just a matter of bringing shame on the family or the clan. Wrongdoing is sin. Sin is breaking the laws of God. God is the one who has determined what is good and what is evil. God is the judge, and God has decided what is right and what is wrong without referring to culture or tradition. His definition of good and evil is called the moral law of God. This law is summarized in the Ten Commandments (Exodus 20:1–17). It is explained more fully in the New Testament epistles. Sin is defined by God, not by what we think is shameful. What is shameful in one culture may not be shameful in another.

Some people become confused about the love and justice of God. They think that God should somehow overlook man's sin, In the way a corrupt judge often overlooks wrongdoing for a bribe. They think that somehow God's love should be able to cancel his holiness and justice.

God is not corrupt like so many human judges. He does not overlook sin. He does not show partiality (Col. 3:25). One attribute of God cannot cancel another attribute. He is loving but he is also just. His love cannot cancel his justice (Gen. 18:25). Neither can his justice cancel his love (Song of Solomon 8:7).

God loves the people he created (Jer. 31:3, John 3:16). He was not willing for people to be cut off from himself forever because of their sin. God's love longed for man to be close to him and to have fellowship with him. But God's holiness and justice demanded that people be judged and punished for their sin. God could not tolerate sinful human beings in his holy presence.

Jesus said that left to their own efforts, people could not save themselves (Matt. 19:25–26) from the wrath of God against their sin. There is no work a person can do which is good enough to release that person from God's death sentence for sin (Gen. 2:17, Rom. 6:23).

However, because God is omnipotent and omniscient, nothing is impossible for him, not even mankind's salvation (Matt. 19:26). God was able to make a way to carry out his punishment against human sin, and at the same time to show his love and his forgiveness towards people.

How could God accomplish this? How could he continue to be just and holy, and punish sin, and at the same time release sinners from the judgment they had earned? A story from school will help us understand how God did this:

Baba, a student at Teachers' College, had an expensive radio that he had worked hard to pay for. One day it was stolen from his room. Baba was very angry. He suspected another student called Adamu. He had seen Adamu enter his room more than once when no one was there. He also knew that Adamu needed money to pay for his brother's school fees. One day Baba secretly went into Adamu's room. He did not see the radio, but he found a large amount of money in Adamu's box. Baba became angry.

Adamu had a friend named Isa, who heard of the situation. Isa felt very bad because both Adamu and Baba were his friends. Isa decided he would pay Baba for the radio, but he would have to sell his own new bicycle in order to get the money. After he sold his bicycle, Isa went to see Baba. He told Baba what he had heard and that he wanted to pay for the radio that Adamu had taken. He did not want Baba to be angry with Adamu. Baba felt great pain at what Isa had done for Adamu. He decided to accept the payment from Isa who had already sold his bicycle. He could not refuse Isa who was his closest friend. Isa paid Baba the full price of a new radio.

Baba called Adamu and told him about the radio and about the money he had found in Adamu's room. Adamu became nervous. Baba was a strong fellow. He could be dangerous if he became angry. Adamu knew he was caught. He admitted he had stolen the radio but what was he to do? He had sold the radio and had already used part of the money, so he could not return the radio and did not have the money. Adamu was afraid and began to tremble.

Baba looked at him seriously. Then he told Adamu what Isa had done. He told him that, since the radio was paid for, he would forgive him and forget the matter. Adamu was speechless. He began to weep. Baba told Adamu there was only one thing he wanted him to do. He wanted Adamu to go to Isa and to thank him for what he had done, and then to change his ways. Adamu wasted no time in looking for Isa but when he found him he didn't know what to say. He felt embarrassed and ashamed. He had no money to pay him back for the radio. Isa told him he did not want to be repaid. Instead, he wanted Adamu to change his ways. Then Isa hugged Adamu and Adamu began to weep again.

From that time on Adamu was ready to do anything Isa asked. In fact, he spent the rest of his time in college trying to help Isa in many ways. They became lifelong friends. The matter greatly affected the relationship between Adamu and Baba. Baba kept his word and never brought the matter up again. Baba and Adamu became good friends because of the relationship each of them had with Isa, and because of what Isa had done.

B. HOW WAS MANKIND'S SALVATION ACCOMPLISHED?

This story gives us a suggestion of how mankind's salvation was accomplished. It also illustrates several words which are used in the Bible to explain salvation, such as mediator, forgiveness, reconciliation, propitiation and sanctification. The meaning of these words will be explained later in this chapter.

In the story, Adamu's sin against Baba broke their relationship and brought the anger of Baba against Adamu. Baba was determined to make Adamu pay for his wrongdoing. By paying for the radio, Isa was able to overcome the wrong which Adamu had done. Isa made it possible for Baba to forgive Adamu. But it cost Isa his bicycle to secure that forgiveness. The intervention of Isa restored the relationship between Baba and Adamu. It also made Adamu very grateful and devoted to Isa.

Although it is not an exact illustration, we can compare this story to the story of our salvation in Christ. Adam's sin against God broke the close relationship between mankind and God and brought God's anger against our sin. God's justice required that people must be punished for their sin. By taking the Father's punishment for our sin, Jesus was able to protect us from the holy anger of God. Jesus made it possible for God the Father to forgive people for their sins, but it cost Jesus his life to secure that forgiveness. Jesus' sacrifice makes it possible for the relationship between human beings and God to be restored. If we really understand what Jesus has done for us, it will make us willing to serve him the rest of our lives.

When Adamu saw what Isa had done for him, it touched his heart so deeply that it caused Adamu to turn away from his sinful behaviour. When we really understand what Jesus had done for us, it will motivate us to turn away from our pride, selfishness and sinful behaviour. This is what the Bible means by the repentance that leads to salvation (2 Cor. 7:10). In gratitude for what Isa had done, Adamu become a lifelong, devoted friend of Isa. If we have this kind of gratitude and devotion to Jesus, God will use it to change our sinful character into a godly and holy character (2 Cor. 5:15).

In the story, Isa became a mediator between Baba and Adamu. If Isa had not come between them and paid for the radio, Baba would have taken Adamu to court and made him pay for the radio himself. In most African societies, in order for a young man to marry a girl, he must have a mediator to meet with the parents of the girl. In the story, Isa became the mediator between Baba and Adamu, to restore their broken relationship.

According to God's word, Jesus Christ is the only mediator who can restore the broken relationship between God and man. A witch-doctor cannot do it. A Muslim teacher cannot do it. The virgin Mary cannot do it. The Bible says, 'For there is . . . one mediator between God and men, the man Christ Jesus' (1 Tim. 2:5). He is the only one who can bring God the Father and sinful human beings back together into a close relationship.

The Bible says that the wages of sin is death (Rom. 6:23). The death penalty for sin has affected every part of man's life and activity on earth. Individuals are corrupt and evil in their words and behaviour. Husbands and wives fight with each other because of their selfish and sinful attitudes. They betray their promises of faithfulness and commit adultery. Students steal and cheat in school. Children grow up to be liars like their parents. Clans and tribes fight with each other because of their pride and desire for revenge. Countries go to war for similar reasons. The world groans with sickness, suffering, unhappiness, bitterness, betrayal, broken homes, crime, violence, hatred, misery, injustice, murder, rape, wars, and ultimately death – all because of man's sin.

THE SACRIFICE OF CHRIST

The bitter truth about man's salvation was that God himself would have to suffer if human beings were to be saved. No human being could qualify to take God's punishment for sin earned by others, because every human being has earned the death penalty for his or her own sin. The Bible says that God himself took his own holy wrath against the sin of mankind (1 Peter 2:24). The holy, innocent and perfect One, would have to suffer the condemnation, judgment and punishment which we deserve (Isa. 53:4–6, 9–10). The Bible says, 'He (Jesus) himself bore our sins in his body on the tree, so that we might die to sin and live for righteousness' (1 Peter 2:24).

By doing this, God could be both a just judge and a merciful Saviour. He could fully punish our sin by punishing himself on the cross in our place. The Bible says, 'God made him who had no sin to be sin for us, so that in him we might become the righteousness of God' (2 Cor. 5:21).

By taking the terrible wrath of God against our sin on the cross, Jesus released us from the judgment and punishment we deserved because of our sin (Rom. 3:24–26). Through Christ's suffering on the cross, those who now trust in Jesus are able to come close to God once again and to be made holy. This was dramatically pictured during the crucifixion of Christ when the curtain of the temple was supernaturally torn from top to bottom (Matt. 27:51). The torn curtain exposed the most holy place, which was the presence of God in the temple (Heb. 9:7). At the cross of Christ, both God's justice and God's love were satisfied.

Sacrifice is a common theme in African traditional religions. There is a strong similarity between some traditional ideas of sacrifice and what the Bible teaches about the sacrifice of Christ. There are usually four or five categories of sacrifice in traditional practice. These would include propitiatory sacrifice, substitutionary sacrifice, mediatory sacrifice, communion sacrifice and gift sacrifice. The first two of these have a traditional meaning which can increase our understanding of the sacrifice of Christ for our sin.

In the propitiatory sacrifice, there is usually some great crisis or problem which has caused the elders to seek advice from the traditional diviner. They ask what can be done to save the situation. What sacrifice will propitiate (turn away) the anger of the ancestors or divinities causing this great crisis? A sacrifice is then prescribed to solve the problem. If the crisis or problem is severe it is often a costly sacrifice. With some groups in the past, a human sacrifice would be required for a very severe crisis.

Sin has led to most of the problems and crises which mankind faces. Indeed, a propitiatory sacrifice was urgently needed if God's wrath was to be turned away from sinful humanity. However, it was not men or women who initiated this sacrifice, but God himself. There was nothing they could do to help themselves. The Bible tells us, 'For while we were still helpless, at the right time Christ died for the ungodly' (Rom. 5:6–NASB).

The good news of Jesus Christ is this: By the propitiatory sacrifice of Christ, not just one problem or crisis has been solved, but sin, the very root of all human suffering and sorrow, has been overcome. The final result of sin is death (Rom. 6:23). The Bible tells us that Jesus Christ has, 'abolished death, and brought life and immortality to light through the gospel' (2 Tim. 1:10).

The substitutionary sacrifice in traditional beliefs is very similar to the propitiatory sacrifice. When someone is believed to be under the wrath of a divinity or an evil spirit, the trouble will continue until that person dies, unless a substitute is provided on behalf of the suffering person. The substitute prescribed as sacrifice is often a sheep. Jesus made it clear that sin is the root of mankind's problems, even in the case of some inexplicable disasters (Luke 13:2–5). The Bible warns us that our sins will find us out (Num. 32:23). Our sins will trouble us right to our death. 'The soul who sins will die' (Ezek. 18:4–NASB).

God has provided the complete substitutionary sacrifice for man's sin in Christ. Just as the blood of the Passover lamb protected the Israelites from God's judgments against Egypt (Ex. 12:5–13), so the blood of Jesus, the Passover lamb of God, protects us from God's judgment for our sins (1 Cor. 5:7). When John the Baptist saw Jesus coming towards him, he said, 'Behold, the Lamb of God who takes away the sin of the world' (John 1:29–NASB)!

THE BIBLICAL MEANING OF SIN

The Hebrew word most frequently translated 'sin' in the Old Testament is *chata*. This word means to miss the mark. In the New Testament, a Greek word *hamartia* has a similar meaning and is translated 'sin'. From these words, sin means to miss the mark of God's holiness. We fail to live up to what God wants us to be and expects us to be. God is holy and pure. We are unholy and unclean.

Because we know that we have failed to be what God wants us to be, we feel ashamed and try to hide from God. We try to cover our spiritual nakedness by blaming circumstances or other people for the way we are. Something similar happened to our first parents. Adam and Eve failed to obey God when they ate the fruit which God had forbidden them to eat. Instead of admitting their sin and asking God to forgive them for the wrong they had done, Adam blamed his wife and even God for his failure (Gen. 3:11–12), and Eve blamed the serpent instead of admitting her sin (Gen. 3:13).

Because they had sinned, they felt ashamed and tried to hide from God (Gen. 3:7–10). They realized they were physically naked, and tried to cover themselves with fig leaves (Gen. 3:7). They probably did this to cover their shame for disobeying God. In a similar way, people who have committed a crime will compulsively or symbolically wash their hands. They think this will somehow take away their guilt. Pontius Pilate, who ordered Jesus to be crucified, washed his hands in this way (Matt. 27:24).

Adam and Eve lost their close relationship with God when they sinned. Because they had disobeyed God, he put them out of the garden of Eden (Gen. 3:23).

In most African societies, a person feels ashamed and unacceptable to the clan if he or she does not act in the way expected by the clan. More than almost anything else, African people want to be accepted and honoured by their own people. The pain of disapproval and shame is great when a person knows he has disgraced his people. When a person dishonours his own people, he loses the close relationship he had with them and will look for a way to become acceptable again.

To restore the broken relationship between God and man, Jesus took our sin and shame on the cross (1 Pet. 2:24). Because Christ was made sin for us, God the Father had to reject him on the cross. That is why Jesus cried out, 'My God, my God, why have you forsaken me' (Matt. 27:46). On the cross, Jesus was despised and rejected both by God the Father and by men (Isa. 53:3–4). Jesus took the shame and rejection which we deserved from God (Isa. 53:5). He was rejected in our place. Because Jesus took our shame and rejection on the cross, God is now able to accept us and to forgive us.

Some people are only concerned about the approval of their clan and of their ancestors. Such people should remember that if it was important for our first parents to be accepted and forgiven by God, it is just as important for each of us to be accepted and forgiven by God. The Bible says that God has taken away the condemnation of those who belong to Christ (Rom. 8:1).

Because of Jesus' death, man can now be saved from death and eternal punishment (John 3:16) by repenting of his sin and receiving Christ (John 1:12). Those who trust Christ become joined to him spiritually. The Bible says they have become part of his body (1 Cor. 12:27). They will live forever with him in heaven (John 14:1–3). Christ has triumphed over sin, shame, death, and Satan (Col. 2:13–15). This is the gospel. This is the good news of our salvation. This is the best news man has ever heard!

There is nothing more important in life than salvation. In eternity, people will not care who was first to walk on the moon, who was the head of state in a particular country, or who won the football world cup in a particular year. All the honour, glory, thanks, and praise will go to the One who accomplished our salvation, Jesus Christ our Lord.

How can a person be sure his sins are forgiven and that he will be saved?
This important question has to do with assurance of salvation. Is it possible for a person to be certain that he or she really has forgiveness of sin and will go to heaven? Some churches teach that a person can never be sure of it.

A person will not earn eternal life by his good behaviour. A person will not gain eternal life by going to church, having a Christian name, giving gifts to the poor, or even by being baptized. Salvation is a gift from God which no person in the world can earn (Eph. 2:8–9). A person can have eternal life only by repenting of his or her sin and putting his or her faith in Jesus Christ as Lord and Saviour (Mark 1:15). It is God, not man, who promises that those who do this will be saved and will live with Christ in heaven. If we can believe God's words, we can have assurance that our sins are forgiven and that we will be with God in heaven.

If it is not possible to be sure of salvation, why then did Jesus make so many strong statements about assurance of salvation (e.g. John 3:16, 5:24; 6:37; 10:9, Rev. 3:20)? Is God a liar? Can we believe what God promises to us or not? The most famous verse of the Bible is John

3:16. This verse says, 'For God so loved the world that he gave his one and only Son, that whoever believes in him shall not perish but have eternal life.' There is another assurance of salvation which is given to a Christian who has been made alive by the Holy Spirit (regenerated). This is the witness of the Holy Spirit in the heart of that Christian that he or she belongs to Christ. The Bible says, 'The Spirit himself testifies with our spirit that we are God's children' (Romans 8:16).

C. WHAT IS THE MEANING OF SALVATION?

The word salvation means deliverance or rescue. To be saved means to be delivered or rescued from something. To be saved from a fire means to be rescued from the fire. It means you don't get burned to death!

What kind of rescue or deliverance does salvation mean in the Bible? The salvation of Christ means deliverance from sin and the terrible consequences of sin. It is a supernatural act which God alone can accomplish. It means to be rescued from sin in the past, in the present, and in the future.

It means that Christians are now delivered from the condemnation of sin and from the punishment their sin deserves (Rom. 8:1). It means that they can now be delivered from the power of sin in their minds, their emotions, their behaviour and their relationships (Rom. 6:14). It means that in the future, they will even be delivered from the effects of sin in their bodies and in the world itself (Rom. 8:21–23).

SALVATION IN THE PAST

By his death, Jesus rescued us from the death penalty for sin (Rom. 6:23). Because of Jesus' sacrifice, we will not be condemned and punished by God for our sin if we are joined to Christ by faith (Rom. 8:1). We have been spared from the terrible wrath of God against sin (Rom. 5:9). We have been cleansed and declared righteous in God's eyes (2 Cor. 5:21). This is the reason God can now forgive us our sins. In Revelation 1:5 it says, 'He has freed us from our sins, by his blood.' This is salvation from sin in the past (1 Cor. 6:11).

SALVATION IN THE PRESENT

Even when our sins are forgiven, we still have a problem. We still live in a body of flesh and blood with a sinful nature. What are we to do about that? How can we get victory over the downward pull of our sinful nature? By his resurrection and by the power of his Holy Spirit, Jesus has provided us with the spiritual strength to overcome the power of sin in our lives! We can overcome sin's corruption and control when we are controlled by the Holy Spirit (Rom. 8:11–13). We can receive God's help through the power of the Holy Spirit by faith (Rom. 8:11, Gal. 3:14). To have this victory, we must yield our bodies and minds to Christ (Rom. 12:1–2) instead of yielding them to the desires of our sinful nature (Gal. 5:13–16).

There is a real conflict for the Christian if he is to have victory over the control of sin in his daily life. This inward struggle can be very intense (Gal. 5:17). But God promises to help us by his Holy Spirit if we will choose to yield to him instead of yielding to the desires of our flesh (Rom. 8:12–13). The very word victory implies a battle. Victory means that the battle has been won!

The secret to this victory is the resurrection power of Christ, made available to us through the Holy Spirit who lives in the Christian. The Bible says, 'If the Spirit of him who raised Jesus from the dead is living in you, he who raised Christ from the dead will also give life to your mortal bodies through his Spirit who lives in you' (Rom. 8:11). This is salvation from sin in the present (Rom. 5:10).

SALVATION IN THE FUTURE

At his return and the establishment of his kingdom, Jesus will provide us with deliverance from the very presence of sin and its horrible effects on the world (Rom. 8:18–25). In that future day, our salvation will be complete. We will have resurrection bodies like Christ's body (1 Thess. 4:16–17, Phil. 3:20–21). Even the world itself will be changed into a place of perfect peace and beauty (Isa. 65:17–25, Rom. 8:21). For this reason Paul says, 'our salvation is nearer now than when we first believed' (Rom. 13:11). This is salvation from sin in the future (1 Pet. 1:5).

D. WHAT ARE THE RESULTS OF SALVATION?

What are the results of salvation? What happens to the person who has repented of sin and received Jesus as Lord and Saviour (Mark 1:15, John 1:12, Acts 20:21)?

The key word in the Bible to describe the results of salvation is 'new'. Paul wrote, 'if anyone is in Christ, he is a new creation; the old has gone, the new has come!' (2 Cor. 5:17). Have you ever seen a brand new bicycle, a brand new robe, a brand new piece of furniture or a brand new dress? There is something very beautiful about things when they are new and unspoiled. So it is with salvation. We have been given a new quality of life, a new power for living, a new hope, a new joy, a new song of thanksgiving, a new peace, and an abundant life through Jesus Christ (John 10:10). Here are some of the most important things we have received with this new life in Christ:

Forgiveness: Forgiveness means we will no longer have to pay the terrible price for the sins we have committed. Baba forgave Adamu and forgot about the radio because it had been paid for by Isa. Those who put their faith in Christ have been forgiven of all their sin because Jesus has paid the full price for their sin (Eph. 1:7).

Reconciliation: Reconciliation means the healing of a broken relationship. Adamu's relationship with Baba was restored because of what Isa did. When a married couple separates and then is brought together again, they are reconciled. Those who have put their faith in Christ have been reconciled to God. They have been brought back into a loving personal relationship with God as their Saviour after being separated from him because of their sin (Col. 1:21–22, Rom. 5:10).

Redemption: This is a word taken from the ancient slave market. The slave was put up for sale. To own the slave, a person had to purchase (redeem) the slave with money. We were slaves to sin and condemned to death. Jesus purchased (redeemed) us for himself at the price of his own blood, paid to the holy justice of God the Father (Heb. 9:11–12). Because of this, the Bible says we no longer belong to ourselves, but to God. We were bought by Christ at the awesome price of his own blood (1 Cor. 6:20, Eph. 1:7, Rev. 5:9).

Justification: To be justified means to be declared legally 'not guilty' concerning some accusation. We have been declared 'not guilty' of our sin in God's judgment court (Rom. 5:1,9). This is because Jesus took our sin on the cross. Jesus was declared guilty for our sins by God the Father (2 Cor. 5:21). Therefore he suffered our death sentence. Since there is no longer a death sentence left for us to suffer, we are declared 'not guilty' by God! We have been justified!

Because God himself has declared us not guilty, no one else, including Satan, can declare us guilty before him (Rom. 8:33)! We are no longer condemned for our sins before God (Rom. 8:1). Some people remember the word justified with the saying, 'just-as-if-I'd never sinned.'

Propitiation: This is a word which means to satisfy or turn away the wrath of God against our sin. In the story, Isa propitiated the anger of Baba against Adamu by repayment of the price for the radio. In other words, it turned away Baba's anger against Adamu for his wrongdoing. In traditional religions, certain sacrifices are made to the spirits in order to propitiate (turn away) their anger. Christians no longer have to make such sacrifices. Christ's blood satisfies the anger of God against our sin (Rom. 3:24–25, 1 John 2:2). No one in eternity will be able to condemn the Christian whom God himself has forgiven (Rom. 8:33–34).

Regeneration: When we believe in Christ, an amazing thing happens. We are brought from spiritual death to spiritual life (Eph. 2:1,4–5). Jesus said, 'I tell you the truth, a time is coming and has now come when the dead will hear the voice of the Son of God and those who hear will live' (John 5:25). Jesus was speaking about the miracle of regeneration. A few moments later he added that he will one day also bring back to life all the physically dead (John 5:28–29).

This transformation is called the 'washing of rebirth and renewal by the Holy Spirit' (Titus 3:5). In regeneration, the triune God himself comes to live in a Christian (John 14:16–17,23, Rom. 8:9). What an amazing thing! Through regeneration, God actually comes to live in his people! Without regeneration, we cannot enter the kingdom of God (John 3:5) and we do not belong to Christ (Rom. 8:9).

The indwelling presence of God makes a total change to the Christian's life. Through his presence in our lives, we are empowered to live the new and abundant life that Jesus promised (John 10:10b). The presence of God can help us get victory over temptation and our sinful tendencies. This is why the gospel of Christ changes evil men into good men. This is why the majority of good works towards the outcast, hurting, and needy people of the world were originally started by Christians over the last 2000 years of history. To be regenerated means to be made alive by the Spirit of God!

Grace: This is one of the most beautiful words in the Christian vocabulary. It is related to a word meaning, 'to freely give.' Grace refers to the undeserved kindness which God has shown to mankind, especially in Jesus Christ. The Bible says, 'it is by grace you have been saved, through faith' (Eph. 2:8). In other words, we have been saved because of God's great love, mercy and goodness given to us in Christ, which was entirely undeserved. Because of God's grace, we can be forgiven of our sins. Because of God's grace, we can be accepted by God and become his people. Because of God's grace, we can have eternal life. Some people remember the word grace with the acrostic – God's **R**iches **A**t **C**hrist's **E**xpense.

Grace also includes all the other acts of kindness of God towards the human race, and especially to his own people. It is the love, goodness, and help of God in our daily lives. The rain is a gift of his common grace to all people. The strength, encouragement and help of the Holy Spirit in the life of Christians, and his answers to our prayers, are evidences of his special grace to his redeemed people.

Adoption: Orphans are often put up for adoption because their real father and mother are dead. When an orphan is adopted, a man who is not the child's father, becomes his or her new father. The orphan becomes a legal member of a new family. So it is with the salvation of Christ. We are adopted by God and he becomes our new Father (Rom. 8:15–16, Eph. 1:5). We become the children of God in God's family (1 John 3:1–2). We are transferred from Satan's kingdom to God's kingdom (Col. 1:12–13).

Inheritance: Because we have become the children of God, we take part in the privileges and responsibilities of God's family, the church. We will discuss these privileges and responsibilities further when we study the church. Because we are now God's children, we will one day inherit all that belongs to God as joint heirs with Christ (Rom. 8:16–17, Eph. 1:11,14)! How much is that? Since God owns everything, we will share in everything (1 Cor. 3:21–23)! Our human minds cannot grasp what this means, but we can be sure it will be better than anything we have ever imagined (1 Cor. 2:9, Rev. 21:6–7).

Prayer: At one time we prayed in uncertainty or even despair, or didn't pray at all. Now we can come to God in the name of Jesus in complete confidence that he will hear our cries for help (John 16:23–24). If you wanted to see the head of state of your country personally about some matter, you probably could not do it. If it was possible at all, you would have to make an appointment far in advance and pass through many officials. Even then, you would have a very short time in his busy schedule, and he might not be able to help you.

People of every culture and every religion pray, but only Christians have assurance from God that their prayers will definitely be answered when they pray according to God's will (1 John 5:14–15). As Christians we can come to God at any time, praying in the name of Jesus (John 16:24). Indeed, we are encouraged to come boldly to God's throne to get his help in our time of need (Heb. 4:16). As Christians we now bear the name of Christ. We belong to him. Because we belong to Christ, God urges us to bring every matter to him in prayer, at all times (Eph. 6:18, Phil. 4:6). God has the desire as well as the power to answer our prayers (Mark 11:22–24), but we must learn to pray according to the will of God (1 John 5:14–15). We can learn about God's will by studying the Bible (John 15:7).

Eternal Life: Eternal life is not a place. It is a personal relationship with Jesus as our Lord and Saviour and with God as our Father (John 17:3). Eternal life does not begin when we die. It begins at the time we first put our faith in Christ. Later when our bodies die, our relationship with God continues right on into our new home, which is heaven (John 14:3)!

The Church: When we put our faith in Christ, we become a part of his body, which is called the church (Col. 1:18,24). The local church is not a building, but a group of people. The church is made up of all the people on earth and in heaven who have put their faith in the Lord Jesus Christ (Gal. 3:26–28, Eph. 3:15). We become a part of the body of Christ when we are baptized into his body by the Holy Spirit, a result of our faith in Christ (1 Cor. 12:13). Water baptism, which the Lord commanded to be done (Matt. 28:19), is an outward, visible sign of what has already taken place spiritually through our faith in Christ and God's work of regeneration in us. Water baptism does not save us or make us part of the church. Rather, it is a public testimony that we have been spiritually joined to Christ by faith and have already become part of his church.

E. WHAT ARE SOME WAYS IN WHICH SALVATION APPLIES TO THE NEEDS FELT IN AFRICA?

The death and resurrection of Jesus Christ meets the deepest spiritual needs of all people in the world. Whether they realize it or not, the greatest need of all men is forgiveness of sin from God and a personal relationship with him. This forgiveness and this relationship is made possible by the death and resurrection of Christ. His death secured forgiveness for our sins. His forgiveness has made reconciliation with God possible, so that people can now experience a close relationship to God as their Father and shepherd.

If a person is reconciled to God and has a personal relationship with Christ as his or her Lord and Saviour, then the deepest needs felt by Africans will be abundantly met (John 10:10b). Take for example the great need felt for acceptance by the community. The community of an earthly extended family is very important, but it will only continue during this earthly life. By contrast, the community of God's chosen people, the church, is an eternal community which will last forever and ever. When we enter into a personal relationship with God through Jesus Christ, we become a part of this eternal community of God's people. We are accepted by God into his eternal extended family, and become part of a fellowship of brothers and sisters in Christ who will live together forever in heaven. No earthly community can give this eternal acceptance.

Consider the need felt in Africa for protection from evil spirits and powers. The resurrection of our Lord Jesus Christ guarantees to every Christian the protection of the One who has been lifted to the highest place of authority and power in the universe (Matt. 28:18, Eph. 1:20–22, Phil. 2:8–9). There is no witch, sorcerer, ancestral spirit, divinity, demon, or even Satan himself, who will dare to challenge the King of Kings. All creatures in the universe must bow in submission and fear to the One who has become the Christian's great God and Saviour, Jesus Christ (Phil. 2:10, Titus 2:13). A Christian can be fully set free from the fear of witches and evil spirits.

Consider the desire for life force. The Bible tells us that life is a gift from God (Zech. 12:1, Acts 17:25). If life is a gift from God and the Christian is the child of God (1 John 3:2), it must certainly be true that God wants to bless his own children with the fullest gift of life. Indeed, Jesus said, 'I came that they might have life, and might have it abundantly' (John 10:10b–NASB). Christians are given the life-giving power of the Holy Spirit when they are regenerated (born of God) (Titus 3:5). It is the power of the Holy Spirit which raised Jesus Christ from the dead (Rom. 8:11)! That is the supreme life force! What greater life force could a person possibly have than the very presence of the Creator of life in his heart (John 14:16–17)? Truly the gospel of Jesus Christ meets the very deepest needs of the African heart.

F. WHAT IS SANTIFICATION?

The word sanctification means the process of consecration or setting apart for a holy purpose. In the Old Testament, certain objects were said to be sanctified when they were set apart for holy use in the worship ceremonies of the tabernacle (Lev. 8:10, Num. 7:1). In the Old Testament, blood and anointing oil were used to set apart (sanctify) objects (Lev. 8:15), clothes (Lev. 8:30), and people (Lev. 8:23–24, Num. 8:17) for God. Even the seventh day of the week was made holy (sanctified), set apart for God's use (Gen. 2:3, Ex. 20:11). The important idea in sanctification is separation from the world unto God. In Leviticus 20:26 God said, 'You are to be holy to me because I, the LORD, am holy, and I have set you apart from the nations to be my own.'

When we are sanctified, we are set apart from the world to be God's holy people. As we become more holy we become more like God. We begin to reflect his glory. That is exactly what God wants (1 Pet. 2:9). He wants people to be holy like himself (1 Pet. 1:15–16). This is why he created man in his image in the beginning (Gen. 1:27). God wants to restore his image in his people (Eph. 4:24, Titus 2:14). The process by which he does this, through the power of the Holy Spirit, is called sanctification (2 Thess. 2:13). Thus sanctification is the transforming work of the Holy Spirit in the Christian's life and holiness of character is the result of this work. Like salvation, the process of sanctification has a past, a present and a future aspect.

SANCTIFICATON IN THE PAST

Sanctification in the past has to do with the way God now sees us in relationship to Christ. Because we have believed in Christ, God the Father now sees us as being spiritually inside Christ, and thus separated from the world (Rom. 6:3– 6, Col. 3:3). He sees us as being holy, because when he looks at us now, he sees Christ who is holy instead of seeing us. For this reason, the Bible says that Christ, 'became to us wisdom from God, and righteousness and sanctification' (1 Cor. 1:30). Jesus himself is our sanctification. God has declared us to be holy in Christ (Heb. 10:10).

For this reason, the Bible says that we have already been sanctified (1 Cor. 6:11). That is our lawful position before God, even though it is not a completed reality in our daily experience. We are now set apart for God because we have been made holy by the blood of Christ (Rom. 5:9).

SANCTIFICATION IN THE PRESENT

In the present, our sanctification is a process of gradually becoming more holy in our behaviour, day by day. In the story of Baba and Adamu, Isa said that he did not want to be repaid for the radio, but only wanted Adamu to change his ways. So it is with our salvation in Christ. We can never repay Jesus for what he has done for us. Instead, Jesus wants us to change our ways. He wants us to put away sin from our daily lives (Col. 3:5–9). He wants us to begin to do good (Col. 3:12–14, Titus 2:14). This process of becoming more holy, day by day, is called present or progressive sanctification (1 Thess. 5:23, 1 Pet. 1:14–16).

We need to understand the relationship between past sanctification and present sanctification. An illustration will help us. Suppose you were appointed to be your country's ambassador to the United Nations. From the very day of this appointment, you would be the legally designated ambassador. However, it would almost certainly take some months of careful preparation and training before you could actually begin the duties of this assignment. There would be a distinct difference between the legal fact of your appointment and the daily experience of actually being the ambassador. In a similar way, there is a very great difference between being declared holy by God (past sanctification), and the experience of becoming holy in our day to day behaviour (progressive sanctification). Past sanctification takes places at the very moment we put our faith in Christ. Present (progressive) sanctification is a lifetime process.

God uses several ways to accomplish progressive sanctification in our lives. The most important ways are the word of God (Eph. 5:26), the work of the Holy Spirit (2 Thess. 2:13) and the discipline of the Lord (Heb. 12:10). We will consider first the purifying effect of the word of God on our lives. The word of God was given to us to teach us what to believe, to rebuke us for sin, to correct us when we go astray, and to show us how to live a holy life (2 Tim. 3:16, John 17:17).

However, knowing what is right and actually doing what is right are two different things. It is easy to learn what is right. It is very much harder to do what is right. That is the biggest problem of mankind. People know what is right but they don't do it. Some years ago a group of state government officials came to a local government council (LGC) and sacked the entire LGC for a long list of corrupt practises. A few years later, some of these very same state government officials were sacked for some of the very same corrupt practises. They knew quite well what was right but they could not do it themselves.

The power to do what is right comes from the Holy Spirit who lives in us, once we have believed in Christ (Rom. 8:9–14). It is the Holy Spirit who gives us the inner strength to obey God's word and to do the will of God (Rom. 8:4). It is the Holy Spirit who makes us want to do the will of God in the first place (Phil. 2:13). Because of our sinful human nature, we do not have the power to do the will of God without the work of the Holy Spirit within us (Rom. 7:18, Rom. 8:11).

Another means which God uses for our present sanctification is discipline and suffering. God disciplines us as a faithful father would discipline his son (Heb. 12:5–10). Though it is a hard experience and not enjoyable (Heb. 12:11), God's discipline works very well. His discipline enables us to become more holy (Heb. 12:10). Closely related to this is the matter of suffering in general. God sometimes allows believers to suffer to help them become more holy and pure (1 Pet. 4:1–2).

In addition to the word of God, the work of the Holy Spirit, discipline and suffering, there are several other means which God uses to accomplish our progressive sanctification. These include faith (Acts 26:18, Eph. 3:17), our spiritual union with Christ (Rom. 6:4–5) and the local church fellowship of regenerated believers (Heb. 10:25).

By faith we believe the purifying truth of the word of God. We apply the work of the Holy Spirit in our lives by faith. We experience the reality of our spiritual union with Christ by faith. We accept the discipline of God and the suffering which he allows in our lives by faith.

In addition to these means of sanctification, we become accountable for our behaviour to brothers and sisters in Christ by being a part of the local church. God uses our participation in the local church as an important part of his process of progressive sanctification. The function of the local church is very similar to the way clans and tribes maintain their traditional values. Individuals in the clan are not free to do just anything they want. They must behave in ways that are acceptable to the traditions of their people. In a very similar way, there are biblical standards for the community of God's people in the local church. It is the responsibility of the church elders to see that these standards are maintained. This process makes everyone in the local church accountable to the others in their local fellowship. In this way God uses the local church fellowship for our progressive sanctification.

We have discussed present salvation and present sanctification. What is the difference between present salvation and present sanctification? The difference is this: Present (progressive) sanctification is the process of becoming more holy. Present salvation is the goal of present sanctification. The goal is that we should not be controlled or dominated by sin in our lives.

SANCTIFICATION IN THE FUTURE

There is also a future aspect to sanctification. We will be perfectly holy only when we meet Jesus in heaven, or when Jesus returns to this world, whichever takes place first (Eph. 5:27, Heb. 12:23). We can never become completely holy in this life because of our sinful human nature. Some people claim they have become completely holy and free from sin in this life. People who say this do not understand the word of God (Rom. 7:21–23, Gal. 5:17). The Bible says, 'if we claim to be without sin, we deceive ourselves, and the truth is not in us' (1 John 1:8). The truth is that God is working progressive sanctification in our lives, day by day, at the present time. One day when we meet the Lord at death or at his return, the work of our sanctification will be completed. We will finally be completely holy (1 John 3:2, Jude 24).

The salvation of God is accomplished by the death and resurrection of Jesus Christ, by the coming of the Holy Spirit, and by the glorious return of Christ. We have carefully examined the death of Christ and the results of his death for mankind. We will now focus our attention on the resurrection of Christ.

G. HOW DO WE KNOW IF CHRIST REALLY ROSE FROM THE DEAD?

The resurrection of Christ is the cornerstone of Christianity. It is one of the facts which sets Christianity apart from every other religion in the world. The whole truth of the gospel depends on the resurrection of Christ. Paul wrote, 'If Christ has not been raised (from the dead), your faith is futile; you are still in your sins' (1 Cor. 15:17). All other religious leaders and prophets who died, remain dead to the present time. Only Jesus Christ has been raised from the dead. According to the testimony of literally millions of Christians all over the world, both now and in past generations, Jesus is very much alive. How do they know? Because he answers their prayers and because he still performs the signs and miracles he promised to perform (Mark 16:17–18, John 15:7, Heb. 2:4).

Many skeptics doubt the resurrection of Christ. How do we know whether or not Jesus really rose from the dead? To answer this question we must carefully examine the historical record. Can we prove from history that the resurrection really happened? What are the means by which a historic event is proven? What evidence would be acceptable in a court of law?

When trying a case, a court of law usually accepts two types of evidence:

(a) The testimony of eyewitnesses to the event.
(b) The circumstantial evidence surrounding the event.

Let us use these standards to test the evidence for the resurrection of Christ. By doing this, we will find that it is possible to legally prove the resurrection of Christ.

Consider the testimony of the eyewitnesses of Christ's resurrection. There were different kinds of eyewitnesses. First, he was seen by devoted women who had come to put spices on his body on the morning of the resurrection. They persisted in their testimony in spite of the disbelief of the other disciples. Second, the disciples who saw him during the 40 days after his resurrection were eyewitnesses (Acts 1:3). The proof of their witness is that they were willing to suffer and die for the risen Lord they had seen (Acts 4:20, Acts 7:59, Acts 12:1–2). Then there were the soldiers who were guarding the tomb. The proof of their witness is that they had to be bribed to say that the disciples came and stole the body of Jesus (Matt. 28:12–13).

The way the gospel stories of the resurrection are written, shows us that they were given by eyewitnesses. The very fact that each of the four stories is slightly different is evidence that they were written by simple eyewitnesses. There is agreement about the main event, but there are some differences in the details of what took place. This supports the truth of the four gospel stories.

If you were to ask four people at a football game to describe the game, they would all agree on which teams played and who won. However, each person would describe the game from his own perspective. Each observer would be watching different players at different times. It is just this way with the four gospel stories of the resurrection of Christ. Each gospel writer describes different details of the story with which he was familiar, so that each story is just a bit different, but the four stories agree about the main event of the resurrection of Christ.

In addition to the eyewitness character of the resurrection stories, we also need to understand that Jesus was seen alive after his resurrection by many individuals and groups, in different circumstances and at different times. He was not just seen at one time or in one place. He was not seen just from far away, but at close range. He walked, talked and ate with his disciples (Luke 24:13–43). In fact he was seen for a period of 40 days after his resurrection and had some long discussions with the disciples during that time (Matt. 28:16–20, Luke 24:13–43, John 21:1–23, 1 Cor. 15:4–7). He did not just appear as a spirit, like many people in Africa have seen. He made a point to prove that he had a resurrection body of flesh and bones (Luke 24:36–43).

Among the eyewitness testimonies, the record of the Apostle Thomas is especially important because this man strongly refused to believe the eyewitness testimony of his close friends about seeing Christ alive from the dead (John 20:24–25). A week later Thomas himself saw the risen Lord and spoke with him. He was so amazed that he said, 'My Lord and my God' (John 20:24–29)!

The second kind of proof for the resurrection of Christ comes from the circumstantial evidence associated with his resurrection. Here is a summary of some of this evidence.

1. The fact of the empty tomb. What happened to the body of Jesus? Many non-Christians have attempted to offer explanations for the empty tomb, but every one of these explanations fails to account

for what actually took place. Note an example of this in number seven below.

2. There was a consistent and unanimous testimony by the apostles of Christ that Jesus rose from the dead. The apostles saw Jesus alive after his resurrection and they proclaimed this fact whenever they preached the gospel (e.g. Acts 2:32). This was true throughout the book of Acts, and it has been true throughout church history.

3. There was an amazing change in the character and attitude of all the followers of Jesus from fear and unbelief to courage, joy, and certainty about his resurrection. What happened to produce this change if not the resurrection of Christ? The fact that the apostles of Christ changed from fear and despair at the crucifixion, to courage, joy, and bold testimony after the resurrection, even in the face of torture and death, is the strongest possible proof that the resurrection really took place (Acts 5:29–42, Acts 12:1–2). Such an unnatural, total change in character in a large group of people simply cannot be accurately explained apart from the reality of the resurrection. People are just not willing to suffer torture and death, as the early apostles did, for something they know or suspect to be a lie. It can only prove the resurrection.

4. The remarkable conversion of Saul of Tarsus, a murderous enemy of all Christians, also proves the resurrection of Christ (Acts 9:1–19). What happened to Saul that changed this man completely, if he did not see and hear the risen Christ on the road to Damascus (Acts 9:3–7)?

5. Jesus keeps his promises and answers prayer today, and gives life-changing power to those who are converted. How is that possible if he is dead? Every true Christian in the world can testify from answered prayer that Jesus Christ is very much alive.

6. There was a change in worship from the seventh day of the week to the first day of the week by the Jewish apostles. This change indicates that something very, very unusual happened on the first day of the week. Such a change was unthinkable for a Jew (Luke 24:1–8, Acts 20:7–8).

7. One of the most obvious proofs of the resurrection is the fact that the Jewish religious leaders had to bribe the Roman guards who were assigned to guard Christ's tomb. They were bribed to say that the disciples stole his body (Matt. 28:11–15). This fact proves several things. First, it proves that Jesus' body was indeed gone from the tomb and that the stone was removed at sunrise. Second, it proves that his body had been placed in Joseph's prepared tomb where the guards were, and had not been moved to another place,

as some non-Christians have tried to say. Third, it proves that the resurrection really occurred, for if someone else had removed Jesus' body, the guards would have said so.

If the apostles had stolen his body, as the guards were bribed to say, then it meant that the disciples invited themselves to suffer torture and death for a lie about a dead man whom they knew to be dead. They would have had his decaying body with them. No group of people in the world would all agree to such madness. Eventually someone would expose the secret. But there was no secret to expose in the resurrection of Christ. Not only would the disciples have absolutely nothing to gain through such a deception, they would experience severe suffering instead. And indeed they did experience bitter persecution and death as a result of their testimony about Jesus' resurrection.

8. Many books have been written by non-Christians attempting to disprove the reality of the resurrection of Christ. The theories of these people have been carefully studied and very well answered. It is interesting that the resurrection of Christ is probably the most strongly denied event of history by non-Christians. Yet all the attempts by non-Christians to disprove the resurrection have failed. It is impossible to disprove an event which really took place. Some people who have purposely set out to disprove the resurrection have been converted to Christ when they carefully examined the historical evidence.

The abundant evidence of history proves the resurrection of Jesus Christ. He rose from the dead as he said he would do (Luke 18:32–33), and he is alive for ever and ever (Rev. 1:18). What is the meaning of this amazing event which has changed the history of the whole world? What are the results of the resurrection for the Christian and for all mankind?

H. WHAT DOES THE RESURRECTION OF CHRIST MEAN FOR THE CHRISTIAN TODAY?

By his death and resurrection, Jesus Christ conquered sin, Satan, and death. What does this mean for a Christian living today? Here is a summary of what was accomplished through the resurrection of Christ and what his resurrection means to Christians.

1. As a result of Christ's resurrection, we now have a living hope, the certainty that we will go to heaven when we die (1 Peter 1:3–4). By his resurrection, Christ abolished death and made eternal life and

immortality available to all who believe in him (2 Tim. 1:10, John 11:25, John 14:19).

2. The resurrection proves to us that Jesus Christ is the God-man, that is, the man who was God, and the God who became a man (Rom. 1:4, Heb. 1:8 Col. 2:9).

3. The resurrection proves that Christians will have resurrection bodies like Christ's resurrection body (Phil. 3:20–21). The Christian does not look forward to become an ancestral elder spirit, as in the teaching of traditional religions. He looks forward to being raised in the very resurrection likeness of Christ himself.

4. The resurrection of Christ proves that there will be a resurrection of all human beings, for Jesus promised that he will raise everyone from the dead (John 5:28–29). Some will be raised to a resurrection of life and others to a resurrection of judgment (John 5:28–29).

5. The resurrection proves that all of Christ's promises, words and predictions were true (Mark 8:31, John 11:25–26).

6. The resurrection of Christ assures the believer of resurrection power available to live the Christian life (Eph. 1:19–22, Eph. 3:20).

7. The resurrection of Christ proves that we really do have forgiveness of sins (1 Cor. 15:17–20).

8. The resurrection gives us assurance that we now have a high priest interceding on our behalf at the Father's right hand in heaven (Rom. 8:34).

9. The resurrection proves that there will be a general rebirth of the whole physical creation (Rom. 8:19–23).

10. The resurrection proves that God the Father has fully accepted the sacrifice of Christ for our sins (Rom. 4:25).

11. The resurrection proves that there will be a final judgment of all men. (Acts 17:31). The resurrection proves that the Bible is the perfect and accurate word of God. Thus all the doctrines taught in the Bible are also true

I. WHAT WAS THE PURPOSE OF THE ASCENSION OF CHRIST AND WHAT IS HE DOING NOW?

After Jesus' resurrection from the dead, he appeared to his disciples many different times, over a period of 40 days (Acts 1:3). During this time the Bible says he spoke to them about the things concerning the kingdom of God. Jesus continued the relationship he had with his disciples during this final period before his ascension in order to tell them what their responsibilities would be after his departure to heaven.

The main difference during this period was that Jesus was in his resurrection body, which was not limited by time and space. Because of this, he would appear among them out of nowhere even when the doors were locked (John 20:19). Some people in Africa can understand these appearances of Christ since they believe they have seen the spirits of their ancestors who have died.

There was a major difference, however, in the post-resurrection appearances of Christ to his disciples. It was not just the appearance of his spirit. As Jesus told his disciples in Luke 24:39, it was the Lord himself in his resurrection body of flesh and bones (Luke 24:41–43).

During this period of time, all the questions and doubts of the disciples were removed, as in the case of doubting Thomas (John 20:24–29). By the time Jesus ascended into heaven, the disciples were ready not only to proclaim the gospel of his death and resurrection to all men, but they were prepared to suffer and die for him when necessary (Acts 5:29–32,40; Acts 7:56–60). Jesus' work on earth for men's salvation was finished. Now the task was left for his disciples of all generations, including us, to proclaim his salvation to all tribes and nations on earth (Isa. 45:22, Matt. 28:19–20).

Having finished his work of salvation and the training of his disciples, Jesus ascended into heaven in his resurrection body, in full view of his disciples (Acts 1:9–11). Two holy angels appeared and reminded the disciples that Jesus would return to the world just as he had departed, visibly and in his resurrection body. In chapter eighteen we will consider his return in some detail.

Now that Jesus had completed God's plan of salvation for the world, it was time for him to be exalted to the highest place in the universe. The arrival of the triumphant Christ in heaven must have been the most awesome event ever witnessed by the holy angels! The Bible says, 'Therefore, God exalted him to the highest place, and gave him the name that is above every name, that at the name of Jesus every knee should bow, in heaven, and on earth, and under the earth' (Phil. 2:9–10). Not only did Christ arrive in triumph, but he brought with him a vast multitude of Old Testament believers who had been waiting for heaven to be opened by the death of Christ (Psalm 68:18, Eph. 4:8–10).

God the Father has also given this same exalted position, far higher than the angels, to his church (Eph. 2:6). It is because of this position which believers have been given with Christ, that Christians now have authority over Satan and his demons (Luke 10:19, Eph. 1:20–21). From this position of authority, Christians will one day judge the world and even judge angels (1 Cor. 6:2–3).

What is Jesus now doing in his exalted position as King of Kings?
From Scripture we learn that Jesus is presently completing his plan to reach every tribe and people group on earth. Here we can only briefly summarize these activities.

(a) He is upholding and sustaining the universe (Heb. 1:3).
(b) He is the Lord and head of his church (Eph. 1:22–23, Eph. 4:15–16, Col. 1:18).
(c) He is building his church throughout the whole world (Matt. 16:18, Matt.28:20, Eph. 2:19–21). Through the Holy Spirit, Christ is giving spiritual gifts and gifted men to his church on earth (1 Cor. 12:4–7, Eph. 8:4–12).
(d) He is praying for his people (Rom. 8:34, Heb. 7:25). An example of how Jesus intercedes for his people is found in John 17:1–26.
(e) He is preparing a place for his people in heaven and waiting for his enemies to be subdued (Psalm 110:1–2, John 14:2–3).

J. WHO WILL BE SAVED?

There is one more question to consider. Who will be saved? Can any person be saved, or is the salvation of Christ only intended for certain people? Will all people be saved, as some suggest? What does the Bible say?

The question about who will be saved is a very hard question in Africa. Because of strong extended family and clan relationships, it is extremely difficult for people to consider the possibility that some of their extended family or ancestors may not be together with them in heaven. The question is often asked why a God of love would keep anyone out of heaven? This is an emotional question which we have to treat with the greatest sensitivity. Unfortunately, because it is such an emotional issue, there have been a number of theologians who have been eager to present a theology in which everyone will be saved. This theology is called universalism, and it has been widely accepted and believed in Africa.

The question, however, is not what our emotions say, but what does our gracious and loving God say? He gave his Son for the salvation of mankind. To find the truth about who will be saved, we must read the Bible and accept the revelation of God.

The Bible tells us that God made a provision for the salvation of all mankind through the death of Christ. The Apostle John wrote, 'he is the propitiation for our sins: and not for ours only, but also for the sins of the whole world' (1 John 2:2–KJV). Does this mean that all men will therefore be saved?

It was pointed out in the introduction to this book, that a theology which is biblical must consider everything the Bible says on a subject. It is not safe to construct a doctrine on just one verse of Scripture, unless the Bible has nothing else to say on that subject. To understand God's truth, we must consider all the verses which address the issue. What does the Bible teach about who will be saved? In particular, what did Jesus himself say?

When we carefully consider what the Bible says, we learn that all people will definitely not be saved. If we think about it for a little while, we will see that it could not really be any other way. We certainly want all those of our own extended family to be in heaven, but when we think about some of the more evil people in history, we soon realize that heaven would cease to be heaven if such people were there, unless they were very greatly changed in character. It is this change in character which the gospel of salvation in Christ is all about. We know from sad experience that there are a great many people in the world who want nothing to do with Christ and who want no part in such a change in character and behaviour.

A clear picture of this difference between human beings was seen at the crucifixion of Christ. On one side of Christ, a bitter and unrepentant criminal abused Christ with his last words (Luke 23:39). On the other side of Christ was another criminal. But this man was broken by his sin, and expressed repentance as he spoke to Jesus (Luke 23:40–42). In response to these two men, Jesus promised only the repentant thief that he would be with him in Paradise. This event is a small picture of the human race. Some will repent, believe and be saved. Many others will scoff at Christ, will never repent, and will be lost.

In Luke 13:3 Jesus said, 'Unless you repent, you too will all perish.' Later in the same chapter, Jesus' disciples asked the question, 'Lord, are only a few people going to be saved' (Luke 13:23)? In response to this question, Jesus said, 'Make every effort to enter through the narrow door, because many, I tell you, will try to enter and will not be able to' (Luke 13:24). A little later in the same conversation, Jesus added that he would say to some people, 'I don't know you or where you come from. Away from me, all you evildoers! There will be weeping there, and gnashing of teeth when you see Abraham, Isaac and Jacob and all the prophets in the kingdom of God, but you yourselves thrown out' (Luke 13:27–28). Indeed it was Jesus, more than anyone in the Bible, who spoke about the terrible reality of hell. When he spoke of that place, he plainly stated that there would be people there.

In Matthew 7:13–14 Jesus said, 'Enter through the narrow gate. For wide is the gate and broad is the road that leads to destruction, and many enter through it. But small is the gate and narrow the road that leads to life, and only a few find it.' In the book of Psalms, God says, 'The wicked will return to Sheol, Even all the nations who forget God' (Psalm 9:17–NASB).

Yet, the sacrifice of Jesus on the cross is sufficient to provide salvation for everyone who will repent of his or her sins and put their faith in Christ (1 John 2:2). Unfortunately, many people in this world never repent and put their faith in Christ. It is for us who believe in Christ to preach the gospel to all people (Mark 16:15), and to persuade those who are willing, to repent of their sins and to believe in him (2 Cor. 5:11).

From our study of the death and resurrection of Christ, we learn that God has made salvation possible for all who will receive Christ. The Bible says, 'to all who received him, to those who believe in his name, he gave the right to become children of God' (John 1:12). This verse does not say that all men will be saved. What it does say is that each one who personally believes and receives Christ will become a child of God. In Acts 20:21 we read that Paul went about preaching 'that they must turn to God in repentance and have faith in our Lord Jesus Christ.' Repentance toward God and faith in Christ are the necessary conditions for salvation.

Who will be saved? The answer is that all who will repent of their sins, personally trust in Jesus Christ, and receive him as their Lord and Saviour, will be saved.

Many people ask about the fate of those who never had an opportunity to put their faith in Christ. This would apply to all those who die without hearing about the salvation of Christ. The answer to this question is that God is a just judge (Gen. 18:25). He does not judge men unfairly. He judges men on the basis of the light which they have received, not on what they have not received (Rom. 1:18–21). Romans 1:20 says, 'Since the creation of the world, God's invisible qualities, his eternal power and divine nature have been clearly seen, being understood from what has been made, so that men are without excuse.' We must also remember that the cross of Christ shows us that God loves all mankind.

The sad truth is that people do not live according to the light which they have been given, because of their sinful natures. In the end, we must simply accept that God knows the heart of every person who has ever lived. He deals with them according to what is in their hearts. Christians are commanded to preach the gospel to people of all nations on earth.

SUMMARY

Sin has left the human race in a terrible mess. God's plan for mankind is to be saved from sin. In both the Old and New Testament, God pleads with people to call to him to be saved (Isa. 45:22, Rom. 10:13). It is not possible for man to save himself. Only God was able to make a way of salvation through the death and resurrection of Jesus Christ. In Christ, God took his own wrath against our sin, and this made it possible for us to be forgiven and declared righteous.

In most African traditional religions, salvation means acceptance by the community. Along with this, salvation would include deliverance or protection from witchcraft and evil spirits and the possession of life force. Each of these ideas can be compared with a truth about the salvation of God. God's salvation means that because of what Jesus did for us on the cross, we can be accepted by God the Father (John 1:12, Eph. 2:12–13). It means we are accepted into the extended family of God's people, the church (Eph. 2:19–20). God's salvation also means that we have God's Holy Spirit living within us (Rom. 8:9). Because of the Holy Spirit's presence, God can protect us from witchcraft and evil spirits (2 Thess. 3:3, 1 John 4:4). He can also give us supernatural life force for holy and abundant living (Eph. 3:20, Phil. 2:13). Thus God's salvation meets the deepest needs of the African heart.

DISCUSSION QUESTIONS AND PROJECTS BASED ON CHAPTER SEVEN

1. Explain fully why it is not sufficient just to be sincere in one's faith in God in order to be saved. Give Scripture verses.

2. Explain how God's just condemnation of man's sin was satisfied by the death of Christ. Give Scripture verses.

3. How can a Christian overcome the weakness of his sinful nature?

4. Clearly explain why all people will not be saved.

5. Write a brief essay to explain the verse which says, 'Salvation is found in no one else, for there is no other name under heaven given to men by which we must be saved' (Acts 4:12).

6. What will salvation mean in the future? Give two Bible verses which refer to salvation in the future.

7. Divide the class into pairs of people. Imagine that one partner is an old man from your village who is interested in learning more about Christianity. Take turns to explain the results of salvation to him in a culturally meaningful way. The terms to explain are: regeneration, adoption, redemption, justification, and propitiation.

8. Explain the past, present and future aspects of sanctification. Explain why we cannot be perfectly holy until we reach heaven.

9. Discuss holiness, shame and guilt in the African context. Then relate these to the biblical revelation of holiness, shame and guilt.

10. How would you answer a person who claims that because of Christ's death and resurrection, all men will be saved?

11. Let the group discuss the centrality of the cross in the African concept of salvation, love and forgiveness.

12. How would you relate the sacrifice of Christ on the cross to the African concepts of sacrifice and food offerings?

SUGGESTED FOR FURTHER READING

Adeyemo, Tokunboh. *Salvation In African Tradition*. Nairobi: Evangel Publishing House, 1979.

Drury, Keith W. *Holiness For Ordinary People*. Grand Rapids, Michigan: Asbury Press, 1987.

Graham, Billy. *Peace With God*. Carlisle: OM Publishing, reprinted 1995.

Marshall, I.H. *The Work of Christ*. Carlisle: Paternoster Press, 1994.

Stott, John. *The Cross of Christ*. Leicester: InterVarsity Press, 2nd edn 1989.

8

The Holy Spirit – The One Who Sanctifies and Strengthens Christians

John Newton was one of the most evil men of his day. He was a slave-trader who earned his money by selling human beings. Yet this is not what we remember John Newton for. We remember him, instead, as the godly church leader who composed many beautiful hymns, including the hymn, *Amazing Grace*. Who brought about such a great change in John Newton, and in many others like him? It was the Holy Spirit. The Holy Spirit has the power to change people's character and behaviour, and to help them become more and more like Christ (2 Cor. 3:18, Eph. 3:20).

By reading the book of Acts, we discover that it is the Holy Spirit who is most active in the world today, although the world is almost totally unaware of his presence and activity (John 14:17). The four gospels focus on the life and works of Christ. The book of Acts focuses on the work of the Holy Spirit through the members of the early church. The gospel of Luke mentions the Holy Spirit 12 times. This is the most frequent mention of the Holy Spirit in any of the four gospels. The same writer, Luke, mentions the Holy Spirit 42 times in the book of Acts.

From this it is clear that it is primarily the Holy Spirit who is at work in the church and in individual Christians today. It may come as a surprise to some Christians, but the Bible teaches that the Holy Spirit is also actively at work among non-Christians. In John 16:8 Jesus said, 'When he (the Holy Spirit) comes, he will convict the world of guilt in regard to sin and righteousness and judgment.' From this verse it is clear that it is the Holy Spirit who persuades people about their sin and points them to Jesus Christ to find forgiveness for their sin. The Holy Spirit is present all over the world, at all times, and no one can hide from him. Psalm 139:7–10 says, 'Where can I go from your Spirit? Where can I flee from your presence? If I go up to the heavens, you are there; if I make my bed in the depths, you are there. . .if I settle on the far side of the sea, even there your hand will guide me, your right hand will hold me fast.'

Because of all that the Holy Spirit would do when he would come to the church at Pentecost, Jesus said that it was for our good that he (Jesus) should leave the world. If Jesus did not leave, the Holy Spirit would not have come, but if Jesus left, he would send the Holy Spirit to his people (John 16:7). Why was it good for Jesus to leave and for the Holy Spirit to come? Simply because Jesus was present in only one place at one time, even in his resurrection body. Only the people around Jesus could experience the blessing and power of his presence at a given time. Today the Holy Spirit is present everywhere in the world where Christians are present. Because this is true, the blessing of the Lord's presence can be experienced wherever there are Christians.

Who is the Holy Spirit? Is he really a person, or just a kind of power, as some people believe? Is the Holy Spirit really God? If he is God, is he really a different person from God the Father and God the Son? What does the Holy Spirit do in the world today? How can we recognize his presence and activity? What does it mean to be filled with the Spirit? In this chapter we will seek to answer the following questions:

A. How do we know that the Holy Spirit is a person?
B. How do we know that the Holy Spirit is God?
C. Is the Holy Spirit a different person from Jesus and the Father?
D. What do we learn about the Holy Spirit from the images used in the Bible to describe his work?
E. What does the Holy Spirit do among unbelievers today?
F. What does the Holy Spirit do for Christians?
G. What is God's plan for every Christian?
H. How does the Holy Spirit change Christians to become like Christ?
I. What is the Holy Spirit's plan for all Christians as a group?
J. What does it mean to be filled with the Spirit?

A. HOW DO WE KNOW THAT THE HOLY SPIRIT IS A PERSON?

Some people think that the Holy Spirit is not a person, but just an influence or a type of power. The Bible teaches that the Holy Spirit is a person. The Greek word for Spirit, *pneuma*, is neuter in gender, but the Bible speaks of the Spirit with the personal pronoun 'he', as in John 16:13: 'When he the Spirit of truth comes, he will guide you into all truth.' Thus the Bible identifies the Holy Spirit as a person.

As he is described in the Bible, the Holy Spirit has the mind and will of a person. He does what a person does. He spoke and gave instructions when he called Paul and Barnabas to be missionaries

(Acts 13:2). The Holy Spirit reveals things to his people. He revealed to Simeon that he would not die until he had seen God's Messiah (Luke 2:25–26). The Holy Spirit also revealed the deception of Ananias and Sapphira to Peter in Acts 5:1–9, when they lied about the price they were paid for their property. The Holy Spirit decides which spiritual gifts he will give to each Christian (1 Pet. 4:10).

Besides having a mind and a will, the Holy Spirit has the emotions of a person, such as love (Rom. 15:30), joy (Rom. 14:17), and grief (Eph. 4:30). The Holy Spirit revealed his grief and anger against the Israelites because of their rebellious attitude toward God during the 40 years of wandering in the wilderness (Isa. 63:10).

B. HOW DO WE KNOW THAT THE HOLY SPIRIT IS GOD?

Many people, including some Christians, have the idea that the Holy Spirit is less than God. What does the Bible say?

The Holy Spirit is presented in the Bible as being equal with God the Father and God the Son. When Jesus gave the great commission to his disciples, he said to them, 'Go and make disciples of all nations, baptizing them in the name of the Father, and of the Son, and of the Holy Spirit' (Matt. 28:19). If there are three persons, there should have been three names. However, there is only one name, because there is only one God. The name of God is the Father, the Son and the Holy Spirit. Jesus stated that the three persons of God are equal. The Father is God, the Son is God and the Holy Spirit is God.

In the book of Acts, Peter told Ananias that he had lied about the amount of money for which he had sold a certain property. Then Peter told Ananias, that he had lied to the Holy Spirit (Acts 5:3), and in doing this, Ananias had lied to God (Acts 5:4). Peter called the Holy Spirit God. Other passages in the Bible, such as Isaiah 9:6, teach the same thing. In 2 Corinthians 3:17 Paul said, 'The Lord is the Spirit'. The Holy Spirit is called the Spirit of the Lord in Isaiah 61:1 and Acts 8:39 and the Spirit of God in 1 Samuel 10:10 and Romans 8:14. Thus the Holy Spirit is identified as God in both the Old and New Testaments.

C. IS THE HOLY SPIRIT A DIFFERENT PERSON FROM JESUS AND THE FATHER?

Some people think that the Holy Spirit is just another name for God the Father or for Jesus. What does the Bible say? To answer this, let us recall the story of Jesus' baptism. On that occasion, John the Baptist explained how he knew that Jesus was the Messiah. John said, 'I saw the Spirit come down from heaven as a dove and remain on him' (John

1:32). John saw a visible appearance of the Holy Spirit at the same time he saw Jesus. John went on to say, 'I would not have known him (Christ) except that the One who sent me to baptize with water told me, "The man on whom you see the Spirit come down and remain is he" ' (John 1:33).

Not only did the Holy Spirit come down in the form of a dove and rest on Jesus, but God the Father also spoke from heaven at the same time, and said, 'This is my Son whom I love; with him I am well pleased' (Matt. 3:16–17). On this occasion, all three persons of God were present and active at the same time. This clearly shows us that the Holy Spirit is a different person from Jesus and the Father.

Recall that in the great commission, Jesus commanded his followers to baptize people in the name of the Father, the Son and the Holy Spirit. This again shows that the Holy Spirit is a different but equal person, together with the Father and the Son. In John 16:7 Jesus said, 'If I go, I will send him (the Holy Spirit) to you.' Here Jesus distinguished between himself and the Holy Spirit.

D. WHAT DO WE LEARN ABOUT THE HOLY SPIRIT FROM THE IMAGES USED IN THE BIBLE TO DESCRIBE HIS WORK?

The Holy Spirit is identified in the Bible by several visual images in addition to direct references to him as the Spirit of God. Each of these visual images gives us additional understanding of the Holy Spirit and his work.

THE HOLY SPIRIT AS FIRE (ACTS 2:3)

At Pentecost, when the Holy Spirit came upon the followers of Jesus, one of the indications of his presence was the appearance of 'what seemed to be tongues of fire' (Acts 2:3). In the Old Testament, the presence of the Spirit of God had been manifested as fire in more than one situation. When the Israelites wandered in the Sinai desert for 40 years, the indication of the Lord's presence among them was a pillar of cloud by day and a pillar of fire by night (Num. 14:14). When God spoke to Moses in the desert, he spoke from a burning bush where the fire did not consume the bush (Ex. 3:2).

When Nadab and Abihu, the two sons of Aaron the priest, took it upon themselves to offer unauthorized fire before the Lord at the tabernacle, the Bible says that, 'fire came out from the presence of the LORD and consumed them, and they died before the LORD' (Lev. 10:2). In this situation the fire indicated God's judgment on these two priests for doing something they were evidently not authorized or commanded to do (Lev. 10:1).

When Elijah challenged the priests of Baal to see whose God would answer prayer and consume the sacrificial ox by fire, God sent fire to consume the sacrifice which Elijah had placed on his altar, after the priests of Baal had prayed all morning with no results (1 Kings 18:23–39). In this case, the fire seemed to combine acceptance of Elijah's sacrifice and an indication of judgment on the traditional priests of Baal.

Fire purifies and purges from undesirable elements, as when fire is used to purify precious metals by melting out the impurities. The purifying (sanctifying) work of the Holy Spirit seems to be suggested in Scripture by his appearance as fire. The prophet Malachi indicated that Christ's ministry (done in the power of the Holy Spirit) would have the effect of a 'refiner's fire' (Mal. 3:2). John the Baptist spoke of Jesus as the one who would baptize believers 'with the Holy Spirit and with fire' (Matt. 3:11), again suggesting purification from sin (sanctification).

THE HOLY SPIRIT AS LIVING WATER (JOHN 7:38)

When Jesus spoke to the needy and disillusioned woman of Samaria, he told her that he would give her living water to drink which would satisfy her deepest inner longings (John 4:10–14). On the last day of the Jewish Feast of Tabernacles, Jesus said that for those who were still thirsty (unsatisfied), he would provide water which would not only satisfy their own deepest longings, but also be a river of living water to meet the needs of others (John 7:37–38). Jesus identified this living water as the Holy Spirit (John 7:39), who would be given to those who believed in him.

In the book of Ezekiel and in the book of Revelation, the Holy Spirit's presence in heaven is seen as the river of the water of life, pure as crystal, flowing from the throne of God, and bringing life wherever it flows (Ezek. 47:1–9, Rev. 22:1,17). In these passages, the Holy Spirit is seen as living water, satisfying the deepest longings of the human heart, and bringing life and fruitfulness to situations where there is no life, just as physical rain and water bring life to a desert.

Perhaps because the Holy Spirit is pictured in the Bible as living water, we are commanded to be physically baptized in water (Matt. 28:19) as a sign that the Holy Spirit has baptized us and placed us into the body of Christ (1 Cor. 12:13). In 1 Cor. 12:13 it says we are all made to 'drink (the living water) of one Spirit' through the Spirit's baptism.

THE HOLY SPIRIT AS A DOVE (JOHN 1:32)

At the baptism of Jesus, the Holy Spirit descended on Christ in the form of a dove (Luke 3:22). The dove is a sensitive, gentle and harmless bird. In the book of Hebrews we are told that Jesus was, 'holy, harmless and undefiled' (Heb. 7:26–KJV). Beyond all persons, Jesus was filled to the utmost with the Holy Spirit. The descent of the dove at his baptism suggests the harmless, gentle and sensitive heart of the Spirit of God in Christ who understands and cares about the needs of the human heart in a way that no human being could ever do.

A dove was also the least sin offering which a poor person could bring under the Law of Moses (Lev. 5:7). This suggests the fact that Christ was a sin offering, through the Holy Spirit (Heb. 9:14), available even to the poorest person on earth.

THE HOLY SPIRIT IN THE SACRED ANOINTING OIL (LUKE 4:18).

In the Old Testament, God ordered the making of a holy anointing oil which was to be used for anointing the objects of the tabernacle and the priests themselves, to make them holy (Ex. 30:22–30). It was not to be duplicated or used for any other purpose (Ex. 30:32–33). Jesus said, 'The Spirit of the Lord is on me, because he has anointed me to preach good news to the poor. He has sent me to proclaim freedom for the prisoners and recovery of sight for the blind, to release the oppressed, to proclaim the year of the Lord's favour' (Luke 4:18–19). As the verse states, Jesus had these ministries because he was anointed by the Holy Spirit. The anointing oil as a picture of the Holy Spirit cannot be mistaken when the symbolic rituals of the Old Testament ceremonial law are studied and understood.

Kings were also anointed with a sacred anointing oil in the Old Testament. In the case of King David, the Bible plainly states that from the very day Samuel anointed the boy David with the sacred anointing oil in the presence of his father and brothers, 'the Spirit of the LORD came upon David in power' (1 Sam. 16:13).

The seven-branched lamp of the tabernacle gave continual light from pure olive oil (Ex. 27:20). The Holy Spirit is the secret inner presence in the life of a Christian which enables the believer to be moral and spiritual light to a world darkened by sin (Matt. 5:14–16). Oil symbolizes the Holy Spirit throughout the Bible. It suggests to us that the indwelling Holy Spirit is a hidden source of spiritual power and light in the life of a Christian. Through the Spirit's presence, Jesus was the light of the world (John 8:12). The Bible says, 'God anointed Jesus of Nazareth with the Holy Spirit and power, and . . . he went around doing good and healing all who were under the power of the devil, because God was with him' (Acts 10:38).

THE HOLY SPIRIT AS WIND (JOHN 3:8)

The Greek word *pneuma* can be translated either as 'wind' or as 'spirit' depending on the context of the verse. Jesus used this similarity of meanings in talking with Nicodemus, when he told Nicodemus, 'The wind blows wherever it pleases. You hear its sound, but you cannot tell where it comes from or where it is going. So it is with everyone born of the Spirit' (John 3:8).

Wind can be gentle and refreshing, or a mighty, irresistible force. The picture of God's Holy Spirit as wind is very meaningful. Just as the wind is invisible, but its effects can easily be seen, the Holy Spirit is the mighty, invisible wind of God who has spread the gospel of Christ throughout the whole world. On the day of Pentecost, one indication of the Holy Spirit's coming was the 'sound of a rushing, mighty wind' (Acts 2:2–KJV). He is also the unseen refreshing spiritual breeze to Christians who need revival from the Lord.

E. WHAT DOES THE HOLY SPIRIT DO AMONG UNBELIEVERS TODAY?

THE HOLY SPIRIT RESTRAINS MUCH EVIL IN THE WORLD

If it were not for the presence and activity of the Holy Spirit in the world today, life in this world would be unbearable. We do not fully understand how evil the hearts of people really are, and what they will do, given the opportunity.

The Holy Spirit restrains much of the evil that people would like to do. He is probably the One referred to in 2 Thess. 2:7, who restrains lawlessness. In Genesis God told Abimelech, the King of Gerar, that he had restrained him from committing adultery with Abraham's wife, Sarah, when Abimelech had taken her as a wife (Gen. 20:6).

It is clear that the Holy Spirit does not restrain all evil from taking place. The world still has much crime and violence. However, if the Holy Spirit were to suddenly stop his restraining work, the world would become almost unbearable.

The Holy Spirit uses different ways to restrain evil. Sometimes he uses the government, the laws and the police (Rom. 13:3–4). He also uses the holy angels of God in response to the prayers of Christians (Acts 12:3–8). We will learn more about the work of the holy angels in chapter ten. Probably the most general way in which the Holy Spirit restrains evil in the world is by speaking to people's hearts about right and wrong, and convicting them of guilt for doing wrong. Jesus said, 'When he (the Holy Spirit) comes, he will convict the world of guilt in regard to sin and righteousness and judgment' (John 16:8). This refers to the work of the Holy Spirit in a person's understanding of right and wrong, the conscience. It is only because of this work of the Spirit that people realize they are sinners who need forgiveness.

THE HOLY SPIRIT CONVICTS PEOPLE ABOUT THEIR SIN AND DIRECTS THEIR ATTENTION TO CHRIST

Closely related to the Holy Spirit's work of restraining evil is his work of bringing people to Christ. The Holy Spirit persuades people that there will be a judgment when they will have to give an account of their sin. As the Spirit convicts people with a sense of guilt concerning their sin, he also warns them that there will be a judgment and reckoning for their sin. On the basis of this truth, he pleads with people to repent and to turn to Christ (John 16:8–13).

If the Holy Spirit did not faithfully perform his work in people's hearts convicting them of their guilt for sin and their need for Christ, none of them would ever repent or put their faith in Christ. It is impossible to come to faith in Christ apart from the work of the Holy Spirit (John 6:44, Rom. 8:9).

The fact that people are even willing to think about Christ and consider what he did for them, is a work of the Holy Spirit. Jesus said, 'He (the Holy Spirit) will bring glory to me, by taking from what is mine and making it known to you' (John 16:14). To glorify someone means to call attention to the admirable qualities of that person. The Holy Spirit does not draw attention to himself. Instead, he draws the attention of people to Christ, and what Christ has done for them (John 15:26).

Unfortunately, it is possible for people to resist this work of the Spirit and to harden their hearts against God. God warns people not to harden their hearts (Heb. 3:15). If they harden their hearts, it will be impossible to bring them to repentance (Heb. 6:6) and they will be lost. It is a sad fact, but the Bible speaks of those who have so hardened their hearts that their consciences have been seared (burned) and hence they no longer listen to the Spirit's voice (1 Tim. 4:2). Pharaoh was a person who hardened his heart against God (Ex. 5:2; 8:15). The Pharisees and Jewish leaders in the New Testament did the same thing (Acts 7:1–58).

When people harden their hearts against God, they lose a true sense of right and wrong. That is why we see people today committing such terrible acts of crime and violence with no great concern over the evil they have done. Our world is becoming increasingly violent and wicked because people are hardening their hearts to the voice of the Holy Spirit.

When people harden their hearts like this, they become deceived into thinking that good is evil and evil is good (1 Tim. 4:2–3). This is one reason for the increase in sexual immorality and abortion in recent years. Because people are becoming increasingly hardened to the voice of God's Spirit they no longer think that these terrible sins are wrong. In many cases they have heard about Christ but they have rejected him. When a person rejects Christ, he loses all hope of salvation and he also becomes increasingly corrupt. It is becoming common to hear convicted criminals give their final testimony with no indication of sorrow for what they have done.

F. WHAT DOES THE HOLY SPIRIT DO FOR CHRISTIANS?

We have just seen that no one can come to repentance for his sin and have faith in Christ if not for the work of the Holy Spirit. The Spirit convicts a person about his sin and persuades him to believe that judgment will come (John 16:8–11). The Spirit also persuades people to believe that Christ is the only one through whom a sinner can find forgiveness for his sin. Thus it is the Holy Spirit who brings a person to the point of conversion.

It is also the Holy Spirit who performs the actual work of conversion. Jesus said to the educated Jewish religious teacher named Nicodemus, 'I tell you the truth, no one can enter the kingdom of God unless he is born of water and the Spirit. Flesh gives birth to flesh, but the Spirit (i.e. the Holy Spirit) gives birth to spirit' (John 3:5–6). The spirit of an unconverted person is dead because of sin (Eph. 2:1–2) and it is only the Holy Spirit who has the power to give birth and life to his dead human spirit. The act of giving spiritual life to a person who is spiritually dead is called 'the washing of rebirth and renewal by the Holy Spirit' (Titus 3:5). This is just the beginning of many things the Holy Spirit does for individual Christians.

Some Christians wrongly think that conversion is the goal of God's work. The truth is that conversion is only the beginning of God's plan for a person's life. Conversion is like arriving at the international airport of a new country. We don't land at the airport just to stay in the airport. The airport is just the starting point of a whole new experience in a new country.

It is like that with conversion to Christ. Conversion is only the beginning of a new experience in a new kingdom – the kingdom of God. Formerly we lived in the kingdom of this world under the rule of Satan (Eph. 2:2). By believing in Christ we become the children of God (John 1:12). We are transferred into the kingdom of God under the rule of Jesus Christ. The Bible says, 'He has rescued us from the dominion of darkness, and brought us into the kingdom of the Son he loves' (Col. 1:13).

In order to understand what the Holy Spirit does for the Christian, we must understand God's plan for each believer. We must also understand his plan for all believers together as a group (the church). The things which the Holy Spirit does for us are all related to that plan.

G. WHAT IS GOD'S PLAN FOR EVERY CHRISTIAN?

God's plan for every Christian is that he or she be changed in his character to become like Jesus Christ (Rom. 8:29). The Bible says, 'we . . . are being transformed into his likeness with ever increasing glory, which comes from the Lord, who is the Spirit' (2 Cor. 3:18).

The Apostle Peter was an example of this kind of change. He was an unknown fisherman along the shores of the Sea of Galilee. He was an emotional, impulsive person (Matt. 16:22, John 21:7), and he had a bad temper (John 20:10). He boasted of his loyalty to stand by Christ, and even to die for him (John 13:37). Then, a few hours later, in front of a slave girl, he denied that he even knew Christ (John 18:17).

But the Holy Spirit did a great work in Peter's life. He became the one to give the first evangelistic message of the Christian church to the very men who murdered Christ. At this sermon 3000 people were converted (Acts 2:14–41)! Later he became such a great leader that the Roman Catholic Church declared that Peter was the first pope. One of the most famous church buildings in the world (St. Peter's in Rome), was named after him.

That is not all. The Bible says Peter's name is on one of the very foundation stones of the eternal city of God in heaven (Rev. 21:14). The work of the Holy Spirit was so great in Peter that he changed this unknown common fisherman into a great Christian leader who will be respected for all eternity. The same could be said about the change which the Holy Spirit produced in the life of the slave-trader, John Newton, mentioned earlier.

Millions of African people can testify to the same life-changing power of the Holy Spirit. He has rescued them from witchcraft, demon possession, criminal violence, sexual sin, drug addiction, and from a thousand other sins, and he has given them a whole new life in Christ. Every true Christian is an example of the life-changing power of the Holy Spirit. It is God's purpose to change wretched, sinful men into the character of Christ by the power of the Holy Spirit.

H. HOW DOES THE HOLY SPIRIT CHANGE CHRISTIANS TO BECOME LIKE CHRIST?

How does the Holy Spirit change us into the image of Christ? The Bible says he does it by making his home in the heart of every believer (John 14:16–17). When the Holy Spirit comes to live in our hearts, he opposes our sinful desires, so that Christians find a great conflict going on within themselves. Galatians 5:17 says, 'the sinful nature desires what is contrary to the (Holy) Spirit, and the Spirit what is contrary to the sinful nature.' It is the Holy Spirit dwelling in us who gives us the desire, as well as the strength, to change and to be like Christ (Phil.

2:13), even though our sinful nature strongly resists those changes (Gal. 5:17).

However, God will not overrule our freedom to choose. We must choose to obey the urging of the Holy Spirit if we are to be changed. This explains why many Christians do not show much change in their character. They are resisting the urging of the Holy Spirit. Hence the Bible urges us to 'live by the Spirit, and you will not gratify the desires of the sinful nature' (Gal. 5:16). It is only when we ourselves choose to obey the urging of the Holy Spirit that God gives us the strength to change. Philippians 2:13 says, 'It is God who works in you to will and to act according to his good purpose.'

The situation can be illustrated as switching on an electric light. Pushing the switch could be compared to making a decision to change our behaviour. If there is power going through the wires, the light will come on, but if there is no power, no light will come on. In the case of the non-Christians, they may choose to change their ways (pushing the light switch in our illustration). But if there is no power to change their characters (just like a power failure in the wires), they may change for a while, but soon sinful desires gain control of their lives again.

In contrast, when the Christians chooses to change their behaviour, the power of the Holy Spirit is present in their lives to actually help them to change. When they decide to obey God, the Holy Spirit helps them. They can then become light to others as well. Jesus said, 'Let your light shine before men that they may see your good deeds, and praise your Father in heaven' (Matt. 5:16).

We are sanctified, or set apart from the world, in order to show forth the glorious character of Jesus Christ. Paul wrote, 'God chose you to be saved through the sanctifying work of the Spirit and through belief in the truth. He called you to this . . . that you might share in the glory of our Lord Jesus Christ' (2 Thess. 2:13–14). The work of setting apart miserable sinners like us to become the people of God, is the greatest proof in the world that Christianity is the truth. No other religion or philosophy has ever consistently accomplished such changes in character because only God can enable sinful people to become like Christ.

In order to accomplish this great work of changing sinful men and women into the holy image of Christ, the Holy Spirit does many things for the Christian and in the Christian. Here is a list of some of the things which the Holy Spirit does in Christians:

Regeneration: This work was defined in chapter seven. The Holy Spirit gives spiritual birth and new life to those who put their faith in Christ. This work is illustrated in the New Testament by several word images. In Titus 3:5 it is called 'the washing of rebirth and renewal by the Holy Spirit.' In John 3:3 it is called being 'born again.' In 1 Corinthians 12:13 it is called baptism by the Spirit, and drinking of the

Spirit, by which we become members of the body of Christ. These expressions all refer to the same great miracle that takes place at conversion, in which our dead human spirits are made alive to God by the Holy Spirit.

Sealing: The Holy Spirit's indwelling presence in the heart of a Christian places a seal of ownership on that Christian, so that our membership in the family of God is guaranteed forever (2 Cor. 1:21–22, Eph. 1:13–14). This invisible seal of ownership assures us that we now belong to Christ. We are secure in his protection. It is also a guarantee that we will some day experience the completion of God's salvation and receive a resurrection body at the return of Christ (Eph. 4:30). In this sense, the Holy Spirit's sealing presence in a Christian is like the deposit or pledge (a partial payment) which a person might make when buying a bicycle or a piece of property. The deposit guarantees that the person will make the full payment later. The Holy Spirit's presence is God's deposit (guarantee) in our lives which guarantees that he will one day complete his work of salvation in us (2 Cor. 1:22).

Strength and Encouragement: The Holy Spirit strengthens and encourages the Christian (John 14:16, Eph. 3:16). Jesus spoke of the Holy Spirit as the 'helper' (NASB) or 'counselor' (NIV), *parakletos* in Greek (John 14:16,26; 15:26; 16:7). The meaning of *parakletos* is someone who comes alongside to give help, encouragement, strength or counsel. The Apostle Paul said that it was this work of God's Spirit which enabled him to carry out the difficult labours of his ministry (Col. 1:29, 1 Cor. 15:10). In the Old Testament, the Holy Spirit gave such great physical strength and courage to Samson and David that they both killed lions bare-handed (Judges 14:5–6, 1 Sam. 17:36–37). In the New Testament, the Holy Spirit primarily gives spiritual and moral strength to the Christian (Eph. 3:16,20). However, he also gives physical strength and endurance for the work of the gospel when it is needed (Col. 1:29).

Prayer: The Holy Spirit helps the Christian to pray, because we often do not know just what to pray for. The Holy Spirit himself actually prays for the Christian, or interprets his prayers to God the Father (Rom. 8:26). By doing this, the Holy Spirit enables the Christian to pray according to the will of God (Rom. 8:27). In some cases the Holy Spirit prays by actually using the tongue and lips of the Christian in a manifestation of the gift of tongues (1 Cor. 14:14–15).

Illumination of Scripture: The Holy Spirit reminds us of the words of Scripture (John 14:26) and illuminates the meaning of God's truth to the Christian (John 16:13, 1 Cor. 2:10–12).

Witness and Service: The Holy Spirit motivates the Christians to serve the Lord (Phil. 2:13). He also empowers the Christian's witness and ministry for Christ (Acts 1:8, Col. 1:29). The Apostle Paul recognized the need for this power and boldness in his own ministry, and he asked his fellow Christians to pray that God would open up the doors for ministry to him and give him this power (Col. 4:3, Eph. 6:19–20). This is what Christians should regularly pray for missionaries and evangelists.

Fruit of the Spirit: It is the Holy Spirit who produces the beautiful character qualities of Jesus Christ in the Christian. These character qualities are called the 'fruit of the Spirit' (Gal. 5:22–23). They include love, joy, peace, patience, gentleness, goodness, faithfulness, humility and self control. God is very pleased when these qualities mature in his people.

Guidance: The Holy Spirit guides the Christian in his or her daily life and service to the Lord (Rom. 8:14). A practical example of this was when Paul and Silas tried to preach in Bithynia, on Paul's second missionary journey, but were forbidden by the Holy Spirit to go there (Acts 16:6–7).

Signs and Miracles: The Holy Spirit sometimes confirms the truth of the gospel by performing signs and miracles, especially where there are resistant unbelievers. Hebrews 2:3–4 says, 'This salvation, which was first announced by the Lord was confirmed to us by those who heard him. God also testified to it by signs, wonders, and various miracles, and gifts of the Holy Spirit, distributed according to his will.' God does not perform miracles to please people. He performs miracles to glorify Jesus Christ and to draw people to believe in Christ. An example of this was the miracle of blindness which Paul pronounced on Elymas the magician (Acts 13:8–12) because Elymas actively opposed preaching of the gospel by Paul and Barnabas to the Roman proconsul of Cyprus. This miracle confirmed the preaching of Paul and brought the proconsul, Sergius Paulus, to faith in Christ (Acts 13:12).

Inner Witness of the Spirit: The Holy Spirit witnesses to Christians in their hearts that they are the children of God and that they belong to Christ (Rom. 8:16, 1 John 5:10).

Anointing: The Holy Spirit anoints those who preach and teach the word of God so that they can effectively edify the people of God (1 Cor. 12:28, 1 Cor. 14:4, 1 John 2:27).

Calling to Ministry: The Holy Spirit sets people apart for the ministry of the gospel, as he did with Paul and Barnabas in Acts 13:2. He will often confirm this calling by the testimony and encouragement of others in the person's local church.

Spiritual Gifts: The Holy Spirit gives every Christian one or more spiritual gifts (1 Pet. 4:10–11). Spiritual gifts are God-given spiritual abilities which will help the church in some way. The purpose of spiritual gifts is to build up (strengthen and edify) the local church (Rom. 12:4–6, 1 Cor. 12:4–11). More will be said about the gifts of the Spirit in chapter nine.

Overcoming Temptation: The Holy Spirit, in answer to prayer, helps Christians resist the temptations and direct attacks of Satan (Matt. 26:40–41). The Apostle John wrote, 'the one who is in you is greater than the one who is in the world' (1 John 4:4). John and Paul also spoke about the Spirit's protection from Satan (1 John 5:18, 2 Thess. 3:3). More will be said about the Christian's conflict with the powers of darkness in chapter twelve.

Love: The Holy Spirit pours the love of Christ into the hearts of Christians (Rom. 5:5). This is the explanation for the many works of mercy and help started by individual Christians and by Christian organizations through the centuries. Again and again, history records that Christians were the first to help the poor, the blind, the handicapped, the sick, and the hurting people of the world. This happened because the Holy Spirit poured the love of Christ into the hearts of these believers. One of the clearest indications of a local church where the members are living according to their sinful natures and not according to the Holy Spirit, is a church were there is backbiting, division, tension, resentment and unforgiveness.

Christian Unity: The Holy Spirit creates unity and fellowship among Christians (Eph. 4:3–4). When there is division in the local church, it is because the Christians in that church are living according to their sinful nature and not according to the Holy Spirit (Rom. 8:5–6). Where there is unity, forgiveness and love in the local church, the Christians in that church are 'walking by the Spirit' (Gal. 5:16, Col. 3:12–14).

I. WHAT IS THE HOLY SPIRIT'S PLAN FOR ALL CHRISTIANS AS A GROUP?

It is God's plan that as a group, God's people (the church) should show forth the beauty of a society of people who live and act in the way God intended people to live when he created them in the beginning (Gen. 1:27–28 cf., Eph. 4:22–24). The moral and social order of this world has become totally corrupted by sin. The world in which we live is a moral and social mess. God wants to reveal through the church that there is a far better way for people to live together in a community based on love for God and love for one another. The local church is to be a testimony of righteousness and love to the selfish, evil people of the world.

For this reason the church is called 'a holy nation.' The Apostle Peter wrote, 'But you are a chosen people, a royal priesthood, a holy nation, a people belonging to God, that you may declare the praises of him who called you out of darkness into his wonderful light' (1 Pet. 2:9). The people of God are to speak his praises with their lips (Psalm 34:1) and to live lives of love and good works towards one another and towards the world (Titus 2:14). This is God's great plan for his people. We will study the plan of God for his church in more detail in chapter nine.

J. WHAT DOES IT MEAN TO BE FILLED WITH THE SPIRIT?

To be controlled or possessed by a spirit is a common experience in Africa. Most people have witnessed someone under the control of a spirit. When a person is under the control of a spirit, his character and behaviour may be dramatically changed. He or she may have unusual physical strength and endurance. The person may speak in a strange language which is not his own language. He or she may speak prophecies or messages from an ancestor or a divinity. In some cases the person will seem to be untouched by certain types of physical pain, such as the cutting of a knife or burning by fire. The subject of spirit possession will be discussed more fully later in this book.

The Bible speaks of a condition where a person is so controlled by the Holy Spirit of God that he or she is said to be 'filled with the Spirit'. There are some points of comparison between the control of the Holy Spirit and the control of an ancestral spirit. Control by ancestral spirits results in temporary total obedience to the will of that spirit. Control by the Holy Spirit results in temporary total obedience to the will of God. Control by ancestral spirits almost always affects the people around the controlled person in some way. Control by the Spirit of God almost always affects the people around the person filled with the Spirit. The differences between control by an ancestral spirit and control by the Holy Spirit comes from the character of the controlling spirit.

When a person is filled with the Spirit of God, his or her character and behaviour may be dramatically changed. An uneducated and slow person may become very bold in his witness for Christ before very educated people, as the fishermen Peter and John were in front of the Jewish leaders who had killed Christ (Acts 4:13). Some people in the Bible who were filled with the Spirit of God became physically very strong (Judges 15:14–15). Some people spoke in languages which were not their own (Acts 2:4). Some people spoke prophetic messages from God (Luke 1:41–43). Unlike the control of an ancestral spirit, the control of the Holy Spirit in a Christian's life always brings blessing to the people of God and blessing to the person filled with God's Spirit. The filling of the Spirit brings honour and praise to God.

The filling of the Holy Spirit has been a subject of much disagreement in recent years. As with all truth about God, the only way to be sure about it is to examine the teaching of the word of God. To do this we will study several examples given in the Bible where people were described as being filled with the Holy Spirit.

There are many such examples. In the Old Testament, when God set apart Bezalel and gave him special skill to construct the furniture of the tabernacle, the Lord said, 'I have filled him with the Spirit of God' (Ex. 31:2–3). When the Spirit of God who was on Moses was given to the 70 elders of Israel, they prophesied (Num. 11:25). In the case of Othniel (Judges 3:10), Gideon (Judges 6:34), Jephthah (Judges 11:29), Samson (Judges 14:6) and others in the Old Testament, the Bible says the Spirit of the Lord came mightily upon them, usually to lead God's people against God's enemies.

In the New Testament, when the angel Gabriel spoke to Zechariah about the birth of John the Baptist, he said John would be filled with the Holy Spirit from the time he was in his mother's womb (Luke 1:15). At the birth of John the Baptist, the Bible says Zechariah was filled with the Holy Spirit as he prophesied (Luke 1:67). When the disciples spoke of the mighty works of God at Pentecost in different languages, the Bible says they were all filled with the Holy Spirit (Acts 2:4). When Peter spoke to the Jewish leaders who crucified Christ, the Bible says Peter was filled with the Holy Spirit (Acts 4:8). When Stephen preached to the angry Jewish leaders about their murder of Christ, the Bible says Stephen was full of the Holy Spirit (Acts 7:55). When Paul brought God's judgment of blindness on Elymas the magician, the Bible says Paul was filled with the Holy Spirit (Acts 13:9–11).

In Acts 1:8, Jesus said, 'You will receive power when the Holy Spirit comes on you, and you will be my witnesses in Jerusalem, and in all Judea and Samaria, and to the ends of the earth.' From this verse it is clear that a believer cannot have power for evangelism without being filled with the Holy Spirit.

What do these examples reveal to us? In each case, the filling of the Spirit gave power or ability to work for the Lord. Sometimes the Spirit's fulness was given to make the truth of God clear and persuasive. Sometimes his fulness was given to confirm the word of God by works of power. Sometimes the Spirit's fulness was given to empower the leaders of God's people, or to enable them to carry out a specific task for God's people, as with Bezalel and some of the judges.

For some people, being filled with the Holy Spirit was a temporary experience where God filled them with his Spirit for a certain work. This seemed to be true at certain times in the Old Testament, as in the case of Gideon (Judges 6:34) and Samson (Judges 14:6). In the case of some men such as John the Baptist (Luke 1:15), Stephen (Acts 6:5), Barnabas (Acts 11:22–24) and some of the Old Testament prophets

(Dan. 6:3, Micah 3:8), the fulness of the Spirit seems to have been a continuing experience.

HOW MAY A CHRISTIAN BE FILLED WITH THE HOLY SPIRIT?

It is important to understand that we are commanded by God to be filled with the Spirit. Ephesians 5:18 says, 'Do not get drunk on wine. . . .Instead, be filled with the Spirit.' Thus it is clearly God's desire that his people be filled with his Spirit. Being filled with the Spirit was one of the qualifications for those who were chosen as deacons in the early church (Acts 6:3). Stephen was such a man (Acts 6:5).

We can be sure that it is God's will for all Christians to be filled with the Holy Spirit when they are living as God wants them to live. In Ephesians 3:15–19 Paul was speaking about all the believers at Ephesus when he said, 'I pray . . . that you may be filled to all the measure of the fulness of God.'

In some cases in the Bible, God chose to fill someone with the Holy Spirit without the person asking, because God wanted to accomplish a special purpose through that person. Bezalel (Ex. 31:2–3) and John the Baptist (Luke 1:15) were examples of this.

In the New Testament Jesus encouraged us to ask for the fulness of the Holy Spirit. He said that God is willing to grant the presence and power of the Holy Spirit to those who ask him. In Luke 11:13 Jesus said, 'If you then, though you are evil, know how to give good gifts to your children, how much more will your Father in heaven give the Holy Spirit to those who ask him!' It is important for believers to experience the reality of being filled with the Holy Spirit, which is the will of God for their lives.

According to Romans 8:9, everyone who truly belongs to Christ has the Holy Spirit. This is because it is the Holy Spirit who gives new birth at the time of a person's conversion (John 3:3,5, Titus 3:5). However, every Christian is not necessarily filled with the Holy Spirit. Otherwise we would not be commanded by God to be filled with the Spirit (Eph. 5:18), and Paul would not have needed to pray this for the Ephesian Christians (Eph. 3:15–19).

As with all prayer made to God, a person must pray for the fulness of the Holy Spirit from a clean and sincere heart. Any hypocrisy or sin in a person's life will keep this prayer from being answered. Isaiah 59:1–2 says, 'Surely the arm of the Lord is not too short to save, nor his ear too dull to hear. But your iniquities have separated you from your God; your sins have hidden his face from you, so that he will not hear.'

If we do pray for the fulness of the Holy Spirit from a clean and sincere heart, we may be sure that God is willing to answer this prayer. As we have just seen, it is God's will for Christians not just to have the

Holy Spirit, but to be filled with his Spirit. The Bible assures us that if we ask for things which are in God's will, he hears our prayer and he answers us (1 John 5:14–15).

HOW MAY WE KNOW IF WE ARE FILLED WITH THE HOLY SPIRIT?

There is considerable disagreement among Christians as to how we can know if a person is filled with the Holy Spirit. Some Christians believe that a person will speak with another language (the gift of tongues) when filled with the Holy Spirit. They believe this because some Christians in the book of Acts, especially at Pentecost and shortly afterwards, did speak in other languages on certain occasions when they were filled with the Holy Spirit (Acts 2:4; 10:44–47; 19:2–6). Speaking in another language may be an indication of the fulness of the Spirit in some cases.

If we carefully study each of the situations in Acts where people spoke in tongues, we will discover something important. In each case, a new group of people was being included in the church, and the sign of tongues was miraculously given as a confirmation to the Jewish Christians that the new group was indeed part of the body of Christ (Acts 11:15–17 cf., 1 Cor. 1:22).

Is there any universal sign of the fulness of the Spirit which is true in all situations? If we take all the examples given in the Bible where people were said to be filled with the Holy Spirit, the one characteristic common to every situation seems to be that there was a clear indication of the Holy Spirit's power at work through that person's words or actions. In other words, the Spirit's fulness was always recognized by the evidence of God's presence and power at work through the person's words and actions. A modern day example of this would be the great evangelist, Dr. Billy Graham, who has led thousands of people to Christ through his Spirit-filled preaching.

What about the ordinary Christian who is not in a special ministry? What is the evidence of the Spirit's fulness in his or her life? Even in the simple things of everyday life, a person who is filled with the Holy Spirit will give clear evidence of a Christ-like character (Gal. 5:22–23), a strong and effective witness for Christ to friends and family (Acts 1:8), and a power-filled prayer life (Rom. 8:26–27). These qualities of life were very likely seen in the life of Stephen (Acts 6:5) and Barnabas (Acts 11:22–24), who were described as men filled with the Holy Spirit.

God wants all his people to have power in their ministry to others, so that the church will mature and grow strong. To have this power, one must be filled with the Holy Spirit. Since it is God's will for his people to be filled with the Holy Spirit, it is right to ask God in prayer to be filled with his Spirit (Luke 11:13), just as Paul prayed for his friends at Ephesus to be filled to the fulness of God (Eph. 3:15–19).

WILL A CHRISTIAN BECOME SINLESS AND PERFECT IF HE IS FILLED
WITH THE HOLY SPIRIT?

Some groups of people teach that a Christian will become sinless and
perfect when he or she is filled with the Holy Spirit. This idea cannot
be supported from the Bible. The Apostle John says, 'If we claim to be
without sin, we deceive ourselves, and the truth is not in us' (1 John
1:8). John goes on to say, 'If we confess our sins, he is faithful and just,
and will forgive us our sins, and purify us from all unrighteousness' (1
John 1:9). We can be forgiven and be purified, but we cannot become
sinless in this life.

It is a sad fact that some people in the Bible who were filled with the
Holy Spirit fell into tragic sin. For example, Samson was filled mightily
with the Holy Spirit to perform God's judgment on the Philistines
(Judges 15:14–15), but shortly after this he committed immorality with
a prostitute (Judges 16:1). King David was so filled with the Holy
Spirit that he wrote over half of the Psalms (Matt. 22:43–44), yet
David committed both adultery and murder! Speaking by a revelation
from God, Peter gave a powerful testimony that Jesus was the Messiah
(Matt. 16:16–17). Then, just a moment later, Peter expressed the
voice of Satan by trying to discourage Christ from his purpose for
coming into the world (Matt. 16:22–23).

Because we are human beings with a sinful nature (Rom. 7:14–18),
we will continue to struggle with sin in this life (1 John 1:8–9). But we
can thank God, because he has given us his Holy Spirit to help us to
overcome our sinful nature in this continuing struggle (Rom. 8:12–13,
Gal. 5:17–18).

In conclusion we may ask, should all believers seek to be filled with
the Holy Spirit? The answer is yes. If every member of each local
church were filled with the Holy Spirit, our world would be a very
different place, and the church would already have fulfilled the Great
Commission. However, we should not seek to be filled with the Holy
Spirit in order to have some sort of emotional experience. Instead, we
should seek to be filled with the Spirit in order to exalt Jesus Christ, to
build up his people, and to win the lost to Christ (John 16:14, 1 Cor.
12:7, Acts 1:8).

SUMMARY

The Holy Spirit is the unseen presence of God in the world, in the
church, and in the heart of every Christian. He is the One who convicts
people of their sin, who draws people to Christ, who makes people
new persons in Christ, and who helps them to change so they will
become more like Christ. He places a seal of ownership on every
believer when he has made them a part of the body of Christ. He bears
witness with our human spirit that we have become the children of

God after we have believed in Christ. He helps us to pray. He helps us to resist temptation and he guides us. He is God, but he is a different person from God the Father and God the Son.

He inspired the writing of the Bible. He illuminates the minds of Christians as they read the Bible and he helps Christians recall the truth of the Bible for the everyday needs of life. He is represented in the Bible by the symbols of oil, water, wind and fire. The Holy Spirit gives spiritual gifts to God's people so that the church of Jesus Christ will be built up to maturity. He calls people to the ministry of the gospel and he empowers those he calls to carry out their ministry. He sometimes performs signs and miracles to confirm the truth of the gospel. He pours out the love of God into the hearts of Christians, so that they are moved to share God's love with other people. He fills Christians with his presence and his power so that they can effectively witness to others about Christ. He is the One who encourages God's people. He is the One who sanctifies and strengthens the children of God so that they will bring honour to God by their lives.

DISCUSSION QUESTIONS AND PROJECTS BASED ON CHAPTER EIGHT

1. Explain God's plan for each individual Christian and how the Holy Spirit works to accomplish that plan. Give Bible references.

2. Explain God's plan for all of his people together (his church), and how the Holy Spirit works to accomplish that plan. Give Bible references.

3. A pagan student points out the fact that some traditionalists and some Muslims have better character than some Christians. How would you explain to him why there is only a small change in the behaviour of some true Christians?

4. Divide into groups of four students each to study four situations in the Bible where people were described as being filled with the Holy Spirit. Describe the evidence given by others that the person was filled with the Spirit.

5. Discuss together the ways in which the Holy Spirit helps us as we pray.

6. Let people give testimonies about incidents in their own life in which they experienced the guidance of the Holy Spirit or the strength and encouragement of the Holy Spirit.

7. Let people give testimonies about incidents in their own life when they saw the Holy Spirit confirm the truth of the gospel with supernatural power or miracles (Heb. 2:3–4).

8. Ask several students to describe to the class the way in which God called them into the ministry.

9. Let the group make a list of the specific ministries of Christian love and mercy to the needy in their country. These might include ministries to the poor, the hungry, the blind, the handicapped, the sick and widows or orphans.

10. Divide into small groups to study Acts 8:17–24. Ask each group to relate the power of the Holy Spirit to the African concept of spirits, mystical powers, spells, and omens. What was the great sin of Simon the magician, and what warning is this for African Christians?

11. Differentiate between the evidence of the power of the Holy Spirit and the evidence of the power of evil spirits and demons.

12. Sometimes different groups of Christians get into hurtful arguments over the work of the Holy Spirit. Discuss some ways in which these conflicts can be eliminated from the body of Christ.

SUGGESTED FOR FURTHER READING

Graham, Billy. *The Holy Spirit*. London: Fount, 1980.

Green, Michael. *I Believe In The Holy Spirit*. London: Hodder, 1985.

Packer, J.I. *Keep In Step With The Spirit*. Leicester: InterVarsity Press, 1984.

Packer, J.I. *A Passion for Holiness*. Cambridge: Crossway, 1992.

Pytches, David. *Come Holy Spirit*. London: Hodder, 2nd edn 1995.

Smail, T. *The Giving Gift*. Darton: Longman & Todd, 1994.

Stott, J. *Baptism and Fullness*. Leicester: InterVarsity Press, 1964.

9

The Church – The Extended Family of God

'King Herod arrested some who belonged to the church, intending to persecute them. He had James, the brother of John, put to death with the sword. When he saw that this pleased the Jews, he proceeded to seize Peter also. . . . After arresting him, he put him in prison, handing him over to be guarded by four squads of four soldiers each. . . . So Peter was kept in prison, but the church was earnestly praying to God for him. The night before Herod was to bring him to trial, Peter was sleeping between two soldiers, bound with two chains, and sentries stood at the entrance. Suddenly an angel of the Lord appeared and a light shone in the cell. He struck Peter on the side and woke him up. "Quick, get up!" he said, and the chains fell off Peter's wrists . . . "Wrap your cloak around you and follow me," the angel told him. Peter followed him out of the prison, but he had no idea that what the angel was doing was really happening; he thought he was seeing a vision' (Acts 12:1–9).

Pastor Paul called the church together for a special meeting. As the church gathered in the small building, the pastor quickly came to the reason for the meeting. Maichibi and Ramatu had been having problems in their marriage. Ramatu came from a bad family background with many problems. Six weeks ago, Ramatu had left Maichibi and their two children and had gone back into prostitution. Maichibi continued to attend church but his heart was very heavy. Maichibi came to his pastor for help. Maichibi asked whether there was anything Pastor Paul could do. After discussing the matter with the church elders, and with Maichibi's permission, Pastor Paul decided to call the church together to pray for Ramatu. Now, with the small congregation gathered together, the Pastor related Maichibi's story and a brief summary of their family problems.

Pastor Paul asked the congregation to divide up into groups of four or five people each to pray, and to ask the Lord to touch Ramatu's heart with repentance, and to bring healing to the marriage. The church members prayed fervently for the couple for over an hour. Four weeks later Ramatu appeared in church once again with Maichibi and their children. She confessed her sin and stated her desire to be reconciled to her husband. As in the book of Acts, God had answered the prayers of the local church.

God hears and answers the prayers of his people when they pray according to the will of God with one heart and one voice, without sin and division in the congregation. Because this is true, stories similar to these two true stories have been repeated down through church history. Just what is the church? What relationship do the members of the local church have to each other in the plan of God? Why does the church have unusual power in prayer before God? What is God's plan for the local church and how has God planned for the church to function? In this chapter we will seek to answer the following questions:

A. What is the church?
B. Who are members of the church?
C. Which church is the true church of Christ?
D. Where is the temple of God?
E. What are three important applications of the fact that the church is the body of Christ?
F. How can a Christian discover which spiritual gifts he has been given?
G. What is God's plan for the church in relation to mankind?
H. What is the purpose of the church?
I. What are the main illustrations used in the New Testament to describe the relationship between Christ and his church?
J. Why are there so many different denominations and churches?
K. What ceremonies (sacraments) did Jesus give to his church?
L. What are the main types of church government?
M. What are the main leadership positions in the local church, according to the New Testament?

A. WHAT IS THE CHURCH?

Lumumbe: 'Would you like to go to church with me?'

Odozi: 'Which church do you go to?'

Lumumbe: 'I attend the Good News Church. There are many young men there like you and me. I think you would enjoy it.'

Odozi: 'Why are there so many different churches? Why don't you all attend the same one, since you say you all believe in Christ? What is the church anyway?'

Many people think of a church as a particular building. Others think a church refers to a certain denomination, like ECWA or Baptist. The word church is commonly used by people today to refer to a building or to a denomination. How is the word church used in the New Testament? What does the Bible mean by the church?

The New Testament speaks of the church in a worldwide sense, as in Colossians 1:24–25. It also speaks about local churches in certain places, such as the church at Antioch (Acts 13:1) and the church at Corinth (1 Cor. 1:2). In both the worldwide and local sense, the church refers to a group of people. In Acts 5:11 it says, 'Great fear seized the whole church and all who heard about these events.' The church is a group of people, whether it is referring to all Christians everywhere in the world or just to those Christians who regularly meet together each week in a certain place.

The church consists of all those who have trusted in Jesus Christ as their Lord and Saviour, regardless of their race, nationality, denomination or position in life. Galatians 3:26–28 says, 'You are all sons of God through faith in Christ Jesus. . . . There is neither Jew nor Greek, slave nor free, male nor female, for you are all one in Christ Jesus.' All the people who have trusted in Christ in this way have been regenerated (made spiritually alive in Christ) by the Holy Spirit (Titus 3:5–7). By trusting in Christ we have been spiritually joined to Christ, and have become part of his spiritual body. Romans 6:5 says, 'If we have been united with him like this in his death, we will certainly also be united with him in his resurrection.'

The church is a very special group of people. It is the extended family of God, because the members of the church are the children of God, and God is their Father. The Apostle John wrote, 'How great is the love the Father has lavished on us that we should be called children of God! And that is what we are'. (1 John 3:1) The church is a worldwide community of brothers and sisters in Christ. Jesus told his followers, 'You are not to be called "Rabbi", for you have only one Master, and you are all brothers' (Matt. 23:8).

The church is the largest extended family in the world. It is very important that Christians come to understand that there is an even more lasting community than their earthly extended family. Family and clan are very important in this life, but someone who has believed in Christ has become part of a much more enduring family than even his earthly family. He has become part of the eternal family of God. When this physical life is over, a Christian will live with God's family (i.e. other believers) in heaven for ever (Rev. 21:3). In the next life, he or she will only live with those members of his or her earthly family who have personally trusted in Christ as their Lord and Saviour. A Christian is someone who has entered into an extended family relationship with brothers and sisters in Christ from around the world.

This relationship will one day be stronger than any earthly family relationship, and it will last forever.

B. WHO ARE MEMBERS OF THE CHURCH?

All Africans know there is a God. Many of the ideas about God in African traditional religions and in Islam are correct. However, it is one thing to know the truth about God, and quite another thing to know God personally, that is, to have a personal relationship with him.

People of many religions claim to be the children of God. Many Africans believe that God is the Father of all people, and that all people are his children because God is the Creator of mankind. What does the Bible say? Who does God himself say are his children?

John 1:11–12 says, 'He (Jesus) came to that which was his own, but his own did not receive him. Yet to all who received him, to those who believed in his name, he gave the right to become the children of God.' These verses teach us that it is only those who have personally received Jesus Christ into their lives as their Lord and Saviour who have become the children of God. Jesus said, 'I know my sheep and my sheep know me' (John 10:14).

In his prayer for his own people, Jesus said, 'This is eternal life, that they may know you, the only true God, and Jesus Christ whom you have sent' (John 17:3). According to Jesus' own words, it is only those who have a personal relationship with Christ who belong to him. It is those who have such a relationship with Christ who have been regenerated by the Holy Spirit. For this reason Jesus said to the Jewish religious teacher, Nicodemus, 'I tell you the truth, no one can see the kingdom of God unless he is born again' (John 3:3). This is the reason Jesus warned in Matt. 7:21, 'Not everyone who says to me Lord, Lord will enter the kingdom of heaven, but only he who does the will of my Father who is in heaven.' Concerning those people who outwardly profess to be Christians but have no personal relationship with him, Jesus said that he will say to them, 'I never knew you' (Matt. 7:23). Thus the true church is composed of those who know Christ personally as their Lord and Saviour; who have been made alive in him by the Holy Spirit (regenerated).

In a hot argument with the strict Jewish leaders concerning whose Father God really was, Jesus declared to these Jews that it was not God, but Satan, who was their real father (John 8:44)! In the same discussion, Jesus said that if God were their father, they would love him (Christ), (John 8:42). Thus Jesus made it very clear that God is not the Father of all men, but only the Father of those who love and receive Christ.

Some people think that being baptized, attending a local church, having Christian parents or having a Christian name, makes them Christians. The Bible says it is only those who have personally invited Christ into their lives and made him their Lord and Saviour, who have become the children of God (John 1:12, 2 Pet. 1:10–11, 2 Pet. 3:18, Rev. 3:20). If you are reading these words and you have never personally invited Christ into your life to be your Lord and Saviour, why don't you stop right now and ask Jesus to forgive all your sins? Invite him through prayer to come into your heart to be your Saviour from sin and the Lord of your life. If you sincerely repent of your sins, and put your faith in Christ by asking him to be your Lord and Saviour, you will be saved and will become a part of the true and eternal Church.

C. WHICH CHURCH IS THE TRUE CHURCH OF CHRIST?

Different denominations claim to be the true church of Christ. Which group is the true church?

The true church does not have a denominational name such as Africa Inland Church, Sudan Interior Church, Evangelical Churches of West Africa, Anglican, Methodist, Baptist and so forth. Members of the true church are probably found in all church denominations. At the same time, many of the people who attend these churches are not part of the true church, for they have never been regenerated and made alive by the Holy Spirit (Titus 3:5). The true church is composed of all those people who have repented of their sins and put their faith in Christ.

D. WHERE IS THE TEMPLE OF GOD?

Local churches sometimes meet in large or small buildings, sometimes in homes, and sometimes just under a tree. The building and the location are not important. The people, however, are very important to God. He calls his people who meet in this way, 'a holy temple in the Lord' (Eph. 2:21). He calls the individual Christians the 'living stones' which make up this temple. The Apostle Peter reminds us, 'you also, like living stones, are being built into a spiritual house' (1 Pet. 2:5). Thus all Christians are the building blocks, or 'living stones' which form the present temple of God. The church is therefore, 'a dwelling in which God lives by his Spirit' (Eph.2:22).

To better understand this truth, it is worthwhile to review the special dwelling places of God's Spirit in the past. The first such place, designated by God, was the tabernacle. The tabernacle was a movable tent-like structure which God commanded the Israelites to put up in different places in the Sinai Desert during their 40 years of wandering and later in the promised land (Ex. 40:1–34, Josh. 18:1, 2 Sam. 7:5–6). The next location designated by God was the beautiful temple building in Jerusalem, built by King Solomon (1 Kings 8:10–12, 2 Chron. 7:1–3). Unfortunately Solomon's temple was destroyed by the Babylonians because of Israel's idolatry. This was symbolic of the fact that God's presence had already departed from their midst because of their sins (Psalm 44:9–16, Isa. 1:13–15; 21–25).

In the gospels, the dwelling place of God's Spirit was the earthly body of Jesus Christ (John 1:32–33). After Jesus had ascended to the Father, the Holy Spirit was sent into the hearts of Christians at Pentecost (Acts 1:8, Acts 2:1–4) to give birth to the church. Jesus told his disciples that the hearts of believers would be the dwelling place of God's Spirit from that time on (John 14:16). According to Scripture, the church is made up of all those people on earth and in heaven (Heb. 12:23) in whom the Spirit of God now lives (Eph. 2:20–22).

Those who have received Christ into their lives are spiritually joined to him (John 17:21, 1 Cor. 6:17). This is not just an illustration, but a truth so real that the Bible refers to those who believe in Christ as his body. Christians are the parts of his body. In 1 Corinthians 12:27 Paul says, 'Now you are the body of Christ, and each one of you is a part of it.' As a group, all of God's children make up the parts of his spiritual body, known as the church (Col. 1:18,24). Christ is the head, and we are his body (1 Cor. 12:27, Col. 1:18).

E. WHAT ARE THREE IMPORTANT APPLICATIONS OF THE FACT THAT THE CHURCH IS THE BODY OF CHRIST?

COMMUNITY

The Church is an eternal community. As the body of Christ, Christians are spiritually joined to Christ as the head and therefore spiritually joined to each other as parts of his body. Since they are joined to each other in this way, they are the extended family of God both in this life and in the life to come. They are members of the kingdom of God, and the King of Kings is their Master. As a believer, a Christian is part of a worldwide family of brothers and sisters from every tribe and nation. God has given to this family an eternal inheritance in heaven (1 Pet. 1:3–5).

This extended family of God has been joined together for all eternity by the blood of Christ. Jesus is not only their Saviour from sin, but their Master and their King. They have his name. He owns them. Jesus has purchased his people with his very own blood. Revelation 5:9–10 says, 'You (Jesus) were slain, and with your blood you purchased men for God from every tribe and language and people and nation. You have made them to be a kingdom and priests to serve our God, and they will reign on the earth.'

In many African societies, when a person is initiated, he is initiated into someone's name. He becomes legally and spiritually joined to that person. In a similar way, when we put our trust in Christ and confess him as our Lord and Saviour, we become legally and spiritually joined to Christ. He becomes our Master and our owner. And who is this Jesus who now owns us, protects us and provides for us? He is the King of Kings and Lord of Lords (Rev. 19:13–16). He is Lord of all creation (Phil. 2:9–10, Col. 1:16–17). He is the God of heaven and earth (Matt. 28:18, Titus 2:13).

Because of the social structure of life in Africa, it is very easy for us to understand what God's intentions were in creating the church. In Africa, a person's extended family and ethnic community are the most important realities in his or her life. The family is the group of people where we feel at home, where we belong, where people know us, speak our language and understand our way of thinking. It is the group of people where we are accepted. It is the community where brothers and sisters care for each other, and where even distant cousins are called brothers and sisters. It is the group of people whom you can count on to help you when you are in need or in trouble.

It is to be this way in the local church. The members of the church are the people who know us and speak our spiritual language. They understand our way of thinking. The local church is the community where we can be accepted regardless of racial, social or ethnic background because we are all equally forgiven sinners before God. The local church is the community where people are obligated to support and care for each other because they are brothers and sisters in Christ. We belong to each other because we belong to Christ. It is therefore God's intention that the church be the community where people can count on their brothers and sisters in Christ to help them and encourage them when they are in need or in trouble. The church is God's people. Our fellow church members are our brothers and sisters in God's family.

There are other points of comparison between the African extended family and the community of the local church. The extended family is the community where you get your values and beliefs and your early training in life. It is the community where you establish the deepest and most enduring relationships of life. It is the group of people from which you derive your name and your identity as a person. It is the community in which you find a sense of purpose in life because you help to make it what it is.

Likewise, the church is the community where you are to get your values and beliefs and your early training in the Christian life. It is the community where you will establish the deepest and most enduring relationships in life. It is the group of people from which you derive your name as a Christian and your identity as a child of God. It is the community from which you find a sense of purpose in life because you help to make it what it is by serving God and serving others.

An African family has as its leader a wise old man – usually the eldest father in the family. The family is the community where we are corrected and disciplined if we misbehave. It is the community where we learn things by sitting around the fire at night and telling stories about the great heroes of the clan who lived in former years. It is the community where decisions are made by sharing ideas and discussing things together. We come to one opinion which can be submitted to the eldest father for his blessing. It is the community where we have special times of family celebration, such as childbirth, naming ceremonies and weddings. It is the family where we eat together and often share food from the same dish.

So, too, in the church, our leader is Christ himself, 'who has become for us wisdom from God – that is, our righteousness, holiness and redemption' (1 Cor. 1:30). The church is the community where we are to be corrected and disciplined if we misbehave. It is the community where we are to learn the principles of godly living by telling the stories about the great heroes of the faith found in the Bible. The church is the community where decisions are made by discussing things together. By sharing ideas we come to one opinion, which can be brought before God in prayer for his blessing. It is the community where we have special times of celebration, such as dedication of children to God, baptisms, weddings and also Christmas and Easter. It is in the church family where we eat bread together from the same dish and drink from the same cup in remembrance of the Lord's death for our sins.

The reason people in Africa have such total loyalty to their clan and culture group is because their identity, security and meaning in life has to do with being a part of their extended family and clan. The same is true concerning the church, but in a much deeper way. Most clans and tribes have a name based on a great and respected ancestor. Members of the tribe are proud to bear the name of this ancestor. A Christian has identity, security and meaning in life because he or she belongs to the very God of heaven and earth, the King of Kings. He is the one who poured out his life blood on earth to purchase his people. We bear the name of our great God and Saviour, Jesus Christ (Acts 11:26). We are his people. We are Christians.

In Africa, the life and well-being of the extended family is all important to the life and well-being of the individual. Therefore the individual has unconditional loyalty to his extended family, clan and tribe. An even greater degree of loyalty to the extended family of God must be true for a Christian, because God's family will endure for eternity. The highest loyalty of a Christian must be to Christ as Lord and Saviour, and to Christ's body, the church, as his or her spiritual family. To become a Christian, is to become a part of the everlasting kingdom of God.

There is a very important application of the truth that the church is the body of Christ in relation to prayer. Does God the Father hear and answer the prayers of Jesus Christ? Yes, he does (John 11:41–42). But what about the prayers of the local church? As the body of Christ, the church bears the name of Christ. When the church prays according to the will of God as revealed in the Bible, with united and pure hearts, she has the authority of Christ in prayer. In these circumstances God will hear and answer the prayers of the church (the body) even as he will answer the prayers of Christ (the head).

Who does God listen to? People of every religion pray at one time or another, but what group of people can pray to God with assurance that their prayers will be answered? The only group of people to whom God has made definite promises that he will answer their prayers, is the church (Matt. 18:19–20, Mark 11:22–24, John 16:23–24, 1 John 5:14–15). Only the church bears the authority of the name of Christ before God the Father. Jesus said, 'You did not choose me, but I chose you, and appointed you . . . that whatever you ask of the Father in my name, he may give to you' (John 15:16–NASB).

Jesus said that wherever two or more Christians are gathered together in his name, he is present in their midst (Matt. 18:20). In other words, Christ (the head) and his body (the church) is present in that place. When Christians understand the will of God from Scripture and are pure and united before the Lord, the local church is able to pray to the Father with confidence that their prayers will be heard and answered. God has promised to answer their prayers (Matt. 18:19, John 16:23–24) provided there is no sin or unforgiveness to hinder their prayers from being heard (Mark 11:25, Isa. 59:2). The Apostle John wrote, 'This is the confidence we have in approaching God: that if we ask anything according to his will, he hears us. And if we know that he hears us – whatever we ask – we know that we have what we asked of him' (1 John 5:14–15).

The answers God gives may not come in the way we expect or at the time we anticipate, but the answers will most surely come (John 15:7). When the early church prayed for Peter in prison, it is possible they were praying for Peter to have strength to suffer and die for Christ, because James had just been killed (Acts 12:2). They did not seem to expect Peter's release from prison (Acts 12:12–16), but that was God's answer to their prayers.

Jesus said that the gates of hell would not overcome the church (Matt. 16:18). In other words, the gates into Satan's kingdom would not be able to stand against the invasion of the church. Jesus was saying that Satan's kingdom would be overpowered by the church. The truth of this statement has been repeated countless times in the history of the expansion of the church, as Christianity has grown from a small group of believers in Jerusalem to a church across the entire world.

Christians are commanded to pray for their government leaders (1 Tim. 2:1–2) so that God's will may prevail over Satan's will and the will of sinful men, in the decisions made by the government. Because praying for government leaders is the revealed will of God, God will answer the united prayers of his people when they pray for their government leaders. The most dramatic example of this in recent history has been the collapse of communist leadership in many parts of the world in answer to the specific prayers of Christians in communist countries. Because of her access to God in prayer, the church is the only group of people who can consistently change the course of history from wrong to right.

The stories at the beginning of this chapter also illustrate some of the ways in which God answers the united prayers of the local church. Jesus taught his followers to pray that God's will would be done on earth as it is done in heaven (Matt. 6:10). Praying like this in specific situations in life, is praying according to the will of God.

The unity between Christ and his church is so real that when Jesus spoke to Saul on the Damascus road, he said to him, 'Saul, Saul, why do you persecute me' (Acts 9:4)? Why did Jesus say this to Saul? Saul was not persecuting Jesus himself, but the followers of Jesus. However, Jesus went on to say, 'I am Jesus whom you are persecuting' (Acts 9:5). Jesus was speaking about a spiritual reality. Jesus (the head) and the church (his body) are spiritually joined together as one, so that whatever happens to Christ happens to his people, and whatever happens to his people, happens to Christ. Jesus told his followers, 'If the world hates you, keep in mind that it hated me first. . . . If they persecuted me, they will persecute you also. If they obeyed my teaching, they will obey yours also' (John 15:18–20). Paul said, 'We were therefore buried with him through baptism into death in order that, just as Christ was raised from the dead through the glory of the Father, we too may live a new life. If we have been united with him like this in his death, we will certainly also be united with him in his resurrection' (Rom. 6:4–5).

One application of the unity between Christ and his people is that Christians are called the ambassadors of Christ (2 Cor. 5:20). An ambassador is the official representative of his government to another country. The official words of the ambassador carry the same authority as the official words of the head of his government when those words are spoken in accordance with the policy (will) of his government. So it is with the church. The church has the authority to pray in the name of Christ, to speak in the name of Christ, and to act on behalf of Christ in this world. The prayers, the words and the actions of the true church of

Jesus Christ, when spoken and done in agreement with the word of God, carry the authority of Christ himself. No other individual, tribe, nation, or group of people on earth has this authority. Only the church of Jesus Christ speaks for God in this present world. It is for this reason that Jesus made the amazing statement, 'Truly I say to you, whatever you shall bind on earth shall have been bound in heaven; and whatever you loose on earth shall have been loosed in heaven' (Matt. 18:18 – NASB).

This delegated authority can be seen in the way the prayers of the early church brought about the supernatural release of Peter from prison. The little church group prayed fervently for Peter (Acts 12:5), but they did not expect to see Peter released, according to Acts 12:15. What they didn't realize was that their prayers included someone much greater than themselves. Jesus himself was pleading with the Father for Peter through the prayers of his people. To the amazement of the little church, God sent his angel and released Peter from prison (Acts 12:7–11)!

So it is throughout the world when the true church prays with one heart and mind to the Father in the name of Jesus, without a barrier of sin. Jesus himself pleads with the Father through his body – his people – and God answers! This is why Jesus said, 'If two of you on earth agree about anything you ask for, it will be done for you by my Father in heaven. For where two or three come together in my name, there am I with them' (Matt. 18:19–20).

Church history is filled with many examples of God's answers to the united prayers of his people. A small group of Christians met each Saturday to fast and pray in Kaduna, Nigeria, asking the Lord to resist the growth of secret societies in Bendel State, Nigeria. In a few weeks time, the Bendel State government passed a law making secret societies illegal. In 1994, a group of Christians met to pray and ask the Lord to prevent the death and suffering of many people in Haiti on the very night an American invasion was being launched against that country. On that very night, the Haitian military leaders agreed to step down. The invasion was called off even as the paratroop planes were on their way to invade. The truth is this: God answers the united prayers of his people when they pray from clean hearts, according the will of God (1 John 5:14–15).

Unfortunately most local churches do not use their privilege of united prayer nearly as often as they should. If they did, they could promote the kingdom of God much more effectively than they do. They could do much more good in the world than they do. They could also do much more to hinder and resist the forces of evil in the world than they do.

How much could a local church accomplish through their united prayers, if they really acted on their authority in Christ? The answer is, they could greatly change the world around them, because they could cause God's will to prevail over the plans of evil men and even over the plans of Satan. Jesus taught us to pray, 'Thy will be done, On earth as it is in heaven' (Matt. 6:10–NASB). Why would Jesus teach his people to pray this way unless God intended to answer such prayers?

The problem is that local churches rarely pray about the great problems of their country or the world. Instead, they usually pray for themselves and for their own needs, rather than for the needs of the suffering world around them. If they did pray more for the world, the church could greatly speed the preaching the gospel of Christ to the ends of the earth. Jesus commanded, 'Therefore go and make disciples of all nations' (Matt. 28:19). He also said, 'Ask the Lord of the harvest therefore to send out workers into his harvest field' (Matt. 9:38).

The fastest growing missionary church in the world today is found in Korea. Why is that? Because the church in Korea takes prayer very seriously.

God's people could be delivered from many evils and many of Satan's attacks could be thwarted if the whole church waged spiritual warfare in prayer. Jesus taught his people to pray, 'deliver us from the evil one' (Matt. 6:13).

SPIRITUAL GIFTS

As members of the body of Christ, each Christian has been given one or more spiritual gifts by the Holy Spirit (1 Pet. 4:10). He or she has been given these gifts so that the church will grow strong and also be able to carry out God's purposes in the community.

God wants each member of the church to use his spiritual gift in order for the local church to grow and function properly (1 Cor. 12:12–20). In 1 Corinthians 12, Paul compares the function of each believer in the church to the function of the parts of the human body. Each part of the human body is both necessary and important for the proper function of the body. In a similar way, each Christian is both necessary and important for the proper function of the local church.

In order to make the church grow and function properly, God has given special abilities to each member of the local church. These abilities are the gifts of the Holy Spirit (1 Cor. 12:4–7). The Apostle Peter said, 'Each one should use whatever gift he has received to serve others, faithfully administering God's grace in its various forms. If anyone speaks, he should do it as speaking the very words of God. If anyone serves, he should do it with the strength God provides, so that in all things, God may be praised through Jesus Christ' (1 Pet. 4:10–11).

According to Peter's statement, the gifts of the Holy Spirit are divided into two categories. There are speaking gifts and there are serving gifts. Examples of speaking gifts would include gifts such as prophecy (Rom. 12:6), teaching (Rom. 12:7), encouraging others (Rom. 12:8), words of wisdom (1 Cor. 12:8), tongues and the interpretation of tongues (1 Cor. 12:10). Examples of serving gifts would include gifts such as leadership, giving, showing mercy (Rom. 12:8), healing (1 Cor. 12:9), and the identifying of spirits (1 Cor. 12:10). God wants the members of the local church to use these gifts to strengthen and help one another (1 Pet. 4:10, 1 Cor. 12:7, 1 Cor. 14:12). It is important for Christians to discover which spiritual gifts God has given them so that they can use their gifts to build up the local church.

F. HOW CAN A CHRISTIAN DISCOVER WHICH SPIRITUAL GIFTS HE HAS BEEN GIVEN?

In order to discover your own spiritual gift, you could do four things:

(a) Study and understand the individual gifts from the places in Scripture where they are discussed, such as 1 Corinthians 12 and Romans 12.
(b) Study how the spiritual gifts were used in the book of Acts in order to be able to recognize the gifts when they are being used in the local church.
(c) Find out what you can do in the local church which God seems to use and bless for the good of the congregation.
(d) Confirm your gift by asking other members of your local church what they think your spiritual gift seems to be.

In addition to the spiritual gifts given to each believer, God has also given certain multi-gifted people to the church. These people include apostles (church planters), prophets, evangelists, pastors and teachers (Eph. 4:11). God wants these gifted people to equip (enable) others in the church to be better able to serve the Lord (Eph. 4:12).

G. WHAT IS GOD'S PLAN FOR THE CHURCH IN RELATION TO MANKIND?

Some people think God has little to do with the world today. Others think he just sustains the world by providing rain and crops for mankind, but not much else. Many people believe that God created the universe, but now he just lets it run by itself, like someone who wound up a clock and then let the clock run down. What does the Bible say?

The Bible reveals that the main business of God in the world today is related to building his church. Jesus said, 'I will build my church, and the gates of Hades will not overcome it' (Matt. 16:18). Jesus is building his church out of men and women from every tribe and nation on earth (Rev. 5:9). God promised 4000 years ago to Abraham that he would do this. Here is the promise: 'Now the Lord said to Abram, I will make you a great nation, and I will bless you, and make your name great, and so you shall be a blessing. . . and in you all the families of the earth shall be blessed' (Gen. 12:1–3).

How could God bless all the families on earth through one nomadic cattle herder? The answer is given in Galatians 3:7–9, which says, 'Therefore be sure that it is those who are of faith that are sons of Abraham. And the scriptures, foreseeing that God would justify the Gentiles by faith, preached the gospel beforehand to Abraham saying, "All nations shall be blessed in you." So then, those who are of faith are blessed with Abraham the believer.' Abraham was the ancestor of Christ. He was also the man who believed God, so he is the spiritual father of all those who have faith in Christ. In other words, beginning with Abraham, God has extended the blessing of salvation through faith to all people.

All those who have faith in Christ are blessed, as Abraham was blessed for his faith. As the church expands into all tribes and nations of the world, families from those tribes and nations will be blessed as people put their faith in Christ and become part of his church.

Some people in Africa and other places have the idea that God has favoured the Jews but not them. That idea is false. There is no partiality with God (Acts 10:34–35, Rom. 2:11). The Lord revealed this truth through Paul, who had been a strict Jewish Pharisee, with these words: 'For there is no difference between Jew and Gentile – the same Lord is Lord of all and richly blesses all who call on him' (Rom. 10:12).

Seven hundred years before Jesus commanded his followers to take the gospel to all nations of the world (Matt. 28:19), God spoke through the Jewish prophet Isaiah and said, 'Turn to me, and be saved, all the ends of the earth; For I am God, and there is no other.' (Isa. 45:22). God loves all people, and desires them all to turn to him in repentance and faith. God does not prefer the Jew, the African, the Chinese or anyone else. It is simply that in God's plan of salvation for all mankind, the Jewish nation had a special role to play (Rom. 9:4–5).

God is calling out a people for himself from every tribe and nation to complete the building of his holy temple, the church. At the very first council of the Christian church, the Apostle James summarized this great plan of God with these words: 'Brothers, listen to me. Simon (Peter) has described for us how God at first showed his concern by taking from the Gentiles (the non-Jewish nations) a people for himself' (Acts 15:13–14). God is at work in the world today. He is calling out a special people for himself who will reveal the excellences of his holy character (1 Pet. 2:9). He is building a church for his own glory with men and women from every tribe and nation in the world. One day this great work of God will be complete.

H. WHAT IS THE PURPOSE OF THE CHURCH?

What does God want to accomplish through his special holy people whom he bought with the blood of Christ? What are God's purposes for the church?

THE PRAISE AND WORSHIP OF GOD

A primary purpose of the church, which will continue for all eternity, is that God might be given the praise and worship he deserves by his people. In Isaiah 43:21 God's people are described as 'the people I formed for myself, that they may proclaim my praise.' In Ephesians 1:12 it says that believers exist for 'the praise of his glory.'

EVANGELISM AND WITNESS

The church also exists to win people over to Christ and to show the world how God wants them to live. The church is God's means to reveal the character of Jesus Christ to the world so that God will be glorified (1 Pet. 2:9–12). Jesus said that his people are the light of the world (Matt. 5:14–16). Light eliminates darkness. God wants the church to be a light for him in a dark world. He wants the church to show the world what is right and what is wrong, and how people ought to live.

To really understand how God wants them to live, people must first have a personal relationship with him. Since that relationship has been broken by sin, people must first be reconciled to God. Hence the most important part of the church's witness as light to the world, is to tell people how they can be reconciled to God through Jesus Christ and find forgiveness for their sin (Luke 24:46–47). The church must by all means seek to bring people to repentance and faith in Christ.

GOOD WORKS

The New Testament says we are 'God's workmanship, created in Christ Jesus to do good works, which God prepared in advance for us to do' (Eph. 2:10). Jesus said Christians are 'the salt of the earth' (Matt. 5:13–14). Salt and good works are related ideas. Salt is used to bring out the best taste in food and to prevent food from spoiling. In a similar way, the church is intended to bring out the best in God's plan for mankind. God's plan for mankind should be seen in the lives of his people. By their good works, Christians reveal how people ought to live in their marriages, their families, their work, their communities, and in all the relationships of life.

History has consistently shown that the people of Christ have always been at the forefront of those movements in society which reveal the mercy, goodness and justice of God. An example of this was the abolition of slavery in Britain by William Wilberforce. He was encouraged by fellow-Christians who saw the injustice and evil of slavery. Orphanages, schools for the blind and deaf, ministries to the handicapped, needy and downtrodden have been promoted by Christians wherever the church has been planted in the world, often through legal and social reform.

Salt is also used to prevent food from spoiling. God plans for the church to keep society from becoming totally evil. Through its good works of mercy and kindness, and through its prayers, God wants the church to restrain the world from becoming even more evil. God plans for the good works of his church to touch all parts of human life. The presence of the church is one of the ways in which the Holy Spirit restrains evil in this world.

It is Jesus' plan to reveal the knowledge of himself, his salvation, his goodness, his love and his glory to all the world through the church (Psalm 67:1–2,7; 98:2–3, Eph. 3:1–11). Christ is building his church with men, women, boys and girls from every tribe, race, and language group on earth (Matt. 28:19–20, Rev. 5:9–10; 7:9–10). When this work is finished, Jesus will return and establish his kingdom on the earth, with his church ruling the world along with him (Rev. 5:9–10, Rev. 11:15).

FELLOWSHIP AND EDIFICATION

Another very important purpose of the local church is fellowship and mutual encouragement among God's people (Acts 2:42). A burning stick will burn well when it is with other burning sticks in a fire. If, however, it is removed from the fire and burns alone, it may die out. This illustrates the Christian's need for fellowship with other believers in the local church. By sharing their experience in the Lord (Acts 2:42), by the teaching of the word of God (Col. 2:7), and by using the gifts of the Holy Spirit (1 Cor. 12:7–30), members of the local church are to build each other up in the love of God and in their faith in Jesus Christ (Eph. 4:15–16).

AN ETERNAL INHERITANCE IN CHRIST

Jesus plans to give his people an eternal inheritance (Rev. 21:7). The Bible says we are joint heirs with Jesus Christ of what belongs to God. God plans for the church to share in the inheritance of Christ (Rom. 8:17, Eph. 1:9,11). Galatians 4:7 says, 'since you are a son, God has made you also an heir.'

Parents normally pass on to their children the wealth and property they have acquired during their lifetime. We call this an inheritance. It is not something the children have worked for. Even when the parents don't leave a will for the distribution of their property, many governments have laws which assign the parents' property to their children. In a similar way, the children of God are heirs of God. It may be difficult to believe, but the Bible teaches that along with Christ, Christians will inherit all that belongs to God. Paul wrote, 'For all things belong to you, whether . . . the world or life or death or things present or things to come; all things belong to you, and you belong to Christ; and Christ belongs to God' (1 Cor. 3:21–23).

Some parts of this inheritance are given to the Christian right from the moment of his or her new birth, such as the promise of God to hear and answer prayer made in Jesus' name (John 16:24). Some parts of this inheritance will be received later, such as the promise of a resurrection body similar to the resurrection body of Christ (Phil. 3:21).

I. WHAT ARE THE MAIN ILLUSTRATIONS USED IN THE NEW TESTAMENT TO DESCRIBE THE RELATIONSHIP BETWEEN CHRIST AND HIS CHURCH?

There are several illustrations used in the New Testament to describe the church, and the relationship between Christ and his church. Here is a summary of these illustrations:

(a) Christ is the head and the church is his body (Col. 1:18, Eph. 1:22–23).
(b) Christ is the cornerstone and Christians are the individual building blocks of the temple of God (Eph. 2:19–22, 1 Pet. 2:5–7).
(c) Christ is the bridegroom and the church is the bride of Christ (2 Cor. 11:2, Eph. 5:25–27,32, Rev. 21:9).
(d) Christ is the good shepherd, and the church is his flock of sheep (Psalm 100:3, John 10:1–16, 1 Pet. 5:2–4).
(e) Christ is our high priest, and the members of the church are all priests before God (Heb. 8:1, 1 Pet. 2:5, Rev. 5:10).
(f) Christ is the vine and the members of the church are the branches of the vine (John 15:1–6).
(g) Christ is the King and the church is his kingdom (Matt. 25:34, Luke 12:31–32, Luke 22:29–30).

J. WHY ARE THERE SO MANY DIFFERENT DENOMINATIONS AND CHURCHES?

Christians worldwide basically agree on who Christ was and what he accomplished by his death and resurrection. Critics of Christianity often point out how many different churches there are, with many claiming to be the only true church. Why are there so many different denominations?

The answer is not hard to find. Although Christians agree on the primary truths revealed in the Bible about Christ and his salvation, they often have different opinions on less important matters such as church government and various church practices. Differences of opinion about how the church should be organized, the method of water baptism to be used, the method of celebrating holy communion and other issues have caused men to form different denominations. Some of these secondary matters are mentioned in the Bible in a way that leaves room for a difference of opinion. In life, people tend to gather together with others who hold the same opinions.

It is important to realize that different does not necessarily mean wrong concerning some matters. It just means different. As an example, people wear different kinds of clothes and eat different kinds of food. It is likely that God is not very concerned about the fact that there are different denominations so long as Christians from different denominations continue to have fellowship with each other and to show love and respect for one another. What grieves the Holy Spirit is when different groups of Christians attack and criticize each other instead of standing together in Christ. When they criticize and fight with each other they greatly dishonour God, and the testimony of Christ is weakened or destroyed in that place.

Africans sometimes wonder why so many different churches and mission agencies have started work in the same country or even in the same local area, disregarding what others are doing or have already done. The reason for this is sometimes the conviction of church and mission leaders that other groups working in the area have not given a full or correct explanation of the Bible to the local people. Such reasons may be based on fact since, unfortunately, some churches or missions do not really rely on the Bible for their teaching. Sometimes it happens just because a church or mission group wants to set up their own policies and practices regarding secondary matters.

This kind of duplication can cause confusion and doubt about Christianity among local non-Christian people. The best thing to do where this situation exists, is to seek to establish acceptance and fellowship among the Christian groups working in the area. It can then be explained to non-Christians that Christians sometimes have different preferences about secondary matters, but they have a common faith in the saving death and resurrection of Christ.

K. WHAT CEREMONIES (SACRAMENTS) DID JESUS GIVE TO HIS CHURCH?

Although there were many ceremonies, sacrifices and festivals which God commanded the Israelites to perform in the Old Testament, there were really only two ceremonies given to the church by Christ in the

New Testament. These two ceremonies were water baptism (Matt. 28:19) and Holy Communion (Matt. 26:26–28).

WATER BAPTISM

Water baptism was not a new thing to the Jews. Gentiles who wanted to follow the Jewish religion were baptized in water. The origin of the word for baptism means to submerge something in water. In the gospels, we see John the Baptist with a ministry of water baptism indicating repentance from sin (Mark 1:4). The idea of conversion and public confession concerning a person's religious faith was already understood in the sign of baptism at the time when Jesus began to preach publicly.

The baptism commanded by Christ added a deeper spiritual significance to the Jewish idea of conversion through baptism and to the baptism performed by John. Jesus commanded that his followers be baptized in the name of the Father, the Son and the Holy Spirit (Matt. 28:19). This is a clear reference to the truth of the Trinity, since there is one name, but three persons. Christian baptism also carries the idea that a person has been changed (regenerated) by passing from spiritual death to spiritual life.

Christian baptism is intended as a public testimony of conversion to faith in Christ. Galatians 3:26 says, 'All of you who were baptized into Christ have clothed yourselves with Christ.' Many traditional cultures have rites of passage, or ceremonies, which mark initiation into adult life. These rituals usually take place at the time young people mature sexually into adults. The procedure and rituals followed often carry important information about the beliefs and practices of that tribe. In a somewhat similar way, Christian water baptism is a rite of passage, which testifies that a person has passed from spiritual death without Christ to spiritual life in Christ. Churches in some countries make an important public ceremony and celebration out of Christian water baptism.

It could be a good practice for local churches to make a major public celebration out of water baptism in tribes where traditional rites of passage carry deep meaning about traditional religious beliefs. By doing this, the church will be able to show the clear difference between the spiritual truth and world-view of the Bible and the traditional religious beliefs and world-view of their people. By doing this, they can help new Christians in the tribe to make a clean break with the beliefs and practices of African traditional religion. More will be said about the problem of initiation rites in chapter thirteen.

Different church groups practise different forms of baptism. Some of these are related to the different views about the meaning and purpose of baptism held by different denominations. Thus Roman Catholics, Anglicans, and Lutherans baptize infants, whereas Baptists, the African Inland Church, the Evangelical Churches of West Africa and many kinds of Pentecostal Churches only baptize adults and children who make a public confession of Christ. Methods of water baptism include immersion, pouring water over the person, or sprinkling water on the person's head. The method is not important. The sign of new life in Jesus Christ and a covenanted relationship to the living God by the baptized person, is what makes baptism important.

A question which sometimes puzzles Christians is the relationship between the baptism of the Holy Spirit, by which we are placed into the body of Christ (1 Cor. 12:13), and water baptism, which is a testimony of our conversion to Christ (Gal. 3:27). This is worth considering as the Bible says that there is only one baptism (Eph. 4:5). Which baptism, water baptism or Holy Spirit baptism, is the one true baptism?

Clearly the baptism by the Holy Spirit (1 Cor. 12:13) into the body of Christ is the one true baptism, since that is a supernatural act of God which makes us part of the church. Water baptism has no supernatural power by itself to make us part of the church, as some people incorrectly think. Consider, however, the thought that water baptism is a testimony of what happened at conversion.

If we think about this, we see that water baptism is an outward physical symbol of what the Holy Spirit has done by making us a part of Christ's body. As we saw earlier, the church is where the Holy Spirit now lives (Eph. 2:22). The church is the present temple, or dwelling place of God's Spirit.

As we saw in chapter eight, water is sometimes used as a symbol of the Holy Spirit in the Bible. In John 7:37–39 Jesus said, ' "If anyone is thirsty, let him come to me and drink. Whoever believes in me, as the scripture has said, streams of living water will flow from within him." By this he meant the Spirit, whom those who believed in him were later to receive.' Thus the sign of being baptized by the Holy Spirit is accurately illustrated in the New Testament by being baptized with water. From this we can see that the one true baptism is the baptism by the Holy Spirit, performed by God himself. This baptism is symbolically illustrated by water baptism. The Holy Spirit's baptism makes us part of the church. Water baptism is therefore consistently used in the New Testament as a sign of this work of the Holy Spirit, by which we received new life in Christ.

To summarize, water baptism does not make us a part of the church. Instead, water baptism is an outward, visible testimony that the Holy Spirit has made us a part of the church.

HOLY COMMUNION

The second ceremony which Christ commanded his followers to practice was the celebration of Holy Communion. This ceremony is called the Eucharist (thanksgiving) by Roman Catholic and Anglican churches. Jesus established this ceremony at the last supper with his disciples (Matt. 26:26–28, Luke 22:17–20). It is called the Lord's Supper by Paul in 1 Cor. 11:20. Over the centuries the church has been divided over the precise meaning of the elements of the bread and wine which Christ shared. The Roman Catholic Church teaches that the bread and wine become the actual body and blood of Christ during the communion service, by a miracle, while the Protestant churches teach that the bread and wine are symbols of his body and blood.

All Christian groups agree that the celebration of Holy Communion is a ceremony remembering the death of Christ for our sins. The broken bread testifies to his broken body (Matt. 26:26) and the cup testifies to his blood, poured out for the forgiveness of our sins (Matt. 26:28). Paul stated that the Lord's Supper was to be a regular practice of the local church (1 Cor. 11:23–32). In Paul's discussion of the Lord's Supper, he makes a strong point that believers are to examine their own hearts before the Lord and to judge any sin in their lives before they take the communion elements. Otherwise they will bring God's judgment upon themselves (1 Cor. 11:27–30).

Because of this warning, some Christians refuse to participate in the Lord's Supper. This is not good and it does not please God. Instead, God wants us to confess our sins and receive his forgiveness (1 John 1:9) and then take part in the Lord's Supper with thanksgiving to God for what he has done.

How often should Christians celebrate the Lord's Supper? There is no rule given in the New Testament. Common sense suggests that it should be celebrated often enough to keep the truth of the Lord's sacrifice fresh in the hearts of his people, but it should not become a meaningless ritual.

L. WHAT ARE THE MAIN TYPES OF CHURCH GOVERNMENT?

There are three main forms of church government among Christian churches. Most churches use a combination of, or variation on these three types of government.

THE EPISCOPAL FORM OF CHURCH GOVERNMENT

This form of church government comes from the Greek word *episkopos*, meaning bishop or overseer. The episcopal form of government is based on a well-defined structure of church officials. In this form of government there is usually a clear line of church authority from leaders to church members. At the top is an individual leader, called a pope, archbishop, bishop, or some other title. There is an order of leaders from the highest ranking down to the local church members. In churches which have this form of government, the ordinary church members do not usually have administrative authority, although they may exercise their spiritual gifts in various ways. There is sometimes a distinction made between the clergy (the paid officials) and the laity (the ordinary church members). Denominations which use this form of government include the Roman Catholic, Anglican and Methodist Churches.

THE PRESBYTERIAL FORM OF CHURCH GOVERNMENT

The presbyterial form of church government comes from the Greek word *presbuteros* which means elder. This form of government relies on the leadership of a group of elders in each local church. These elders are either appointed or elected, and they represent the interests of the rest of the congregation in church business meetings. Often these churches are associated into larger groups in a particular geographical area. These groups may be called a district church council, a local church council, a synod or a presbytery. The Africa Inland Church, the ECWA Church, the Presbyterian Church and the Christian Reformed Church have church governments of this kind.

THE CONGREGATIONAL FORM OF CHURCH GOVERNMENT

This form of church government has a strong association with the political idea of democracy. In the congregational form of church government, church administrative business is carried out in congregational meetings in which everyone has an equal vote. Each local church is usually independent of other churches, except for loose types of association for fellowship. Congregational type churches usually form their own policies without reference to other churches or associations. Groups which use this form of government include the Baptist Church, the Congregational Church and most Independent Bible Churches.

M. WHAT ARE THE MAIN LEADERSHIP POSITIONS IN THE LOCAL CHURCH, ACCORDING TO THE NEW TESTAMENT?

When discussing why there are different Christian denominations, we observed that there are many different opinions as to how the church should be organized. In any discussion of leadership positions in the church, we should be aware of these differences of opinion. Such differences should not be allowed to interfere with our fellowship with brothers and sisters from other denominations.

There are at least two types of leadership positions described in the New Testament, with qualifications given for each position. These are the positions of elder and deacon. These two offices appear to refer to different leadership roles in the local church. This can be seen by comparing Philippians 1:1 and 1 Timothy 3:1–7 with 1 Timothy 3:8–13.

Some Christians feel there are at least two more positions of leadership described in the New Testament, in addition to deacons and elders. These would include bishops (overseers) and pastors. These four terms (elder, deacon, bishop, and pastor) are used commonly throughout the New Testament. We will examine the ministry associated with each of these titles.

Those who believe that elders and deacons are the only two positions would teach that bishops (overseers) and pastors are simply certain selected elders. This seems to be the pattern in the churches established by Paul.

ELDER (GREEK *PRESBUTEROS*)

The terms elder (*presbuteros*) and overseer (*episkopos*) are used interchangeably in the New Testament (Titus 1:5,7). When Paul called the elders (Acts 20:17) from the church at Ephesus he stated that God had made these elders to be overseers (bishops) of that church (Acts 20:28). The term elder suggests the spiritual maturity of the person, while the term overseer (bishop) suggests the type of spiritual responsibility the person has in the church. In other words, a person had to be an elder (spiritually) in order to be an overseer. An overseer was not to be a new convert (1 Tim. 3:6).

The biblical qualifications for overseers (and hence elders) are given in 1 Timothy 3:1–7 and Titus 1:5–9. They are to be spiritually mature men of excellent character. In both places, the very first qualification is that they be people who are above reproach. In other words, there must be nothing that is questionable in their character or their behaviour.

The second qualification is that they must be the husband of only one wife. This would eliminate those who are polygamists and those who have been divorced and remarried. This does not mean that Christian polygamists or remarried persons are not godly people. It simply means that God wants an example of his perfect will for marriage (Matt. 19:3–6) to be displayed in the leadership of the church.

In addition, overseers must be men who show moderation in everything. They must be self-controlled, prudent (wise and careful), respectable (having a good reputation), hospitable, able to teach, not given to drinking, gentle, not quarrelsome, and not lovers of money (1 Tim. 3:2–3). They must manage their own homes well, and not be recent converts (1 Tim. 3:4–7).

There was always more than one elder in each local church in the New Testament (Acts 14:23). If we are to follow this example, the leadership of any local church should be in the hands of a group of elders, and not just one person. Because of our sinful human tendencies, it is not wise for just one person to have absolute control over a local church. Everyone in a local church should be accountable to other members of the church. The church belongs to Christ and not to any one person. Christ alone is the head of his church.

Elders have responsibility to lead and to teach the church (1 Tim. 3:2). Hence it would appear that those appointed as elders should give evidence of leadership and teaching gifts from the Holy Spirit. These men should be responsible for instructing the congregation in the word of God (1 Tim. 5:17).

In many smaller churches, only the paid pastor does the preaching and teaching because he may be the only elder with formal Bible training. It is important for a church to recognize those people who have speaking gifts from the Holy Spirit and to encourage such people to get formal Bible training.

Overseer or bishop (Greek *episkopos*)

This function of appointed elders of the early church had to do with spiritual leadership in the church. This leadership included the teaching of the word of God as well as the administrative duties of running the church (1 Tim. 5:17). It also involved ministries of counseling (Titus 1:9) and church discipline (1 Cor. 5:12–13). The qualifications for overseers have been discussed under the heading of elders.

Pastor or Shepherd (Greek *poimen*)

The word pastor means shepherd. This title has to do with the responsibility of the church elders to take care of the local church members (the flock). Christ himself is the chief shepherd (1 Pet. 5:4) of all his sheep. Jesus has planned for local churches to have one or more shepherds (1 Pet. 5:1–3). Christ is to be the role model for each local shepherd, or pastor.

If the pattern of a single paid pastor is followed, it is important for the pastor to share the leadership responsibilities of the church with his fellow elders. All elders, including a paid pastor, are to be subject to one another (Eph. 4:1–3, Phil. 2:1–5, 1 Pet. 5:5).

Just as Jesus cares for his people, local pastors are to be examples of loving care, humility, patience, and concern for their flock. Pastors are specifically warned by the Apostle Peter not to use their position of leadership for personal power or financial gain (1 Pet. 5:2–3).

DEACON (GREEK *DIAKONOS*)

The word *diakonos* means servant. All Christians are to be servants of Christ (John 12:26). However, there seems to have been a special group of appointed servants (deacons) in the early church, because particular qualifications are given for this office in 1 Timothy 3:8–13.

Also, a distinction is made between overseers and deacons in Philippians 1:1.

The list of qualifications for deacons is similar to the list of qualifications for elders but not quite as long. Deacons are to be people worthy of respect, blameless, temperate, sincere, not given to drinking, and not pursuing dishonest gain (1 Tim. 3:8). They are to hold the faith firmly, and to be of proven good character (1 Tim. 3:9). Men who are deacons are to have only one wife, and to manage their homes well (1 Tim. 3:12). It makes sense that those appointed to be deacons should give evidence of having serving gifts from the Holy Spirit.

There are many kinds of service deacons may do. The seven men described in Acts 6:1–6 could be considered deacons of the early church. They were appointed to distribute food. It is interesting that these seven men had to be filled with the Holy Spirit and with wisdom (Acts 6:3). There was a special commissioning service for their ministry (Acts 6:6).

From the above discussion it can be seen that the two categories of spiritual gifts given by the Holy Spirit (speaking gifts and serving gifts) (1 Pet. 4:11), seem to correspond to the two leadership offices in the church. That is, elders need speaking gifts along with leadership ability, and deacons need serving gifts.

SUMMARY

The church is the body of Christ. It is the eternal, extended family of God. It is the community of all those people on earth and in heaven, from many tribes, races and nations, who have put their faith in Jesus Christ as their Lord and Saviour. The true church is not one particular denomination. Rather, it consists of people from many denominations who have been regenerated by the Holy Spirit because they have put their faith in Christ. The church is the dwelling-place of the Holy Spirit in the present age.

Because of the social structure of African life, it is easy to understand God's plan for the local church. In Africa, a person's extended family and tribal community are the most important realities in his or her life. It is God's plan that the local church should become the most important community in the life of a Christian. It is the group of people who belong to each other as spiritual brothers and sisters, regardless of tribal or social connections, because they each belong to Christ as their Lord and Saviour. As the community of God's holy people, the members of the local church have a responsibility to care for one another. They also have the great privilege and responsibility to pray for themselves and for the world, and to live by the power of the Holy Spirit. By doing this, God will cause his will to be done on earth through their prayers and his glory to be seen in the world through their good works. No other community in the world has such a privilege or responsibility.

The purpose of the church in this world is to bring true praise and worship to God, to provide fellowship, growth and support for Christians, and to cause God's truth to be known to a lost world through the words of witness and actions of love of God's people. The church's relationship to Christ is pictured in the New Testament by illustrations such as the bridegroom (Christ) and his bride (the church), the good shepherd and his sheep, the head and the parts of the body and the king and his kingdom.

Jesus gave two important ceremonies to his church. These are water baptism, a testimony of a person's regeneration in Christ, and Holy Communion, a remembrance of the death of Christ to secure forgiveness of sins for his people. Different churches have different forms of church government. These differences are not really important, so long as Christians from different denominations love, respect and accept each another. The New Testament describes various positions of leadership and service in the local church. These positions include elders (overseers), pastors, and deacons. People appointed to these positions of leadership must fulfill the requirements of spiritual maturity and character described in the New Testament.

DISCUSSION QUESTIONS AND PROJECTS BASED ON CHAPTER NINE

1. Which church is the true church of Jesus Christ?

2. How may a person become a member of the true church of Christ?

3. Which kind of baptism is the one true baptism for all Christians?

4. Why are there different denominations?

5. Let the group discuss these questions:
   (a) How does the concept of the church relate to African community life?
   (b) In what ways does the church strengthen African community life?

6. List the purposes of the church in God's plan. How does your own local church fulfil these purposes?

7. What is the church going to inherit from Christ?

8. Divide into groups of four each. Let each group discuss why there is more power in prayer when several believers gather together in Jesus' name, than when just one believer prays? Give Scripture references to support the answer.

9. Arrange for seven students from different local churches to each give a testimony about prayer in their local churches. They should give details of how God answered specific prayer.

10. Divide into tribal groups. Let each group make a list of the most urgent prayer needs for their tribe or people group. Then pray together in the group for each of these requests.

11. Divide into groups of four each. List the most urgent prayer needs for your country and for your church leaders. Let each group pray together for these needs.

12. Stage a debate between two persons on the benefits of the episcopal form of church government as compared with the congregational form of church government. After the debate, allow the class to respond to the ideas that were given.

13. Hold two discussions on the use of spiritual gifts. The discussion for the first day will be on speaking gifts. The discussion for the second day will be on serving gifts. Each day the discussion leader should list gifts in that category on the chalkboard. Let participants give examples of how the gift was used in the New Testament and how the gift might be used in their own local church. After these two days of discussion, let students write down what they consider to be their own spiritual gifts.

14. Let the class adopt a people group in their country as a prayer project. This should be a group which is unreached with the gospel or very resistant to the gospel. Information on such groups is available from church or mission leaders. The group should pray for their targeted group at least once a week. The focus of prayer should be that God would send the needed evangelists to the people and that he would open the hearts of the people to receive the gospel when they finally hear it.

SUGGESTED FOR FURTHER READING

Green, Michael. *Freed to Serve*. London: Hodder, 1988.

Johnstone, Patrick. *Operation World – You Can Change The World*. Carlisle: O.M. Publishing, 1994.

Martin, Ralph P. *The Family And The Fellowship*. Exeter: Paternoster Press, 1979.

Rye, James and Nina. *The Survivor's Guide to Church Life*. Leicester: InterVarsity Press, 1992.

Watson, David. *I Believe in the Church*. London: Hodder, reprinted 1993.

10

The Christian and the Spirit World

Mbweni had become deeply involved in the rebel movement. He felt sympathy for their cause and wanted to help them in whatever way he was able to. He had worked at the large mission station about 10 km from his village for several years. He knew who lived in each house on the compound and the schedules which each family kept. He had even been inside several of the houses and knew the layout of the rooms. No one else in the group knew the mission compound as well as Mbweni.

The time had come to carry out the raid his group had so carefully planned for several weeks. By the end of this night no one would be left alive on the mission compound. He and his group were well prepared. They were many and they were well armed. They could easily overcome the two old night-guards who slept and took turns walking around the compound.

As Mbweni and his large group silently approached the compound fence they suddenly stopped in amazement and fear! Where had this large number of guards come from? Had the people on the compound been warned about Mbweni and his group? And what strange swords that glowed with fire, did the guards hold in their hands? The guards looked strong and there were many of them. After a short discussion in whispers, Mbweni and his men decided to cancel the attack. The guards clearly outnumbered their group.

Some months later Mbweni was put into prison by the government for his participation in the rebel movement. Two years after the incident took place, a missionary from that compound was visiting the prison. As the missionary talked with Mbweni, Mbweni related how his group had been frightened away by the large number of guards with their strange swords. Mbweni asked the missionary how they had learned of the attack and where they had hired so many guards. To Mbweni's amazement, the missionary said that no extra guards had been hired and that only the two regular night guards had been on duty that night.

This story reveals that there is indeed a spirit world. There are times when the spirits in that world are directly involved in the affairs of our world.

Traditional people spend much of their time thinking about the spirits around them. They are often just as concerned about their relationship to their ancestors and to other spirits as they are to the people in their village. They are well aware of the fact that many things which happen in the world they can see are related to things which take place in the world which they cannot see – the world of the spirits.

To the person following traditional religion, it is all-important in life to do or say what is right in relation to the spirits of the unseen world. By contrast, very few people in Europe or North America gave much thought to spirits until recent years. That situation has changed somewhat in the past 30 years because many Europeans and North Americans have become involved in the demonic world of the occult. However even today, most Europeans and North Americans spend little or no time thinking about spirits. Western people are generally preoccupied with the things they can see. Africans often think about the things they cannot see. This reflects a very basic difference between the world-view of the European person and the world-view of the African person.

What does the Bible say about the spirit world? How much concern should we have for the spirits around us? Are there nature spirits of sky and earth? Are there other kinds of spirits who affect our lives more than we think? In this chapter we will seek to answer the following questions:

A. What does the Bible say about the spirit world and our relationship to that world?
B. Who are the angels?
C. What are the angels like?
D. What are the different kinds of angels?
E. What are the characteristics of the holy angels?
F. What are some of the ways in which the holy angels help the people of God?

A. WHAT DOES THE BIBLE SAY ABOUT THE SPIRIT WORLD AND OUR RELATIONSHIP TO THAT WORLD?

The Bible tells us quite a lot about the spirit world. Since the Bible is the word of God, we must compare all ideas about the spirit world with what the Bible reveals to us. It was shown in chapter two that the Bible is the word of God. If God says something is true, then it is true, whether it fits our world-view or not. Likewise, if God says an idea is false, we must reject that idea, no matter how strongly we have been taught to believe it. Otherwise we will be deceived.

Almost everyone in Africa believes in God. The Bible reveals that God is a spirit and that our worship of God must be spiritual worship. In other words, our worship must not include images or idols of any kind. The Bible says, 'God is spirit, and those who worship him must worship in spirit and truth' (John 4:24–NASB). A common practice of non-Christian religions is to represent spirit beings with idols or images. God forbids this in the Bible. In Exodus 20:4 God says, 'You shall not make for yourself an idol in the form of anything in heaven above or on the earth beneath or in the waters below. You shall not bow down to them or worship them.'

The Bible says that all spirits in the universe were created by Jesus Christ. They are all under his power and authority. Colossians 1:16 says, 'For by him all things were created, things in heaven and things on earth, visible and invisible, whether thrones or powers or rulers or authorities, all things were created by him and for him.' From this verse and other verses of Scripture, it is clear that there is a world of spirit beings. It is also clear that these spirits were created by Christ and that they exist for his purposes. They are all subject to him without exception. These created spirits have a significant degree of power and authority. They can have a very real effect on what takes place in the visible world.

The spirit world is a world of great importance and every African understands this. However, some African ideas about the spirit world do not agree with the teaching of the Bible. What does the Bible teach about spirits?

B. WHO ARE THE ANGELS?

The Bible teaches that before God created man or the earth, he created a vast number of spirit beings called the heavenly host (Psalm 148:2–5). The word host means a large company of persons, as with an army. The heavenly host may include all the creatures God created before he began his creation on earth. How many creatures and how many different kinds of created beings there are, we do not know. We do know that there are many. In Revelation 5:11, God is worshipped by angels numbering in the millions. Nehemiah 9:6 says, 'You give life to everything, and the multitudes of heaven worship you.' According to Psalm 103:20–21 and Psalm 148:2, the heavenly host are the angels. The word angel comes from the Greek word *angelos*, which means messenger. In the Bible, angels are sometimes referred to as 'stars' (Job 38:4,7; Rev. 12:4,9). Perhaps they are called stars because of their radiant appearance (Luke 24:4, Rev. 10:1). Angels were also called the 'sons of God' in Job 1:6 and in Job 38:7.

There are two main groups of angels described in the Bible. The larger number are the holy angels. These are the powerful and faithful servants of God (Psalm 103:20–21, Mark 8:38). The smaller number (perhaps one third, according to Rev. 12:4) are the evil angels, who fell in rebellion along with Satan (Matt. 25:41).

Angels are spirits according to Hebrews 1:14. There are different kinds of angels. It is quite possible that the Bible does not even reveal to us all the many kinds of spirits that make up the heavenly host. From what the Bible does reveal, we know that there are different kinds of angels with different degrees of power and authority. Some of these spirits are described as having an unusual form. Seraphim (singular seraph) are full of eyes and have six wings (Isa. 6:2 cf. Rev. 4:7–8). Cherubim (singular cherub) are described as having human form, but with four faces and four wings (Ezek. 1:1,5–8; 10:20–22). Some angels have the ability to appear in human form as men. Angels appeared like this to Abraham (Gen. 18:1,22,19:1) and at the tomb of Christ (Luke 24:4). Demons, who are probably fallen angels, can also assume a physical appearance (Rev. 16:13).

The ability of angels to appear in a physical form suggests something important about mankind's relationship to the spirit world. It is clearly possible for spirit beings to make themselves visible to human eyes. Whether they do this to help people or to deceive them, depends on the kind of spirits they are. We must recognize that because spirits have this ability, it is possible for evil spirits to deceive people. It is probably through such visual appearances of evil spirits that people of many religions of the world have been deceived. If you saw a spirit being with your own eyes, you would most likely believe what you saw. You would probably also believe what the spirit told you (1 Tim. 4:1).

C. WHAT ARE THE ANGELS LIKE?

Angels are not the spirits of the departed dead, nor glorified human beings. They are a separate category of highly intelligent and powerful beings created by God. There is a distinction made in the Bible between the spirits of the departed dead and the angels (Luke 16:22, Luke 20:34–36, Heb. 12:22–23). Angels are a higher level of created beings than human beings (Psalm 103:20).

Like people, angels are persons who speak, and do things (e.g. Matt. 28:2–7). Unlike people, they are persons of a resurrection order who cannot die (Luke 20:36). Angels do not marry and have families (Mark 12:25). However, they are able to speak and relate to ordinary men, as when an angel spoke to the Lord's disciples at his ascension (Acts 1:10–11). In some cases, angels appeared to men in their heavenly glory and were majestic in their appearance (Rev. 10:1–2). Daniel saw an angel in this way (Dan. 10:4–8). It was an awesome and overpowering experience for Daniel (Dan. 10:8).

It is correct to assume that angelic spirits can have a direct effect on the course of human events and even on nature. In 2 Samuel 24:15–16, an angel of God struck down 70,000 people of Israel with a plague as judgment against King David. An angel of God, in one night, struck down 185,000 Assyrian soldiers who had been besieging the city of Jerusalem (Isa. 37:36). In the book of Job, Satan, a fallen angel, caused a violent storm (with God's permission) which killed all ten of Job's children (Job 1:12,19). In the book of Revelation, the angels of God affect the winds (Rev. 7:1), the earth (Rev. 8:6–7), the sea (Rev. 16:3–4), and the sun (Rev. 16:8), as they carry out the judgments of God against the world.

Some traditional African beliefs in divinities or nature gods are similar to the truth about angels revealed in the Bible. However, there are important differences between the traditional concept of divinities and the angels of the Bible. According to Scripture, the activity of the holy angels is ordered directly by God alone (Psalm 103:20–21). According to some traditional religions, people can persuade divinities to act on their behalf. In the Bible, human beings are strongly warned not to worship angels (Rev. 19:10, Rev. 22:8–9). This would include making sacrifices and offerings to them. The spirits and divinities of traditional religions, however, often receive or even require, sacrifices and offerings.

If people make sacrifices or offerings to spirits, they will almost certainly fall into the hands of Satan or one of his fallen angels. Satan has the power to appear as an angel of light (2 Cor. 11:14) and he has done so in human history. Worship is just what Satan wants (Matt. 4:8–9). People have been kept from knowing the truth about God and his salvation in Jesus Christ by making sacrifices and offerings to spirits who indicated that they require such acts of worship. Such acts of obedience or worship break the very first of God's commandments (Ex. 20:3–5). Any spirit or divinity of traditional belief who requires a ritual sacrifice or offering from human beings is a fallen angel. The holy angels of God will never require such acts of worship (Rev. 22:8–9).

The Bible teaches that man is to worship God and God alone (Matt. 4:10, Col. 2:18–19). God wants people to seek him directly in order to get help (Isa. 55:6–7). He does not want them to go through intermediary spirits or human specialists such as medicine men or witch-doctors. The only mediator between God and men whom God accepts is Jesus Christ (1 Tim. 2:5). In Deuteronomy 32:16–17 Moses says, 'They made him (God) jealous with their foreign gods and angered him with their detestable idols. They sacrificed to demons which are not God.' This passage in Deuteronomy reveals the deadly deception in traditional religions. The spirits who pretend to be divinities and ancestors are none other than carefully disguised demons of Satan.

If people are to get help from God, they are commanded to make their requests and prayers directly to God in the name of Jesus Christ (John 16:23–24, Heb. 4:14–16). God will take care of how he works out the answer. If God uses the holy angels to help people, the angels will be directed by God (Psalm 103:20–21), and not by people. If people try to request help from spirits other than God, or from witch doctors, they risk becoming controlled by demons, as stated in Deuteronomy 32:16–17. In Deuteronomy 6:13–15 the Bible says, 'Fear the Lord your God, serve him only, and take your oaths in his name. Do not follow other gods, the gods of the peoples around you.' This statement is just as important in Africa today as it was to the Israelites 3300 years ago.

The people of non-Christian religions who seek the favour of gods or spirits other than the true God, will eventually be deceived and brought into slavery by Satan and demons. The apostle Paul warned us, 'the sacrifices of pagans are offered to demons, not to God, and I do not want you to be participants with demons' (1 Cor. 10:20). This is true no matter how 'kind' the spirits may seem to be to people who seek for help. Demons are very skilled in pretending to be what they are not.

Some people believe that everything which happens is the result of the activity of some spirit. The Bible does not teach that everything which happens is the result of the work of angels or demons. Jesus indicated in Luke 12:54–55 that there is a regular and predictable occurrence of things in nature. It is only in certain situations where good or evil angels intervene in the affairs of life. We must learn to base our world-view (our view of reality) on what the Bible teaches rather than on traditional cultural ideas. More will be said about the interaction between spirits and people in chapter twelve, which deals with spiritual warfare.

D. WHAT ARE THE DIFFERENT KINDS OF ANGELS?

When God created the angels, they were all holy and beautiful beings (Ezek. 28:12–13), just as everything from God's hand was good and perfect (Gen. 1:31). There were different kinds of angels created by Jesus Christ (Col. 1:16). At least eight different Greek words are used in the New Testament to describe the different ranks of angels. Some ranks of angels are of greater power and authority than others, although the Bible does not describe each category in detail. The highest rank of angel seems to be the archangel. The only person in the Bible specifically called an archangel is Michael (Jude 9). Daniel 10:13, however, suggests that there may be others in this category.

Another group, the cherubim, seems to have had a special place guarding the throne of God (Ezek. 10:1–19, Ezek. 28:14).

E. WHAT ARE THE CHARACTERISTICS OF THE HOLY ANGELS?

First of all, they are holy (Mark 8:38). They obey God without question. In keeping with their pure character, they are swift to follow the orders of God. Psalm 103:20 says, 'Praise the Lord you his angels, you mighty ones who do his bidding, who obey his word.'

Angels have very great knowledge, power, ability, and strength (2 Pet. 2:11). Angels are of an order of creation greatly superior to human beings. Consider the great knowledge of the angel who told Zacharias the priest all the details about the birth and ministry of the unborn son (John the Baptist) who would be born to Zacharias and his wife Elizabeth (Luke 1:13–17). Think about the power of the angel in the book of Revelation who will turn all the sea and fresh water into blood as sign of God's judgment (Rev. 16:3–4). Consider the ability of the angel who made the iron chains fall off Peter, and who caused the gates of the prison to open by themselves (Acts 12:7,10).

The strength of angels is far beyond human strength. Consider the following examples of their great strength. One angel alone killed 185,000 Assyrian soldiers in one night (Isa. 37:36). One angel shut the mouths of a group of hungry lions and prevented them from touching Daniel in the lions' den (Dan. 6:22). One angel easily rolled away the huge stone at the grave of Christ (Matt. 28:2). At the close of this age, one angel will bind Satan and cast him into the abyss for 1000 years (Rev. 20:1–2). These are the very angels God has sent to be the unseen helpers of the children of God (Heb. 1:14)!

F. WHAT ARE SOME OF THE WAYS IN WHICH THE HOLY ANGELS HELP THE PEOPLE OF GOD?

1. Angels guard and protect the people of God in many situations (Psalm 34:7, Psalm 91:11). It was an angel who brought the apostles out of jail when they had been imprisoned by the high priest (Acts 5:17–19). It was an angel who stood by Paul and encouraged him in a storm at sea (Acts 27:22–24). It is likely that many Christians have been helped by holy angels at various times in their life without knowing it, thinking that it was just some helpful stranger (Heb. 1:14, Heb. 13:2). It was clearly a group of God's holy angels who protected the mission compound in the story at the beginning of this chapter. There are many testimonies of someone who gave a Christian urgently needed help and then disappeared suddenly after the help was given. The angel dis-

appeared like this after he had helped Peter to escape from prison (Acts 12:10).

2. Angels physically and mentally strengthen the people of God. It was an angel who strengthened Jesus in his earthly body when he was in agony in the garden of Gethsemane (Luke 22:43). It was an angel who strengthened Daniel in his extreme weakness (Dan. 10:16–18). It was an angel who prepared unusual food for Elijah and strengthened him for his 40-days flight from Jezebel (1 Kings 19:5–8).

3. Angels guide believers, especially in evangelism. In Acts 8:26 an angel told Philip to take a certain road to Gaza so that Philip would meet the Ethiopian official who came to believe in Christ as a result of Philip's preaching. In Acts 10:3–7, an angel told Cornelius to send messengers to Joppa to find Peter so that Peter could come and preach the gospel to Cornelius. Sometimes angels hinder foolish people from pursuing their sin, as in the story of Balaam and his donkey (Num. 22:21–28).

4. Angels deliver Christians from human and demonic danger. Psalm 34:7 says, 'The angel of the Lord encamps around those who fear him, and he delivers them.' The angels rescued Lot and his family from the wicked men of Sodom (Gen. 19:9–11) and later from the destruction of the city (Gen. 19:16). Angels delivered Elisha and his servant from the attacking Syrians (2 Kings 6:17–18). A holy angel fought with an evil angel to bring a message to Daniel (Dan. 10:13,20).

   Some people may ask the question why the holy angels rescue God's people in some situations, but not in others. Daniel was rescued from the lions (Dan. 6:21–22) but many early Christians were torn apart by lions in the Roman Coliseum. In the book of Hebrews, God tells us that some heroes of the faith had dramatic escapes from death (Heb. 11:32–35) but others were allowed to glorify God through suffering and death (Heb. 11:36–37). One group was not better than the other. Only the Lord knows the reason for each of these situations. In the case of each of the heroes of faith mentioned in Hebrews 11, the person trusted God for his situation. Thus God was glorified through what took place. The important thing is not whether we live or die, but that whether we live or die, Jesus Christ might be exalted through what takes place. This is also what Paul taught in Philippians 1:19–21.

5. Angels are often the agents through whom God answers prayer. We must remember that prayer plays a very important part in whether or not God's angels are free to work. An angel came to Daniel in direct response to Daniel's prayer (Dan. 10:12). Jesus was strengthened by an angel in response to his agonized prayer in the garden of Gethsemane (Luke 22:42–43). An angel came to

Peter's rescue as a direct result of the united prayers of the early church (Acts 12:5,7). If we fail to pray, it is very possible that we may limit the help that God might have given us through his angels.

Lack of prayer may explain why certain tragic events take place. The Bible says, 'Your enemy the devil prowls around like a roaring lion, looking for someone to devour. Resist him, standing firm in your faith' (1 Pet. 5:8–9). One way we may resist the devil's attack is through prayer. If we fail to pray, we may leave ourselves unprotected by God's angels. Hence the Bible tells us to 'pray continually' (1 Thess. 5:17), and to 'pray in the Spirit on all occasions, with all kinds of prayers and requests' (Eph. 6:18).

6. Angels remind the people of God about things and deliver messages to them from God. An angel awakened Elijah and told him to eat the food prepared for him (1 Kings 19:5–7). The angel Gabriel brought a message to Zacharias about the son he would have (Luke 1:11–20). Later Gabriel brought a message to Mary about the birth of Jesus (Luke 1:26–37). An angel told the women at Jesus' tomb that he had risen from the dead (Mark 16:4–6).

7. Angels escort believers to heaven at the time of their death. When the beggar Lazarus died, an angel carried Lazarus to the place where Abraham was (Luke 16:22). Many Christians at the point of death have testified to those around them that the holy angels were coming to take them.

8. Angels carry out the judgments of God. Two angels brought down fire and brimstone from heaven on the cities of Sodom and Gomorrah and turned them into ashes (Gen. 19:13). An angel destroyed 70,000 Israelites when God judged David for counting his people (2 Sam. 24:10–16). Angels are very active in God's final judgments against sinful men at the close of this age (Rev. 8; 9; 16).

9. Angels will accompany Christ at his return. The angels will gather up all those who cause evil on earth and cast them into the eternal fire (Matt. 13:41–42, Matt. 25:41,46). The angels will gather together the elect saints of God from all over the earth (Matt. 24:31).

10. Angels delight in the worship of God and very likely join the people of God on earth whenever they gather together to worship the Lord (Matt. 28:5–8, Rev. 5:11–14).

SUMMARY

The Bible teaches that human beings are surrounded by a vast number of spirit beings, both good and evil, called angels. These spirits are similar in some ways to the spirit beings described in some African traditional religions, but there are also important differences. The angels are a higher order of creation than man. They are very great in strength, in intelligence and in many other ways. Angels are not all the same. They have different appearances and different degrees of rank and authority. They have different responsibilities, such as the cherubim and the seraphim. They have different degrees of power. Angels are not the spirits of departed human beings.

Unlike people, they are timeless, created beings who do not reproduce or change in number. Although they are mostly unseen in their activity, they frequently interact with people. The holy angels are directed by God to minister to the people of God. However, the people of God are strictly forbidden to worship angels. Spirits who suggest or require worship from men are fallen angels. We must remember that the Bible gives us the truth about the spirit world. Therefore all other ideas about the spirit world must be compared with the revelation given to us by God in the Bible. We should only accept and believe those truths about spirit beings revealed to us in the Bible lest we be deceived by Satan.

DISCUSSION QUESTIONS AND PROJECTS BASED ON CHAPTER TEN

1. Discuss and note the similarities and differences between the concept of nature gods in some African traditional religions and the angels of the Bible.

2. List and discuss seven ministries which the holy angels carry out on behalf of Christians.

3. Let the group discuss the following questions:
   (a) Why do you think people are rarely allowed to see angels doing their work?
   (b) Why are people rarely allowed to speak with angels?
   (c) In what ways are humans and angels similar? In what ways are they different?

4. Divide into groups of three to four each to discuss the following questions, and provide Bible references to prove the answers:
   (a) What relationship are people intended to have with angels in this present life?
   (b) What relationship will people have with angels in heaven?

5. Divide into groups of three to four each to conduct an inductive Bible study on Daniel 10:1–21 to discover the answers to the following questions about angels:
   (a) What are the characteristics of angels?

(b) What are the powers of angels?
(c) How do angels minister to God's people?
(d) What reaction do human beings have when they are in the presence of angels?
(e) Which specific holy angels and fallen angels are mentioned in this passage?
(f) What is the nature of the conflict between God's angels and Satan's angels?

SUGGESTED FOR FURTHER READING

Graham, Billy. *Angels – God's Secret Agents*. London: Hodder, reprinted 1995.
Moreau, Scott. *The World Of The Spirits: A Biblical Study In The African Context*. Nairobi: Evangel Publishing House, 1990.

11

The Origin of Evil and the Strategies of Satan

An African newspaper reported a story about a terrible lorry accident in which many people were killed and injured. The next day a group of people publicly claimed that the cause of the accident was a curse which their group had placed on the lorry and its occupants, the very day of the accident. By what power was this group able to carry out such an evil plan?

People are aware of the real and evil power of witches and sorcerers who bring tragedy and harm to other people. We are also aware of people in secret societies who do terrible things in their meetings. In the daytime these people may appear to be respectable businessmen. At night they do very evil things. What powers motivate people to act in such wicked ways?

Why is there evil in the world? Where did evil come from in the first place if the universe was created by God who is altogether good and holy? In this chapter we will discuss the following questions:

A. What is the origin of evil?
B. How did other angels become involved in Satan's rebellion?
C. Who controls the present world system of values?
D. What is the origin of non-Christian religions?
E. What are demons?
F. What are the works of demons, according to the Bible?

A. WHAT IS THE ORIGIN OF EVIL?

The Bible suggests a shocking story about a rebellion against God which took place long ago before mankind was on the earth. This story might explain the origin of evil in the universe and why the world is so tormented with evil today.

A statement is presented in Ezekiel 28:11–18 which, at face value, is addressed to the king of Tyre. However, a careful reading of the statement reveals that the central figure of the story cannot be the king of Tyre. For example, in Ezekiel 28:13 it says that the person addressed 'was in Eden, the garden of God,' and was a created being. The Bible says that only God, Adam, Eve and Satan were present in the garden of Eden. In Ezekiel 28:14 and 16 it is stated that the person addressed was a cherub, which is a type of angel. From these hints, it seems that the real person being described in Ezekiel. 28:11–18 is an angel imaged in an earthly king. The point of similarity between the earthly king of Tyre and the angel is a problem of pride.

According to the story, one of the created angels of God was apparently a guard near the throne of God (Ezek. 28:14). This angel was created very beautiful and very wise, but became very corrupt as a result of pride (Ezek. 28:17). In the New Testament, the Holy Spirit revealed through the Apostle Paul in 1 Timothy 3:6 that the fall and condemnation of Satan came about through his conceit (arrogant pride). Putting this evidence together, there is a strong suggestion that the real person being described in Ezekiel 28:11–18 is Satan, although he is not identified by this name in the passage.

How did this angel become so consumed with pride? According to the story, he began to think about the great beauty and wisdom God had given him at his creation (Ezek. 28:13,17). Perhaps he began to think more about himself than about God, and thus he became conceited. As his conceit grew, he began to worship himself instead of worshipping God. We learn from Jesus' encounter with Satan in the wilderness (Matt. 4:1) that Satan's real desire was to have God (Christ) worship him (Matt. 4:9)! It seems that Satan had literally gone insane because of pride. He wanted God to worship him, the creature, instead of him worshipping God, the creator!

In Isaiah 14:12–14 there is a passage very similar to Ezekiel 28:11–18. This passage is addressed to the king of Babylon, but again seems to apply to someone more than the king of Babylon, with similar ambitious pride. In Isaiah 14:12 a person identified as Lucifer, 'morning star, son of the dawn', is revealed to have an ambition to rule all the angels and to make himself like God (Isa. 14:13–14). There seems to be a strong possibility that Ezekiel 28:11–18 and Isaiah 14:12–14 are talking about the same angel, and that this angel is Satan.

Perhaps Satan thought about what a magnificent and wise creature he was, as worthy of worship and leadership as God is. Perhaps he thought why God's angels shouldn't worship and follow him, instead of worshipping and following God. If this was true, Isaiah revealed the inner thoughts of Satan when he wrote that the angel said to himself, 'I will raise my throne above the stars (angels) of God . . . I will make myself like the Most High' (Isa. 14:13,14). Because of his pride, this angel planned a coup against God!

Through his pride and his carefully planned decision to rebel against God, Satan seems to have introduced evil into the universe. Pride was the root from which all other sins came. Why? Because pride puts self first, and hence leads to rebellion against God. Rebellion against God cuts a person off from the life and holiness of God. God is the source of all life, goodness, and holiness. The absence of life is death. The absence of good is evil. The absence of God's holiness is sin. Satan's rebellion created the conditions for evil and sin to develop in the universe. Thus the pride and conceit of Satan led to the existence of evil and death.

Satan's deliberate choice to rebel against God was the most terrible event in history. God is the source of life and of all that is good and holy. When Satan chose to rebel, he separated himself from God. By doing this, he separated himself from the only One who could continue to make him holy and good. Satan's decision was a dreadful act of self-destruction. That is why the Bible says, 'Pride goes before destruction' (Prov. 16:18). Foolish human beings who choose to worship themselves instead of God and to rebel against God as Satan did, will end up destroying themselves as Satan did. In addition, they will share in Satan's final punishment in hell (Matt. 25:41).

Without God's holiness and life, Satan became corrupt and evil, and died spiritually. A simple illustration may help explain how this happened. A mango will grow into a beautiful and delicious piece of fruit as long as it remains connected to the branch of the tree. When it is removed from the branch it is cut off from the life-giving sap of the tree and it slowly begins a process of decay. After a while, the process of decay causes the mango to rot and smell bad. Eventually it dies completely and changes into lifeless waste. This process of decay and death applies to all living things when life is removed.

In a spiritual sense, this is what happened to Satan and the angels who rebelled with him. Life is a gift from God. Separation from God results in death. Once Satan and other rebel angels were cut off from the life and holiness of God, they became totally evil and corrupt. The same is true for human beings and their separation from God through the sin of Adam and Eve. The world is in a great mess because of sin and rebellion against God. Jesus said that Satan, the enemy, is the father of lies and a murderer (John 8:44). This statement reveals the terrible consequences of Satan's pride and willful rebellion against God.

Satan's consuming desire now is to deceive and destroy (1 Pet. 5:8). He has become the enemy of God, the enemy of God's people, and the enemy of all that is holy and good. He will attempt to destroy anyone he can, although he cannot act without God's knowledge and permissive will (Job 1:6–19, Job 2:1–6, Luke 22:31). When Christ returns to this world, Satan will be thrown into the lake of burning sulphur and will be tormented for ever and ever (Rev. 20:10). The eternal fire was created as punishment for Satan and his fallen angels (Matt. 25:41).

From what has been said, it should be clear why God says again and again in the Bible that he hates pride (Prov. 6:16–17; Prov. 8:13). God says pride goes before destruction (Prov. 16:18). It is because of pride that evil first entered the universe through Satan. It is because of pride that the Pharisees rejected Christ and planned his murder (Matt. 26:4, John 7:1). Jesus stated that these Pharisees were children of Satan (John 8:44). He said they would not escape the punishment of hell (Matt. 23:33). It is because of pride that people still turn away from God today and go their own foolish way to destruction.

B. HOW DID OTHER ANGELS BECOME INVOLVED IN SATAN'S REBELLION?

It is worth considering for a moment how the rebellion of the other angels probably came about. The Bible does not tell us directly, but it does offer some clues. As with Satan, pride may likely have been involved. Perhaps under Satan's suggestion, they wanted to gain a higher position than God had assigned to them.

The fall of other angels is mentioned in 2 Peter 2:4, Jude 6, and Revelation 12:4. In Revelation 12:4, it is stated that the dragon (i.e. Satan cf. Rev. 12:9) swept away a third of the stars (angels) with him. Apparently a third of the angels in heaven were deceived into rebellion against God by Satan's strategy. Early Jewish rabbis identified the angelic rebellion mentioned in Jude 6, and 2 Peter 2:4, with the events described in Genesis 6:1–4. Here the 'sons of God' married the 'daughters of men.' The 'sons of God' may refer to angels according to Job 1:6, Job 2:1 and Job 38:7. If this is true, then these 'marriages' were unlawful relationships between fallen angels and human beings resulting in a generation of monstrous and very evil human beings. Such an idea may be suggested in Genesis 6:4–5. This would explain why God decided to destroy all mankind with the flood except for the family of Noah.

Someone may well ask the question how Satan could possibly have thought he could succeed in opposing God? The answer is not given in the Bible but perhaps there is a hint in the story of King David's son, Absalom. Absalom tried to overthrow his own father, King David. The method of Absalom was to draw away the hearts of the Israelites by making attractive promises to them (2 Sam. 15:3–6). There is a suggestion in Ezekiel 28:16 that Satan may have done something like this. Absalom also cast doubt in the minds of the Israelites about David's character (2 Sam. 15:4). Did Satan have a similar plan to cast doubt in the minds of the angels about God's character? He certainly tried to create doubt about God's character with Eve in the garden of

Eden (Gen. 3:3–5). Perhaps Satan thought that if he could draw away the hearts of enough angels, he could rob God of the loyalty of his angels.

It seems quite possible that Satan used the same strategy with the angels who fell into rebellion as he used in the garden of Eden with man. Satan's strategy in the garden of Eden was to lure Adam and Eve away from obedience to God by deception and lies about God (Gen. 3:4–6).

Having been close to the throne of God, Satan must have understood, better than we do, the great heart of love which God has for all his creatures. He certainly knew that God's love was unchanging. He probably counted on the idea that because of his love for his creatures, God would not use violent force to bring him and other angels back if they rebelled.

It is a fact that God does not use ruthless force or violence to gain the obedience of his creatures. He made us, and he wants us to love him by our own choice (Deut. 6:5). God knows it will be good for us to obey him (Deut. 6:24). He wants our love and fellowship to come from a heart of appreciation to him as our creator. He wants us to love him for who he is, not because we are forced to love him. In this sense, human parents reflect the heart of God as a Father when they desire the same free choice of obedience from their children. They know it will be good for their children to choose to love and obey them as parents.

C. WHO CONTROLS THE PRESENT WORLD SYSTEM OF VALUES?

With his great army of fallen angels, Satan set up an invisible rebel movement in this world. The present world system of values is not God's will. It is Satan's will. Satan is now called the 'prince' of this world by Christ (John 12:31, John 16:11) and the 'god' of this world by Paul (2 Cor. 4:4). In this capacity he controls the present world system of values. Since the present world system of values is under the control of Satan and other evil angels, Christians are warned that they must not love (desire) the world. If they love the world, the love of God the Father is not in them (1 John 2:15). The present world system is based on pride, selfishness, lust and greed (1 John 2:16).

Satan is called the devil, meaning accuser or slanderer (of the people of God). Satan accuses the people of God in the presence of God (Job 1:8–11; 2:3–5, Rev. 12:10). He probably does this so that God will be required by his justice to bring punishment on his own people whom he loves (Heb. 2:2; 10:26,27). Satan is also called the 'evil one' (Matt. 13:19), the 'tempter' (Matt. 4:3) and the 'ruler of the kingdom of the air' (Eph. 2:2).

There is a suggestion both in Scripture and from history, that Satan may use his power to influence the leadership of both political nations and tribal groups (Dan. 10:13,20). It is likely that evil angels seek to influence nations and tribes of people for evil purposes. The Bible refers to these evil angels as 'spiritual forces of evil' in Ephesians 6:12 and 'the power and authorities' in Colossians 2:15. Evidence of demonic influence can be seen in the evil practices of some traditional religions and in the demonic behaviour of some governments. Such behaviour has been seen in the twentieth century in the ghastly killing of six million Jews by the Nazi government of Germany in World War II, by the ethnic genocide in the former Yugoslavia, and in the tribal slaughters of Rwanda. Hitler, the evil leader of the Nazi government, was deeply involved with Satan through his involvement with occult persons in his secret service.

From the preceding discussion, we have come to understand that the governments of this world are influenced by a vast host of evil angels, who control the world system of values under Satan. However, a much greater number of holy angels, who are fully obedient to God, have been given the task of caring for the people of God who live in this evil world (Psalm 103:20–21, Heb. 1:14). This should be a source of great encouragement to all who love the Lord.

D. WHAT IS THE ORIGIN OF NON-CHRISTIAN RELIGIONS?

Non-Christian religions have arisen in the world for a combination of reasons. The main reasons have probably been wrong concepts of reality, resulting from superstition and ignorance. These wrong ideas have been actively given to human minds through the deceiving lies of Satan and demons (1 Tim. 4:1).

Truth, however, eliminates superstition and deception just as light eliminates physical darkness. This is why Jesus said, 'I am the light of the world; he who follows me shall not walk in the darkness, but shall have the light of life' (John 8:12–NASB). Jesus was the light of the world because he came 'to bear witness to the truth' (John 18:37). Paul stated that Jesus had called him to preach to the Gentiles, 'to open their eyes and turn them from darkness to light, and from the power of Satan to God, so that they may receive forgiveness of sins and a place among those who are sanctified by faith in me' (Acts 26:18).

In the Old Testament, the pagan people who surrounded the Israelites had patron gods or goddesses who were known to them by name. For example, the Moabites worshiped a god they called Chemosh and the Ammonites worshipped a god they called Molech (1 Kings 11:7). The Philistines worshipped an agricultural god they called Dagon (Judges 16:23). The Sidonians worshipped a fertility goddess called Ashtoreth (1 Kings 11:15). The Assyrians worshipped a god they called Nisroch (2 Kings 19:36–37). These spirits often required evil practices, such as human sacrifice (Jer. 32:35) and sexual immorality (Jer. 2:20, Ezek. 16:25). It seems that each ethnic group had one or more traditional spirits whom they were required to worship and obey. Even God himself describes these pagan spirits as the particular 'gods' of each of these people (1 Kings 11:33).

To most people these gods may seem to be nothing more than pagan idolatry and superstition. However, God identified these traditional gods which were represented by idols, as demons. Note what God said about the Ammonite god Molech (Jer. 32:35), whom some Israelites had begun to follow, 'They mingled with the nations and adopted their customs. They worshipped their idols, which became a snare to them. They sacrificed their sons and their daughters to demons' (Psalm 106:35–37). Here God says that in making human sacrifices to Molech, the Israelites were in fact making sacrifices to demons. God reveals a demonic source behind superstitious idolatry.

Missionaries entering groups of people who have had no contact with Christ, often report severe conflict with demons, especially in the early days of their ministry. This supports the idea that demons seek to exercise influence or control over people, especially in the area of their religious beliefs. The Bible speaks about ideas and beliefs which have a demonic origin (1 Tim. 4:1). Beyond this, Satan (and very likely his demons) seeks to be worshipped (Matt. 4:9). This is one reason why God strictly forbids all the practices of pagan religion (Deut. 18:9–12). God says in Deuteronomy 32:16–17, 'They made him jealous with their foreign gods and angered him with their detestable idols. They sacrificed to demons which are not God.' This is the reason for the first commandment: 'You shall have no other gods before me' (Ex. 20:2).

Traditional African people know that certain spirits demand practices of ritual worship and obedience from the people under their influence. Sometimes these spirits have visually appeared to them with such demands, sometimes they have appeared in dreams, and sometimes they have communicated these demands through a possessed person or through a diviner. The evidence all points to the same fact that non-Christian religions involve contact with Satanic powers of darkness.

The origin of non-Christian religions involves superstition and ignorance. In addition there seem to be fallen angels (1 Tim. 4:1 cf., Col. 2:18) who seek the worship of people and seek to control their lives (Matt. 4:8–9). As many Africans know, evil spirits threaten men with sickness, tragedy and other punishments if they don't obey them.

Such demons are very clever in their deception. They deceive people by pretending to be divinities or the spirits of dead ancestors. Since people are supposed to respect divinities and the spirits of their ancestors, they obediently do what these deceiving spirits tell them to do. Note the warning which God gave to the Israelites about being deceived by such spirits: 'They have been led astray by false gods, the gods their ancestors followed' (Amos 2:4). It is significant that concern for the spirits of ancestors is found in non-Christian religions in many parts of the world. This is not surprising, because people feel a strong emotional attachment to their ancestors and relatives. Traditional religions throughout the world which seek the help of ancestral spirits, reveal a consistent pattern of belief which has very effectively deceived people. Such beliefs have kept many people from finding a personal, saving relationship with Jesus Christ.

It is significant that Jesus commanded that his gospel be brought to all nations of people (Matt. 29:19). The word for nations in this verse, *ethne*, refers primarily to ethnic groups with the same culture and language. For the plan of Christ's redemption to be completed on earth, Satan's control over every tribal group on earth must be broken by the power of the gospel. Therefore, making disciples from all groups of people on earth is a priority for the church. The church must finally include people from every tribe, tongue, and nation on earth (Matt. 28:19, Rev. 5:10; 7:9). The Great Commission will not be completed until believers have been discipled in every ethnic group.

E. WHAT ARE DEMONS?

Demons (evil spirits) are mentioned in many places in the Bible. Who are these evil spirits? In the teaching of some traditional religions, evil spirits are thought to be the spirits of long dead ancestors of evil character. What does the Bible have to say?

We learned in chapter six that at death God separates the spirits of the dead from the living. After death, human souls are restricted to a place where God has assigned them (Luke 16:19–31). Hence the idea that the spirits of long dead ancestors may still be around as evil spirits to influence or trouble people, does not find support in Scripture. This is important to understand, because God alone, not the teaching of traditional religion, can truthfully reveal to us the mysteries which surround physical death. God has revealed these mysteries in the Bible.

There are several theories about who demons are and where they come from. We learned in chapter ten that angels are a created order of spirits of various kinds (Col. 1:16). We have also learned that there was a rebellion by a large number of angels (Rev. 12:4). Among the various theories about who demons are and where they come from, it seems most likely that demons come from among the fallen angels who rebelled with Satan against God. In Matt. 12:24, the Pharisees accused Christ of casting out demons by Beelzebub, the prince of demons. In Matt. 12:26 Jesus replied by saying, 'If Satan drives out Satan, he is divided against himself.' Here Jesus identified Satan as the prince of demons. A similar comparison is found in Luke 10:17–18, where Christ described Satan as falling from heaven in the context of the disciples of Jesus casting out demons. Finally, in Revelation 12:7, Satan and his angels are described as fighting against Michael and his angels. Although we cannot be absolutely certain about it, these verses suggest that demons come from among the ranks of fallen angels.

The evil character of demons and their works is plainly taught in the Bible. As we have just seen, Satan is their ruler (Matt. 12:24–26). Hence there is no important difference whether we speak of the work of Satan or the work of demons. Just as God uses the holy angels to carry out his will, so Satan uses demons to carry out his plans.

F. WHAT ARE THE WORKS OF DEMONS, ACCORDING TO THE BIBLE?

The Bible has much to say about the activity of demons. An entire book could be written on this subject. In this book we will only summarize the types of activities in which demons engage. In chapter thirteen we will focus in more detail on several ways in which demons deceive millions of people who follow non-Christian religions and even deceive some Christians.

TYPES OF DEMON ACTIVITY

Deception: Probably the most widespread work of demons in the world is the work of lying and deceiving people. The works of demons are like the works of their leader, Satan. Jesus said that Satan was the father of lies (John 8:44). Thus demons also lie and persuade people to believe lies. They can do this by false suggestions just as people can communicate true or false suggestions to each other. When demons suggest false ideas or lies to our minds, we will probably think it is something we thought up ourselves. We will almost never realize that the suggestion came from a source outside our own minds. Because of this, the Bible warns us to, 'take captive every thought to make it obedient to Christ' (2 Cor 10:5). The way to do this, is to evaluate every idea or thought we have in the light of God's truth. Does it agree or disagree with what God says in the Bible? If it agrees with the word of God, we may accept it. If it does not agree with the word of God, we must reject it.

Demonic lies are often directed to the minds of people who are emotionally weak. Have you ever heard the lie which often comes to mind when you are having a serious problem – God doesn't love you; God doesn't care about your problems. This thought cannot come from God, because God loves human beings infinitely more than any person has ever loved another person. Such thoughts must therefore come either from our own sinful nature or from demons. In both cases we must reject such thoughts and replace them with the truth of God. What is the truth of God? The Bible says, 'For God so loved the world, that he gave his only begotten Son, that whosoever believeth in him should not perish, but have everlasting life' (John 3:16–KJV). In the Old Testament, God said, 'I have loved you with an everlasting love' (Jer. 31:3). The thought that God does not love us is a lie, whatever the source of that thought.

Some demonic lies are directed to large numbers of people, such as the teachings of false religions. The Bible says that demons promote false teaching (1 Tim. 4:1). Many people in Africa have been deceived by the false ideas of traditional religion and by false prophets who claim to speak from God. According to 1 Kings 22:22, the deception spoken by false prophets can come from lying spirits. One specific issue in false religion in many parts of the world has to do with beliefs about ancestors. We will take a closer look at this problem in chapter thirteen.

Demons can also lie through the lips (words) of a demonized person in order to deceive people. They will lie in order to promote false beliefs which will keep people from the truth of God. For example, some people are sure of the pre-existence of human souls because they witnessed a spirit speaking through a person to confirm that it was indeed the soul of a former human being. The spirit may have given accurate details of the former life. But how do we know that the spirit was not lying? The fact is, such spirits lie in order to deceive people, because Satan, their leader, is the father of lies (John 8:44). Because of this, the words of a spirit speaking through a demonized person's lips cannot be trusted. There is therefore no value in speaking with evil spirits who possess people and speak through their mouths. The power of lies can be very great indeed.

Murder: Jesus described Satan as a murderer (John 8:44). We may thus expect demons to bring violence, physical harm and death, if they are able to carry out their desires. One wonders how many crimes of murder, tribal wars, religious wars and national wars have been brought about in history by the suggestions of demons to the minds of men? In the gospels we see the Gerasene demoniac cutting himself with stones (Mark 5:5). We see a demon trying to physically kill a possessed boy by throwing him into the fire and into water (Mark 9:22). In Job, Satan or some of his demons brought a violent storm and killed ten of Job's children (Job 1:12,19).

In Africa are many known cases of curses placed on people who experienced violence, tragedy or death, just as in the story at the beginning of this chapter. Demons are certainly involved in such curses and tragedies. This is a very important reason why Jesus taught his followers to pray, 'deliver us from the evil one' (Matt. 6:13).

People are afraid of spirits. They have good reason to be afraid if they are not spiritually joined to Jesus Christ, who is the Lord of all spirits. This is an important reason why Christians must preach Christ as both Lord and Saviour. Only when people know the truth and the saving power of Christ as their Lord as well as their Saviour, can they be delivered from the fear of Satan and evil spirits.

Torture: Short of death, demons can torture people with partial handicaps, such as blindness, dumbness (Matt. 12:22), deformity (Luke 13:11–17), physical sickness (Job 2:7, Acts 10:38), and mental illness (Luke 8:27–29). How many people in mental hospitals today are suffering from demonic madness? How many people suffer from bitterness, resentment, depression, anger against God and other forms of mental torture because they believe and obey the lies of demons instead of believing and obeying the truth of God?

Sexual Uncleanness and Violence: Evil spirits in the Bible are often referred to as unclean spirits. The Greek word used for unclean, *akathartos*, means unclean, either in a ceremonial (ritual) way, or in the moral sense of being evil, sexually impure or vicious. In the New Testament, the word is primarily used to describe demons as vicious, evil, or sexually impure (Matt. 10:1, Mark 1:23; 7:25, Eph. 5:5). In Revelation 17:4, a closely related Greek word, *akathartees*, is specifically used to mean sexual uncleanness in relation to adultery. Immoral sex and vicious violence often occur together, as in the crime of rape. Violence and immoral sex are often seen together in films of the cinema industry. These facts suggest the presence of unclean demons.

Concerning possible demonic sexual impurity in the Bible, recall that Jesus cast seven demons out of Mary Magdalene (Luke 8:2), who had been a prostitute. King Solomon with his 1000 wives and concubines was clearly preoccupied with sex (Ecc. 2:8). This may be related to the fact that Solomon sinned against the Lord by participating in the pagan worship of Ashtoreth, the Sidonian female goddess of fertility, even building a shrine for her (2 Kings 23:13).

Sexual uncleanness is one part of life where demonic suggestion and temptation finds ready cooperation from the sinful heart of man. Surely the current preoccupation of North American and European culture with sex has a demonic shadow.

Influence in Human Governments: It is clear from the titles given to the fallen angels in Daniel 10:12–21, that demons attempt to influence and even control human governments for evil purposes (Rev. 16:14). The Bible says, 'the god of this age (Satan) has blinded the minds of unbelievers' (2 Cor. 4:4). This is probably an important reason why we are specifically commanded to pray for government leaders (1 Tim. 2:2). The prayers of God's people help to free the minds of these leaders from the strong suggestions being made to them by Satan and demons. When their minds are thus free from Satan's evil thoughts, such leaders will be able to hear the gentle voice of the Holy Spirit, who can give them wisdom to govern properly. We only bring harm on ourselves when we fail to pray for political leaders, whether they are Christians or not.

Hindrances to the Work of the Gospel: In 1 Thessalonians 2:18 Paul revealed that Satan effectively prevented him from making a journey he intended to make for the cause of Christ. A person does not have to be in the work of the gospel very long to realize that one is being seriously opposed by evil spirits (Eph. 6:12). For this reason, constant, persistent, faithful prayer is absolutely necessary, if the ministry of the gospel is to prosper.

Hindrances to Prayer: One of the most important ways in which demons oppose the servants of God is to hinder or delay answers to their prayers. Demons strongly oppose prayer, since prayer will bring their downfall. Recall how the evil angel opposed the answer to Daniel's prayer in Daniel 10:12–13, and how the apostles kept falling asleep when Jesus asked them to pray with him in the garden of Gethsemane (Matt. 26:38–43).

General Harassment of the People of God: Demons make it their business to harass, trouble, disturb, frustrate and discourage the people of God whenever they can. Paul revealed that a messenger of Satan was the source of his distress in 2 Corinthians 12:7. Jesus said that Satan demanded to sift Peter like wheat (Luke 22:31).

Promotion of Idolatry, Witchcraft and Various Pagan and Occult Practices: According to Scripture, idolatry is directly related to demonic influence (Psalm 106:35–37). The Bible indicates that demons are involved in urging people to participate in various non-Christian practices including traditional sacrifices, communication with the dead, divination, witchcraft and many other things (Deut. 18:9–12, Deut. 32:16–17, 1 Sam. 15:23, Rev. 18:2). The evil supernatural power exercised by witches and sorcerers must come from demons since it does not come from God.

The Working of Strange Occurrences and Deceiving Miracles: The history of mankind is full of strange stories about supernatural events which have no scientific explanation. Objects have been seen to move through a room by themselves. Spirits and ghosts have been seen and even photographed. Objects and even people, have suddenly burst into flame with no fire present. People under spirit possession have performed impossible feats of strength with no ill effect such as bending solid steel or enduring the pain of walking on burning coals at more than 1000 degrees Fahrenheit. How can such things happen? The Bible reveals to us that Satan and his demons have the power to perform deceiving miracles (2 Thess. 2:9, Rev. 16:13–14). Just as Jesus performed miracles so that men would believe in him and be saved (John 5:36; 10:38), so Satan and his demons also perform miracles in order to deceive people and to keep them from believing the truth about God.

Slandering and Accusing Christians Before God: Just as Satan is actively engaged in slandering and accusing Christians before God (Rev. 12:10), so it is very likely that demons assist him in this process, probably by gathering information for bringing charges against God's elect (Rom. 8:33,38–39).

SUMMARY

God, who is good and holy, created the universe. As part of his perfect creation, he created a great company of angels who were also good and holy. These angels were independent creatures with great intelligence and freedom of choice. One of these angels, a cherub close to the throne of God, became preoccupied with his own beauty, wisdom and importance and apparently decided to elevate himself in the sight of the other angels to become equal with God. It seems that he determined to draw the hearts of the other angels, and mankind, away from devotion to God.

When he cut himself off from God, the only source of goodness and holiness, he went insane because of his pride and became totally corrupt, evil and violent, demanding to be worshipped just as God is worshipped. Thus Lucifer introduced evil into God's perfect universe and became Satan, the enemy of God and of God's people. Satan also persuaded other angels to join him in his rebellion against God. This group of fallen angels set up an invisible rebel movement in the world. The false suggestions of demons are one of the reasons for non-Christian religions.

Some of the fallen angels appear to be demons which are very active in the world today. Demons give supernatural power to evil people like witches and sorcerers who use their power to harm other people. The work of demons can be recognized in religious deception, in the worldwide increase of crime (especially murder) and sexual immorality, in the cruelty and terrorism of some governments, in the power of witches and sorcerers, in the opposition that Christians experience in doing the Lord's work, and in many other kinds of evil in the world today. We are therefore taught by Jesus to pray, 'deliver us from the evil one' (Matt 6:13).

Christians should not be discouraged by this army of evil spirits in the world, because an even greater army of God's holy angels are assigned by God to help and protect God's children. In addition, every believer has God himself (the Holy Spirit) dwelling in his heart, and God's Spirit is incomparably more powerful than any evil spirit. When Christians understand their position in Christ, they can effectively oppose the evil work of demons through their prayers and by using the weapons of spiritual warfare.

DISCUSSION QUESTIONS AND PROJECTS BASED ON CHAPTER ELEVEN

1. Which sin in the heart of Satan led to all other sins? Give a Scripture reference.
2. What was the plan in Lucifer's heart according to Isaiah 14:13–14?
3. What was Satan's strategy in the garden of Eden to bring about the ruin of mankind?
4. The Bible says, 'Pride goes before destruction' (Prov. 16:18). Divide into smaller groups to discuss these questions:
   (a) How does pride lead to destruction?
   (b) What kinds of evil in African life can be traced to pride?
   (c) What is the relationship between tribalism and pride?
5. What are the spiritual weapons against Satan?
6. Have the group listen to the world news for one week. Then discuss and identify those world events which reflect the activity of Satan and evil angels.
7. On what evil values is the present world system based?
8. The devil is called 'the accuser of our brothers' (Rev. 12:10). About what would the devil accuse us before God? According to 1 John 1:9, what can a Christian do about these accusations?
9. Why are there non-Christian religions?
10. Divide into tribal groups. Each group should seek to identify those beliefs and practices in the traditional religion of their tribe which appear to come from demons.
11. Divide into smaller groups and let each group list as many types of deceptions by demons as they can.
12. Let the whole group discuss the nature of demonic fear and its extent in Africa. How should a Christian respond to this kind of fear?

SUGGESTED FOR FURTHER READING

Green, Michael. *I Believe in Satans' Downfall*. London: Hodder, 1995.

Hillstrom, Elizabeth L. *Testing the Spirits*. Downers Grove: InterVarsity Press, 1995.

Koch, Kurt. *Occult Bondage And Deliverance*. Grand Rapids, Michigan: Kregel, 1986.

12

Spiritual Warfare

'They went across the lake to the region of the Gerasenes. When Jesus got out of the boat, a man with an evil spirit came from the tombs to meet him. This man lived in the tombs, and no one could bind him any more, not even with a chain. For he had often been chained hand and foot, but he tore the chains apart and broke the irons on his feet. No one was strong enough to subdue him. Night and day among the tombs and in the hills he would cry out and cut himself with stones. When he saw Jesus from a distance, he ran and fell on his knees in front of him. He shouted at the top of his voice, "What do you want with me, Jesus, Son of the Most High God? Swear to God that you won't torture me!" For Jesus had said to him, "Come out of this man, you evil spirit!" Then Jesus asked him, "What is your name?" "My name is Legion," he replied, "for we are many." And he begged Jesus again and again not to send them out of the area. A large herd of pigs was feeding on the nearby hillside. The demons begged Jesus, "Send us among the pigs; allow us to go into them." He gave them permission, and the evil spirits came out and went into the pigs. The herd, about two thousand in number, rushed down the steep bank into the lake and were drowned' (Mark 5:1–13).

The doctor and his companion were the first two missionaries ever to enter the rainforest village. There was no church among these people and there were no Christians among them. The two men had a local companion who was able to translate for them. Through their translator the two men asked the chief if they could stay in the village for some days to tell the people some stories about God and his love for them. The chief agreed, and each man was given a small separate building to spend the night in. Each room had an opening for a door and an opening for a window. As the men lay down to sleep they were both excited about finally arriving in this place for which they had been praying so many days. They could not sleep because of their excitement. It was a bright moonlit night.

They could see clearly in their rooms because the light of the moon shone in through the door- and window-openings.

Suddenly the doctor felt two strong-as-steel cold hands grasping him by the throat, choking him to death. He immediately reached back to grab the strangling hands and shake himself loose, but there was nothing to grab! The hands tightened their grip. He could see that there was no one in the room. Gasping for breath, he choked out the name JESUS, and immediately the hands released their grip. The next morning while eating breakfast, the doctor related his experience to his companion. His companion looked at him in astonishment and proceeded to relate his own identical experience. The two men bowed their heads and thanked the Lord for his protection.

As Christians we are engaged in a spiritual war. This war can become very intense when the servants of God attempt to take the gospel of Christ to people who are bound by Satan. The above true story from Malaysia is similar to other stories which have accompanied the preaching of the gospel to unreached people throughout the world. The Christian is opposed by the demons of Satan in many different ways (Eph. 6:12–13).

Sometimes the opposition comes in the form of negative thoughts and discouragement. Sometimes the opposition comes in the form of temptation. Sometimes the opposition comes in the form of severe health, family or emotional problems. Sometimes the opposition comes in the form of great political and economic trouble in the country, or in crime, violence or war.

Whatever the means, opposition from Satan and his demons is real and can be both discouraging and dangerous. There are two other strong enemies which the Christian must face in his spiritual life. Perhaps the most discouraging enemy is right within himself. It is the weakness and corruption of his own sinful nature. The Apostle Paul said, 'I know that nothing good lives in me, that is, in my sinful nature. . . . the evil I do not want to do – this I keep on doing' (Rom. 7:18–19). Further, the Christian is daily surrounded by the corrupt values of the present world system which encourages pride, selfishness, greed, and lust.

The spiritual war is not a game. The world holds a strong attraction for us, our sinful human nature is corrupt, and Satan is a cruel and powerful enemy. We must take this war seriously if we are to overcome the three enemies of God's people. These enemies are the world, the flesh, and the devil. How is a Christian to win against such enemies? In this chapter we will consider the following questions:

A. How can a Christian overcome the downward pull of his sinful nature?

B. How can a Christian overcome the temptations of the world?
C. How can a Christian overcome the attacks of Satan?
D. What are the weapons of spiritual warfare and how are we to use them?

A. HOW CAN A CHRISTIAN OVERCOME THE DOWNWARD PULL OF HIS SINFUL NATURE?

How does the Bible say we are to deal with our corrupt human nature and its sinful desires (the lusts of the flesh)? The answer is to stop doing something and to start doing something in order to overcome our sinful tendencies. The power to make these changes will not come from ourselves. It can only come from the Holy Spirit who lives in every Christian. By the power of the Holy Spirit we must stop doing the things which are wrong. By the power of the Holy Spirit we must start doing the things which are right. We must learn how to replace sinful behaviour with what God wants us to do.

If a person stops doing what is wrong but does not replace his corrupt behaviour with godly behaviour, he will soon go back even more deeply into the same sins. An example of this is the drunkard who decides to give up drinking. He gives it up for a while but he does not replace his drinking habit with a godly substitute. Sooner or later he will go back to drinking even more severely. This is the meaning behind the story Jesus told in the gospels, of a man from whom an evil spirit departed. When the evil spirit left the man it found no home. Soon it returned to the man with seven other spirits worse than the first one (Matt. 12:43–45). The spirit found that the man's house (his soul) had been swept clean (Matt. 12:44). But the man's soul had not been filled with better things. So eight evil spirits moved in instead of the original one.

A specific example of how to replace sinful actions with godly actions is given in Ephesians 4:28. This verse says, 'He who has been stealing must steal no longer, but must work, doing something useful with his own hands, that he may have something to share with those in need.' The thief must stop stealing. But if he is to overcome the downward pull of his sinful desire to steal, he must replace stealing with something godly. He must start working with his hands and then share the benefit of his work with those in need. By doing this, the sinful habit of stealing will finally be broken. God will give the former thief lasting joy in helping others. The brief, guilty pleasure of stealing will be replaced with the lasting, joyful pleasure of helping those in need.

The principle of replacing sinful behaviour with godly behaviour is the only way to permanently overcome sinful habits. The principle is stated in six words in Psalm 34:14. This verse says, 'Turn from evil and do good.' With careful thought, prayer and counsel, this verse can be applied to every kind of weakness in our sinful nature.

For example, every young man struggles with sexual desires. How may this principle be applied to overcome the temptation of lust and sexual immorality? The answer is found in the story of Joseph in the book of Genesis. Joseph was a young man. He was severely tempted to commit sin. The wife of Potiphar, the captain of Pharaoh's guard, begged Joseph again and again to sleep with her (Gen. 39:1–16). How many young men have had a woman beg them over and over to sleep with her?

The temptation was very strong for Joseph. He was strong and handsome (Gen. 39:6). He was not married. He was very far from home. No one knew or cared about him in Egypt. His brothers had sold him as a slave and abandoned him (Gen. 37:28). Potiphar's wife was attracted to Joseph and invited him to come to bed with her (Gen. 39:7). Who would know? Who would care?

The principle of Psalm 34:14 as applied to lust is found in 2 Timothy 2:22. This verse says, 'flee from youthful lusts, and pursue righteousness, faith, love and peace, with those who call on the Lord from a pure heart.' A man must flee (run away) from lust. He must physically remove himself from the temptation. This could mean leaving a cinema, throwing away a magazine with the wrong kind of pictures, or refusing to be alone in the dark with a girl who is not his wife. But a man must also do something righteous to replace his temptation. He must begin to actively pursue righteousness, faith, love, and peace with others. In principle, Joseph did these two things.

Although Joseph never read 2 Timothy 2:22, he followed the same two principles. He literally ran away from Potiphar's wife (Gen. 39:12). Why did he do that? The reason can be found in his statement to the woman: 'How then could I do such a wicked thing and sin against God?' (Gen. 39:9). Evidently Joseph wanted to please God more than he wanted to please himself. He was willing to deny himself in order to be pure before God. As it is stated in 2 Timothy 2:2, he had determined to pursue righteousness, as one who called upon God from a pure heart.

Deuteronomy 6:5 says, 'Love the Lord your God with all your heart, and with all your soul, and with all your strength.' Joseph had determined to love the Lord his God with all his heart. Joseph wanted God's blessing and fellowship more than he wanted short-lived pleasure. He wanted to be sure God would answer his prayers more than he wanted to enjoy sin for a few minutes. He replaced his immediate desire for pleasure with his long-term desire for God's blessing on his life.

The Holy Spirit can give a young man the strength to be pure. Part of the fruit of the Holy Spirit is self-control (Gal. 5:23). The power of the Holy Spirit can give a young man the willingness to 'flee youthful lusts' (2 Tim. 2:22). But fleeing youthful lusts is not enough. There must be a desire to live your life for something greater than personal pleasure. The willingness to say no to one's own desires comes from having a greater desire to please God than to please yourself. This is what it means 'to love the Lord your God with all your heart' (Deut. 6:5).

The Holy Spirit will give us the desire to please God more than ourselves if we are serious about being like Christ (Psalm 119:9–10, Phil. 2:13). He will give a devoted Christian a greater desire to honour the Lord than to satisfy his or her own desires. It was God who gave Joseph the strength to resist this great temptation because Joseph was willing to deny his own desires in order to please God.

B. HOW CAN A CHRISTIAN OVERCOME THE TEMPTATIONS OF THE WORLD?

The world's system of values is based on pride, selfishness, lust and greed (covetousness). How does God say we are to deal with the world's system of values? As with our sinful nature, the Bible tells us to stop doing something, and to start doing something. We must 'turn from evil, and do good.' The Bible says, 'Do not love the world, or anything in the world. If anyone loves the world, the love of the Father is not in him' (1 John 2:15). We must stop setting our hearts on the things of the world. How can we do that? Only if we start setting our hearts on something different, something better.

The Bible says, 'Since then you have been raised with Christ, set your hearts on things above, where Christ is seated at the right hand of God' (Col. 3:1). We must start setting our hearts on the enduring things of God such as growing in godly character, helping others, showing kindness and generosity, praying, telling people about Christ and serving God in various ways. These are the 'things above'.

When we are busy helping and encouraging others, we will not be concerned with running after the things of this world. God will give greater satisfaction and joy in serving him than we could ever find in serving ourselves. The reason why so many people in the world are so unhappy is that they spend all their time and strength trying to please themselves instead of trying to please God and serving others. God made us to find our highest pleasure in pleasing him and in helping others, not in pleasing ourselves.

Covetousness is closely related to lust. We lust because our natural desires have been corrupted by sin. We covet because we see things with our eyes and want to have them. Our values and desires have been corrupted by the value system of the world around us. The world tells us to get everything we can and to forget about other people and their problems. God says, 'Give and it will be given to you. A good measure, pressed down, shaken together and running over, will be poured into your lap' (Luke 6:38). How are we to be set free from loving the things of the world? The answer is to replace our desire for the things of this world with a desire for the things of God. We must discover that there is more pleasure in serving God than there is in serving ourselves.

The world says that to be happy, you must be important, you must preserve your pride, and you must be greater than others. Jesus said, 'Not so with you. Instead, whoever wants to become great among you must be your servant, and whoever wants to be first must be your slave – just as the Son of Man did not come to be served, but to serve, and to give his life as a ransom for many' (Matt. 20:26–28). The proof that the value system of this world is a deceptive lie from Satan can be discovered by examining the lives of some immoral, rich people, such as many actors and actresses in the cinema industry. These people have more wealth, fame and pleasure than most people in the world. Yet, their personal lives are an unhappy mess. Their lives are often destroyed by marital unfaithfulness, divorce, drinking and suicide. God did not make human beings to live for selfish pleasure, but to glorify him by living to serve God and others.

To overcome the temptations of the world we must deliberately choose to follow God's value system. The important question is: On what have we set our hearts? Have we set our hearts on accumulating money, education, and earthly importance or have we set our hearts on serving God and showing his kindness to others? If we are to overcome pride, greed and selfishness in our hearts, we must reject the value system of the ungodly world around us and choose to follow the value system set forth in the Bible. That is the meaning of Colossians 3:1, 'Set your heart on things above, where Christ is.'

C. HOW CAN A CHRISTIAN OVERCOME THE ATTACKS OF SATAN?

As if the attraction of the world's value system and the downward pull of our sinful natures were not enough problems for the Christian, we are also faced with deadly enemies in the persons of Satan and his vicious demons. The Bible says Satan goes about, 'like a roaring lion, seeking someone to devour' (1 Pet. 5:8–NASB).

Every Christian will almost certainly be tempted by Satan or his demons at some time in his or her life. He or she may also be directly attacked by Satan or his evil angels. How does the Bible say we are to deal with Satan? In order to answer this question we must first understand where Satan gets his power. We learn from Colossians 2:15 that evil angels were 'disarmed' when Jesus was crucified. How were they 'armed' before the cross? The answer is given in Colossians 2:14 where it says that Christ, 'cancelled the written code, with its regulations that was against us.'

Like the prosecutor before a judge, prepared with his case against the accused criminal, Satan and his demons were armed with a record of our sins against God (the 'written code'). As the one who accuses people before God (Rev. 12:10), the weapon of Satan against mankind is his legal demand that human beings be judged and punished by God for their sins. Satan demands this because he knows we have earned God's condemnation and judgment by breaking the laws of God. Colossians 2:14 says the 'code' consists of the laws of God which we have broken. The penalty for our sins prescribed in the 'regulations', is death. The Bible says, 'the wages of sin is death' (Rom. 6:23). Satan had a lawful right to accuse us before God. Because God is just and holy, God was required to accept this accusation and to punish us according to his justice.

When Jesus came he took the death penalty for our sins on the cross (Heb. 2:9) so that, 'through death, he might render powerless him who had the power of death, that is the devil' (Heb. 2:14–NASB). The basis for Satan's accusations against us was removed by Jesus' death on the cross for those who believe in Christ. That is why the Bible says, 'They overcame him (Satan) by the blood of the lamb' (Rev. 12:11). Romans 8:1 says, 'Therefore, there is now no condemnation for those who are in Christ Jesus.' Those who are in Christ by faith, are eternally saved (John 5:24; 10:28)

But Satan is a clever enemy. He knows that even though he does not have the power to snatch Christians out of the mighty hand of God (John 10:28), he can tempt Christians to continue to sin after they have believed in Christ. If we continue to sin we will have to be disciplined for those sins in this present life (Heb. 2:2). The writer of Hebrews warns us, 'For if we go on sinning wilfully after receiving the knowledge of the truth, there no longer remains a sacrifice for sins, but a certain terrifying expectation of judgment, and the fury of a fire which will consume the adversaries' (Heb. 10:26,27–NASB).

Satan knows this fact well, therefore he and his demons make it their business to tempt Christians to continue to sin. When we continue to sin after putting our faith in Christ, Satan continues to accuse us before God for these sins (Rev. 12:10). Satan demands that we be disciplined according to God's justice (Heb. 10:26–27). By doing this Satan can gain a legal right to attack the Christian. This happened in the case of the immoral man mentioned in 1 Corinthians 5:1–5. The Bible says that because this church member refused to turn away from his immorality Paul delivered him over to the power of Satan to discipline him for his sin (1 Cor. 5:5). He did not lose his salvation (1 Cor. 5:5), but he could have lost his physical life in Satan's savage attack.

From this example we can see that the realm of Satan's power is sin and rebellion against God. This is one reason why the Bible has so much to say about a life of personal holiness. If Christians willingly participate in sin, they give Satan 'a foothold' in their lives (Eph. 4:27).

Concerning the unforgiving servant in Matthew 18:21–35, Jesus clearly stated that he was 'handed over to the torturers' (NASB). This must certainly include demons, who delight in torturing people, as we saw in chapter eleven. It is therefore very important for Christians to continue to confess their sins and failures, so that they can be forgiven. With this, the basis for Satan's accusations and attacks against them is removed (Prov. 28:13). The Bible says, 'If we confess our sins, he is faithful and just and will forgive us our sins and purify us from all unrighteousness' (1 John 1:9).

From this discussion it is clear that the basis for Satan's power and activity is sin. Sin is disobedience to God, and Satan was the original rebel against God. If a Christian participates in wilful sin, he opens himself up to the attack of Satan and his demons. This is one reason why many Christians seem to be bound by sinful habits and attitudes, such as resentment and unforgiveness. They can be free from these if they are willing to confess and renounce their sins and receive God's forgiveness. By this they will overcome Satan's influence over them. The Bible says, 'He who conceals his sins does not prosper, but whoever confesses and renounces them finds mercy' (Prov. 28:13).

To have victory over Satan's attacks, we must stop doing something and start doing something. The key to victory over Satan is found in James 4:7. This verse says, 'Submit yourselves, then, to God. Resist the devil and he will flee from you.' The first part says we must submit ourselves to God. In the words of Psalm 34:14, we must 'turn from evil'. We must obey the word of God. Only then can we resist Satan with God's authority.

To overcome the temptation of Satan in the wilderness, Jesus first submitted himself to God the Father by choosing to obey the word of God rather than his own desires. This is why he repeatedly quoted Scripture and said, 'It is written. . .' (Matt. 4:4,7,10). It was only after Jesus had submitted his will to the word of God that he was in a position to resist Satan and to order him to leave (Matt. 4:10). A Christian must do the same thing if he is to resist Satan and to order him to leave, by God's authority.

When we submit ourselves to God, Satan loses the basis of his power over us, which is our sin and rebellion against God. Satan got victory in the lives of Adam and Eve because he persuaded them to rebel against God. Without submission to the Lord, a Christian will be unprotected from Satan's attacks. On the other hand, when we submit to God and his word, we have the delegated authority of Christ to stand against Satan and his demons (Luke 10:19, Eph. 6:11–18). A true story from Zambia will illustrate this.

> *One Saturday our Christian group was having a time of fellowship when a girl began to manifest demons by the characteristic screaming. Her eyes were white and clear, but as soon as the demons manifested themselves, her eyes turned bloodshot, red, and her facial expression became abnormal. Her voice also changed. We took her to another room to pray for her. After a few minutes we stopped, as we often did in a situation where we saw no results. The Lord gave us a word of wisdom (1 Cor. 12:8), and told us that she was holding on to many things. When we asked her, she said she had some medicines (of witchcraft) at home. We agreed to meet the following day after fasting.*
>
> *The following day when we went to her flat, we asked her about the medicines so that we could burn it (Acts 19:19). She collected it all and filled a big bag. Then, after two minutes of praying, she was set free.*

The situation with non-Christians is different. While true Christians are owned by Christ for eternity, non-Christians are the lawful property of Satan. They have no personal relationship with Christ. They are therefore the slaves of Satan whether they are aware of it or not. Non-Christians can only find freedom from this slavery by repenting and putting their faith in the Lord Jesus Christ. That is why Jesus told the Jews, 'If therefore the Son shall make you free, you shall be free indeed' (John 8:36). Only Jesus can release people from the control of sin, death, and bondage to Satan.

DIRECT ATTACK BY DEMONS

A Christian is not helpless in the face of a direct satanic attack (Eph. 6:13). What is the Christian to do when confronted with a direct attack by demons as in the opening story of this chapter? For beyond temptation, Satan sometimes has power, under God's sovereign permission, to attack believers, as Satan attacked Job (Job 1; 2) and Paul (2 Cor. 12:7). In such situations, Christians have been given a position of authority over Satan and his demons (Eph. 1:19–22, Eph. 2:6). Jesus told his disciples, 'I have given you authority . . . to overcome all the power of the enemy' (Luke 10:19). This included the authority to cast out demons (Luke 9:1, Luke 10:17).

When we consider direct spiritual conflict with Satan and demons, we must avoid two extreme viewpoints. First, some Christians are inclined to blame every difficulty on Satan, and so they become preoccupied with casting out demons. This viewpoint is unbalanced and unbiblical. The truth is that our sinful natures are responsible for the majority of our problems (Rom. 7:14–23). Sins must be confessed and renounced (Prov. 28:13). However, the reality of Satan greatly adds to the problems we already have because of our sinful natures.

Second, some Christians fail to recognize Satan's presence and activity, especially in opposing the Lord's work. Many Christians have the idea that, because Satan was legally defeated at the cross of Christ, he is no longer active or powerful in the world. That is simply not true. Such people do not understand how serious the spiritual battle with Satan really is. As a result they do not recognize the satanic source of many problems and therefore do not know how to deal with them. Christians, especially missionaries who are trying to bring the gospel to the unreached, are often fiercely attacked by demons. Sometimes they seem helpless to defend themselves. What can a Christian do about such attacks?

Ephesians 6:13 speaks about the need to take up the full armour of God. When the servants of God are directly attacked or resisted by demons, they need to know how to confront these spirits and to resist them, in the same way as Jesus drove off Satan in the wilderness temptation (Matt. 4:10). This situation is called a power encounter. It is an encounter between the power of God and the power of Satan. An example of an important power encounter occurred in the Old Testament when Moses came against the pagan priests of Egypt with their demonic magic (Ex. 7:11). With the rod of God which turned into a snake, God defeated these demonic powers (Ex.7:12). Another occasion involved Elijah's confrontation with the pagan priests of Baal on Mount Carmel. In this situation God defeated the powers of darkness in the activity of the priests of Baal, through Elijah's prayer (1 Kings 18:21–40).

In the New Testament, Paul pronounced God's judgment of blindness on the false Jewish prophet, Elymas, for hindering the preaching of the gospel (Acts 13:10–12). He also cast a demon out of a fortune-telling girl in Philippi who was hindering the preaching of the gospel (Acts 16:16–18).

Christians have Christ's power over Satan and his evil angels because they are spiritually joined to Christ, as stated in 1 Corinthians 12:27. This places Christians in a position of authority above all principalities and powers of darkness (Eph. 1:20–21; 2:6). The Bible says we are the ambassadors of Christ, imploring people to be reconciled to God (2 Cor. 5:20). An ambassador is the official representative of his government in another country. We are the official representatives of Jesus Christ in this world. When speaking on official business, an ambassador speaks for the head of state of his own country. In such official statements his words have the same authority as the words of the head of his government. The church speaks for

God in this world. The words of God's people, when in agreement with the Bible, have the authority of God himself (Matt. 18:18–20).

In Luke 10:17, the 70 followers of Christ seemed surprised to find that this delegated authority of Christ was real and that demons were subject to them in Jesus' name. By this delegated authority Christians have authority to cast out demons (Matt. 12:29; 18:18–20, Luke 10:19). There are occasions in spiritual warfare when a serious problem will not be solved until the demons involved are cast out in the name of Jesus (Acts 16:18). This is especially true when the gospel is being brought to a people group for the very first time. Satan does not give up his territory without a fight.

It may also be necessary to cast out demons where they have gained a stronghold in a person's life due to demon-related pagan or occult practices, sinful addictions, or abuse in childhood. In such cases it is very important to remember that Satan has power because of sin and rebellion against God. Unless people are willing to confess and renounce the sin in their lives, it is useless, and often very dangerous (Acts 19:16), to cast out demons. Demons know who they own, and will only give up their hold on those who sincerely renounce their sins. Concerning child abuse, it is significant that some of the demonized people whom Jesus helped, were children (Mark 9:17–21).

Direct conflict with Satan and demons can be a deadly and dangerous business (Acts 19:14–16). It is best not undertaken by individual Christians, but rather by the whole church or by a group of Christians together. The group should pray for the situation and all the people concerned, continually calling on the Lord for his protection and his deliverance (Psalm 50:15, Matt. 6:13). All known sin in the group should be confessed and forsaken. The group can divide into two so that one part can continue to pray while the other part casts out the demons. Christians involved in casting out demons should sing songs of praise to the Lord (Psalm 96:1–9). Demons cannot endure an environment of praise to Jesus because the Lord is present where his people praise him (Psalm 22:3, Matt. 18:20).

SPIRITUAL WEAPONS FOR SPIRITUAL WARFARE

In order to fight a spiritual war, Christians must use spiritual weapons. Physical weapons are useless in such a war. A tragic example in history of trying to fight a spiritual war with physical weapons, was the Crusades. The Crusades were wars fought between European Christian knights (soldiers) and Muslim forces in the Holy Land (Palestine) from 1095 AD to 1272 AD. The Christians thought they should use military force to drive the Muslims out of Jerusalem because it was the Holy Land of Christ. These wars lasted for 177 years with many deaths on both sides. In the end, there were no Muslim converts to Christianity and Jerusalem was again in the hands of the Muslims. To this day Muslims are bitter against Christians because of the Crusades. What can we learn from this?

The European knights made a great mistake in trying to fight a spiritual war with physical weapons. Some Christians do not learn from history and try to do the same things today. When they do, the tragic results are the same because it is not the will of God for Christians to use physical weapons to destroy the enemies of God. Instead, Christians are told to pray for their enemies (Matt. 5:44).

When Peter tried to use a physical weapon to defend Jesus, the Lord told him to put away his sword (John 18:10–11). When Jesus was surrounded by his enemies he did not use physical force to oppose them, although he could have easily done so. We do well to listen to the words of Christ to Peter, 'Put your sword back in its place, for all who draw the sword will die by the sword' (Matt. 26:52).

The reason why physical weapons are useless in a spiritual war is because the real enemies are not people of flesh and blood, but spiritual powers of wickedness (evil angels) (Ephesians 6:12).

D. WHAT ARE THE WEAPONS OF SPIRITUAL WARFARE AND HOW ARE WE TO USE THEM?

In a passage dealing specifically with spiritual warfare (Eph. 6:10–19), the spiritual weapons are listed as: truth, righteousness, the gospel of peace, faith, salvation, the word of God, and prayer

TRUTH

The Christian is told to put on the 'belt of truth' to counteract the lies of Satan (Eph. 6:14). If a Christian studies and understands the truth of God found in the Bible, he will be much less likely to be deceived by the lies of Satan in the world's system of values, in non-Christian religions and elsewhere.

RIGHTEOUSNESS

The Christian is told to put on the 'breastplate of righteousness' (Eph. 6:14) to protect his heart from the sin which tempts him. A Christian can only resist Satan with a clean and holy heart, submitted to God. This is just what Christ did in his wilderness encounter with Satan. He submitted himself to God by submitting to the Old Testament Scriptures (Matt. 4:4–10). Thus Christ put on the 'breastplate of righteousness' in his encounter with Satan.

From his position of submission to the Father, Jesus resisted Satan and cast him out (Matt. 4:10–11). Our prayers will not be answered by God unless they come from a clean heart (Isa. 59:1–2). If our hearts are not clean we can change that situation. The Bible says, 'If we confess our sins, he is faithful and just and will forgive us our sins, and purify us from all unrighteousness' (1 John 1:9).

THE GOSPEL OF PEACE

We are instructed to put on the shoes of the 'readiness that comes from the gospel of peace'. Shoes are used for walking, for going somewhere. The Christian is not simply to defend the faith or to protect himself from Satan. He is to actively take the gospel of peace to those who have no peace with God and no personal relationship with Christ.

FAITH

The Christian is told to take up the 'shield of faith' (Eph. 6:16) to stop the fiery arrows of Satan. Faith is a defensive weapon to protect us from the attacks of Satan. These fiery arrows may come in many forms. They may come as discouragements, bad news, problems, persecution, sickness, accidents, crime, disappointments, and many other ways. In every case, we are told to take the shield of faith to stop these arrows. We are to believe the promises of God instead of the doubts and fears which these problems bring into our minds when Satan attacks us.

Our faith may be strengthened in several ways. Romans 10:17 says 'faith comes from hearing . . . the word of Christ.' We may strengthen our faith as we study the word of God and see how God, in the past, helped believers who had trusted in him. We will begin to understand that if he was willing to help them, he must also be willing to help us with our needs today.

A second way to increase our faith, is to put the promises of God into practice. Our faith will increase when we see God keep his promises. For example, do you have a question about what to do in a difficult decision? God has promised wisdom (James 1:5) and guidance (Psalm 32:8) for such decisions. As you trust God for the wisdom and guidance you need, you will see God give you the wisdom and guidance you were seeking. When you see this, it strengthens your faith in his promises for the next decision you have to make. The same thing happens when you take the other promises of God seriously.

A third way we may increase our faith is to keep a written record (a journal or diary) of how God has answered our prayers. When we look at the written record of God's faithfulness to us in answering past prayers, it will strengthen our faith as we pray about new matters. Jesus said, 'whatever you ask for in prayer, believe that you have received it, and it will be yours' (Mark 11:24).

SALVATION

The 'helmet of salvation' is intended to protect the head. The head is the most critical part of the body. If the head is destroyed, the whole body will die. The assurance of salvation protects our minds from every fear, every uncertainty, every trial and every difficult situation in life. When we have certainty about our eternal salvation, it doesn't matter what may happen to us in this life. We know where we are going and no person or power can change that. We know that when our life ends, we will be with the Lord forever, in heaven. The comfort of eternal salvation is expressed in Psalm 27:1: 'The Lord is my light and my salvation. Whom shall I fear?' When we know we have forgiveness for our sins and the certainty of heaven, it gives us stability and purpose in our lives. There is a goal. There is a graduation day into glory. Our minds are protected by the 'helmet of salvation'.

THE WORD OF GOD

The word of God is called the 'sword of the spirit' (Eph. 6:17). The sword was an offensive weapon used to destroy the enemy. All of our enemies, whether problems, people, or powers of darkness may be overcome by the promises of the word of God. God has given us promises and principles in his word which apply to every need we will face in life. The word of God is our guidebook for living.

PRAYER

The Christian is told to 'pray . . . on all occasions' (Eph. 6:18). Prayer brings the help of God's Spirit and God's angels into every situation we face. In many Psalms the writer prays that God will deliver him from his enemies. These Psalms are given to us as a pattern for our prayers. We will always have a struggle with our sinful nature, the present world system, and Satan. In Psalm 50:15 the Lord says, 'Call upon me in the day of trouble. I will deliver you, and you will honour me.' In Psalm 143:9 the writer prays, 'Rescue me from my enemies O LORD, for I hide myself in you.'

Jesus taught his disciples to pray 'Deliver us from the evil one' (Matt. 6:13). If we will pray these prayers in faith and humility of heart, God will send us the help we need. Prayer connects us to the power of God. Prayer moves the hand that made the world. There is no situation where it will not be possible to pray. And when we pray, God will hear, and God will answer, when we pray with clean hearts according to the will of God.

Why Pray?
(a) Because prayer brings the help of God to us in every situation (Psalm 3:3–4, Psalm 34:4,6).
(b) Because prayer is God's chosen way to oppose the power and work of Satan (Matt. 6:13, Eph. 6:12,18).
(c) Because prayer is the means of finding peace in the midst of very fearful circumstances (Phil. 4:4–7).

(d) Because prayer can be the means of changing the hearts and attitudes of other people (Neh. 2:4–8).

(e) Because prayer can be the means of physical and emotional healing (James 5:14–15).

(f) Because prayer can remove obstacles and barriers (Mark 11:23–24).

(g) Because prayer can bring inner courage and strength when someone is discouraged and defeated (Col. 1:9–11).

HUMILITY

One final aspect of spiritual warfare concerns humility. Humility is the opposite of pride. The Christian is told to humble himself before the Lord (James 4:10, 1 Peter 5:6). In this way we can escape the condemnation which came upon Satan and all others who set themselves against God because of their pride (1 Tim. 3:6).

SUMMARY

The Christian life is not an easy road. The Christian struggles with three great enemies of the soul. These enemies are the world (the corrupt world system of values), the flesh (our own sinful human nature), and the devil (a fallen angel who controls many other fallen angels). If Christians did not have the power of the indwelling Holy Spirit, they would surely be overcome by these three great enemies.

But the gospel is good news, not just for the forgiveness of sins in the past, but for having the power of God available to help the Christian live victoriously over these three enemies in the present. The ways to have victory over each enemy are similar. A Christian must put away those attitudes, behaviours and beliefs which are contrary to the Bible, and replace them with those attitudes, behaviours and beliefs which are commanded in the word of God.

Concerning our sinful human nature, we must replace sinful habits with godly habits. The principle is stated in Psalm 34:14, which says, 'Turn from evil and do good.' With careful thought, prayer and counsel, this verse can be applied to every kind of weakness in our sinful nature. The Holy Spirit will give us the desire to please God more than to please ourselves, when we are serious about following Christ. He will help us to follow godly actions and words instead of following our sinful human desires.

Concerning the temptations of the corrupt values of the world around us, we must learn to set our hearts on the things of God instead of setting them on the things of this world. When we are serious about following Christ, the Holy Spirit will help us to desire the things of God more than the things of this world.

Concerning the attacks of the devil, we must understand that the area of Satan's power is sin and rebellion against God. When we learn to make holiness the top priority in our lives, Satan will lose his influence in our lives. The key to victory over Satan is found in James 4:7, which says, 'Submit yourselves, then, to God. Resist the devil and he will flee from you.'

What should the Christian do when directly attacked by demons, as in witchcraft or demonic curses? For such spiritual attacks, the Christian is given spiritual weapons of warfare in the New Testament. These weapons can be used against the direct attacks of demons. Three of these weapons are the promises of the word of God, prayer and faith. According to the promises of the word of God, Christians have authority to cast out demons by the power of the Holy Spirit. By prayer and by faith in the promises of God, the attacks of the devil can be overcome.

DISCUSSION QUESTIONS AND PROJECTS BASED ON CHAPTER TWELVE

1. What are the two things we must do to achieve a lasting victory over the downward pull of our sinful nature?

2. What decision must a Christian make if he is to be free from covetousness?

3. Make a costume as object lesson for teaching children about the seven weapons used in spiritual warfare. This should include a belt labeled truth, a helmet labeled salvation, a sword labeled the word of God, and so forth.

4. What must a Christian do which Jesus himself did to resist Satan?

5. Explain how Elijah's contest with the priests of Baal on Mount Carmel was a power encounter.

6. Divide into small groups of three or four each. Let each group list as many ways as they can think of, by which God helps his people through prayer.

7. Let each person in the group start to keep a prayer journal. On one side of the page write 'Matters committed to prayer.' On the opposite page write, 'The way in which God answered.'

8. There are many cases of demon possession mentioned in the Bible. Have a discussion in class to determine what conditions may have led to people being demonized.

9. List some ways by which a new Christian can increase his faith.

10. In what specific way does the Holy Spirit help a single person to get victory over the temptation of lust? Develop a teaching lesson for youths, based on the story of Joseph in Gen. 39:6–20.

11. What are some of the symptoms of demon possession?

12. How may a Christian determine the difference between demon possession and mental illness?

SUGGESTED FOR FURTHER READING

Duewel, Wesley L. *Mighty Prevailing Prayer*. Grand Rapids, Michigan: Zondervan, 1990.

Duewel, Wesley L. *Touch The World Through Prayer*. Grand Rapids, Michigan: Zondervan, 1986.

Foster, Richard. *Prayer*. London: Hodder, 1992.

Parker, Russ. *The Occult*. Leicester: InterVarsity Press, 1989.

Sherman, Dean. *Spiritual Warfare*. Seattle, Washington: Frontline Communications, 1990.

Warner, Timothy. *Spiritual Warfare*. Wheaton, Illinois: Crossway Books, 1991.

13

The Bible's Perspective on Traditional Beliefs and Practices

'After six days Jesus took with him Peter, James and John the brother of James, and led them up a high mountain by themselves. There he was transfigured before them. His face shone like the sun, and his clothes became as white as the light. Just then there appeared before them Moses and Elijah, talking with Jesus. Peter said to Jesus, "Lord, it is good for us to be here. If you wish, I will put up three shelters – one for you, one for Moses and one for Elijah" ' (Matt. 17:1–4).

Yakubu was returning home from a visit with his relatives. He had spent three weeks in his uncle's village helping with the farmwork. As he drew near to his home village he approached a small stream. Crossing the stream he met an old man named Baba Yinusa whom he had known for many years. He greeted the old man and asked him about his family.

Strangely, Yinusa did not return his greeting. Yakubu spoke to him again, and again Yinusa ignored his greeting. Yakubu was very troubled. He asked Baba if something was wrong but again Baba refused to answer him. Yakubu continued on the way to his village. Arriving home, he related the incident to his family and asked if they knew of any problem in Yinusa's family. Yakubu's family looked at him in great surprise and then said, 'Oh, That's right! You have been away for three weeks and did not know. We buried Baba Yinusa three days ago!'

Yakubu's story raises many questions concerning traditional beliefs, practices and experiences. What is real and what is not real? Which beliefs in African traditional religions are correct and which are not?

In African traditional religion, there is a very important relationship between the living and those who have recently died (the living dead). Many aspects of traditional life have to do with the relationship between the living and the living dead. In the belief of many groups of people, the moral and social stability of the clan is considered to be the responsibility of the tribal elders who have died and who have been elevated to the status of ancestral spirits. It is a serious offense to ignore the will of the ancestors in matters which relate to the culture and social order of the clan.

The story of Jesus speaking to Moses and Elijah on the Mount of Transfiguration clearly confirms the belief of traditional religions that those who have died have a conscious existence after physical death. Moses had died more than 1200 years before Christ and Elijah had been taken from the earth about 700 years before Christ. However, on this occasion the Apostles Peter, James and John see Moses and Elijah talking with Jesus. Thus the African world-view that physical death is a door into the spirit world is quite accurate according to the word of God. However, some of the beliefs and practices of traditional religion which result from the reality of the spirit world are quite wrong, and almost always result in drawing people away from a personal relationship with God through Jesus Christ.

Satan has many ways of deceiving people. In non-Christian religions throughout the world there are certain practices which we need to understand in the light of what the Bible teaches. These practices include communicating with the dead, black and white magic (medicine, spells, and charms), spirit possession, divination (ways of explaining present events or foretelling the future), initiation rituals, and other practices. People are attracted to these practices by the power involved. People want power so that they can control their world.

Although life in present-day Africa is changing, the question of traditional beliefs and practices is still a very important issue. In what ways do traditional beliefs help a person understand the truth of God and in what ways do they lead people away from the truth of God? What does the Bible say about the spirits of the dead? What happens to the dead after they die? Does God want the living to have any relationship with the dead? What is the explanation for experiences such as Yakubu's encounter? What is the biblical perspective on matters such as divination, magic and mystical powers? How should a Christian look at initiation practices such as female circumcision? Although much more will have to be written on these issues in other books, this book will lay a biblical foundation for the following questions:

A. What does the Bible teach about the spirits of the dead?
B. What does the Bible say about how a Christian should relate to his ancestors?
C. What is real concerning the spirits of the dead and what is the result of deception by demons?
D. What is the Bible's perspective on spirit possession?

E. How may Christians help those who are influenced or controlled by demons?
F. What does the Bible teach about heaven and hell?
G. What does the Bible say about communication with the dead?
H. What is the Bible's perspective on traditional initiation practices?
I. What does the Bible say about magic?
J. What does the Bible say about divination?

A. WHAT DOES THE BIBLE TEACH ABOUT THE SPIRITS OF THE DEAD?

Many groups of people in Africa have strong beliefs concerning the spirits of their ancestors. For most tribes, there is a necessary relationship between the living and the living dead. What does the Bible say about the condition of those who have died and our relationship to them?

As the conversation between Jesus, Moses and Elijah reveals, it is correct to say that those who have died are conscious and continue to exist. They remember what took place during their life and they also seem to have additional knowledge, as revealed by the fact that Moses and Elijah were speaking with Jesus concerning his death which was soon to take place at Jerusalem (Luke 9:31). Jesus' story about the rich man and Lazarus in Luke 16:19–31 gives us similar insight into what happens after death, as well as other important information about the condition of the dead. For example, after the rich man died, he was painfully aware of the great mistake he had made in not serving God. He very much wanted Lazarus to be sent to tell his brothers about his mistake (Luke 16:25–28). However, this request was not granted (Luke 16:29–31). In Jesus' conversation with Moses and Elijah on the mountain, the apostles did not talk to them although they saw and heard the ancient prophets.

These stories reveal a truth which is consistently taught throughout the Bible. God does not want the living to speak with the dead. In Deuteronomy 18:10–11, the Lord warns, 'Let no one be found among you who . . . consults the dead. Anyone who does these things is detestable to the Lord.' The reason for this warning will be discussed in this chapter.

The story in Luke 16:19–31 also reveals that at death there is a permanent separation between the spirits of those who loved and served God and those who did not. Lazarus was evidently a poor man who loved God. At his death he was accompanied by holy angels to a place of comfort (verses 22, 25). The rich man evidently loved only himself. He went to a place of torment (verses 23,24). Here Jesus revealed the sobering truth that there will be a separation of people at death, and that there will be torment for those whose sins are not forgiven.

In a story in the Old Testament, King Saul wanted to talk with the spirit of the dead prophet Samuel (1 Sam. 28:8–19). King Saul knew he was doing something wrong by consulting the dead, since he himself had earlier forbidden this practice in Israel in accordance with the law of God (Lev. 19:31, 1 Sam. 28:9). Now Saul was seeking to speak with the dead out of desperation (1 Sam. 28:15). When Samuel's spirit did appear to Saul, Samuel gave him a strong word of condemnation and told him that he should have obeyed God (1 Sam. 28:16–19). God evidently allowed Samuel to speak to Saul in this unusual case, not to encourage or help Saul, but to condemn him. From this story we can also see that God does not want living people to contact the dead. We see that contact with the dead cannot be a source of help or encouragement from God, as taught in many traditional religions. Instead, any such contact condemns us.

What happens to Christians who die? According to the words of Jesus to the dying criminal (Luke 23:41–43), and according to Paul's words (2 Cor. 5:1–8), Christians go into the presence of Christ in Paradise (heaven) at their death. In this intermediate state before the resurrection of all the dead, believers are given a heavenly form in which they can speak and relate to one another (2 Cor. 5:1–4). The heavenly forms of Moses and Elijah were both seen and heard by Peter, James and John, as Jesus spoke to the prophets on the mountain (Luke 9:28–32).

Protestant Christians have not accepted what is taught by the Roman Catholic Church, namely that very, very few, if any, Christians go to be with the Lord directly at death. The Catholic Church teaches that Christians first go to a place of purging (cleansing by fire) for their earthly sins and only later go to heaven. The place of purging is called purgatory. The idea of purgatory disagrees with several statements made in the New Testament. Paul stated that he desired, 'to be absent from the body and to be at home with the Lord' (2 Cor. 5:8). Paul also taught that Christ died for us so that whether we are physically alive or physically dead, we will still live together with Christ (1 Thess. 5:10). Jesus told the thief who was dying on the cross next to him, 'today you will be with me in Paradise' (Luke 23:43). These and other verses in the Bible indicate that at death a forgiven sinner goes directly into the presence of Christ in Paradise.

What happens to people who die without a personal, saving relationship with Christ? Jesus himself answered this question when he said to the Jews, 'I told you that you would die in your sins; If you do not believe that I am the one I claim to be, you will indeed die in your sins' (John 8:24).

What is the result of dying without forgiveness of sins? In the story of the rich man and Lazarus, Jesus revealed what happens after death. He described the condition of two people who had died. In the case of the rich man, who was apparently selfish and unconcerned about serving God and the needs of other people, Jesus said this godless man went to a place of torment and suffering (Luke 16:23–24). In a related comment about the final judgment of the human race, Jesus again indicated that those who did not belong to him would go to a place of torment and suffering (Matt. 25:31–46).

B. WHAT DOES THE BIBLE SAY ABOUT HOW A CHRISTIAN SHOULD RELATE TO HIS ANCESTORS?

Traditional religions often require elaborate relationships between the living and the living dead. These relationships can include rituals, sacrifices and offerings which must be made to satisfy or to persuade the ancestors. They also include communication with the dead: through divination, or directly through words from spirit possessed people. These traditional beliefs almost always cause the living to look to their ancestors or other spirits for guidance, help, correction, and blessing, instead of looking directly to God. By doing this, such people break the first of God's commandments to have no other 'gods' before him (Ex. 20:3).

Traditional beliefs and practices involving ancestral spirits are not from God. They are part of a subtle plan by Satan to deceive people and to bring them under God's judgement for breaking his commandments. Beliefs and practices relating to ancestral spirits have kept many people from a personal relationship with God through Jesus Christ.

What does the Bible say about a person's relationship to parents and the elderly people of the community? The Bible gives a general guideline: 'You shall rise up before the greyheaded, and honour the aged, and you shall revere your God; I am the LORD' (Lev. 19:32–NASB). This statement from the Law of Moses reveals that it is right and pleasing to God for people to show respect for the elderly at all times. There is even a hint in this verse that showing this kind of respect is related in some way to showing reverence for God himself.

What about a person's relationship to his or her own parents? The fifth commandment says, 'Honour your father and your mother' (Exodus 20:12). This commandment shows us that it is the will of God that all people should bring honour to their parents. They can do this by showing them respect and by carefully considering their advice (Prov. 1:8). They can show honour to their living parents by showing submission and obedience to them in every way that does not cause them to disobey the teaching of God's word (Eph. 6:1, Col. 3:20). The highest form of honour they can give to their parents is by living holy lives of godly character and behaviour.

What does the Bible say about the relationship of the living to the dead? Some of the principles just given concerning our relationship to living parents also apply to honouring those who have died. We may bring honour to the members of our family who have died by living holy lives of godly character and behaviour, by showing respect for their names, by honouring the good works which they did during their lives on earth and by walking in their faith if they were Christians.

However, Christians must be very careful that when they honour their ancestors they do not return to the beliefs and practices of traditional religion. They must be very careful not to honour their ancestors in place of honouring God, which is commonly done in non-Christian religions. A Christian must look only to God, through Jesus Christ, for guidance, correction, help, and for blessing upon his or her life. When someone has a problem, that person needs to pray to God the Father in the name of Jesus Christ. A person must not seek the blessing, guidance or help of any ancestor, divinity, or spirit other than God himself. The psalmist wisely warns us, 'The sorrows of those will increase who run after other gods. I will not pour out their libations of blood or take up their names on my lips' (Psalm 16:4).

While they are required to honour the members of their family, the living must never try to contact the dead or seek the help of dead relatives (Deut. 18:10–11). God does not want his people to offer food or drink offerings to their ancestors (Deut. 26:14). Making such food or drink offerings would be following the pagan practices of non-Christian religion. It is a form of idolatry which God forbids (Deut. 20:18). As seen in chapter eleven, when such sacrifices and offerings are made to ancestral spirits, the real persons receiving these offerings are not ancestors at all, but demons (Deut. 32:16,17, 1 Cor. 10:19,20).

God has commanded that his people must burn and destroy the objects associated with traditional religions which place ancestors or any other spirits before God. In addition, they must totally abandon such beliefs and practices. God warned his people Israel, 'This is what you are to do to them: Break down their altars, smash their sacred stones, cut down their Asherah poles and burn their idols in the fire' (Deut. 7:5). God repeated this order later in the same chapter (Deut 7:25). They were forbidden to have the objects of non-Christian religions in their houses (Deut. 7:26). In the New Testament, the people of Ephesus understood that this was included in their repentance from sin. As a result, the Ephesian converts physically burned the objects associated with their non-Christian beliefs and practices (Acts 19:18–19). African Christians today must learn to do the same.

Failure to make a definite and permanent break with the beliefs and practices of traditional religion has greatly weakened the church in Africa. Failure to completely put away non-Christian practices is a serious sin and brings God's judgment. It can bring the loss of God's protection over a person's life. When the Israelites refused to completely deny the traditional religions of the people around them, God said, 'you have forsaken me and served other gods; therefore I will deliver you no more. Go and cry out to the gods which you have chosen; let them deliver you in the time of your distress' (Judges 10:13,14–NASB). This may be part of the explanation why so many African Christians suffer from problems which arise out of tribalism and syncretism.

C. WHAT IS REAL CONCERNING THE SPIRITS OF THE DEAD AND WHAT IS THE RESULT OF DECEPTION BY DEMONS?

Spirits have been seen by people in most parts of the world at one time or another. These spirits often claim to be ancestors. They may look exactly like dead relatives and even talk like them. In some places they are called ghosts.

Who are these spirits? We saw in chapter six that God assigns a definite place to the spirits of those who have died and he restricts them to that place (Luke 16:24–26, 2 Cor. 5:8). They are not free to leave those assigned places apart from his special permission (as in the case of the prophet Samuel – 1 Sam. 28:15–19). Hence the possibility is not great that the appearance of a spirit is actually the appearance of the ancestor.

Since demons have the power to appear to human eyes in any chosen form (2 Cor. 11:14, Rev. 16:13), and since demons are much more powerful and intelligent than people, it should not come as a surprise that demons have the ability to imitate the appearances and voices of dead relatives. There are many testimonies by those who claim they have seen the spirits of the dead, just like the true story at the beginning of this chapter.

Why would demons imitate dead relatives? They do it to increase the deception of non-Christian religions which lead men to trust in ancestors or other spirits instead of trusting in Christ. It would be very difficult to say with certainty whether a particular appearance of a spirit was actually the spirit of the person who had died or just a visionary appearance by a demon. However, biblical revelation would suggest that most cases are intentional visionary deceptions by demons.

In recent years, doctors have been able to bring some people back from near-death experiences by reviving them after their hearts had stopped beating. Some people who have had this experience have told stories about their spirits being separated from their bodies. They claim to clearly remember what they did and who they saw while their spirits were separated from their bodies. Some claim to have seen heaven or hell.

In some of these stories told by non-Christians, the testimony of the person does not agree with the Bible teaching on what takes place after death. For example, some of them deny that there is such a place as hell, or suffering for sin after death. Such false testimonies may happen for many reasons. In some cases, the person's brain may have been affected when his or her heart stopped beating. In other cases, the person may have been deceived by a demonic experience. We must also understand that there is a difference between such out-of-the-body experiences and true death, as described in the Bible. At true death, a person's human spirit leaves his or her body permanently.

Some people claim they have spoken with the dead. In such cases, if the words of the 'dead' do not agree with the word of God, those who claim they have spoken to the dead have been deceived. Our own minds can deceive us. Demons can easily deceive people. Demons especially deceive those who purposely try to speak with the spirits of the dead. We should not underestimate Satan's power. The Bible is the word of God, and God tells us the truth.

Why does God warn people not to contact the dead? From what has been said, we can see that those who disobey God and insist on contacting the dead, open themselves up to deception by demons. They may contact a spirit whom they think is their relative and who claims to be their ancestor. The spirit may offer secret information which seems to prove that it is the real person. But remember, demons are very intelligent and powerful. They serve their master, Satan, whom Jesus said was the father of lies (John 8:44). By trying to contact the dead, a person may come into contact with a lying spirit. In addition, a person will come under God's judgment for trying to contact the dead because God has condemned this practice (Deut. 18:11–12). A Christian must avoid this practice at all times.

D. WHAT IS THE BIBLE'S PERSPECTIVE ON SPIRIT POSSESSION?

Spirit possession is a common occurrence in many parts of the world. When people are possessed by a spirit, they may display unusual strength, endurance or tolerance of pain. They will often speak with a different voice (the voice of the spirit who indwells them). These voices may claim to be ancestors or to be bringing messages from ancestors. What is the reality behind spirit possession?

Many scientists and anthropologists believe that spirit possession is simply a state of self-induced behaviour or a form of play-acting. According to this theory, people may act in a certain way in order to escape a personal problem, to draw attention to themselves, or for some other reason. The supposed spirit possession makes them the centre of attention in a way which is accepted and believed by their people. This explanation may be true in some cases.

In addition to this, the Bible describes many cases of people who were definitely possessed by spirits who are described as evil or unclean (Mark 1:23; 5:8; 9:25). Jesus dealt with many such cases (Matt. 8:16; 9:32, Mark 7:25, Luke 9:42). There is no indication in these cases that Jesus was simply accommodating local superstitions or applying psychology to a play-actor. Indeed, the spoken responses of these spirits to Jesus' presence reveals that the spirits recognized Jesus' true identity as the Holy One of God (Mark 1:24) long before the disciples understood this truth (Matt. 16:15–16). The unclean spirits revealed their great fear of Jesus' power. Most important, they acknowledged his coming judgment upon them (Matt. 8:29). It is evident from these stories that the spirit-possessed people involved were not play-acting. They had evil spirits within.

In the case of the Gadarene man, the demons begged Jesus to allow them to enter some nearby pigs (Matt. 8:31). When Jesus allowed this, the pigs went mad and destroyed themselves, showing that the evil spirits had moved from the man to the pigs (Matt. 8:32). The Bible recognizes the reality of evil spirits possessing people and even animals. How and why does such possession take place?

In chapter eleven it was pointed out that the area of Satan's power is sin and rebellion against God. People who participate in sin or wilful rebellion against God, unknowingly open a place for demonic influence in their lives. In Ephesians 4:26–27 Paul reveals that unrighteous anger can give Satan a foothold in a person's life. How much stronger a foothold might Satan gain in the life of a person who willingly places other gods before the true God (as in the practice of non-Christian religions)? In the rituals of many traditional religions, spirits are sought and invited to possess a person. Unfortunately, demons are quite willing to take control of those who invite them to do so, even if the people inviting them think they are only inviting kindly ancestral spirits or benevolent divinities.

How great a foothold can Satan gain in the life of people who give themselves over to sin? The brutality of man's history is one answer to this question. We can only wonder how many crimes of murder, tribal war, torture and rape were suggested by demonic presence in people's lives. One area of evil concerns non-Christian parents who introduce their children to sin either by their example, their suggestions, or their abuse. The Bible speaks about the sins of parents being visited upon children to the third and fourth generation (Ex. 34:7). This is especially true where parents have given spirits other than God's Spirit a place in their lives (Ex. 20:5). This may be one reason why some children experience spirit possession and other indications of demonic influence very early in their lives.

The Bible makes it clear that spirit possession is the work of demons. In a summary statement about Jesus' ministry of healing people from spirit possession, the Bible says, 'When evening came, many who were demon-possessed were brought to him, and he drove out the spirits with a word and healed all the sick' (Matt. 8:16). Here the spirits possessing people were clearly identified as demons. In the book of Acts, Jesus' ministry of healing and driving spirits out of people is summarized in the words, 'You know of Jesus of Nazareth, how God anointed him with the Holy Spirit and with power, and how he went about doing good, and healing all who were oppressed by the devil; for God was with him' (Acts 10:38–NASB).

E. HOW MAY CHRISTIANS HELP THOSE WHO ARE INFLUENCED OR CONTROLLED BY DEMONS?

Christians have been given authority by Christ himself to cast out demons in Jesus' name (Mark 16:17, Luke 9:1, Luke 10:17,19). This authority is available because Christians are spiritually 'seated' with Christ (that is, spiritually joined to Christ as his body) in a position above all principalities and demonic powers (Eph. 1:19–22, Eph. 2:6). When spirit possession is the result of demonic influence and not simply acted behaviour, there will be a power encounter if a Christian attempts to cast out the demons.

Since the basis for demon presence is sin in a person's life, there will be no permanent deliverance from the influence of demons until the demonized person is willing to confess and forsake his sins and renounce his non-Christian beliefs and practices. It is both unwise and dangerous to try to cast demons out of a person who is not willing to make such a confession and renunciation. Specific sins must be confessed and renounced before any effective deliverance will take place.

Some people can be so completely under the influence of demons (demonized) that the demons will speak instead of the person (Mark 5:9–10). When this happens, Christians may have to bind, silence or cast out such demons in order to deal with the people themselves about their sin and their need for repentance. Counseling demonized people requires first finding out the root sin by which the demons gained their influence or foothold. To do this, the persons must be at least temporarily released from the demon's grip on their mind and senses. Thus there may be a need to silence or cast out the demons in the name of Jesus. However, it is not useful or even wise to speak with demons, since they are liars and experts in deception.

The basic issue is sin, which must be exposed, confessed and renounced before a person will experience permanent deliverance from demonic influence. That is why the Bible speaks mainly about sin and very little about demons. Repentance really includes the renunciation of all sin and all the works of Satan. Such renunciations were commonly practiced in the early Christian church as part of a person's conversion with the statement, 'I renounce you, Satan, and all your works and ways.'

In some cases today this may include renouncing the sinful influence or abuse of parents or other relatives, including those who may have already died. Once a person has renounced his or her sins, that person must be patiently instructed and encouraged in the Christian life, lest he or she turns back to former sins and thereby invite an even greater demonic invasion.

Demons become angry when they are driven from the people they have controlled. They tend to attack and harass their former victims in many ways. People who have been delivered from demons need to learn much about self-discipline in obedience to God's word. They also need support, prayer and discipling by other Christians.

When Paul preached in Ephesus, those who followed the non-Christian religion of that place demonstrated their willingness to forsake and renounce their practices by confessing them and burning the objects of their religion (Acts 19:18–19). A similar confession and open renunciation of pagan or sinful practices must take place if a person is to be fully delivered of Satan's control over his or her life.

When God called Gideon to deliver Israel from the oppression of the Midianites (Judges 6:11–14), it was first necessary for Gideon to destroy the pagan shrine which his people had built (Judges 6:25–27). God would not empower Gideon to overcome the Midianites until Gideon had put away all the idols of his family's false religion. So also today, God will not enable a person to overcome Satan until that person puts away the beliefs and practices of non-Christian religion along with other known sins in his or her life.

Such a renunciation must be followed by serious discipleship in following Christ and growing in obedience to his word. Without such follow-up and discipleship there is a danger that the new believer may turn back to the practices of his or her non-Christian religion in times of personal crisis. It is for lack of careful discipleship that so many professing Christians in Africa have turned back to traditional practices in times of personal need. The great need of the church in Africa today is for discipleship and growth into maturity in Christ through obedience to the word of God.

F. WHAT DOES THE BIBLE TEACH ABOUT HEAVEN AND HELL?

The Bible teaches that heaven and hell are real. Heaven is the blessed place where God dwells. Jesus spoke of heaven as Paradise. Because one of the two thieves crucified next to Jesus repented of his sin and believed in Christ, Jesus told him, 'Today you will be with me in Paradise' (Luke 23:43). The Apostle Paul said, 'I know a man in Christ who fourteen years ago was caught up to the third heaven. . . . And I know that this man . . . was caught up to Paradise. He heard inexpressible things, things that man is not permitted to tell' (2 Cor.

12:2–4). In Revelation 21:2–22:15, heaven is described by the Apostle John and is called 'the holy city, the new Jerusalem' (Rev. 21:2).

Some of the people mentioned earlier who claim to have seen heaven and then have returned to their bodies, have described the holy city exactly as it is described in the Bible. The Apostle John gave additional details about the holy city which some people interpret literally and others interpret symbolically (Rev. 21:10–27). The final truth is that the holy city is a greater and more glorious reality than any person could ever describe. More will be said about heaven and the eternal kingdom of God at the end of chapter eighteen.

As we have seen, the Bible teaches that the spirits of the dead either go into the presence of the Lord or to a place of torment (Hades). A permanent separation of the dead is taught in the story Jesus told about the rich man and Lazarus in Luke 16:19–31. Jesus said Lazarus was taken to a place of comfort with Abraham. The rich man went to a place of torment (Luke 16:24). Since the time of Christ's ascension, all Christians who die go into the presence of the Lord (2 Cor. 5:8). The holy angels meet the Christian at the moment of death and accompany his spirit into the presence of Christ. The spirits of these Christians will accompany Christ when he returns to earth, at which time these Christians will receive their resurrection bodies (1 Thess. 4:14–17).

It is interesting to observe that the spirit of Lazarus was carried by holy angels to the place of comfort. Many dying Christians have testified to seeing angels at the moment of death. Perhaps God sends his angels to protect his people from the evil spirits who inhabit this world (Eph. 2:2). No such protection is mentioned concerning the rich man because he did not belong to the Lord.

The most painful and difficult truth in the Bible is the reality of hell. Hell is real according to Christ. In Matthew 18:9 Jesus said, 'If your eye causes you to sin, gouge it out and throw it away. It is better for you to enter life with one eye than to have two eyes and be thrown into the fire of hell.' This warning of Christ is put in the strongest possible words. There is a hell for those whose sins are not forgiven. If gouging out a person's eye could save a person from hell, it would be worth doing. Since sin comes from the heart, nothing such as gouging out an eye can take away a person's sin. Jesus was saying that there is no degree of power, no position of importance, no amount of wealth and no kind of pleasure which is worth having, if it means going to hell as a result (Mark 8:36). Only Jesus can forgive a person's sin and save him from hell (Eph. 1:7, Eph. 2:8–9).

It is important to understand the Greek words which are translated 'hell.' In Matt. 18:9, the Greek word is *gehenna*. In a statement in Mark 9:47, which is parallel to Matt. 18:9, Jesus added the description that in hell (*gehenna*), 'their worm does not die and the fire is not quenched.' This may be the same place called the 'lake of fire' in the book of Revelation (Rev. 20:14,15), where unforgiven sinners are cast after the final judgment of the great white throne (Rev. 20:11–13). The lake of fire is described by God as the 'second death' (Rev. 20:14). The physical death of the body and the departure of the soul to the place called Hades is the first death (Rev. 20:13). Christians interpret the words of Christ concerning hell in different ways. Some take them literally and some take them figuratively. Whatever meaning Christ intended, the fact is that Jesus made it clear that hell is a terrifying reality.

Before the time of the great white throne judgment, the unsaved dead await the judgment in Hades (Luke 16:23, Rev. 20:12–13)). For the unsaved, Hades was also a place of torment, according to Christ's words in Luke 16:23–24. In Jesus' description, there was another part of Hades where the believing dead, such as Abraham, were comforted. Old Testament believers rested in the peaceful part of Hades until Christ took them into heaven at the time of his ascension (Eph. 4:8–9). The Old Testament word *sheol* (the place of the dead), appears to correspond to Hades in the New Testament.

The awful reality is this: There is eternal anguish and suffering after death for those whose sins are not forgiven (Matt. 25:41). Hell is described in terms of darkness, weeping and gnashing of teeth (Matt. 8:12, Matt. 22:13, Matt. 25:30). It is described by Christ in terms of eternal fire, torment and punishment (Matt. 13:41–42, Mark 9:43, Rev. 14:10–11). Jesus said that the suffering of hell was not prepared for mankind, but for Satan and those angels who rebelled with him (Matt. 25:41). Unfortunately, since the garden of Eden, human beings have participated in Satan's rebellion against God. Human beings will share in Satan's punishment unless they repent and receive forgiveness for their sins through trusting in Jesus Christ and his sacrifice on the cross (John 8:24).

For those who find it hard to believe that a loving God would ever send people to hell, they must remember that it was Jesus, who knows all things, who spoke more about the reality of hell than anyone else in the Bible. God is a holy and just judge. He will not tolerate sin. It is for this reason that rebellious angels and people must be punished for their sin (Heb. 2:2). It is also for this reason that Jesus came and gave his life on the cross to pay the death penalty for mankind's sin, so that people could be saved from the anguish and suffering of hell. But it is not enough just to know that he died and rose again. Men and women must repent of their sin and personally believe in Jesus Christ as their Lord and Saviour by receiving him into their lives (John 1:12). Only in this way will they find forgiveness and be saved from God's judgment on sin (Mark 1:14–15).

For those who will not repent of their sin and receive Christ and his forgiveness, there is the reality of hell. That reality should move Christians to urgency in spreading the gospel of forgiveness of sin through Jesus Christ.

G. WHAT DOES THE BIBLE SAY ABOUT COMMUNICATION WITH THE DEAD?

In most African societies, a funeral is a very important event. This is because of traditional beliefs about the responsibility of the living to the spirits of the dead. In some groups, funeral observances are held when the person dies and again many years later in order to fulfill obligations to the spirit of the one who has died. In traditional religions, receiving messages from the spirits of the dead is very important. What does God say about the relationship of the living to those who have died?

No relationship between the living and the dead is suggested or encouraged in the Bible. God specifically forbids the living to speak with the dead in Deuteronomy 18:10–13. Trying to contact the dead is a sin.

As discussed earlier, the most likely reason why God gave this commandment, is because he knows that demons can and will pretend to be dead ancestors and thus deceive people to believe lies. By pretending to be the spirits of dead ancestors, demons can deceive people in order to control them. Since ancestors are beloved and respected, people are very likely to believe and obey whatever such spirits would tell them to do or believe. It is an effective trap of Satan by which he has led many people all over the world to spiritual death.

When the rich man in Luke 16:22–31 wanted Lazarus to tell his living brothers about the reality of hell, Abraham told the man that his brothers could read the Old Testament to find out the truth about what lies beyond death. Reading the Bible is still the only way authorized by God to know about the mysteries of death.

WHAT IS THE CHRISTIAN RESPONSE TO COMMUNICATION WITH THE DEAD?

People practising traditional religions make offerings and sacrifices to their dead relatives to show them respect and to keep their relatives happy. They fear that if the ancestors are not kept happy, they will punish the living with sickness or some other hardship. They also seek to get their ancestors' advice on what to do about various decisions in life, especially concerning marriage, or problems and difficulties, such as childbirth and sickness.

Where does God want us to get guidance for the issues of life? We have seen that God forbids all contact with the dead. The Bible says, 'When men tell you to consult mediums and spiritists, who whisper and mutter, should not a people inquire of their God? Why consult the dead on behalf of the living?' (Isa. 8:19). God solemnly warns his people, 'I will set my face against the person who turns to mediums and spiritists (i.e. those who contact the dead) to prostitute himself by following them, and I will cut him off from his people' (Lev. 20:6).

God knows our need for guidance and help, and he has made a provision to meet those needs. In Psalm 119:105 the Psalmist says, 'Your word is a lamp to my feet and a light for my path.' God wants us to get the guidance we need for daily living through the principles found in his word. In Psalm 32:8 God promises, 'I will instruct you and teach you in the way you should go. I will counsel you and watch over you.' God does this through the Bible and through his Holy Spirit who lives in the Christian.

Concerning the help which ancestors are supposed to be able to give, the word of God plainly states that our help comes from the Lord. Listen to the words of Psalm 121: 'Where does my help come from? My help comes from the LORD, the maker of heaven and earth. He will not let your foot slip – He who watches over you will not slumber; . . . The LORD will keep you from all harm – he will watch over your life; the LORD will watch over your coming and going both now and forevermore' (Psalm 121:1–3,7–8). It is the living God himself, not ancestors or other spirits, who can help man in his need. When a person has a daily relationship with God through Jesus Christ, there is never a need to contact a dead relative. God promises to give us all the help we need.

New Christians may fear the anger of their ancestors if they do not perform the proper rituals and give them the proper attention. Such Christians need to remember that Jesus Christ has all authority in heaven and on earth (Matt. 28:18). As Christians, God is now their loving father. He is also Lord and King over all spirits in the universe, whether ancestors, angels or demons (Heb. 12:9). Christians no longer need to fear any other person or spirit, because God is watching over them (Psalm 121:7–8). Jesus alone is their Lord and Master.

If they fear the anger of any spirit, they only need to ask their Saviour, the King of Kings, to deal with that spirit. It is a source of spiritual strength to remember that evil spirits were terrified in the presence of Jesus Christ (Matt. 8:29). The Psalmist said, 'The Lord is my light and my salvation – whom shall I fear? The Lord is the stronghold of my life – of whom shall I be afraid?' (Psalm 27:1).

H. WHAT IS THE BIBLE'S PERSPECTIVE ON TRADITIONAL INITIATION PRACTICES?

In most African cultures, initiation rituals are the critical rites of passage by which a child becomes an adult. One of the main purposes of initiation is to educate young people into the secrets of sex, reproduction, marriage, and family life. It is often a kind of ritual preparation for marriage and adulthood in which the whole community participates.

Through initiation, the young person is accepted into the adult life of his or her community. Since it is closely connected with a person's sense of identity with his or her extended family and clan, the initiation process is also full of religious and traditional meaning. To refuse to participate in initiation would be a great problem for a young person because acceptance by the community is all-important in Africa.

For the Christian, initiation rituals present serious spiritual problems. First, there is almost always traditional religious meaning associated with initiation practices. Participation in initiation by a young person is therefore a public testimony of his or her acceptance of, and belief in, the non-Christian elements of his people's traditions. Second, many of the values taught and practices followed during initiation are contrary to the teaching of the Bible.

Initiation rituals vary from one tribe to another. Sometimes marks are made on the body which identify the individual as part of his clan or tribe. Sometimes initiation involves circumcision, either for boys, or girls, or for both. This circumcision is almost always done under conditions which are not medically sterile or safe.

A Christian young person and his family are caught in the dilemma of whether they will do what pleases God, and thereby bring rejection from their community, or do those non-Christian things which please the clan and thereby bring judgment from God. No solution to the problem of initiation will really be successful unless it provides an acceptable substitute for the issue of acceptance by the clan.

FEMALE CIRCUMCISION AS A PART OF INITIATION

Female circumcision is a part of the initiation ritual for girls in many parts of Africa. Because there are serious problems with this practice for Christians, we will present a biblical perspective on this practice and on circumcision in general. There are several traditional reasons given for the practice of female circumcision as a necessary part of initiation.

1. The reason most commonly given for female circumcision is that it ensures the wife's faithfulness to her husband in marriage by reducing the woman's sexual desires. It is believed that if she is circumcised, she will not commit adultery with other men after her marriage. From a Christian viewpoint, there are two serious objections to this.

   First, everyone knows that it is men, not women, who are the most troubled by strong sexual desires. This may even be one reason why the only circumcision commanded by God in the Bible was for men and not for women. Second, in many tribes there is an unjust double moral standard, one for women and a different one for men. Female virginity and faithfulness are considered to be important standards to maintain while it is silently accepted that men will be free to seek additional sexual partners when they desire. In the Bible God makes no distinction between men and women concerning the sins of adultery and sexual immorality (Ex. 20:14, Heb. 13:4). They are sinful for both men and women. The double standard is a result of the sinful heart of men, promoted in order to satisfy their self-indulgence.

2. Female circumcision is considered to be a necessary step which takes the girl from childhood into female adulthood and maturity in the eyes of the adults of her clan. As such, the all-important issue of acceptance by clan members as an adult is the reason why this practice continues.

    Cultural acceptance may seem very important. However, we must remember that God accepts people solely on the basis of their faith in Jesus Christ.

3. Another function of female circumcision is that important instruction and training is given in the weeks or months prior to, and following, the actual circumcision ceremony. This instruction includes teaching about adult responsibilities in marriage, childbirth, sex, and family life. Tribal values, customs, and beliefs are emphasized during this period of instruction.

    Cultural instruction concerning adult life is important for young people. However, a Christian young person must remember that the Bible teaches God's standards for all mankind in the matters of Christian marriage and family life. God's standards are often different from tribal customs. Christians must follow God's standards if they are to please God and to have his blessing on their lives.

    There will be times when some traditional practices will come into conflict with the word of God. When this kind of conflict is present, a Christian must obey the teaching of the Bible. To do this can be very difficult, and bring rejection or persecution from the clan. In such a situation, Christians must ask themselves what is most important in life. Are they going to please the traditional people of their culture for the few brief years of this life and thereby bring God's condemnation and judgment? Or are they going to please God, and thereby have God's blessing on their life, both in this world and for all eternity?

    Long ago, Joshua and the Israelites had to make the same choice between following the practices of the traditional people around them, or following the Lord. What was Joshua's response? Joshua said, 'And if it is disagreeable in your sight to serve the LORD, choose for yourselves today whom you will serve: whether the gods which your fathers served which were beyond the River, or the gods of the Amorites in whose land you are living; but as for me and my house, we will serve the LORD' (Josh. 24:15). Joshua chose to serve the

Lord, and God blessed him abundantly for taking this stand for the Lord.

4. Closely related to the issue of adult clan acceptance is the issue of being united to the whole clan, both living and dead. The shedding of blood at the circumcision ceremony or in other initiation rituals is often intended to unite the boy or girl by covenant to the ancestors of the clan.

   The Bible teaches a very different blood covenant by circumcision. God told Abraham that the bloodshed of circumcision was a symbol of God's chosen people being united to God himself by a blood covenant. God said, 'I will establish my covenant as an everlasting covenant between me and you and your descendants after you for the generations to come, to be your God, and the God of your descendants after you' (Gen. 17:7). God went on to say, 'This is my covenant. . . . Every male among you shall be circumcised. You are to undergo circumcision, and it will be the sign of the covenant between me and you' (Gen. 17:10–11).

   The issue of a blood covenant brings up a clear point of conflict between traditional circumcision and the biblical teaching about circumcision. The all-important question is to whom we are to be united by covenant. This is true whether the initiation ceremony involves circumcision or some other ritual. God will not permit us to have any other loyalty or allegiance which replaces loyalty or allegiance to him. A blood covenant which unites a person to his ancestors instead of uniting that person to God, breaks the first of God's commandments (Ex. 20:3).

   As Christians we are united in a blood covenant to our Lord and Saviour Jesus Christ, not by the shedding of our blood but by the shedding of his own blood (Rev. 5:9). Jesus is the one, 'who loves us, and released us from our sins by his blood' (Rev. 1:5).

BIBLICAL TEACHING ON CIRCUMCISION IN GENERAL

1. Circumcision as commanded by God in the Old Testament was restricted to men only. No place in the Bible can be found where females were required by God to be circumcised (note Gen. 17:10).

2. Old Testament circumcision was a sign of a covenant, not among men, but between men and God (Genesis 17:11). It was a covenant to establish God's people in a special relationship to himself (Gen. 17:7). Thus to use this symbol as a covenant within a human clan is a perversion of the purpose of circumcision revealed in God's word.

3. Old Testament circumcision was to be done on the eighth day after birth, not at puberty (Gen. 17:12, Lev. 12:3). In the plan of God, it had nothing to do with puberty and adulthood training. Since it was done to newborn infants, there was no painful memory involved.

4. The meaning of circumcision in the Bible involves a personal covenant relationship with God, resulting in holiness of life. This is what is meant by 'circumcision of the heart' (Deut. 30:6, Col. 2:11). It results from being united in heart and soul to the Lord. Thus true circumcision in the Bible is a spiritual rather than a physical thing. This spiritual meaning of circumcision was taught even in the Old Testament (Deut. 10:16; 30:6, Jer. 4:4; 9:26), where physical circumcision was required.

5. The very first council of the Christian church was called over the issue of whether men in the New Testament age had to be physically circumcised in order to be saved (Acts 15:1–6). The result of this long and difficult meeting was that physical circumcision was abolished forever as a necessary sign of belonging to God's covenant people (Acts 15:8–10, 23–29).

   Paul later pointed out that physical circumcision is of no spiritual value today (1 Cor. 7:19), whereas spiritual circumcision of the heart is all-important (Col. 2:11–13). There is no spiritual reason why physical circumcision should be practiced by Christian men today. There may be medical reasons for male circumcision, but these are unrelated to the spiritual issue. Regeneration through our spiritual union with Christ in his death and resurrection is the meaning of spiritual circumcision of the heart, as taught in Romans 2:29 and Colossians 2:11–13.

6. In the New Testament, the ritual of physical circumcision has been replaced with the ritual of water baptism as the sign that one has become a member of God's covenant people. This can be seen by comparing Romans 6:1–4 with Colossians 2:11–12 and Acts 2:38.

SUMMARY OF THE BIBLE'S PERSPECTIVE ON TRADITIONAL
INITIATION PRACTICES

1. Traditional initiation rituals require a covenant commitment of loyalty to the clan and to its beliefs and practices. Such a covenant commitment should be made to God alone and to his laws as revealed in the Bible. Traditional initiation involves commitments to the beliefs and practices of traditional religion which God forbids. The Old Testament says, 'You must not do as they do in Egypt where you used to live, and you must not do as they do in the land of Canaan, where I am bringing you. Do not follow their practices. You must obey my laws and be careful to follow my decrees. I am the LORD your God' (Lev. 18:3–4). The New Testament says, 'Do not be yoked together with unbelievers. . . . What fellowship can light have with darkness?. . . . Therefore come out from them and be separate says the Lord. . . . and you will be my sons and daughters, says the Lord Almighty' (2 Cor. 6:14–18).

2. Traditional circumcision is a painful and medically dangerous practice when done on young people under non-sterile conditions. For girls it is a seriously harmful form of bodily mutilation. It is not honouring to a Christian girl whose body is the temple of the Holy Spirit (1 Cor. 6:19).

3. Female circumcision makes it difficult or impossible for a girl to experience sexual fulfilment with her husband. Thus she simply becomes an instrument of pleasure for her husband and the bearer of his children rather than a marriage partner. This is a selfish and unacceptable attitude for a Christian husband to adopt. The Bible says, 'Husbands, love your wives, just as Christ loved the church and gave himself up for her' (Eph. 5:25).

4. Traditional circumcision has a serious risk of transmitting the AIDS virus. Female circumcision can produce nerve damage, severe bleeding, pelvic injury and the possibility of death. It adds difficulty, risk and additional pain to childbirth. No Christian medical doctor could or would approve of female circumcision.

A CHRISTIAN ALTERNATIVE TO THE PRACTICE OF TRIBAL INITIATION

The Bible has much to say about Christian values in marriage, family life, sex and adult responsibilities. The Bible makes it clear that it is the responsibility of godly parents to train their own children in the beliefs, practices and standards of the people of God (Deut. 6:6–9). This includes the training of young people for the responsibilities of adult life (Prov. 1:8–9, Eph. 6:4). Such instruction cannot be left to non-Christian tribal elders (as in a traditional initiation situation) or even to secular government authorities (as in the sex education programmes of some modern government schools). Christian parents along with local church leaders must establish their own programmes of Christian pre-marital instruction. If this is done wisely, it can provide a godly alternative for traditional initiation rituals and also for modern secular sex education programmes.

In Deuteronomy 6:1–14, God makes a clear distinction between his people and his truth, and the local traditional people of Canaan and their religious ideas. This gives us a warning that the people of God are to be separated from the people around them in their own practices of initiation. We must replace non-Christian beliefs and practices with Christian truth. Young people must be taught that their highest loyalty is to God and to God's people. Proper responsibility to the extended family and clan must be seen from this perspective.

A Christian solution to the problem of traditional initiation is not likely to be accepted unless it somehow provides a desirable substitute for the sense of tribal acceptance associated with initiation. A Christian solution should include both a substitute for the outward rituals and a substitute for the instruction associated with initiation.

As one possible approach to this problem, parents and church leaders could establish a programme of pre-adult Christian moral training which would take place during the same period when young people undergo initiation rites. The Christian programme should emphasize the differences between traditional and government values, and the beliefs of Christians.

There would be several important areas of comparison between such a programme and the practice of traditional initiation. In African tradition, the community of acceptance is the clan and tribe. Those responsible for instruction are the traditional elders. Moral and ethical teachings of the clan are part of this instruction. In Scripture, the community of acceptance is the redeemed people of God. Those responsible for instruction are Christian parents and church leaders. The moral and ethical teachings of the Bible are the subject of godly instruction.

Such a programme of instruction could culminate in a major public event, complete with certificates, awards, messages and testimonies from Christian elders, special music, dramas and a celebration feast which would emphasize the acceptance of the young person into the adult community of Christian believers. A somewhat comparable celebration has been practiced among the Jews for centuries in the barmitzvah celebration of 12-year-old Jewish boys. The programme proposed here, however, would apply both to Christian boys and girls.

The training programme should be deliberately planned to replace traditional initiation rituals and government sex education programmes. Such a programme could be carried out in cooperation with existing Christian youth organizations such as Battalion or Boys' Brigade and Kadettes or Girls' Brigade. If the entire Christian community became involved in such a programme, an effective functional substitute for Christian young people could be established in the community.

I. WHAT DOES THE BIBLE SAY ABOUT MAGIC?

Magic, according to African understanding, is the use of mystical power by a person to accomplish that person's will or desire. The power of magic, charms, spells, fetishes and medicines is used all over the world. People use these powers to try to protect themselves from misfortune, danger, evil spirits, evil people, sickness, and to get control over other people and situations. Some people use these powers to harm others. People believe in this power and they want it very much.

Medicine is a broad term in Africa which covers many things. It may refer to a physical mixture of herbs, leaves, roots, bark, animal parts or other physical substances. It may refer to purely mystical power used to hinder evil spirits, evil people, or to ward off danger. It most commonly refers to a combination of both the physical and the spiritual, where the powers of physical substances are believed to be strengthened by spiritual powers. We will not discuss the term medicine here in the scientific medical sense, but in the traditional African sense. Medicine can be used by medicine men, witch-doctors, sorcerers, pure herbalists and by ordinary people who are not specialists. Often the outcome of a conflict or struggle between two persons or two groups is thought to be decided by who had the stronger medicine.

Charms are physical objects carried by a person who believes that such objects will bring good luck or prevent evil. Spells are a form of power or influence projected on people to make them behave according to the will of the one casting the spell. Spells are used to control or affect people, such as a spell to cause a business competitor to be unsuccessful in his business. Fetishes or fetish objects are physical objects or collections of physical substances such as bones, feathers or other parts of animals or plants which are believed to be inhabited by a spirit who helps or protects the person who owns the object. Usually the spirit's presence in the object has been arranged by a specialist such as a medicine man, a shaman, or a witch-doctor. Whereas charms are considered to be impersonal objects of power, fetishes are considered to be personal because of the indwelling spirit.

Magic can refer to a wide use of mystical powers. Magic can be practiced by medicine men, witch-doctors, rainmakers, shamans, sorcerers, witches and ordinary people. There is believed to be black (harmful) magic, white (helpful) magic, magic through physical contact (contagious magic) and magic which operates through laws of similarity (homeopathic magic). Stories about the power of medicine and magic abound in Africa. Many claims are made about the powers of various kinds of medicine, magic, charms, spells, curses and fetish objects. The following true story about contagious magic in Ethiopia is typical of countless thousands of similar true stories:

> *A certain boy was in love with a girl, but she didn't love him. The boy went to a sorcerer to ask for magic power to make the girl love him. The sorcerer told the boy to bring him the girl's exercise book, which he did. The sorcerer wrote quotations from magic books into the exercise book in red ink. After this, the girl became irresistibly attracted to the boy. She even resented the attentions of any other girl for him.*
>
> *Later the boy died, but the girl didn't hear about his death immediately. The girl was tortured by evil spirits, until the moment a messenger came to tell her of the boy's death. As she heard of the boy's death, the spirits left the girl.*

Where does the power in medicine and magic come from? In a subject as broad as magic and mystical powers, there is room for almost every opinion. On the one hand, it has been shown many times that what was believed to be magic power was nothing more than clever deception. On the other hand, there are many documented cases of supernatural magic power seen by reliable witnesses. Between these two realities, there are many examples of unexplained occurrences which are attributed to medicine, magic, spells, curses and other explanations. What does the Bible say about such powers? Does God approve of their use? What is the Bible's perspective?

The Bible confirms the reality of supernatural power in the use of magic (Ex. 7:11–12, Deut. 18:10–12), but God condemns the use of this power (Deut. 18:10). He also condemns those who use it (Ex. 22:18, Jer. 27:9–10). Throughout Scripture, God condemns the use of mystical powers by one person to control or manipulate other people or situations. This can include the prayers of many non-Christian people (Prov. 28:9, Isa. 1:15) and in some cases, even the prayers of some professing Christians (James 4:3). Prayer which God approves of, is never an attempt to manipulate people or to force God to do our will. Rather, true prayer is cooperating with God to cause his will to prevail in the affairs of men. Jesus taught his disciples to pray, 'your kingdom come, your will be done on earth as it is in heaven' (Matt. 6:10).

In those cases where there is genuine supernatural power at work in the use of magic, medicine, spells, curses, fetishes and other forms of influence, the origin of this power is not from God but from Satan and his demons. Demons are very willing to share their powers with people who are living in sin and who are looking for mystical power to control others or to protect themselves. When people employ magic, traditional medicine, spells and other such powers, they are in fact employing the power and activity of demons even though the intended purpose of such magic may seem good. Throughout Scripture, the servants of God were always found in conflict with, and opposed to, those who used magic power. Thus Moses opposed the magicians of Egypt (Ex. 7:10–12) and the Apostle Peter opposed Simon the Samaritan magician (Acts 8:18–23).

There are two basic problems with the use of magic. First, whereas true prayer seeks to let God's will be done, magic seeks to cause a person's own will be done. Magic is based upon selfish desire and the desire to promote a person's own will. Second, the person using magic refuses to trust God and to leave the outcome of a situation with him. Instead, the person using magic is determined to cause his own will to prevail by using mystical power. Thus magic is really a form of sin and open rebellion against God.

Since Satan was the original rebel against God, the devil is only too willing, through his demons, to give supernatural power to those who seek it through using magic. This is true regardless of whether it seems to be good (white) magic or evil (black) magic. In Deuteronomy

18:10–12, God says, 'Let no one be found among you who . . . practices sorcery, engages in witchcraft, or casts spells. Anyone who does these things is detestable to the Lord.'

God's reason for condemning these practices is very much like his reason for condemning communication with the dead. It is sin. It leads men into a trap of Satan and from there into spiritual death (Deut. 32:16–18, 1 Cor. 10:20–22). Some weak African Christians still use magic, fetishes or charms. This reveals that they are looking to something other than God to help them in their time of need. This reveals a lack of trust in God. God wants us to trust in him and only in him. Psalm 40:4 says, 'Blessed is the man who makes the Lord his trust, who does not . . . turn aside to false gods.' Psalm 62:8 says, 'Trust in him at all times, O people.' Proverbs 29:25 says, 'Whoever trusts in the Lord is kept safe.'

It is a fearful thought to realize that people who do not trust Jesus as their Lord and Saviour have no protection from the spiritual and physical harm brought by deceiving spirits. People who follow traditional practices wrongly think that charms, medicine, fetishes and magic will protect them from the power of evil spirits and witches. But the painful truth is that by using these powers, such people walk right into the temptation of Satan and from there into sin and spiritual death. The very thing which they trusted to protect them from evil brings them under the direct power of Satan! What a cruel deception this is! Only God can deliver us from evil (Psalm 27:1). That is why we are taught to pray to him alone for protection from evil (Matt. 6:13).

WHAT IS THE CHRISTIAN RESPONSE TO USING MAGIC?

God knows that we will face problems and crises in life. He has not left us without a way to handle these problems. Instead of turning to magic, fetishes and charms, God wants his people to turn to him in prayer for the problems and needs they face. In Matt. 7:7 Jesus said, 'Ask, and it will be given to you, seek and you will find, knock and the door will be opened to you.' In Hebrews 4:16 we are told, 'Let us then approach the throne of grace with confidence, so that we may receive mercy, and find grace to help us in our time of need.'

There is never a time when it is right for Christians to use magic, charms, spells, spirit medicine, fetishes or other secret powers to solve their problems or to gain power over others. These things are sins. They reveal a lack of faith in God. They must be confessed and forsaken or else the judgment of God may come upon a person's life (Prov. 28:13). In Ephesus, the new Christians showed the reality of their repentance and faith in Christ by destroying all the objects of their magic practices (Acts 19:18–19). Christians today must do the same thing with their objects of non-Christian belief. God said to the people in Ezekiel's day, 'I am against your magic charms with which

you ensnare people like birds and I will tear them from your arms'
(Ezek. 13:20).

Christians should also verbally renounce and refuse all contact with
Satan's power in their own lives and in the lives of their ancestors.
According to God's word, the sins of ancestors are visited upon later
generations (Ex. 20:5, Ex. 34:7, Deut. 5:9). Satan knows this and uses
it to attack generations of people. It is important for a Christian to
verbally renounce and reject, in the name of Jesus and by the power of
his blood, the control which Satan has had on his family ancestors.

In the Law of Moses God revealed a relationship between some
cases of present judgment and suffering and the sins of former
generations which were passed down to the present generation. God
said, 'Those of you who are left will waste away in the lands of their
enemies because of their sins; also because of their fathers' sins they
will waste away. But if they will confess their sins and the sins of their
fathers. . . . I will remember my covenant with Jacob and my covenant
with Isaac and my covenant with Abraham, and I will remember the
land' (Lev. 26:39–42).

It is not magic, but only God and his holy angels who can protect a
Christian from the power of Satan (Eph. 6:10–11). The Bible says,
'For he will command his angels concerning you to guard you in all
your ways' (Psalm 91:11). The Christian is told to take up spiritual
weapons like faith, prayer, and the word of God, to defend himself
from evil spirits (Eph. 6:12–18).

J. WHAT DOES THE BIBLE SAY ABOUT DIVINATION?

In Africa, divination is a practice commonly used to discover the person
who supposedly caused someone's sickness, difficulties, or death. It is
used to get advice or to make decisions, such as whom one should
marry, when to plant certain crops, or when to make a particular
journey. It is used to learn how the ancestors have been offended and
how that situation may be corrected. People use divination to find out
which ritual or sacrifice will solve a particular problem. Sometimes
they want to get revenge on an enemy. Divination can also be used in
foretelling the future. It is a common practice in non-Christian
traditional cultures throughout the world. Divination is a way of
getting knowledge or advice about a situation without depending on
God, yet people who have this power often claim that God gave them
this power (Ezek. 13:6,9).

Divination can take place by shaking gourds, observing the organs
of animals, observing the pattern of small sticks or pieces of pottery
thrown on the ground, using a stick swinging over certain code objects,
interpreting dreams and visions, touching the fingers, examining the

lines on the palm of the hand, laying out cards or other objects, observing tea leaves in a cup, and many other methods. A diviner is someone who supposedly has the power to communicate with spirits and to receive secret information from the spirit world for the benefit of his client.

As with some magic and spirit possession, much of what passes for divination is nothing more than deceptive play-acting. A wise old man can give very perceptive advice from the ancestors because he himself knows his people only too well. He understands their relationships, their jealousies, their grudges, their frustrations, their attitude problems and their difficulties with each other. He then proceeds to prescribe solutions to such problems which will resolve the issue in a culturally acceptable way. A great many African diviners probably fall into this category.

In addition to the wise old man who holds the office of diviner in a community, there are also those individuals who do indeed have supernatural powers of secret knowledge beyond their own perception and judgment. The Bible confirms this kind of divination (Deut. 18:10) and indicates that the source of the diviner's secret knowledge is a spirit of divination (that is, a demon). From the story of Paul's encounter with a girl in Philippi who had this power, we learn that the power came from a spirit who lived in the girl (Acts 16:16–19). The girl in this story had the power of divination and certain men used her power to make money. Such people may be able to accurately prophesy future events or give other demonstrations of mystical power. When Paul cast the spirit out of the girl, she lost her power of divination and her owners became very angry because they lost their source of money (Acts 16:18–19).

WHY DOES GOD CONDEMN DIVINATION?

In Deuteronomy 18:10–12 the Lord says, 'Let no one be found among you . . . who practices divination or . . . interprets omens. Anyone who does these things is detestable to the LORD.' In Leviticus 19:26 the Lord says, 'Do not practice . . . divination or sorcery.' The reason why God condemns divination is very similar to the reason why he condemns magic and communication with the dead. As in other practices of non-Christian religion, divination reveals that a person is trusting in someone or something rather than trusting in the living God. When people put their trust in someone or something other than God, they sin by breaking the first commandment (Deut. 5:7). They also expose themselves to the possibility of demonic deception and influence.

Many people, including many Christians, are deceived about divination because it does not seem to be an evil thing. People are inclined to think of those who have such powers as persons who do good and who help others. For the same reasons they also perceive the medicine man or the witch-doctor as the friend of the community. In some places the same person will hold the office of diviner and medicine man. People of the community are likely to ask what could be wrong with finding out who caused their sickness or problem.

Just as with other powers which come from Satan, there is a subtle form of deception in genuine spirit divination. People tend to believe the words of the seer or the witchdoctor. But how can they know if these words are true? Jesus said that Satan is a liar and the father of lies (John 8:44). Since those who have the real power of divination have this power from a spirit, it is likely that those who trust the words of a diviner will be deceived by the lies of a demon.

Divination usually assigns the cause of sickness or misfortune to another person or to an ancestral spirit. The Bible most commonly assigns the cause of our problems to our own sin and rebellion against God (James 5:16). Divination often assumes that our problems come from the displeasure and discipline of the ancestors. The Bible states that it is God, not ancestors, who disciplines his people (Heb. 12:6). Christians need to be concerned about displeasing God, not their ancestors.

Divination also leads to seeking revenge on certain persons who have been identified by the diviner as the witch or sorcerer causing the sickness. Who but God can know if a certain person has really placed a curse on someone? The diviner sins greatly by putting himself in the place of God! Furthermore, we are seriously warned in the Bible not to take revenge, for vengeance belongs to God (Rom. 12:19). Thus the whole foundation of divination is sin and deception, whether it seems to be for the good of the community or not.

WHAT IS THE CHRISTIAN RESPONSE TO DIVINATION?

The Lord wants his people to trust him with the present as well as with the future. Psalm 62:8 says we should, 'trust in him at all times.' The Bible says, 'Trust in the Lord with all your heart, and lean not on your own understanding. In all your ways acknowledge him, and he will make your paths straight' (Prov. 3:5–6). God will give us understanding of what we need to know if we commit our way to him in prayer. God wants us to seek counsel and guidance from him, not from diviners (Lev. 19:26, Psalm 25:12, Psalm 32:8).

God's word, not the advice of a diviner, is the light for our path in life (Psalm 119:105). We are to trust him with what we do not know. The Bible says, 'The secret things belong to the Lord our God, but the things revealed (in the Bible) belong to us and to our children forever, that we may follow all the words of this law' (Deut. 29:19).

SUMMARY

Although life in present-day Africa is changing, the problem of traditional beliefs and practices is still a very important issue. Most traditional religions require a system of intermediaries such as divinities or ancestral spirits to approach God on man's behalf or to solve the problems of life. As a result, belief in rituals, sacrifices, divination, magic, curses, witchcraft and witch-doctors still forms a large part of the worldview of many people today. These beliefs also affect many Christians, especially those who are weak in their knowledge of God and his word.

In times of crisis, many weak Christians still turn back to these practices in order to solve their problems. By doing this, such Christians break the first of the Ten Commandments by putting other 'gods' before God (Deut. 5:7). They also bring trouble on themselves by bringing God's judgment on these sins. They lose God's protection against evil (the very thing they were seeking!) since they put their trust in other 'gods' to deliver them. That is exactly what Satan wants to happen, so he tempts people to use magic, divination, charms, fetishes, witch-doctors and other traditional practices in times of need.

Since Satan is the father of lies, it is Satan's plan to deceive people and to draw them away from Christ by promoting the false ideas of non-Christian religion. Therefore the Bible condemns communication with the dead, magic, divination, charms, spells, non-Christian rituals and sacrifices, and other practices which lead people away from trust in Christ.

It is very important for the Christian to understand that the Bible gives us the one completely accurate view of reality and truth. We must understand and believe the world-view of the Bible before we can deal with the problem of ancestral spirits, spirit possession, initiation practices, divination, magic, curses, witchcraft, witch-doctors and other issues associated with traditional beliefs. It is especially important to understand what the Bible teaches about the dead and what happens after a person dies.

Jesus Christ is King of Kings and God of all creation, including all spirits in the unseen world. In answer to believing prayer, God is more than able to deal with any problem or crisis which evil people or evil spirits may bring. Even if he chooses not to deliver a Christian from the crisis or to directly solve the problem, the Bible teaches that God 'causes all things to work together for good to those who love God' (Rom. 8:28 NASB).

There is a great need in Africa today for Christians to repent of all non-Christian beliefs and practices and to destroy the objects associated with these beliefs. There is a great need for churches to patiently disciple new believers into maturity in Christ through the word of God, so that

when difficulties and problems arise, Christians will know how to lean
on the Lord for his guidance, strength, help and deliverance from evil.

DISCUSSION QUESTIONS AND PROJECTS BASED ON
CHAPTER THIRTEEN

1. Show how Psalm 40:4 explains why God condemns the use of
   magic, charms and spells.

2. What is God's way to solve the problems and crises of life, instead
   of using magic, fetishes, charms and spells? Support your answer
   with verses of Scripture.

3. Why are funerals such important events in the life of traditional
   African culture? What should be the Christian view of funerals?
   Give Bible verses to support your view.

4. Discuss why rituals concerning ancestors are so common in
   traditional religions throughout the world. What is God's view of
   such rituals?

5. Divide into groups of four each to discuss what the relationship
   between ancestor practices and tribalism is?

6. Develop a Sunday School lesson for 9–14 year olds to present the
   Bible's teaching concerning speaking with the dead. Be sure to
   include specific Bible references. Begin the lesson with a story
   about someone who communicated with the spirits of the dead
   through a medium or a diviner.

7. Let someone explain to the group what a Christian's attitude
   should be toward relatives who have died. The speaker should
   support his view with Bible verses related to the subject.

8. Many people ask whether or not those who have died have any
   further opportunity to repent and believe in Christ. Divide into
   groups of four each to find an answer to this question from the
   Bible. Let someone in each group write out the verses they find.

9. Describe heaven according to what the Bible teaches in Revelation
   21 and 22.

10. Discuss what happens at death according to the Bible, both to
    Christians and to non-Christians.

11. Let the group discuss the kinds of magic and spirit medicine which
    are used by their people. Explain why God condemns the use of
    magic.

12. Let the group discuss the main methods which are used for
    divination in their area. Ask two people to explain to the rest of

the group why divination is wrong. Find Bible verses which condemn the use of divination and false prophecy.

SUGGESTED FOR FURTHER READING

Gehman, Richard J. *African Traditional Religion in Biblical Perspective*. Kijabe, Kenya: Kesho Publications, 1989.

Mbiti, John S. *African Religions And Philosophy*. London: SPCK, 1969.

Parrinder, Edward. G. *African Traditional Religion*. London: Sheldon Press, 1974.

14

Five Issues of Importance in Africa: Guidance, False Prophets, Syncretism, Mediators, Government

A policeman in a certain African city was caught by an angry mob in the midst of a riot. As the policeman sought to disperse them and to restore order, he was suddenly attacked by the crowd and trampled to the ground. He realized he might be killed in the next few moments. He cried out to the Lord for help.

As he was on the ground being beaten by the mob, the Lord suddenly appeared to him and told him he would not die. He also told him that when he recovered, he was to leave the police force and to enter Bible College in preparation for the ministry. Some minutes later he was rescued from the crowd.

As he thought over this experience, the policeman felt sure that the Lord had spoken to him through this vision. He proceeded to resign from the police force and to apply to the Bible College of his denomination. He was accepted and he graduated four years later. Today he is serving as a pastor in his denomination. This man is certain that the Lord guided him through this unusual experience and none of those who know him have any reason to doubt his calling.

This story highlights an important question for Christians. Which methods does God use to guide believers today? In addition to guidance, there are some other issues of importance to Christians in Africa which need to be examined. In this chapter, we will seek to answer the following questions:

A. How does God guide Christians today?
B. How may a Christian distinguish between true and false prophets?
C. The problem of syncretism: In which rituals, ceremonies and other cultural practices may a Christian participate?

D. Who can be a mediator between God and mankind?
E. What is a Christian's responsibility to his country's government?

A. HOW DOES GOD GUIDE CHRISTIANS TODAY?

An important issue for every Christian is guidance. How does God guide his people in the present time? A particularly important part of this issue for many people in Africa relates to dreams. When can dreams be trusted as guidance from God?

In Bible times, guidance took many forms. Sometimes God spoke directly and audibly to men, as he did to Abram in the Old Testament (Gen. 12:1–3), and to Paul in the New Testament (Acts 9:5–6). Sometimes God gave guidance through dreams, as when he confirmed to Gideon that he was to attack the Midianite army. In this case God guided Gideon through the dream of a Midianite soldier (Judges 7:9–15). In the New Testament, God guided Joseph through a dream to take Mary and Jesus to Egypt to escape the anger of King Herod (Matt. 2:13).

Sometimes God gave guidance through visions, as when he led Peter by means of a vision to go to the house of Cornelius to preach the gospel to him (Acts 10:10–17). Sometimes God gave guidance through miraculous events, as when he guided the Israelites through the desert by means of the pillar of cloud and fire (Ex. 40:36–37). Sometimes his guidance came through the messages of prophets, as with Samuel in the Old Testament (1 Sam. 15:1–3) and Agabus in the New Testament (Acts 21:10–11). Sometimes he gave guidance through the direct intervention of angels, as in the story of Balaam (Num. 22:21–35) and the story of Philip and the Ethiopian official (Acts 8:26).

What about the guidance of God today? Does he still use the same methods as in Bible times, or different ones? By what methods can we most commonly expect his guidance today?

To answer these questions, we must remember two things. First, in Bible times, printing had not yet been invented, and the ordinary person did not have his own copy of the Bible. People did not have any way to read and study the Bible for themselves in order to receive guidance. Most Jews only heard the Scripture when it was read to them in the synagogue. Second, we need to understand the difference between the circumstances in which guidance was needed by people in Bible times and the circumstances in which people need guidance today.

The Bible tells the story of God's redemption of man. That story often included unusual events. In unusual circumstances God often used unusual methods to accomplish his guidance. In more ordinary times, God usually gave his guidance in more ordinary ways.

As an example of this, when the Israelites were wandering in the trackless wasteland of the Sinai desert, God gave them the encouragement and guidance of the pillar of cloud and fire (Num. 9:16–23). He also provided food for them supernaturally with the supply of manna (Ex. 16:14–21). However, when they entered and settled in the land of Canaan, there was no longer a need for manna, so the miracle of manna ceased (Joshua 5:12). In a similar way, there was no longer the need for guidance by the pillar of cloud and fire when they were settled in the promised land. Thus we do not read of God guiding the Israelites with the pillar of cloud and fire in the land of Canaan.

In the matter of day to day living, God gave the Israelites detailed instructions on how to live and what to do in various situations through the written Law of Moses (Exodus 21:1). Many times in the Old Testament, the people of God were warned to obey these laws and rules (Ex. 23:21–22, Deut. 11:26–28). In the Bible, God emphasizes that obedience to his word is for our good and for our survival. In Deuteronomy 6:24 Moses said, 'The LORD commanded us to obey all these decrees and to fear the LORD our God, so that we might always prosper and be kept alive, as is the case today.'

Some people wrongly think that God's commandments are a burden. God's commandments are not a burden any more than a parents' rules are a burden to their children. Parents make rules for their children's good, and God has made moral laws for the good of mankind. In 1 John 5:3, the apostle says, 'His commands are not burdensome.' The truth is that God made us and he alone knows what is best and what will bring blessing to our lives. Therefore he has given us commandments and instructions to follow in his word. When we obey these commandments and follow these instructions, we will be blessed. When we obey God's commandments we will live as God intended people to live.

Thus it is God's plan to give us the guidance we need through his word. The book of Psalms begins with the words, 'Blessed is the man who does not walk in the counsel of the wicked . . . but his delight is in the law of the Lord, and on his law he meditates day and night' (Psalm 1:1–2). In the Psalms we are told that the word of God is the means by which God wants to guide us. The Psalmist says, 'Your word is a lamp to my feet, and a light to my path' (Psalm 119:105).

These words teach us that the primary way God intends to guide us in our daily lives is through the study of the Bible. This is one reason why daily Bible study is so important for the Christian. The Bible may not give us specific answers for each decision we must make, but it will always give us clear principles by which we can make the right decisions. By making the right decisions, we will bring blessing to our lives and honour to the Lord.

In addition to the principles found in God's word, the Bible suggests in both the Old and New Testament that it is a good thing for a believer to seek the advice of godly counselors. Proverbs 15:22 says, 'Plans fail for lack of counsel, but with many advisers, they succeed.' Colossians 3:16 says, 'Let the word of Christ dwell in you richly as you teach and admonish one another with all wisdom.' The advice of mature Christians is another means of God's guidance concerning the decisions of life.

From the verses quoted above we can see that the primary ways in which God intends to guide us in our lives today is through his word and through the advice of mature Christian friends. Guidance from God's word can be found in the teaching of Christ in the gospels and in the teaching of the apostles in the New Testament epistles. Guidance can be found in the advice given in the book of Proverbs. Guidance may also be found by correctly applying the stories of the Old and New Testament.

In certain circumstances today God may still use more unusual methods of guidance as he did in the case of the policeman at the beginning of this chapter. More unusual methods might include dreams, visions, or special situations involving the direct intervention of angels. Such methods would more likely be used by the Lord when the Bible is not available, as among people who cannot read. God may also use unusual means of guidance in difficult situations like war, imprisonment or natural disasters.

Think over the following story of guidance claimed through a dream:

A Christian young man named Peter was very much attracted to a girl named Talatu. He found that he often met Talatu on the road. She was very friendly to him. Peter decided that it must be God who was causing him to meet Talatu so often. Peter began to wonder if God was leading him to marry Talatu. The more he was with Talatu the more he liked her and the more he thought about her, day and night. Talatu came from a traditional family and she herself practiced the traditional religion of her people.

Although he did not read his Bible very much, Peter began to pray and ask the Lord for guidance concerning whether he should marry Talatu. One night Peter had a very clear dream in which he saw himself married to Talatu. When he awoke from the dream he decided that God had guided him through the dream to marry Talatu in answer to his prayer. Was this the guidance of God?

If Peter had read his Bible carefully, he would have discovered that God had already spoken to Christians about the kind of persons to whom they should be united, whether in marriage, business or in other ways. The Bible says, 'Do not be yoked together with unbelievers. For . . . what fellowship can light have with darkness? . . . What does a believer have in common with an unbeliever?' (2 Cor. 6:14–15). One application of this passage is clearly that God does not want a Christian to marry a non-Christian. Why then did Peter have such a dream?

The reason for the dream in this case was the strong desire Peter felt for Talatu. Most of us do not realize how strongly our emotions affect the way we think and the things we dream about. In this case the dream could not have come from God, for God never contradicts himself. If God has said something in his word, he will not say something different in a dream. No matter how strongly our emotions may move us, we must recognize that no dream, vision, or unusual circumstances can be considered guidance from God when it contradicts God's written word in the Bible. We must obey the written word of God as found in the Bible if we are to find true guidance from God.

When a boy's father wants to tell his son who is away at school what he wants him to do, he will write him a letter. So also, God has written us a letter. He has spoken to us in the Bible so that we will know his will for our lives.

It is true that God sometimes uses dreams to guide believers who come from a culture where dreams are an expected means of communication from God. As a general principle, God may use a form of guidance which is considered normal for a particular culture. He might not use that same means of guidance in a different culture where it is not considered normal. As a safeguard, when a Christian feels that God has spoken to him through a dream, the person should ask the advice of other Christians about the guidance in the dream. He or she should also carefully compare the guidance in the dream with the teaching of the Bible. If the guidance of the dream does not fully agree with the principles found in the Bible, he or she must not accept the dream as guidance from God.

God sometimes guides us through the way circumstances fit together or the way a situation develops. However, we must be very cautious with this kind of guidance. Sometimes circumstances may lead us completely away from the plan of God, as in the story of Peter above. The only time we should trust circumstances as guidance from God is when the situation is in complete agreement with the principles of the Bible and when mature Christian friends also confirm that such circumstances seem to be guidance from the Lord. Whatever the circumstances, God will not fail to make his guidance clear to us. He will choose a means of guidance which we can easily understand and follow.

In summary, we can say that God will always guide us through the teaching and principles of the Bible. He may also guide us through the advice of mature Christian friends. He may sometimes guide us through dreams, visions and other more unusual means. However, these unusual means may only be trusted for guidance when they confirm the teaching and principles found in the Bible. God will never contradict himself. Therefore, a Christian should devote serious time each day to the study of the Bible.

B. HOW MAY A CHRISTIAN DISTINGUISH BETWEEN TRUE AND FALSE PROPHETS?

In New Testament times God spoke through prophets in local churches because the New Testament was not yet complete and there were times when special revelations of God's truth were needed. Africa today is full of people who claim to be prophets of God. Some of these people even have unusual power, like the ability to heal sicknesses or to predict the future. How may we know if these self-proclaimed prophets are really from God or not?

Christians must be careful. Many African prophets are just very clever people who have the ability to speak well and to deceive others with their words and actions. In addition, the Bible says that demons can give people the ability to work miraculous signs (2 Thess. 2:9, Rev. 16:14). Usually such miracle workers claim they are sent by God.

Some people who claim to be prophets of God are false prophets whose powers come from Satan. Such people were also found in Bible times (e.g. Ex. 7:11–12, Acts 8:9–10). They were able to perform miraculous signs by the power of deceiving spirits. One such example is the slave girl in Acts 16:16–18 who was able to predict the future. Paul cast a demon out of this girl. After the spirit left her, she lost her power to predict the future (Acts 16:19).

How can a Christian tell a true prophet from a false one? A person can only be a true prophet when his or her prophecies come from God. How can a Christian recognize when a prophecy is from God? A prophecy that is from God can be identified by answering two questions:

1. Are the prophecies made to bring people to faith in Christ or to strengthen their relationship with Christ? The only true prophecies from God today will be somehow related to faith in Christ. In Rev. 19:10 the Bible says, 'the testimony of Jesus is the spirit of prophecy.' Thus the popular type of prophecy such as 'this popular singer will die in a car accident in the next month', is clearly not from God, even if the event happens. If the prophecy does not draw a person closer to Christ, such predictions are the work of deceiving spirits according to the word of God. This is true regardless of where people say they got their ability to foretell the future.

2. Are the person's prophecies correct all the time? If not, they are not from God according to Deuteronomy 18:21–22. Prophecy that is from God is never wrong, not even once. A prophet of God

makes no guesses or mistakes in his prophesying. A prophecy that is from God must pass both of these tests.

Although the revelation God has made to man about himself and his salvation is now completely contained in the Bible, words of encouragement or rebuke may need to be given to the local church through prophecy. When prophecies of this kind are given in a local church, they should always be carefully compared with the teaching of the Bible. If they agree with the Bible, then such prophecies may likely be from God. If they disagree with the Bible in any way, or if they change the Bible in any way, they cannot be from God.

The greatest need in the church today is for those who can correctly teach and explain the written word of God. The most important ministry of prophecy in the church today is the ministry of correctly explaining the Bible.

C. THE PROBLEM OF SYNCRETISM: IN WHICH RITUALS, CEREMONIES AND OTHER CULTURAL PRACTICES MAY A CHRISTIAN PARTICIPATE?

People who come from a non-Christian background are often tempted to simply add Christianity to the religious system from which they have come. The result is a mixture of both religions. Syncretism is the name given to this mixture of two or more religions.

The Israelites were guilty of this practice. The Bible says, 'They worshipped the LORD, but they also appointed all sorts of their own people to officiate for them as priests in the shrines at the high places. They worshiped the LORD, but they also served their own gods in accordance with the customs of the nations from which they had been brought' (2 Kings 17:32–33). God was very displeased with this. He said to the Israelites, 'Do not forget the covenant I have made with you, and do not worship other gods. Rather, worship the LORD your God; it is he who will deliver you from the hand of all your enemies' (2 Kings 17:38–39).

The Israelites, however, would not give up the practice of syncretism (2 Kings 17:40). It was because the Israelites participated in the pagan practices of the people around them that God sent them into captivity for 70 years as punishment (Jer. 25:5–11). In 2 Kings 17:7–9 we read, 'All this took place because the Israelites had sinned against the LORD their God. They . . . followed the practices of the nations which the LORD had driven out before them. . . . The Israelites secretly did things against the LORD their God that were not right.'

It is therefore very important for a Christian to have nothing to do with those rituals and practices which are associated with the traditional religious beliefs of his or her people. Long ago God warned his people,

'You must not do as they do in Egypt, where you used to live, and you must not do as they do in the land of Canaan, where I am bringing you. Do not follow their practices' (Lev. 18:3).

If a Christian participates in such syncretism, he will bring the Lord's judgment upon himself or herself just as the Israelites brought God's judgment upon themselves. Syncretism is a sin. This is true because many traditional rituals are related to non-Christian religions.

Some rituals can bring a person into contact with evil spirits. Paul said this was happening in the traditional religion of Corinth. He stated, 'the sacrifices of pagans are offered to demons, not to God, and I do not want you to be participants with demons' (1 Cor. 10:20).

The reasons why Africans practice syncretism are not hard to understand. Cultural renewal in Africa has caused many people to rediscover their African past. Since culture and religion are so closely related in Africa, this has led to a return to traditional religious practices. Along with this, emotional concerns for the spiritual welfare of relatives who died before the gospel came, has caused many people, including some leading theologians, to try to justify pre-Christian traditional religions. In the African world-view, God is often seen as distant and unapproachable. It therefore seems quite reasonable that human beings must relate to lesser spirits and divinities for the ordinary problems of life and not bother God. In some cases, the development of 'African Theology' has become an effort to justify the practices of traditional religions as a God-given preparation for the gospel of Christ. This view cannot be supported from the Bible.

The trend towards liberal theology in many older church denominations in Africa has also produced a mentality that it does not really matter what you believe, as long as you are sincere. In addition, among many new Christians, there is little knowledge of the Bible. Hence they do not recognize that God will not tolerate the worship of himself to be joined with the practices of non-Christian religions.

Many who decide to follow Christ do so without a thorough understanding of who he is and why they are following him. Perhaps they understand that Jesus died to provide forgiveness for their sins. But they do not understand that Jesus is also Lord of the universe and has all power in heaven and on earth. They do not realize that Jesus alone is more than able to meet the greatest need or crisis they may ever face.

In a time of personal need they may turn back to ancestral spirits or to mystical powers. Because their parents and ancestors used the practices of traditional religion for so many generations, they think that only these practices have real power to help them in a time of great need. They do not understand that by turning back to these spirits and powers they are putting other gods before the living God. By doing this, they lose the very help and protection they could have had from God himself, and instead they bring God's judgment upon themselves. To those who do this, God says, 'you have forsaken me and served other gods; therefore I will deliver you no more. Go and cry out to the gods which you have chosen; let them deliver you in the time of your distress' (Judges 10:13–14).

The living God will not accept a divided loyalty or help those who look to other 'gods' for help. That is why Jesus said that the greatest of all the commandments is: 'you shall love the LORD your God with all your heart and with all your soul and with all your might' (Deut. 6:5–NASB).

Many African Christians fall into the temptation of syncretism today when they claim to follow Christ but continue to go to the witch doctor for help, or to use fetishes, magic, charms, divination and even sorcery in a time of personal crisis. When Christians combine their Christian belief with these traditional practices they are practicing syncretism.

What does the Bible have to say about sacrifices and rituals? While it is true that many rituals and animal sacrifices were performed in the Old Testament, the Bible teaches us that Jesus alone has made the one sacrifice for sins which God accepts. We learn from the New Testament that the Old Testament sacrifices and rituals could not take away sins (Heb. 10:4).

What then was the purpose of these Old Testament rituals? Colossians 2:17 explains that these things were 'a shadow of the things that were to come. The reality, however, is found in Christ.' In other words, the Old Testament system of sacrifices and rituals were God-given pictures of the sacrifice and salvation of Jesus Christ. The New Testament tells us, 'Day after day every (Old Testament) priest stands and performs his religious duties; Again and again he offers the same sacrifices which can never take away sins . . . because by one sacrifice, he (Jesus) has made perfect forever those who are being made holy' (Heb. 10:12–14).

To take part in rituals is important to many Africans. Jesus commanded a once-for-all ceremony to testify to a person' regeneration in Christ. This is the ritual of water baptism (Matt. 28:19). As discussed in chapter thirteen under initiation, it is especially important in Africa for the local church to give public prominence to the ritual of water baptism. It should be a major event in the church community.

Jesus also commanded another ritual so that Christians would remember his death on the cross for their sins (Matt. 26:26–28). This ritual is practiced at regular intervals by all Christians in the world. It is the celebration of Holy Communion. This ritual should be repeated regularly in order to keep the truth of Jesus' death fresh in the minds of his people.

There are some rituals or ceremonies in African life which are not related to non-Christian religions. Some groups of people have a time of great celebration at the beginning of each new year. Some have a special celebration after a successful animal hunt. Every culture in the world has special customs and traditional practices which accompany weddings and childbirth. In most Western and many modern African weddings there is a certain ritual practice where the bride and groom ceremonially cut the wedding cake together and feed each other a small piece. This is an example of a harmless cultural practice.

How should a Christian decide which rituals to participate in and which ones to refuse?

As a general guideline, it can be said that there is probably no harm participating in a practice not associated with non-Christian religions, and not involving anything which the Bible condemns or which would spoil a Christian's testimony. A Christian should seek to maintain a positive Christian testimony in whatever he does. For the sake of honouring the Lord Jesus Christ, his or her conduct should be above criticism at all times (Phil. 2:15). Jesus said, 'Let your light shine before men, that they may see your good deeds, and praise your Father in heaven' (Matt. 5:16).

Many practices are not mentioned by name in the Bible. If one is unsure about a practice, it would be best to question several mature Christian elders to see how they would evaluate the practice. If the elders have any warning or doubt about the practice, it would be best not to participate in it so as not to commit unconscious sin.

There is another related issue. With practices not specifically mentioned in the Bible, some Christians may feel they can participate without committing sin, while other Christians may consider the practice to be wrong. In such a case, the person who thinks it is not wrong (the 'strong' Christian) should abstain from the practice for the sake of the conscience of the one who thinks it is wrong (the 'weak' Christian). This is what Paul taught in Romans 14:1–16 and 1 Corinthians 8:7–13.

An example of such a situation might be eating the meat of an animal which had not been bled to death, as in the case of an animal struck by a vehicle on the road. All Muslims, and some Christians, based on Leviticus 17:12–14 and Acts 15:29, may feel that it is a sin to eat such meat. Other Christians, based on Mark 7:19, may feel there is no sin involved. In such a case, the Christian who feels there is no sin in eating the meat, should not eat it if another person present would be offended.

In the matter of seeking medical help in time of sickness, it is especially important to avoid those who practice traditional religion along with traditional medicine. Some of those practicing traditional medicine may be pure herbalists or bone specialists. In that case there will be no problem of sin in consulting them, since there is no non-Christian religion involved. Many herbalists, however, seek the help of spirits when they prepare their traditional medicines. A Christian should not take this kind of medicine and unknowingly participate in something involving demons.

On the practical side, the medical help from some pure herbalists may not be safe, even if there is no spiritual danger involved. This is especially true for medicines to produce conception of children and medicines against hepatitis. A Christian must remember that his body is a gift from God to be used for God's glory (1 Cor. 6:19–20). Therefore a Christian should seek to get the best possible medical help available.

D. WHO CAN BE A MEDIATOR BETWEEN GOD AND MANKIND?

Mediators are very important in Africa. Many practices are built around the function of a mediator. A mediator is one who works between two people or two groups to bring them together into an agreement. Many African marriage arrangements and even some business arrangements are accomplished through a mediator. Many traditional religions believe that God cannot be approached directly, but only through a mediator, such as an ancestral spirit.

Who can represent mankind before God and who can represent God to mankind? Is it possible to relate to God directly without using the mediation of lesser spirits? Those who follow non-Christian religions often believe that ancestral spirits, divinities, prophets, or other specialists will act as mediators between human beings and God. Even some Christians think that departed Christians or Jesus' mother, Mary, can act as mediators between them and God. What does the Bible say?

The Bible says, 'There is one God, and one mediator between God and men, the man Christ Jesus' (1 Tim. 2:5). This statement indicates that there is only one official mediator between God and mankind whom God will accept. That person is Jesus Christ (Heb. 9:15). People who seek other mediators are likely to come under the influence of demonic spirits.

This is not to say that Christians cannot pray for their fellow-believers. They can pray and they should pray. However, only Jesus Christ can officially represent mankind before God. And only Christ can officially represent God to mankind. He alone has brought about the reconciliation of God and mankind through his death on the cross (Col. 1:19–20). Furthermore, prayer to God is meaningless unless it is made on the basis of a personal relationship with Christ. This is the meaning of praying 'in the name of Jesus' (John 16:24–27). Only Jesus can let our prayers be heard by God the Father. The whole idea of the need for spirit mediators in order to approach God is a deception of demons (1 Tim. 4:1). This deception has kept some people from a personal relationship with God through Jesus Christ.

E. WHAT IS A CHRISTIAN'S RESPONSIBILITY TO HIS COUNTRY'S GOVERNMENT?

Christians in almost every country of the world complain about the government of their country. It is true that there have been few completely honest government officials in history. What should be the attitude of Christians toward the government of their country. What does the Bible say?

In order to answer this question, a Christian must understand the origin of human government. From a human point of view it is easy to say that any particular government only exists because certain strong men were able to gain power over others through military force or political effort.

The Bible, however, gives us a different perspective on human governments. We learned in chapter four that God has the power to control everything. He is sovereign (Psalm 103:19). One of the ways in which God exercises his sovereignty is in the rise and fall of human governments. In Romans 13:1–2 we read these surprising words: 'Everyone must submit himself to the governing authorities, for there is no authority except that which God has established. The authorities that exist have been established by God. Consequently he who rebels against the authority is rebelling against what God has instituted.' The Bible teaches that human governments are established by God.

Most Christians find this statement very hard to accept, especially when they are living under a very corrupt or oppressive government. These words are all the more surprising when we remember that Paul wrote them to Christians living in Rome. Rome was a very pagan city with some very corrupt and oppressive rulers, called Caesars. Some of these Caesars persecuted the Christians bitterly in the years after Paul's epistle to the Romans.

Yet the Holy Spirit tells us through Paul that there is no government authority except that which God has established. By saying this, the Bible is not saying that every government is good. It is simply stating the fact that human government is God's plan for mankind's good. Human government is God's way of keeping law and order in a country (Rom. 13:3–4). Imagine for a moment what conditions would be like if there was no government at all in a country. People would behave almost completely in accordance with their sinful nature, with no fear of being punished for their behaviour. Crime would be out of control. There would be no postal service or any other government agency. Life would soon become unbearable. In Romans 13:4 we read, 'He (the government official) is God's servant, an agent of wrath to bring punishment on the wrongdoer.'

Some governments are obviously much more corrupt than others. What are Christians to do when they live under the rule of an evil government?

The Bible is very specific about a Christian's responsibility to the government of his country. He is to pray and he is to obey. In 1 Timothy 2:1–2 we are told, 'I urge then, first of all, that . . . prayers . . . be made . . . for kings and all those in authority.' Christians often spend much time complaining about their country's government. But how much time do they spend seriously praying for the government and its officials? This is not just a good idea, it is God's commandment. In fact, it is of first importance. 'I urge . . . first of all,' says the apostle (1 Tim. 2:1–2).

It is a serious sin for Christians to fail to pray for the government of their country. Much unnecessary suffering and bad government is a direct result of a failure by God's people to pray regularly and seriously for their government. It was pointed out in chapter eleven that the devil seeks control over the world through influencing human governments. When we pray for government officials, we hinder Satan's influence on these officials. We also make the wisdom and help of the Lord available to those officials through our prayers. It would be a most worthy practice for every Christian to devote time each week to fasting and prayer for his country's government. If Christians all over the world were to do this, the course of human history could be changed. Local churches should also devote special times to prayer for the government of their country.

God has promised to answer prayer for his people (Matt. 18:19). There is no one else besides Christians who have access to God to get help for the government of their country.

Since God has commanded us to pray for our government leaders, he is ready to answer those prayers. If the government is very bad, God may change it completely. In Daniel 2:21 we read, 'He sets up kings and deposes them.'

God may not always change the entire government in answer to our prayers but he may change the hearts of those in authority. An amazing example of this in recent times, is the way the Lord changed the hearts of many leaders in communist countries. Many of the very men who encouraged communism and imprisoned Christians, renounced communism in the early 1990's. In the former Soviet Union, former atheistic communists actually requested Christians to come and teach Christianity in the public schools! Only God can change human hearts like that!

There were probably several reasons why such great changes took place in the former Soviet Union. The most important reason, however, was the prayers of God's persecuted people. These Christians continued to pray for an end to communist oppression during the 70 years of Marxist rule. God can also change the hearts of African government leaders when his people faithfully pray.

In places where the country has a democratic government, it is a Christian's responsibility to prayerfully take part in the elections of the government. The experience of some democratic governments has shown that when Christians unite their voices about issues that matter, they are able to influence the policies and laws of their government in a righteous way according to the will of God.

The second responsibility which Christians have towards their government is to obey the government and to keep its laws. In 1 Peter 2:13–15 we read, 'Submit yourselves for the Lord's sake to every authority instituted among men: whether to the king, as the supreme authority, or to governors, who are sent by him to punish those who do wrong and to commend those who do right. For it is God's will that by doing good you should silence the ignorant talk of foolish men.'

The only exceptions to the rule that Christians should obey the government of their country, are when the government forbids Christians to speak about Christ, or orders them to do something which breaks the law of God. In Acts 4:17–20, the Apostles Peter and John were forbidden by the Jewish leaders to speak about Christ. They said that they must obey God rather than men in this matter (Acts 4:19–20). In Daniel 3:13–18, the three friends of Daniel were ordered by King Nebuchadnezzar to bow down and worship the idolatrous golden image the king had set up. They refused to break the second commandment (Ex. 20:4–5) and bow down to Nebuchadnezzar's image. As a result, they were thrown into a furnace of fire. But God delivered them from the fire right before Nebuchadnezzar's eyes (Dan. 3:19–27).

By praying for their government instead of complaining about it, and by obeying its laws, Christians will have a good testimony for Christ before the world. They will also 'silence the ignorant talk of foolish men' (1 Pet. 2:15).

SUMMARY

The Bible indicates that God used different ways to guide his people at different times in history. However, these situations occurred before the Bible was written or was widely available to God's people, as it is today. The Bible indicates that the word of God is the primary means by which God leads and teaches his people (Psalm 1:1–2, Psalm 119:105). The Bible also suggests that it is good to seek advice from godly counsellors, including parents (Prov. 1:8, Prov. 11:14, Col. 3:16). In unusual circumstances, and in some cultures where God has used other means of guidance, such as dreams, he may still use such means today. However, when a Christian thinks God is guiding through unusual means, such guidance must be compared with the truth of the Bible. God will never give guidance contrary to his word.

There are many people in Africa today who claim to be prophets of God. How can a person recognize a true spokesman for God? The

Bible says, 'the testimony of Jesus is the spirit of prophecy' (Rev. 19:10). The only true prophets of God today are those who accurately proclaim the truth about Jesus Christ, according to the Bible, and turn people's hearts toward Christ.

What about participation in traditional ceremonies? When does such participation become compromise and syncretism? Because non-Christian beliefs deceive people and lead them away from a direct relationship with God through Christ, God commands his people to completely put away the beliefs and practices of false religion (Lev. 18:3, 2 Kings 17:38–39). For this reason, ceremonies or celebrations which include the elements of non-Christian religion must be avoided. If the issue is not clear, it would be wise to seek the advice of mature Christian elders.

It makes sense in African culture that God should only be approached through mediators. But who is qualified to approach God on behalf of men? Certainly not the demons who say they are ancestral spirits! The Bible says there is only one person who is qualified to represent mankind before God, and God before men. That person is Jesus Christ (1 Tim. 2:5, Heb. 9:15).

What should Christians do who live under an evil or oppressive government? The Bible commands all Christians, in all circumstances, to pray (1 Tim. 2:1–2) and to obey (1 Pet. 2:13–15). The Bible says that it is God himself who established the institution of human government (Rom. 13:1). In answer to the believing prayers of his people (Matt. 6:10) God is well able either to improve a bad government or to replace it with another government. History reveals that God has done both at various times, when His people have faithfully prayed.

DISCUSSION QUESTIONS AND PROJECTS BASED ON CHAPTER FOURTEEN

1. What were some of the ways by which God guided his people in the Old Testament?

2. What two ways did God provide to give guidance to all his people today?

3. Divide into small groups of three each. Discuss the following questions:
   (a) In what sort of situations would you expect God to guide his people through dreams?
   (b) Under what sort of circumstances would you expect God to guide his people through the direct intervention of angels?

4. Let three persons relate how the Lord guided them specifically in decision making through the teaching of the Bible.

5. Let three persons relate how the Lord guided them specifically in decision making through the advice of mature Christian friends.

6. If anyone in the group has experienced God's guidance in an unusual way, such as through a dream or through the intervention of an angel, let the person relate the story to the rest of the group. After the testimony, have a group discussion on why the Lord may have chosen that type of guidance in the situation.

7. Enquire if anyone in the group has listened to the preaching of an African prophet. If there is someone, ask the person to relate what the prophet spoke about and the main point of his message. Let the group decide whether it was a true or false prophet and why.

8. Divide into small groups of about four each. List as many examples as possible of syncretism between paganism and Christianity which the members of the group have personally seen.

9. Ask the same small groups as in the previous question, to discuss why they think the people in each of the situations they have listed, fell into the practice of syncretism. For each of these situations, discuss how the group would counsel the person mixing his Christian beliefs with the practices of traditional religion.

10. What is wrong with the belief held by many Roman Catholics that Jesus' mother Mary can speak to God on behalf of sinners?

11. What are the two main responsibilities which a Christian has towards the government of his country?

12. Suppose the government in a country has a very anti-Christian attitude. Discuss what the response of Christians should be to that situation.

13. What methods do Africans commonly use for seeking guidance? Which of these methods is approved by God? Support your answer from the Bible.

14. Discuss the nature of African rituals, ceremonies and festivals and their role in African life. How do these ceremonies relate to the life of the Christian community?

15. Discuss African intermediaries, gods and divinities in relationship to Christ as mediator.

16. How would you relate the word of God to the counsel of the village elders?

17. What is the African concept of government or authority? How does that relate to modern African society and to the Bible?

SUGGESTED FOR FURTHER READING

Duewel, Wesley. *Let God Guide You*. Grand Rapids, Michigan: Zondervan, 1988.

Hastings, Adrian. *African Christianity*. London: Geoffrey Chapman, 1976.

Hastings, Adrian. *A History of African Christianity, 1950–1975*. Cambridge: Cambridge University Press, 1979.

Hastings, Adrian, *The Church in Africa, 1450–1950*. Oxford: Oxford University Press, 1995.

Kato, Byang. *African Cultural Revolution And The Christian Faith*. Jos, Nigeria: Challenge Publications, 1975.

Pytches, David. *Does God Speak Today?* London: Hodder, 1989.

Yamamori, Tetsumao, and Taber, Charles R. eds. *Christopaganism Or Indigenous Christianity*. Pasadena, California: William Carey Library, 1975.

15

The Church and Cultural Prejudice

'In those days when the number of disciples was increasing, the Grecian Jews among them complained against the Hebraic Jews because their widows were being overlooked in the daily distribution of food. So the Twelve gathered all the disciples together and said, "It would not be right for us to neglect the ministry of the word of God in order to wait on tables. Brothers, choose seven men from among you who are known to be full of the Spirit and wisdom. We will turn this responsibility over to them and will give our attention to prayer and the ministry of the word." This proposal pleased the whole group. They chose Stephen, a man full of faith and of the Holy Spirit; also Philip, Procorus, Nicanor, Timon, Parmenas, and Nicolas from Antioch, a convert to Judaism. They presented these men to the apostles, who prayed and laid their hands on them. So the word of God spread. The number of disciples in Jerusalem increased rapidly, and a large number of priests became obedient to the faith' (Acts 6:1–7).

The married students at the Bible College had been given a large piece of land to grow grain and other crops for their families. Part of the land was especially good for growing rice in the rainy season. An expatriate staff member of the school had been assigned the oversight of the farming needs of the married students. He had appointed a student assistant to divide up the farm land each year. The student assistant had secured two student helpers to help him with the land division. Unknown to the expatriate staff member, all three students on the farming committee came from the same ethnic group.

During the third year of the farming committee, some of the married students came to the staff member and complained about the division of the farm land. They asked him if he was aware that all the best land for growing rice had gradually over the three years been assigned to students from one particular ethnic group? Did he

265

realize that the best farm land was now assigned to members of the same ethnic group as the members of the farming committee? The embarrassed staff member admitted he was unaware of the problem. He dismissed the existing farming committee and appointed a new committee of three men, each from a different ethnic group and a different part of the country. The land was re-divided and impartially reassigned to the married students. Peace was restored.

Although the two incidents above took place at different places and at different times in church history, they have something important in common. They present a serious problem which troubles the church. The problem is cultural prejudice. In this chapter we will take a close look at what the Bible says about a person's cultural identity in relation to being part of the church. We will seek to answer the following questions:

A. What does the Bible say about a Christian's cultural origin (clan, tribe, race, and language)?
B. What are some of the problems in the church caused by multi-cultural membership?
C. How may problems of cultural prejudice in the church be solved?
D. What is God's plan for the church in relation to different cultures, races, and languages?

A. WHAT DOES THE BIBLE SAY ABOUT A CHRISTIAN'S CULTURAL ORIGIN (CLAN, TRIBE, RACE, AND LANGUAGE)?

Different English words are used to describe a person's cultural origin. At different times we speak of a person's clan, tribe, people, race or nationality. Sometimes we use the term ethnic group or ethnic origin. In this chapter we will use the general term ethnic group to refer to the cultural origin of any group of people.

The Bible uses several words to describe the cultural origins of different groups of people. In Revelation 7:9, a great multitude of people is described as coming from 'every nation, tribe, people and language.' In order to understand the way God sees the divisions of mankind, let us compare the popular use of the word 'nation' with the biblical use of the word 'nation'.

The popular use of the word 'nation' refers to the different political countries of the world. In 1980, the United Nations recognized 223 such political nations. The number of such nations changes from year to year. Throughout history, politicians and soldiers have divided people up into political nations in order to achieve their own political or military goals. These divisions usually had little to do with the way the people of an area grouped themselves together by language and cultural similarities. Political borders are usually drawn without considering the cultural similarities or differences of the people concerned. As a result, many countries of the world consist of more than one culture or language group. There is often tension and conflict between the different groups.

In many cases, the same ethnic group is found living in more than one country. In Africa, the Maasai people are found in both Kenya and Tanzania. The Malinke people are found in Senegal, Mali, Guinea and some other countries. The Daasenach people are found in Kenya, Ethiopia and Sudan. The Fulani people are found in many countries from East to West Africa.

What does the Bible mean by the word 'nation'? The word translated 'nation' in the New Testament is the Greek word *ethnos*. According to the *Theological Dictionary Of The New Testament*, *ethnos* refers to, 'a multitude bound by the same manners, customs or other distinctive features.' It is from the word *ethnos* that we derive the English word ethnic. Ethnic is a word which means, 'relating to a racial, national or cultural group.' Thus a nation (*ethnos*) according to the Bible is a particular ethnic group. From this we can see that the biblical use of the word 'nation' is different from the popular use of the word.

God sees the human race as divided according to the language and culture groups to which people belong. The human race developed into different language and culture groups through the descendants of the sons of Noah according to Genesis 10:4, 20, 31–32. Also, the Bible says that at the tower of Babel, 'the LORD confused the language of the whole world. From there the LORD scattered them over the face of the whole earth' (Gen. 11:9). Since people could not understand each other, they separated according to their own languages. From there they formed separate communities based on a common language. It is reasonable to assume that each of these language groups developed their own patterns of culture. Thus the division of the human race into separate ethnic nations was hastened by what happened at the tower of Babel.

With time, many of these original groups probably split into smaller groups with different language dialects and other cultural differences. Today language scholars have identified more than 5000 totally different language groups in the world. Some countries have many such ethnic groups within their political borders. Nigeria, for example, has more than 400 ethnic groups.

From God's point of view, each of these language-culture groups is a separate nation of people. In Acts 17:26 we read, 'From one man (i.e. Adam) he (God) made every nation (*ethnos*) of men that they should inhabit the whole earth, and he determined the times set for them and the exact places where they should live.' In the Great Commission, Jesus commanded his followers to take the gospel to every one of these nations of people, in order to make disciples in each group. In Matthew 28:19–20 Jesus said, 'Therefore go and make disciples of all nations (*ethne*), baptizing them in the name of the Father, and of the Son, and of the Holy Spirit, and teaching them to obey everything I have commanded you.' From this passage we see that it is God's will that the good news of Jesus Christ should be taken to all ethnic groups in the world.

In the book of Revelation we discover that when God's purposes are completed, there will be people from every one of these ethnic groups gathered around the throne of God to worship him. In Revelation 5:9–10 we read, 'You (Jesus) are worthy to take the scroll and to open its seals, because you were slain, and with your blood you purchased men for God from every tribe and language and people and nation.' In Revelation 7:9–10 we read, 'I looked, and there before me was a great multitude that no one could count, from every nation, tribe, people and language, standing before the throne and in front of the Lamb . . . And they cried out in a loud voice: "Salvation belongs to our God, who sits on the throne, and to the Lamb." '

These verses make it clear that God sees every person as belonging to a particular language-culture group (nation). His plan is that people from every one of these groups should believe in Jesus Christ and become a part of his Church. The prophecy in Revelation 7:9–10 makes it clear that God's plan will finally be completed at the end of history, at which time there will be people from every different ethnic group on earth in the body of Christ.

There is no suggestion in the Bible that God considers any culture group superior to all other culture groups. The Israelites were privileged to have been chosen by God (Rom. 9:4–5). They were not chosen, however, because they were superior to other culture groups. In fact, in Deuteronomy 4:37–38, God spoke about driving out before the Israelites nations which were 'greater and stronger' than the Israelites. This statement probably referred to the population and military strength of these other nations, but there is no suggestion here or elsewhere in the Bible that any ethnic group is superior to all other ethnic groups. The idea of racial or ethnic superiority is an idea which has come from man's pride. The Bible says, 'The LORD detests all the proud in heart' (Prov. 16:5). In Christ, God sees all people in the same way. Christians are forgiven sinners regardless of their racial or national origin (Rom. 3:23–25, Col. 2:13).

B. WHAT ARE SOME OF THE PROBLEMS IN THE CHURCH CAUSED BY MULTI-CULTURAL MEMBERSHIP?

In the world, people from different cultures, races and ethnic groups have difficulty getting along with each other peacefully. They often do not trust one another. They often think of themselves as better than other groups. This tendency toward national pride is called ethnocentrism. At times they even despise other people and their cultures. Unfortunately, the situation is not much better in some local churches. It often happens that one of the ethnic groups in a church will break off from the others in order to form their own separate church group.

Differences of cultural origin have caused many problems between different groups of people in the world. Racial, cultural and religious differences have even caused wars. This can be seen in the many conflicts between Arabs and Jews in the Middle East, between Hindus and Muslims in India, between Hutus and Tutsis in Rwanda and between Croats, Serbs and Bosnians in modern Yugoslavia. The Bible has some important things to say about the cultural differences between Christians and the need for unity in the church.

Agreement and unity among Christians is one of the most important characteristics which God wants to see in a local church. There are very few problems which will hurt the witness of a local church as much as disagreement, quarreling, and disunity. The need for agreement is a matter repeatedly mentioned in the New Testament. Paul appealed to the Christians at Philippi to, 'be of the same mind . . . united in spirit, intent on one purpose' (Phil. 2:2). In his letter to the Ephesians, Paul urged the Christians to, 'walk in a manner worthy of the calling with which you have been called . . . being diligent to preserve the unity of the Spirit in the bond of peace' (Eph. 4:1,3).

Jesus prayed for harmony and agreement among his followers when he prayed, 'that they may be one, just as we are one' (John 17:22). In Matthew 12:25 Jesus said, 'Every kingdom divided against itself will be ruined.' This statement by Christ carries a strong warning. When the Christians in a local church are not at peace with each other, their witness will be seriously damaged. They will not experience the blessing and power of the Lord in their church life.

People of the same language and culture naturally tend to gather together into one group where they are known, understood and respected. At the same time, they tend to think of all other people as strangers or foreigners, because they do not understand the language and cultural practices of the others. Because they do not understand other groups, they tend to despise them as being less worthy or less intelligent. This leads to criticism, suspicion, lack of trust, lack of communication, unfriendliness and even open hostility. Church members from different culture groups sometimes feel the same way about each other.

Because of their differences, groups of people tend to withdraw from one another, as they did at the tower of Babel. They also tend to think that their own group and their own culture is the best. Because of this, prejudice and misunderstanding between different cultural groups has been common all over the world throughout history. This kind of prejudice has resulted in many evil practices, such as slavery and war. Land disputes, political oppression and ethnic wars, have resulted from cultural prejudice. In most cases the basic problem is that people just don't like and won't trust others who differ from themselves.

Similar cultural prejudices have existed in the church from the very beginning, as seen in the account at the beginning of this chapter. When the Greek-speaking Jews and the local Hebraic Jews began to have fellowship together in the early church, the Hebraic Jews neglected the Grecian-Jewish widows in the daily serving of food when the believers ate together (Acts 6:1). This early Christian history sounds very similar to the other true incident at the beginning of this chapter which took place almost 2000 years later in an African Bible College! Evidently, the hearts of people have not changed very much!

It is important to understand that God did not want that kind of prejudice to continue. He gave the early church leaders wisdom to work out a solution which would eliminate this prejudiced behaviour (Acts 6:2–6). The apostles decided to set apart seven men of good reputation who were full of the Holy Spirit and godly wisdom. From their names, it appears that these men were Greek Christians. They probably came from the group with the complaint of neglect. They would have the responsibility of making sure that their widows got their fair share of food (Acts 6:2–6). This solution pleased the whole congregation. It enabled the early church to avoid serious disagreement and disunity. As a result of this God-given solution, the church greatly increased in number almost immediately (Acts 6:7). The unified church had a strong witness for Christ.

This true story illustrates the important truth that unity builds the local church and disunity destroys it. The strength resulting from unity is suggested in Ecclesiastes 4:12, which says, 'Though one may be overpowered, two can defend themselves. A cord of three strands is not quickly broken.'

C. HOW MAY PROBLEMS OF CULTURAL PREJUDICE IN THE CHURCH BE SOLVED?

We can see in the account from Acts 6 that God is able to give church leaders the wisdom to solve problems of cultural prejudice. God has promised to give godly wisdom to solve problems when we pray in faith for this wisdom (James 1:5–6). The solution God gave to the problem in Acts 6:1 brought blessing to the church. It encourages us that the presence of cultural prejudice and tribalism is not a hopeless situation. God can provide a solution if his people are willing to follow his leading. What are the general principles for solving problems of cultural prejudice and tribalism?

The first principle which must be understood is that it is a sin to continue with attitudes of prejudice and mistrust, and ill-treatment of fellow-members of the church. The Apostle James stated that showing partiality (i.e. prejudice) is a sin which breaks the law of God. In James 2:9 he said, 'But if you show favouritism, you sin and are convicted by the law as lawbreakers.'

The second principle needed to overcome cultural prejudice, is the principle of unselfish love with humility. We are commanded by Christ to love our fellow-Christians (John 15:12). Paul asked two women at Philippi to learn to work together in harmony (Phil. 4:2). The Philippian church was evidently struggling with their own problem of disunity. He urged them to be of one mind and purpose, regarding others as more important than themselves (Phil. 2:2–3). Pursuing an attitude of humility and cooperation is a practical demonstration of the love of Christ. It pleases the Lord and builds up the church (Eph. 4:15–16).

Love is extremely important. Jesus said, 'By this all men will know that you are my disciples, if you love one another' (John 13:35). Unselfish love and cultural prejudice cannot exist together. If there is unselfish love in an attitude of humility, favouritism and prejudice must be abandoned. If we do not have love for one another, we reveal that we are not really Jesus' disciples. If Christians do not show love to one another, it will ruin their witness before an unbelieving world. Non-Christians will mock Christ and mock the church.

The third principle needed to solve the problem of cultural prejudice is that church leaders must be selected on the basis of Scriptural qualifications rather than on human abilities, education or tribal loyalty. The seven deacons selected to solve the problem of the unfair distribution of food in Acts 6,were chosen because they were men who were wise, who had a good (character) reputation, and who were filled with the Holy Spirit (Acts 6:3). It is only the wisdom and work of the Holy Spirit that can overcome the problem of tribalism and cultural prejudice.

In the time of Christ, Gentiles were all those people who were not Jews. Jews thought they were superior to all other people, so they despised Gentiles. They referred to Gentiles as dogs. When God wanted Peter, the Jew, to take the gospel to the Gentile soldier Cornelius, he had to give Peter a special vision of a sheet full of clean and unclean animals. He did this in order to show Peter that God was able to make the Gentiles spiritually clean (Acts 10:10–28). God had to repeat the vision three times (Acts 10:16) to persuade the prejudiced Peter, for no proper Jew (such as Peter) would ever think of entering the house of an unclean Gentile!

As a result of this experience Peter made an important statement about how God wants us to think about people from other culture groups. Speaking to Cornelius and his friends in Acts 10:28, Peter said, 'God has shown me that I should not call any man impure or unclean.' A little later Peter said to the same group, 'I now realize how true it is that God does not show favouritism, but accepts men from every nation (*ethnos*) who fear him and do what is right' (Acts 10:34–35).

This statement by Peter reveals a great step of spiritual growth in Peter's life. It is a step which God wants every believer in Christ to take. It is God's will that every Christian should be free from cultural, racial and ethnic prejudice. Christians need to see and love other Christians the way God sees them and loves them.

How can Christians enjoy heaven unless they are truly set free from their cultural prejudices? In heaven they will live side by side with beloved brothers and sisters in Christ from every group of people on earth (Rev. 7:9–10).

D. WHAT IS GOD'S PLAN FOR THE CHURCH IN RELATION TO DIFFERENT CULTURES, RACES, AND LANGUAGES?

The Church is the eternal community of all believers in Christ. This includes both those who have died and gone to heaven and those still living on earth (1 Cor. 12:27, Eph. 3:15). Some day the church will consist of men and women from every culture, language, race and ethnic group on earth (Gen. 12:3, Rev. 5:9–10, Rev. 7:9–10).

There is a very important relationship between the church and cultural origins. The church is the multi-cultural, eternal, extended family of God, built upon Jesus Christ. When a person becomes a Christian, he or she is spiritually joined to Christ. By being joined to Christ, he or she also becomes joined to all other Christians from other cultures (1 Cor. 12:20, Eph. 4:25). He or she becomes part of an eternal, worldwide family.

The fact is that death will separate all people into two categories: Those who are joined to Christ and those who are separated from Christ (Matt. 25:31–46, Rev. 21:7–8). In the story Jesus told about the rich man and Lazarus, Abraham stated that, 'a great chasm has been fixed, so that those who want to go from here to you cannot, nor can anyone cross over from there to us' (Luke 16:26).

There will be no separation after death of those who belong to Christ, even though they will come from many different cultures and races. The fellowship of human families is limited to this life unless the family members belong to Christ. The spiritual family of believers in Jesus Christ is not limited to this life. They will be one eternal family, whether they come from the same earthly family or whether they come from totally different cultures and races.

The teaching of many traditional religions concerning human families, is not correct. Many traditional cultures believe in a continuous community of their people which is unbroken even at death. They believe that the spirits of the departed ancestors continue to be active in the affairs of the family and clan. They believe that all the living will one day take their place among the spirits of these ancestors when they die.

The Bible does not teach this. The separation which occurs at death depends on whether or not those who die belong to Christ (Matt. 7:22–23). There will be no continuing relationship between those who belong to Christ and those who do not (Luke 16:26).

It is therefore very important that Christians learn to love and accept their brothers and sisters in Christ in this life, even though they come from cultures very different from their own (Matt. 23:8, Rev. 7:7–9). It will be clearly seen in heaven that the church is an eternal, multi-cultural family who are related to each other because of their relationship to Christ.

God wants that relationship to begin in this life and to continue forever in heaven. As members of the body of Christ, Christians have an obligation of loyalty to the church that is even greater than their obligation of loyalty to their human family, clan or tribe.

The reason people have such strong loyalties to their clans and culture groups in Africa, is because their identity, security and meaning in life is directly related to being a part of their extended family and clan. This is even more true concerning the family of God. A Christian has identity, security and meaning in life because he is part of the family of God. Our relationship to our earthly families is only a small picture of our eternal relationship to the family of God.

The great joy and strength of an extended family is the sense of belonging to one another. It is the same in the family of God. God is our Father, and we belong to each other because we belong to Christ (1 John 3:1–2).

SUMMARY

As members of the church, Christians have a serious responsibility to maintain the 'unity of the Spirit in the bond of peace,' as Paul said in Ephesians 4:3. To do this, believers must learn to love, trust, and respect all members of the church regardless of their culture, race or nationality. Cultural prejudice is a sin. Tribalism is the enemy of the church.

When the local church is divided because of pride, hatred, unforgiveness, cultural prejudice and tribalism, its witness will be weak, its prayers will be powerless and it will accomplish nothing for God. Its members will easily fall into temptation, sin and defeat. On the other hand, the local church will be strong in its witness for Christ, strong in its prayers, and strong to stand against evil in the society, when its members are united in love for one another. An army of men can overcome a strong enemy when it stands together. When the local church is united by the unselfish love and humility of its members, it can accomplish great things for God through its prayers and witness.

In order to give undivided loyalty to Christ, a person must understand that in becoming a Christian, he or she became part of an eternal community of brothers and sisters from every culture in the world. This extended family of God will live together in heaven, worshipping the Lamb of God (Rev. 7:9–10). The word of God describes the nature of this great family of Christians in Paul's words to the Galatians: 'there is neither Jew nor Greek, slave nor free, male nor female, but you are all one in Christ Jesus' (Gal. 3:28). This truth about the church and culture must be faithfully taught if the church is to be strong for Christ and to see God's will done on earth through its prayers.

DISCUSSION QUESTIONS AND PROJECTS BASED ON CHAPTER FIFTEEN

1. Where in the Bible do we find the origin of different languages and ethnic groups?

2. Is there any indication in the Bible that one culture, race or group is superior to any other? What does Galatians 3:28 say to the person who believes that his group is superior to others?

3. Why is it that so many people in the world think their own culture or group is superior to all others? What is the real cause of cultural prejudice and tribalism?

4. Consider the previous question in the light of Proverbs 18:12. How may feelings of cultural, racial or ethnic superiority destroy individuals and weaken the whole church?

5. Let three students give testimonies of actual cases where attitudes of cultural or ethnic superiority weakened or hurt the local church. After the testimonies, divide into groups of four each to discuss ways in which ethnic prejudice could be reduced in the local church. Let the chairman of each group report the results of the discussion in his group.

6. Find three persons who can give a testimony of how a Christian group overcame the problem of cultural prejudice.

7. Divide into ethnic groups. Let each group develop a plan for an evangelistic outreach to a different ethnic group, using methods that will make the gospel meaningful and relevant to the other group. This process is called contextualization of the gospel.

8. Find a verse in the Bible that mentions which ethnic groups will be in heaven.

9. Let the group discuss the meaning of tribe as Africans understand it.

10. What is the place of the local church in the African situation?

11. Discuss the root causes of racism, tribalism, nationalism and class consciousness.

12. Divide into small groups of four each for a Bible study on the Christian solution to racism, tribalism and nationalism according to Ephesians 2:11–19, Galatians 3:28, and Philippians 2:3–8.

SUGGESTED FOR FURTHER READING

Clement, Atchenemou, Raymond Hassan and Moyo Ozodo. *Cross Cultural Christianity*. Jos, Nigeria: Nigeria Evangelical Missionary Institute, 1989.

Lausanne Theology and Education Group. *The Willowbank Report – The Gospel And Culture*. Wheaton, Illinois: LCWE, 1978.

Loss, Myron. *Culture Shock*. Middleburg, Pennsylvania: Encouragement Ministries, 1983.

McGavran, Donald A. *The Clash Between Christianity And Cultures*. Washington, D.C.: Canon Press, 1974.

Stott, John and Cooke, R.T. (eds), *Down to Earth: Studies in Christianity and Culture*. Grand Rapids: Eerdmans, 1980.

16

Marriage, Sex, and Family According to the Bible

'Abraham was now old and well advanced in years, and the LORD had blessed him in every way. He said to the chief servant in his household . . . "I want you to swear by the LORD, the God of heaven and the God of earth, that you will not get a wife for my son from the daughters of the Canaanites among whom I am living" . . .

'Then the servant took ten of his master's camels and left, taking with him all kinds of good things from his master. He . . . made his way to the town of Nahor. He had the camels kneel down near the well outside the town; it was toward evening, the time the women go out to draw water. Then he prayed, "O LORD, God of my master Abraham, give me success today, and show kindness to my master Abraham. See, I am standing beside this spring, and the daughters of the townspeople are coming out to draw water. May it be that when I say to a girl, 'Please let down your jar that I may have a drink', and she says, 'Drink, and I'll water your camels too' – let her be the one you have chosen for your servant Isaac". . . . Before he had finished praying, Rebekah came out with her jar on her shoulder . . . . The girl was very beautiful, a virgin; no man had ever lain with her. She went down to the spring, filled her jar and came up again.

'The servant hurried to meet her and said, "Please give me a little water from your jar." "Drink, my lord," she said, and quickly lowered the jar to her hands and gave him a drink. After she had given him a drink she said, "I'll draw water for your camels too, until they have finished drinking" ' (Gen. 24:1–19).

'Isaac brought her into the tent of his mother Sarah, and he married Rebekah. So she became his wife and he loved her' (Gen. 24:67).

Every culture in the world has its own set of customs and rules concerning marriage, sex and the family. What does God have to say about marriage and the family? What does God have to say about sex? Since it was God who created mankind as male and female, and since it was God who joined the first man and woman together in marriage, it is very important for us to understand what God has to say about marriage, sex, and the family. In this chapter we will seek to answer the following questions:

A. What is God's plan for marriage?
B. What is God's plan for husbands and wives?
C. What is God's plan concerning sex?
D. What is God's plan concerning the family life of Christians?
E. What is the Bible's perspective on polygamy?
F. What does God say about divorce?
G. What are some biblical guidelines for choosing a marriage partner?
H. How should a Christian couple deal with the problem of childlessness?

A. WHAT IS GOD'S PLAN FOR MARRIAGE?

MARRIAGE WAS GOD'S IDEA

From the beginning, marriage was God's idea. It was not man's idea. Marriage was planned by God to meet the human need for companionship, love, mutual encouragement, practical help, and sexual satisfaction (Gen. 2:18, 1 Cor. 7:2–3). It was God's plan that children should be born and raised in the security and love created by one man and one woman in marriage committed to each other for a lifetime (Psalm 127:3, Mal. 2:14–16, Matt. 19:6).

When God created Adam in the Garden of Eden, he created a perfect man. But there was one thing Adam needed. God said, 'It is not good for the man to be alone. I will make a helper suitable for him' (Gen. 2:18). God decided to make a perfect partner for Adam. Adam needed the companionship of another human being. God had made the other creatures male and female (Gen. 6:19). Since Adam was a male, God took one of Adam's ribs and made a female partner for him. By doing this, God gave Adam a lifelong companion and helper and a sexual partner for marriage. Through the physical union of Adam and Eve, God planned for the human race to be continued (Gen. 1:27–28, Gen. 2:24).

MARRIAGE, THE FIRST INSTITIUTION IN HUMAN SOCIETY

Marriage was established by God before all other human institutions. This shows us that marriage is the foundation of human society.

Marriage was established before man's fall into sin. This shows us that marriage is holy.

God is pleased with marriage. The miracle by which Jesus changed water into wine at the wedding feast in Cana of Galilee (John 2:1–11), shows us that God wants people to enjoy marriage to the full. He wants men and women to experience love and acceptance and to be complete. Marriage was made for this purpose.

In God's plan, marriage is the basis for a morally and socially stable society. This is part of the reason why God hates adultery (Ex. 20:14), sexual immorality (1 Thess. 4:3–6), incest (Lev. 18:6ff), and homosexuality (Rom. 1:24–28). These things disrupt and twist God's plan for a stable human society. The Bible warns us, 'God will judge the adulterer and all the sexually immoral' (Heb. 13:4).

Part of the reason why many societies today are morally and socially unstable is because people have determined to live without regard for God's laws. Unfortunately, there are severe consequences for sexual sins. The great increase in divorce and broken homes, and the worldwide epidemic of AIDS are just two of these consequences.

Marriage is God's plan for all people and all cultures in the world (Gen. 2:24, Gen. 12:3, Matt. 19:3–9). The family cannot be replaced by any other institution in God's plan for mankind. If someone corrupts family life, he is interfering with God's plan for the whole human race. It was God who performed the first marriage in the garden of Eden (Gen. 2:21–25). It is people who have spoiled marriage through their immorality and unfaithfulness.

GOD'S DESIGN FOR MARRIAGE

God's plan is that there should be one woman for one man. God made one woman for the man he created (Gen.2:22–24). He intended this partnership between one man and one woman to last for a lifetime. In Matthew 19:6–8 Jesus said, 'For this reason a man will leave his father and mother and be united to his wife, and the two will become one flesh. . .therefore what God has joined together, let not man separate.' This lifetime commitment is important for several reasons.

First, it guarantees care, provision and protection for the wife throughout her life (Col. 3:12–13, 1 Peter 3:7). Second, there is a need for the emotional security and development of the children. Children need a secure and stable environment if they are to grow and develop the way God intended. When parents separate or get a divorce, children feel great emotional pain. Part of God's purpose in establishing marriage was to provide an emotionally stable and loving home environment in which to raise godly children. Malachi 2:15 says, 'Has not the LORD made them one? . . . And why one? Because he was seeking godly offspring. So guard yourself in your spirit, and do not break faith with the wife of your youth.'

Another reason why God planned one woman for one man for a lifetime, has to do with a woman's need for emotional security. A woman needs to know that she is the only woman her husband truly loves. A woman's emotional needs cannot be properly met in a polygamous home. When a man has more than one wife, there will always be jealousy and resentment between his wives. Men and women are equal before God (Gal. 3:28). It is just as important for the husband to meet his wife's emotional needs as for the wife to meet her husband's physical needs.

Polygamy is not the will of God
Since God provided one woman for one man at the creation, polygamy is not the will of God. Polygamy did not have a good beginning. The first polygamist mentioned in the Bible (Lamech) was also a murderer (Gen. 4:23). Polygamy, however, is not the same thing as adultery. In polygamy the husband is responsible to provide for his wives and their children. Polygamy is a common practice in many traditional African cultures.

Like King David, many men whom God used in Bible times, were polygamists. Some people use this fact to justify polygamy in African life. Although God used these men for his purposes, he did not want them to be polygamists. Concerning kings, God said, 'The king . . . must not take many wives' (Deut. 17:16–17). The truth is that God allowed Old Testament polygamists to suffer the consequences for taking more than one wife. This can be seen in the life of Abraham (Gen. 16:1–6).

From the time he took Hagar as a second wife, Abraham had no happiness in his home. There was jealousy between Hagar and Sarah and jealousy between Isaac and Ishmael. The jealousy and hatred between Isaac and Ishmael and their descendants has continued for 4000 years right down to the present day. This can be seen in the hatred between the Jews (the descendants of Isaac) and the Arabs (the descendants of Ishmael). More will be said later about the problem of polygamy in the church.

GOD'S PLAN FOR UNITY IN MARRIAGE

In God's plan, marriage involves a threefold unity between a man and a woman. This threefold of unity corresponds to the threefold nature of human beings as body, mind and spirit (1 Thess. 5:23, Heb. 4:12).

Physical unity
The first kind of unity in God's plan for marriage, is the physical relationship of sexual oneness. When God brought the woman to the man in the beginning, they were both naked and unashamed (Gen. 2:25). The Lord said, 'For this reason a man will leave his father and

mother and be united to his wife, and they will become one flesh'
(Gen. 2:24). The Bible teaches that the physical union of marriage is
good and holy in God's sight (Gen. 1:27–28,31, Prov. 5:18–19, Heb.
13:4)

From the physical unity of marriage, children are born and mutual
responsibility for the home is established. The husband is responsible
to work in order to provide for the family (Gen. 2:15). The wife is
responsible to bear the children and to care for the home (1 Tim.
5:14).

Mental and emotional unity
The second kind of unity in God's plan for marriage, is mental and
emotional unity. Mental and emotional unity comes when two people
live in harmony and agreement. To find this kind of unity, the husband
and wife must have at least some common values, common goals and
common interests in life. The birth of children helps to produce these
common values, goals and interests. Having the same culture and
language encourages mental and emotional unity. It is this kind of
unity which meets people's need for companionship, acceptance, and
value as human beings.

Every person in the world desires to be wanted, loved and
appreciated by someone. A person who feels unwanted and worthless
would rather not live. In order to grow in mental and emotional
oneness, the husband and wife must take time to talk to each other and
to share things with each other. They must take time to do things
together and to care for one another's needs (Phil. 2:4). Concerning
a problem of disunity in the Philippian church, Paul said to the
Philippians, 'Make my joy complete by being like-minded, having the
same love, being one in spirit and purpose' (Phil. 2:2). This statement
is a description of mental and emotional unity. Although Paul was not
addressing the need for oneness in marriage in this statement, the
truth of this passage can be applied to unity in the marriage relationship as well as to unity in the church.

If the husband and wife do not take the time to build mental and
emotional unity, they will soon drift apart. The less close they feel to
each other, the less happy their marriage will be. This will also affect
their physical relationship. A wife does not desire to have sex with her
husband when he does not show interest in her as a person. The
medicine for a sick marriage is for the husband to treat his wife with
the same attention, love, care, and respect as he did in the days of their
courtship. This is part of the meaning of Ephesians 5:25, which says,
'Husbands, love your wives, just as Christ loved the church.'

Spiritual unity
The third kind of unity in God's plan for marriage is spiritual unity.
This is the unity created when both the husband and the wife are

Christians and both of them want to follow the Lord. Because God wants spiritual unity in marriage, he never wants a Christian to marry a non-Christian. The Bible says, 'Do not be yoked together with unbelievers. For . . . what does a believer have in common with an unbeliever' (2 Cor. 6:14–15).

The strongest expression of spiritual unity is when the husband and wife read the Bible and pray together. There is no stronger glue to hold a marriage together than spiritual unity. A popular proverb says, 'The family that prays together stays together.' A husband and wife who are one in the Lord will be able to raise godly children (Deut. 6:6–7). The Bible says that God is seeking godly offspring (Mal. 2:15).

Spiritual unity brings great peace and blessing to a marriage. It will give the family the peace which comes when Christ is the centre of the home (John 14:27). It will also enable the family to be a strong witness for Christ. God wants Christian couples to pray together. The Bible says, 'Husbands . . . be considerate as you live with your wives, and treat them with respect as the weaker partner . . . so that nothing will hinder your prayers' (1 Peter 3:7).

A Christian couple who join their spirits together before the Lord in prayer can have great spiritual power and can accomplish many good works for the kingdom of God. Matthew 18:19 says, 'If two of you on earth agree about anything you ask for, it will be done for you by my Father in heaven.' The Lord is pleased with this kind of spiritual unity. A Christian couple who are united in the Lord is the seed of the local church. Jesus said, 'Where two or three come together in my name, there am I with them' (Matt. 18:20).

B. WHAT IS GOD'S PLAN FOR HUSBANDS AND WIVES?

In order for a marriage to work the way God wants it to, each partner must carry out certain responsibilities God has given.

GOD'S PLAN FOR THE HUSBAND

Christ, in his shepherd leadership of the church, is the leadership example for all husbands to follow in their families (Eph. 5:25).

1. The husband must love his wife unselfishly as Christ loves the church (Eph.5:25). This involves self-sacrifice and self-denial.

2. The husband should gently lead his wife and children, just as Jesus, the good shepherd, gently leads his people (Psalm 23, Eph. 5:23). This is a self-denying, servant leadership, not a dominating leadership as found in the world. Many husbands dominate and abuse their wives and lose God's blessing on themselves and their families as a result.

3. The husband should provide for the family. This includes providing for their social, emotional and spiritual needs, as well as their physical needs (Psalm 23:1, 1 Tim. 5:8).

4. The husband should protect the family (Eph. 5:28–29). Every father should follow the example of Job, and pray for his wife and for each of his children every day (Job 1:5).

5. The husband should honour his wife (1 Pet. 3:7).

6. The husband should edify his wife and encourage her in Christ (Eph. 5:26).

7. The husband should show understanding for his wife (1 Pet. 3:7).

8. The husband must take the responsibility to train, correct, discipline and spiritually disciple his children (Eph. 6:4). This is part of the husband's leadership responsibility in the home. At the judgment, God will hold the husband, not the wife, responsible for the spiritual condition of the home, just as God held Adam, not Eve, responsible for their sin and rebellion in the garden of Eden (Rom. 5:12, 15, 18–19).

GOD'S PLAN FOR THE WIFE

The church is to love Christ and submit to him (Eph. 5:24). In this illustration, the church is the example for the wife to follow.

1. Since men and women are equals in the sight of God (Gal. 3:28), both men and women are to submit to one another in the church out of reverence for Christ (Eph. 5:21). This means that they are to be accountable to each other for their behaviour. This applies to husbands and wives in the marriage relationship as well.

   In addition to this general relationship between men and women, there is order in marriage just as there is order in every institution which God has created. In God's order, the husband is the head of the family, just as Christ is the head of the church (Eph. 5:23). Following that pattern, the wife should submit to her husband as she would submit to Christ (Eph. 5:22–24). This order, however, does not give the husband permission to dominate, abuse or beat his wife as a king might dominate his subjects. On the contrary, the Bible teaches just the opposite. The husband's leadership of the wife and family must be characterized by self-sacrificing service and self-denying love, in the same way that Christ loves and leads the church (Eph. 5:25).

2. The wife should encourage and help her husband. One of the most important ways she can encourage him is to pray for him (Gen. 2:18).

3. She will bear their children (1 Tim. 2:15).

4. The wife should maintain a sweet spirit in the home (1 Peter 3:3–4).

5. The wife should take good care of her household (Prov. 31:37).

6. The wife should maintain a good reputation (Prov. 31:31, Titus 2:3). This includes reaching out to help the needy (Prov. 31:20).

7. Older wives should spiritually disciple younger women including their own daughters, to love and respect their husbands (Titus 2:4).

GOD'S PLAN FOR HUSBAND AND WIFE AS PARENTS

God is the example for all parents to follow in raising their children (Eph. 5:1–2). The first idea of God in a small child's mind is often the image of his or her parents, especially the father.

1. Parents must imitate Christ and set an example of godly living before their children (Eph. 5:1–2). Children will tend to follow the example of their parents rather than their advice.

2. Parents must love their children just as God loves the parents (Eph. 5:2).

3. Parents must teach their children about God and his ways (Prov. 1:7–8). This especially applies to ideas about right and wrong, good and evil, and other basic moral and spiritual values. Christian parents must not leave the moral and spiritual training of their children to traditional leaders or to government school programmes. God requires parents to teach their children about his laws and his ways (Deut. 6:6–7).

4. Parents must discipline their children in love, just as God disciplines us in love. This is the father's responsibility (Eph. 6:4, Heb. 12:9).

5. Parents must provide for their children just as God provides for his people (Psalm 23:1, 1 Tim. 5:8).

6. Parents must protect their children physically, mentally and spiritually, just as God protects us (Psalm 18:2, Psalm 144:2).

7. Parents must guide their children as they grow up just as God guides us (Psalm 32:8).

C. WHAT IS GOD'S PLAN CONCERNING SEX?

When God created people, he created them as male and female for the purpose of sexual reproduction (Gen. 1:27–28). It is important for Christians to understand that sex was God's idea for mankind's good and enjoyment. Within marriage, it is not a sin. According to the Bible sex is both good (Gen. 1:31) and holy (Heb. 13:4). It was given to man before his fall into sin in the garden of Eden (Gen.1:27–28, Gen. 2:21–25). The Bible says, 'And rejoice in the wife of your youth. As a loving hind and a graceful doe, Let her breasts satisfy you at all times; Be exhilarated always with her love' (Prov. 5:18–19–NASB).

There is a widespread belief that the original sin of mankind was that Adam had sex with his wife (Gen. 4:1). This is false. The original sin was an act of disobedience to God's command to not eat the fruit of the tree of the knowledge of good and evil (Gen. 2:17, Gen. 3:6).

Because of sin, man has twisted and corrupted God's plan for sex. According to God's plan, sexual relations are to be strictly confined to husbands and wives within the commitment of marriage (1 Cor. 7:2–5, Heb. 13:4). Practising sex outside of marriage is a serious sin. Many problems in the world today are the result of sinful sex. Practices such as adultery (unfaithfulness to a marriage partner), sexual immorality (sexual relations before marriage), homosexuality (sexual relations between people of the same sex), incest (sexual relations between family members), bestiality (sexual relations with an animal), and other impure practices, are all an abomination to God. In Leviticus 18 and 20:10–21, God gives us a list of those practices which are impure and on which he has pronounced a severe judgment.

Sex is a powerful force. It is like fire. Fire is possible because of the way God made the world. Fire can be very useful. We can use fire to cook our food and to heat our homes. But if a house catches fire, it can destroy the house and even kill the people in it. The same is true about sex. Sex is possible because of the way God made men and women. Under God's guidance, sex is one of God's blessings to married people. It is the means of great pleasure and the means of bringing children into the world. Ignoring God's guidance, sex can destroy the home and ruin human lives.

When people try to satisfy their sexual desires outside of marriage, marriages are destroyed, families are ruined and individual lives are brought under the curse of God's judgment. Forgiveness for sin by God does not mean that there will be no consequences in this life. Indeed, the consequences may be dreadful. If a person kills another person in a rage of anger but later repents with great sorrow, God can forgive him. However, repentance and forgiveness will not bring the dead person back to life. It is the same with sexual sins. In the case of King David, although God forgave his sin of adultery with the wife of Uriah, David's family life was ruined from that time on (2 Sam. 12:11–13).

Some cultures do not condemn certain sexual sins, such as sexual immorality. If a Christian comes from such a culture, he or she must understand that it is God who has condemned sexual immorality and other such sins. The Christian is responsible to God, not to the culture, for his or her behaviour. God's laws are absolute. He will not change them to fit culture.

Something must be said about perverted sex. In some parts of the world today, many people have turned to homosexual practices. This is a total perversion of the way God created the world. Even the animal world is made of male and female creatures. Homosexual people today try to argue that their practices are a reasonable alternative lifestyle. The truth is that these practices are an abomination to God (Lev. 20:13). The Bible says that when people practice sexual perversion, God gives them over to their sin, and they bring God's judgment upon their lives (Rom. 1:24,26). We need to remember that God totally destroyed the ancient cities of Sodom and Gomorrah in judgment for the sin of sexual perversion (Gen. 19:1–25). God has not changed.

What is the proper Christian attitude towards the homosexual? God's people should always show love, patience and compassion to those enslaved to homosexuality and other sinful practices. Christians need to offer such people help and deliverance in Christ. At the same time, Christians must not tolerate the growing idea that there is nothing wrong with this perversion or that this group of people deserve special rights. This sin and all other sexual sins are under the condemnation and wrath of God (1 Thess. 4:3–6).

THE PROBLEM OF LUST

Lust occurs because people's normal desires have been corrupted by sin. Desires by themselves are not evil. Our desires come from the way God made us. For example, God made people to need food to sustain life. Having a desire for food when a person is hungry is not a sin. But a gluttonous craving for food is a corrupted form of the normal desire for food. It is a form of lust.

God made men and women with a natural physical and emotional attraction for each other. That attraction is not a sin. Attraction for the opposite sex is part of God's original creation and God pronounced everything in his creation good (Gen. 1:31).

The problem is that our God-given sexual desire has been corrupted by sin. Since the fall in the garden of Eden, people have become corrupt in every part of their character, including their desires. Because of their sinful natures, men and women are not satisfied with their marriage partners as God intended them to be. Instead they look at other men or women with lust.

LOVE OR LUST?

One question which troubles many young people is the difference between love and lust. Both love and lust include very strong sexual desires. What is the difference between them? One simple test which a person can apply to determine if his or her desire is love or lust, is the test of unselfishness. If a man loves a girl with a godly love, he will be unselfish in his desire for her. He will not want to embarrass or defile the girl he loves by encouraging her to have sex with him before marriage.

This principle comes out clearly in the story of the lust which Amnon, the son of King David, had for his half-sister, Tamar (2 Sam. 13:1–12). Tamar was actually willing to marry Amnon, if necessary, but Amnon was unwilling to wait for marriage to satisfy his desire for her (2 Sam. 13:13–14). Amnon's selfish desire for Tamar was not love but lust. By contrast, the carpenter Joseph was willing to wait for a year of betrothal and for the birth of Jesus, before he had sexual relations with Mary as his wife (Matt. 1:24–25). Joseph was willing to wait patiently for Mary because he had true love for her and because he wanted to obey God. What is the difference between love and lust?

Lust wants to get while love wants to give.

Lust is self-serving while love is self-denying.

Lust is unwilling to wait while love is willing to wait patiently for God's time.

Lust is unwilling to take the responsibility which goes with sex, while love is willing to take responsibility for the loved one and for her children for a lifetime.

Lust seeks pleasure only, while love seeks the happiness and the good of the person who is loved.

Lust doesn't care if it brings shame to the other person, while love will never bring shame to the one who is loved.

Lust is not lasting, but love lasts for a lifetime.

Lust is a great curse of sin, but love is a great blessing from God.

We are warned to flee from lust (2 Tim. 2:22), but husbands are commanded to love their wives (Eph. 5:25).

Lust hurts everyone but love heals and helps everyone.

Lust brings sorrow, bitterness and shame, but love brings happiness, joy and fulfillment.

The origin of lust is the sinful nature of man. The origin of love is holy nature of God.

The problem of lust does not apply to single men and women only. Married people are often troubled by lust. One way for married people to escape lust is to have regular sexual intercourse (1 Cor. 7:3–5). In many African marriages, wives will refuse to have sex with their husbands for up to two years or more after a child is born. This is not good. It leads many husbands into lust and immorality. The Bible says, 'Do not deprive each other (sexually) except by mutual consent and for a time, so that you may devote yourselves to prayer. Then come together again so that Satan will not tempt you because of your lack of self control' (1 Cor. 7:5).

If the wife refuses to have sex with her husband because she is afraid of becoming pregnant again too soon, she and her husband should consult a Christian doctor, dispenser, or medical worker who can offer helpful suggestions on family planning. Planned pregnancies can help the family and the marriage in many ways.

Some husbands hurt their wives emotionally because they use them lustfully instead of loving them. God commands husbands to love their wives as Christ loves the church (Eph. 5:25), but he warns men to flee from lust (2 Tim. 2:22). This means that husbands should show great patience and gentleness with their wives, especially in the sexual relationship. The man who shows the same kindness, love and patience toward his wife after marriage as he did during the days of their courtship will have a happy wife. A husband who seriously tries to love his wife unselfishly, as Christ loves the church, will find that his wife is much more responsive and loving toward him. Husbands should read Song of Solomon 4:1–5:4 for a story of how one husband, inspired by the Holy Spirit long ago, expressed his love to his wife.

For unmarried people, the problem of lust can be very great. There are two principles in the Bible which can help to reduce this temptation. The first principle is that Christians must exercise self-control in what they permit their eyes to see. Men are particularly sensitive to what they see. King David eventually committed adultery with Bathsheba because he looked at her while she was bathing (2 Sam. 11:2). Job said, 'I have made a covenant with my eyes not to look lustfully at a girl' (Job 31:1). Jesus said, 'Anyone who looks at a woman lustfully has already committed adultery with her in his heart' (Matt. 5:28). Christians must be very careful about what books they read and what kind of pictures and films they see.

The second principle has to do with physical touch. Touching each other sexually stimulates both men and women and can lead people into serious temptation. The Bible says, 'It is good for a man not to touch a woman' (1 Cor. 7:1–NASB). Men must be disciplined when they are with young women. The Bible says they should treat them as though they were their sisters (1 Tim. 5:1–2). It is not good for a man to be alone in a private place with a woman who is not his wife.

D. WHAT IS GOD'S PLAN CONCERNING THE FAMILY LIFE OF CHRISTIANS?

1. Christian marriage is used as an image of what the church should be in relationship to Christ (Eph. 5:25–32). The husband is to love his wife unconditionally and sacrificially, as Christ loved the church (Eph. 5:25). The wife is to submit to her husband as she would

submit to Christ (Eph. 5:22). Both of these responsibilities are only possible by the power of the Holy Spirit.

2. The parents' task of raising children includes the responsibility of giving their children thorough Christian instruction in the ways of the Lord (Gen. 18:19, Eph. 6:1,4). In Deuteronomy 6:6–7 the Lord says, 'These commandments that I give you today are to be upon your hearts. Impress them on your children. Talk about them when you sit at home, and when you walk along the road, when you lie down and when you get up.'

   The training and instruction of children is a responsibility committed to parents by God. Proverbs 1:8 says, 'Listen my son to your father's instruction, and do not forsake your mother's teaching.' God wants the home to be a place of security, love, care, provision, training, and loving discipline for children. The Lord said through Paul, 'Fathers, do not exasperate your children; instead bring them up in the training and instruction of the Lord' (Eph. 6:4). The family was planned by God to be the special place where children would grow up in the right way. God is concerned that his people raise children who know him and obey him (Deut. 4:40, Deut. 5:29).

3. Christian parents are responsible to care for the needs of their children. This includes their physical needs, such as the need for food, clothing and medical care. It also includes their emotional needs for love and security. The need for love and security is most fully provided in a home where the parents love each other and live in harmony.

E. WHAT IS THE BIBLE'S PERSPECTIVE ON POLYGAMY?

Polygamy (literally polygyny) is a difficult problem in Africa. Since it involves the commitment and responsibilities of marriage, it is not the same issue as sexual immorality or adultery. There are strong cultural arguments in support of polygamy in African society, such as:

1. Having several wives has been a symbol of power, wealth and influence in traditional African societies for many centuries. The same pattern probably explains why kings in the Old Testament often had several wives. Solomon, the wealthiest king in the ancient world, had 700 wives and 300 concubines (1 Kings 11:3). However, Solomon's many wives led to his spiritual downfall (1 Kings 11:3–5).

2. It is important for a man in traditional society to continue his family name into future generations. Having several wives usually

ensures that he will have many male children to continue his name.

3. Closely related to the continuation of one's family name is the idea that by having many children and grandchildren, one will be remembered and honoured long after death. This is very important in traditional society.

4. In agricultural societies, several wives is a way to ensure having many children and hence the necessary labourers for farming, cattle herding and housework. This includes the provision of help when needed, as when some are sick. A large family community is seen as a sign of strength.

5. Since it is common for many African wives to refuse to have sexual relations with their husband for up to two years after the birth of a child, having several wives is a way for the husband to avoid sexual immorality.

6. Because African culture has very strong community values, having many wives ensures having a large family, which is seen as the way to increase happiness and meaning in life.

7. If a person has many daughters, his wealth will increase significantly through the bride-price at the time of the marriage of such daughters.

8. There is a belief in many tribes that it is very bad to be a single woman and have no children. Because of this, many African women prefer to be one of several wives rather than to be single. There is also the idea that a woman who remains single will be the cause of sexual immorality and bring shame on the community.

9. Polygamy solves the problem of single parent mothers.

10. To have several wives, and many children, makes a person feel secure about his or her care in old age.

As these arguments suggest, polygamy makes sense from a traditional African point of view. However, the Bible is clear that polygamy is not the will of God. Although polygamy is not presented in the Bible as a great sin, it is certainly not approved by God in any way. Polygamy is a man-made arrangement to satisfy the desires of a person with a non-Christian world-view. It represents walking by the flesh rather than walking by the Holy Spirit and trusting God in faith for the needs of life. The Bible says that without faith, it is impossible to please God (Heb. 11:6).

God had promised Abraham that he would have a son (Gen. 15:2–4). When Abraham saw that his wife, Sarah, was barren, he decided to listen to Sarah's suggestion and to have a son by his Egyptian maidservant Hagar (Gen. 16:1–3). So Abraham took another wife for reasons similar to those of the traditional African. From that time on, there was no peace in Abraham's home. God's plan was to give Abraham a son miraculously, not through a second wife (Gen. 17:15–19). The bad effects of having a child by Hagar continued long after Abraham had died. Even in our times, the conflict continues between Jews and Arabs. It cannot be argued from the Bible that polygamy is ever God's plan or God's will.

So also in Africa, the bad effects of polygamy continue from one generation to another in spite of the arguments given in favour of polygamy. The emotional pain, jealousy and competition among the wives and children of polygamous families clearly demonstrates the fact that this form of marriage is a matter of selfish convenience. Polygamy denies a woman the emotional fulfilment God intended her to have by enjoying the undivided love and attention of her husband.

Polygamy is considered a necessary accommodation to African culture by some liberal theologians. In answer to this, it must be pointed out that the cultural reasons put forward in support of polygamy accommodate the non-Christian values of traditional beliefs. Non-Christian traditional beliefs bring God's judgment, not his blessing. The desire for status, for example, is simply a cultural justification for pride, a sin which God hates (Prov. 16:5, 21:4). The same can be said for the continuation of a person's family name in future generations. Traditional beliefs about ancestors do not turn people to faith in Christ but away from Christ. The argument using bride-price reveals greed, another sin which God hates (Isa. 57:17, Matt. 23:25).

Most of the arguments given to support polygamy are based upon a non-Christian world-view. Even the argument that it is a blessing to have a large family must be considered in the light of the Bible's full revelation. Yes, the Bible does indicate that a large earthly family can be a blessing (Psalm 127:4–5). But this blessing will not come when people violate the will of God for marriage. It will not come when polygamous husbands eliminate harmony and peace for their wife and children by taking additional wives. The community of unconditional blessing from God is not a large earthly family, but the large eternal family of God, the church.

The argument based on improving morality deserves special attention. Yes, immorality is wrong, but polygamy is not God's solution to the problem. The solution is regular sexual union between one husband and one wife. If the wife resists this, the husband should seek wise counsel from church leaders or Christian medical workers. Concerning immorality in general, the truth is that many men continue to indulge in adultery whether they have one wife or several wives. The problem of lust is not cured by polygamy. There are many cases where a man commits adultery and then later takes the woman as a wife in order to legalize his adultery. King David did this with

Bathsheba even though he had several wives, but God condemned David for his sin (2 Sam. 11:26–27).

It is not the Christian solution to polygamy to require a converted polygamist to drive away all but his first wife. That would be unjust and irresponsible behaviour from a husband who has made a commitment to care for his wives (Num. 30:1–2,16). Instead, the solution consists of supportive prayer and counsel from the pastor and elders of the local church so that God may work things out in his own perfect way. Only God can work out a solution which will not hurt people unnecessarily. Only God can work out the problem in answer to prayer. God's solutions are always compassionate and perfect but God's way may take many years to work out. Prayer and patience are the ways for a polygamist to find God's answer to his situation.

The problems associated with polygamy are very difficult to solve. Let this be a warning to those who are not yet married. It is a great mistake for a man to take more than one wife.

The question is often asked, whether a polygamist who has turned to Christ should be baptized? The answer comes in a biblical understanding of the meaning of baptism. Baptism is a public testimony that a person has become a part of the body of Christ. Would we deny baptism to someone who had been sexually immoral, an adulterer or a thief before turning to Christ? Certainly not (1 Cor. 6:9–11). All such persons should be baptized if they have truly repented and put their faith in Christ, because they are new creatures in Christ (2 Cor. 5:17). The polygamist is no different. When a person repents of sin and receives Christ as Lord and Saviour, all former sins are forgiven, including polygamy (Col. 2:13, 1 John 2:12).

Though he should be baptized, the polygamist must never be an elder or deacon in the local church. The Bible says, 'Now the overseer must be above reproach, the husband of but one wife' (1 Tim. 3:2). Later the apostle says, 'A deacon must be the husband of but one wife' (1 Tim. 3:12). This is because God wants his plan of one woman for one man in marriage to be visibly seen in the lives of the church leaders.

The matter of polygamy after conversion is very different. Because polygamy is not the will of God, it is clearly an act of rebellion for a Christian to take a second wife. It is a sin and the local church must deal with it. God planned for one man to have only one wife. The Christian who takes a second wife must be disciplined by the local church (1 Cor. 5:11–13).

F. WHAT DOES GOD SAY ABOUT DIVORCE?

In Europe and North America where polygamy is not lawful, unfaithfulness and adultery leads to divorce and often to marriage with the adulterous partner. This is somewhat similar to polygamy, without having the different wives in the same home at the same time. Divorce, however, is usually much more emotionally painful and hard on the injured wife or husband than polygamy, because it involves the outright rejection of one person in favour of another. Divorce is also extremely painful to the children.

God hates divorce (Mal. 2:16). Divorce destroys God's plan for marriage and the family. Children who see their parents' love turn to hatred and eventually see them divorce, are deeply hurt for life. They often become bitter and negative about marriage and angry at everyone. When a divorce has taken place in a home, the children are the ones who are most hurt. The children often develop such a low view of marriage that they repeat the same pattern of immorality and divorce which they saw in their parents.

Although God hates divorce, he recognizes that it takes place. He deals with people where they are. He will forgive this sin, just as he forgives other sins (Psalm 103:3).

Divorce is becoming a serious problem in our world, especially in big cities. Fewer and fewer people are willing to make marriage the lifetime commitment which the Bible teaches (Matt. 19:6). In North America, divorce has now become more common than lifetime marriage. The effect of this trend is also felt all over Africa because many Africans watch American television programmes which are full of sexual immorality and divorce.

When young people are far away from the influence of their extended family, they often lose their moral and spiritual values. They may become involved in sexual immorality and adultery. These are the sins which lead marriages to divorce.

What does God want a person to do when his or her marriage partner has been unfaithful? He wants people to forgive one another (Col. 3:13). Repentance, forgiveness and healing of broken human relationships, is always God's perfect will. Peter asked Jesus, 'Lord, how many times shall I forgive my brother when he sins against me? Up to seven times? Jesus answered, I tell you, not seven times, but seventy seven times' (Matt.18:21–22). This principle of forgiveness can be seen in the life of the prophet Hosea. In the case of Hosea, God told him to bring back his unfaithful wife, Gomer, even though she was a prostitute and had betrayed Hosea many times (Hosea 3:1–3).

PROBLEMS IN MARRIAGE

There are many other problems in marriage besides unfaithfulness. The most common problems come from disagreements about money, tension over loyalty to extended family, cultural differences and the lack of talking things over. Most marriage problems have two sides to the story. An interesting verse in the Bible says, 'The first to present his case seems right, till another comes forward to question him' (Prov. 18:17). This is true in many marriage disputes. One person may claim they have been badly treated by their partner. However, when the whole story is known, the person who was badly treated often hurt the other one by a lack of love, hurtful words, or cruel behaviour.

There is a medicine to cure the problems of marriage. The medicine has two parts. The two parts are called love and forgiveness. Proverbs 10:12 says, 'Love covers over all wrongs.' Colossians 3:13–14 says, 'Forgive whatever grievances you may have against one another. Forgive as the Lord forgave you. And over all these virtues put on love, which binds them all together in perfect unity.'

G. WHAT ARE SOME BIBLICAL GUIDELINES FOR CHOOSING A MARRIAGE PARTNER?

There are some useful biblical guidelines for choosing a marriage partner in the story at the beginning of this chapter. At Abraham's command, Abraham's chief servant, Eliezer, went to search for a bride for Isaac. Eliezer was a mature man. He knew that good character was the most important thing for a wife to have. Eliezer believed that God answered prayer. He prayed a very, very wise prayer. Eliezer prayed, 'May it be that when I say to a girl, "Please let down your jar that I may have a drink," and she says, "Drink, and I'll water your camels too" – let her be the one you have chosen for your servant Isaac' (Gen. 24:14).

Eliezer's prayer was actually a request that God would lead him to a girl who was cooperative, helpful, generous, and hard-working. A girl without these qualities would certainly not have offered to draw water for the camels when she was only asked for a drink. Rebekah knew that the camels had just come from a long journey. Camels drink a lot of water, and it would have taken hard work to satisfy their thirst.

Eliezer used the following principles when he sought a wife for Isaac:

(a) He looked for a woman from among people who had true faith in God as Abraham had. He refused to consider unbelievers (Gen. 24:3).
(b) He sought God's guidance through prayer (Gen. 24: 12–14).
(c) He sought a woman of excellent character (Gen. 24:14).
(d) He sought a wife from among people who were culturally close to Abraham (Gen. 24:3–4).
(e) He had confidence that God had prepared a special person for Isaac (Gen. 24:14).
(f) He had faith that God would lead him to the right girl (Gen. 24:14).

(g) He was actively looking for the answer to his prayer in the circumstances (Gen. 24:17–21).

There are also other important considerations in seeking for a good marriage partner. These can be summarized in the word similarity. The more similar you are to the person you marry, the fewer difficult adjustments you will have to make.

It is certainly not a sin to marry someone from a different tribe, a different nationality, a different language, or a different race. However, if one or more of these major differences is present between the prospective marriage partners, there may be difficult adjustments. In order to find the kind of unity described in this chapter, two people usually need to share similar cultures and values. 'Being like-minded' (Phil. 2:2) is one of the important goals of a godly marriage. With great differences between the marriage partners, like-mindedness can be hard to achieve. Abraham wisely insisted that Eliezer seek for a wife from among his own people (Gen. 24:3–4).

Consider what would happen if people married who spoke different languages. The only way they could speak to each other would be through a third language which was not really close to the heart of either of them. Otherwise one partner would have to thoroughly learn the other partner's language. Neither of these solutions would provide the best kind of communication. In marriage more than in any other human relationship, it is very important to understand each other and to be able to communicate at a deep heart level.

Some other differences which can make oneness difficult to achieve, include different goals in life, big differences of age (especially if the wife is much older), differences of education (especially when the wife has the higher education), different attitudes toward money, and different types of personality. These differences do not mean that a marriage will not work. However, if there are several big differences between the husband and wife, they will have to work much harder to have a harmonious relationship.

H. HOW SHOULD A CHRISTIAN COUPLE DEAL WITH THE PROBLEM OF CHILDLESSNESS?

John and his wife Lydia were devoted Christians who wanted to serve the Lord in the pastoral ministry of their denomination. John was a student in Bible College. He and Lydia had been married for 12 years and they had no children. The neighbours in John's village had warned John several times not to marry Lydia, since she was from a different tribe. Now they kept reminding him that Lydia would have no children because a curse had been placed on her. As each year passed, Lydia became more and more depressed, and John became increasingly angry and bitter. How would you counsel John and Lydia from the word of God? How should a Christian couple deal with the problem of childlessness?

Much of the emotional pain of childlessness in African life has to do with traditional value of children. Some of these values are not Christian ideas. Most African cultures have a very strong sense of community. Children are seen as essential for the continuation of a person's family and for his ancestral status in the spirit world. In some cultures, these values are so strong that a husband would say he has had no children until he has had a male child.

In some cultures, the traditional idea of eternal life is an endless continuation of the person's family line. In such a culture, the ability to have children takes on religious importance. Such cultures believe that a couple is cursed by God if they are unable to have children. These traditional beliefs about childlessness are not found in the Bible. However, Christians from such a community may be influenced by the beliefs of their people without realizing it. It is this influence, and not the teaching of the Bible, which makes them angry and bitter when they cannot have children. If the couple is seeking to follow the Lord faithfully and there is no hidden sin in their lives, the couple is not being cursed by God.

In cases such as this, a Christian couple must learn to not rely on the traditional beliefs of their people, but on the eternal truth of the word of God. These two systems of belief are very different in approaching the issue of childlessness.

The Bible speaks of children as a gift from the Lord (Psalm 127:3). However, the idea that childlessness shows that a couple is cursed by God, is false. Also, it is a totally non-Christian idea to assume that eternal life has anything to do with having children. To the majority of people, God gives the gift of children. But there are some people from whom God withholds children because he knows that for them, bearing their own children would not be a blessing. Psalm 84:11 says, 'The LORD bestows favour and honour. No good thing does he withhold from those whose walk is blameless.'

If they have reason to believe that a curse has been placed upon them by another person, a Christian couple has authority to break such a curse in the name of Jesus (Luke 10:19, 1 John 4:4). In every situation they can pray and ask the Lord for a child. This is what Isaac did for his childless wife, Rebekah (Gen. 25:21). This is what Hannah, the childless wife of Elkanah, did (1 Sam. 1:10– 16).

If God still withholds children from a Christian couple after they have prayed about it, the Lord has a reason for it. It could be that God knows that it would not be a good thing in their case. Perhaps God knows that the wife would die in childbirth, breaking the heart of her husband. Perhaps God knows that a child born to that couple would become sick and die, or be born with a cruel disease or deformity.

Because the Lord is willing to spare his children from unnecessary pain and suffering, he may withhold children from a godly praying couple. There may also be other reasons why God does not grant children. What is the couple to do if the Lord withholds children?

Perhaps one reason the Lord has withheld children is that he would like them to adopt an orphaned child. The Bible has much to say about God's compassion for the widow and the orphan (Deut. 14:29, Deut. 24:19–21). If the couple had their own children, they might not consider the possibility of adoption. In some cultures twins are thought to be evil because of traditional beliefs. When twins are born in these societies, they are either killed or abandoned. A Christian couple can have a beautiful ministry of love by taking an abandoned child and giving that child a Christian home.

Some years ago a missionary doctor and his wife decided to adopt handicapped children. They adopted three such children. They gave them a loving Christian home. Another missionary doctor rescued an unwanted child from a pile of garbage in a city. They gave the girl a loving Christian home and today she has graduated from university. Adoption is a very beautiful Christian solution to the problem of childlessness.

SUMMARY

Marriage is found in all cultures of the world in some form. According to the Bible, marriage was the very first human social institution. It was God himself who planned marriage when he created mankind as male and female and then performed the very first marriage himself. What is God's plan for marriage to all people and all cultures of the world?

God planned for one man to be married to one woman as a lifetime commitment of faithfulness, love, companionship, encouragement, support, enjoyment and mutual help. Other forms of marriage, such as polygamy, are man's idea and not God's will. Because divorce destroys God's perfect plan for human happiness in marriage, God hates divorce. Within the commitment of marriage, sex is holy, pure and blessed by God. It is the way God grants the blessing of children and the means of pleasure for husbands and wives. All sexual relations outside of marriage, such as sexual immorality and adultery, are serious sins which God has promised to punish.

Marriage only works the way God planned for it to work when husbands and wives follow the commandments of Scripture. The example for husbands to follow in leading their wives is the example of Christ himself (Eph. 5:23). The example for wives to follow in submitting to their husbands is the church's relationship to Christ (Eph. 5:24). Husbands are commanded to 'love their wives just as

Christ loved the church' (Eph. 5:25). This is servant leadership and self-sacrificing love. Wives are commanded to submit to their husbands as the church submits to Christ (Eph. 5:24). The secret to this submission is doing it for the sake of Christ. The example for parents to follow in raising their children is the example of God as our heavenly Father, as he loves, provides for, guides, leads, teaches and protects his children (Eph. 5:1-2). These responsibilities can only be fully carried out with the help of the Holy Spirit.

Children are God's blessing in marriage, but the inability to bear children does not indicate that a couple is cursed by God. That idea comes from the false teaching of non-Christian religions. If there is difficulty in conceiving children, a couple should consult a doctor. There is an effective and harmless method of family planning which can increase the possibility of conception for childless couples. The same method can also be used to prevent conception in order to space child bearing. If God prevents conception entirely, a couple may want to consider adoption, by God's leading.

DISCUSSION QUESTIONS AND PROJECTS BASED ON CHAPTER SIXTEEN

1. How would you describe a perfect marriage from God's perspective? Give Bible verses to support your answer.

2. Let the group define a perfect marriage. Then divide into several small groups. Let each small group discuss the kind of things that both husband and wife can do to help create this perfect marriage. Each group should compose a list for husbands, and a list for wives.

3. What sort of things can a husband do with his wife that will strengthen their mental and emotional unity?

4. Explain why God hates divorce.

5. Divide into small groups of four each to discuss ways in which husbands can honour their wives, as commanded in 1 Peter 3:7.

6. What kind of things can a husband do that will build spiritual unity with his wife?

7. Explain why adultery is such a serious sin. What effect does adultery have on a marriage?

8. Priscilla and Aquila were a married couple mentioned in Acts 18 and in some of Paul's epistles. What kinds of unity are suggested in their marriage by the reference in Acts 18:26?

9. Explain how the sexual relationship in marriage glorifies God.

10. A young man comes to you and says he has committed sexual immorality with a girl. He says he loves the girl and is willing to marry her. The girl is not a Christian. How would you counsel this young man? Give Bible verses to support your answer.

11. Explain what you would say to a man who was converted to Christ as a polygamist.

12. Divide into small groups of three each. Discuss what God thinks about trial marriages. (Trial marriage is where two people live together without being married in order to decide if they want to be married for life.) Each group should find verses of Scripture to support their answer.

13. A couple comes to you with the problem that they argue all the time. What counsel would you give them? Give Bible verses to support your counsel.

14. A husband comes to you with the complaint that his wife does not want to have sex with him. What counsel would you give this man, based on Ephesians 5:25?

15. A man in your church comes to you and says that his wife has been unfaithful to him. What would you advise this man to do? Give Bible verses to back up your answer.

16. A pastor has been married for ten years and has no children. The pastor's wife has become very discouraged and does not take an active part in the church any more. The pastor himself is becoming spiritually weak. He has privately admitted to you that he has lost his joy in the Lord. How could you help this hurting couple?

17. Discuss the African concept of family.

18. Ask three people from different tribes to give the traditional cultural viewpoint of their people on sexual immorality and adultery.

19. Define the roles of the husband, the wife, and the children, in the African context.

SUGGESTED FOR FURTHER READING

Cornes, A.J.C. *Divorce and Remariage*. London: Hodder, 1993.

Huggett, Joyce. *Growing into Love*. Leicester: InterVarsity Press, 1982.

Kimathi, Grace. *Courting in Marriage*. Nairobi: Uzima Press, 1983.

Phypers, D. *Christian Marriage in Crisis*. London: Marc Europe, 1985.

Trobisch, Walter. *I Married You*. Leicester: InterVarsity Press, 1972.

17

Suffering and the Related Problems of Sickness, Sorcery, Witchcraft, and Bribery

There are some very hard questions in life. Why do good people suffer? Why does tragedy strike the righteous? Why do some people endure great pain or sorrow and others do not?

A young missionary had just arrived in the country. He had dedicated his life to the Lord's service, and was glad to begin the ministry he had set his heart on doing. He was beginning to get to know a few names and faces and to make some friends. One day he joined another missionary on a routine trip. Suddenly a lorry pulled out from the oncoming lane of the highway to overtake another car. The lorry hit the car with the two missionaries head-on. The older missionary, who was driving the car, was killed instantly. The new missionary was on the front passenger seat. He was thrown from the car. He was rushed to a nearby hospital but there was nothing they could do. His neck was broken. He was paralyzed from the neck down. He would never walk or use his arms or legs again. He would be helpless the rest of his life.

Now, many years later, he is confined to a wheelchair. He looks at the people around him each day and asks, 'Why, Lord?' Why would God allow such a terrible thing to happen to a young man who had dedicated his life and strength to serve the Lord?

There were no answers then and there are no answers today for this man. His story focuses our attention on some of the hardest questions in life. Why do good and innocent people often suffer bitterly? Why do some people suffer great pain and sorrow and others do not? No one but God can answer these questions. But we can learn much about suffering by studying what God has to say in the Bible. In this chapter we will discuss the following questions:

A. What does the Bible say about human suffering?
B. What are the causes of sickness?
C. How can a Christian deal with sorcery, witchcraft, magic, curses and spells?
D. How should a Christian handle the problem of bribery?

A. WHAT DOES THE BIBLE SAY ABOUT HUMAN SUFFERING?

The questions are not new. The book of Job deals with this difficult subject. Job lived at the time of Abraham, about 2000 years before Christ. On two occasions, God himself said that Job was a blameless man (Job 1:8, 2:3). Yet it was God, the only one who is perfectly good (Matt. 19:17), who gave Satan permission to bring great harm and suffering to Job on these two occasions (Job 1:12, 2:6).

Suffering, pain, and natural disasters are problems which deeply disturb everyone. Christians and non-Christians alike find it very hard to understand when good people suffer and evil people go unharmed. Some people think that all suffering and trouble is the direct result of evil persons like witches and sorcerers. Some people think that all suffering comes from evil spirits, or from sin in a person's life. The Bible does teach that much suffering is the result of evil persons, evil spirits, and sin, but the Bible does not teach that these are the reasons for all suffering.

In order to really understand why things happen as they do in this world, we must go back to the events which took place at creation. From Genesis we learn that after God had created everything, including man, he said that it was all very good (Gen. 1:31). We learn from the book of Revelation that when God makes a new heaven and a new earth at the end of this age, there will be no more pain, grief or death (Rev. 21:4). By comparing these two statements, it is clear that the painful conditions which exist on earth today were not God's intention at the creation.

The explanation for the condition of this world is found in the story of man's rebellion against God in the garden of Eden. Sin is responsible for all that we see wrong in the world, including natural disasters. After the fall, God pronounced a curse on mankind (Gen. 3:16–19) which extended to the physical earth. The curse meant that there would be painful physical changes to the earth itself and to what it produced (Gen. 3:17–18). In other words, what God had created as good, and for man's good, was ruined by sin against God. It is what would happen if someone gave another person a new bicycle, and that person ruined the bike through carelessness and abuse.

In Romans, the Apostle Paul explains the condition of the natural world which came about as a result of man's rebellion against God. Referring to the curse on the earth, the apostle explains that, 'the creation was subjected to frustration, not by its own choice, but by the will of the one (i.e. God) who subjected it' (Rom. 8:20–NASB). Paul goes on to say, 'We know that the whole creation has been groaning as in the pains of childbirth right up to the present time' (Rom. 8:22–NASB).

Those who suffer at the hands of others, should remember how God himself in the person of Christ, shared their suffering as an innocent victim in the hands of evil men. The thorns which pierced his head, the beard which was pulled from his face, the whip which tore open his back, and the unfaithfulness of his close friends, all brought the same terrible pain to the Holy God of heaven as it would to one of us. No one has ever endured undeserved suffering like Jesus Christ. The many people in Africa who suffer bitterly without a just cause, can find a deep bond with the holy and innocent Saviour who was nailed to the cross like a common criminal.

Because Adam and Eve believed Satan and obeyed him instead of obeying God, Satan and his fallen angels gained a certain degree of control over the present world. Jesus later referred to Satan as the ruler of this world (John 12:31; 14:30). Jesus also indicated that some of the painful and evil conditions of this world, such as poisonous scorpions and snakes (Luke 10:19), are directly related to Satan's power.

From the statement by Christ in Luke 10:19, it is evident that these painful and evil changes in the world were not a part of the original plan for creation. They came about as a result of mankind's rebellion against God and the power which Satan gained over the world as a result of it. As further evidence for this, we read in the book of Job that Satan was able to bring about a violent storm which killed all ten of Job's children (Job 1:18–19). Thus it can be seen that there are times when even violent and destructive storms and natural disasters may be the work of Satan. This is not to say that all violent storms are the work of the devil. However, such things are now possible because Satan is the 'prince of the power of the air' (Eph. 2:2).

From these and other references in Scripture, it is evident that the pain, suffering and troubles of this world are the result of man's rebellion against God. This rebellion resulted in Satan gaining authority over the present world. It also resulted in a curse on the world. Job observed, 'Man is born for trouble, as sparks fly upwards' (Job 5:7).

The book of Job relates a series of bitter trials in Job's life for which Satan is given responsibility, even though Job had not committed a specific sin to bring about this trouble. In a completely different situation, Jesus healed a woman who had been crippled for 18 years. He stated that the woman was a daughter of Abraham, suggesting her Jewish faith, but he said that she had been bound by Satan during all that time (Luke 13:11–16).

Concerning suffering because of sin, Jesus healed a man who had been sick for 38 years (John 5:5–9). After healing the man, Jesus said to him, 'See, you are well again. Stop sinning, or something worse may happen to you' (John 5:14). In this case, Jesus indicated that the man's sin was related to his disability. In the book of James, the author says, 'confess your sins to one another, and pray for one another, so that you may be healed' (James 5:16). This passage also again suggests that in some cases there can be a relationship between specific sin and sickness.

Many people in North America think that trouble and suffering have nothing to do with evil spirits or sin. They believe that everything which happens is the result of chance. This view cannot be supported from the Bible. For example, in the case of the child in Mark 9:17–27 who was both deaf and dumb, Jesus cast a demon out of the boy and stated that it was a spirit of deafness and dumbness (Mark 9:25). Following the exorcism the boy was healed, showing that the boy's condition was indeed caused by the demon.

In Luke 13:2–4 where Jesus commented on a situation where 18 people had been killed by the falling tower of Siloam, he stated that this event did not occur because the people were worse sinners than those around them. However, Jesus did indicate that all men deserve such suffering and more because of their sins (Luke 13:3,5). In saying this, Jesus implied that some human suffering results from human sinfulness.

In addition to sin and evil spirits, the Bible indicates that there may be other reasons for human suffering. For example in John 9:2–3, the disciples asked Jesus why a certain man had been born blind. 'Who sinned,' they asked, 'this man or his parents, that he was born blind?' 'Neither this man nor his parents sinned,' said Jesus, 'but this happened so that the work of God might be displayed in his life.'

The Apostle Peter reminds us that one very important reason why God allows suffering to come into our lives is to purify our lives from sin (1 Pet. 4:1). Peter goes on to show how these experiences can make us want the will of God in our lives rather than to satisfy the evil desires of our sinful nature (1 Pet. 4:2).

From the above examples it is clear that the individual reasons for suffering can be quite different. Only God knows the full answer in every situation. For this reason it is wrong for a person to consult a diviner or witch doctor when something bad happens. Instead, a Christian should confess and renounce every sin in his or her life and then trust the Lord for his grace and help to deal with the situation (Heb. 4:16).

There is something we are told to do whenever we suffer. In James 5:13 (NASB) we are told, 'Is anyone among you suffering? Let him pray.' This is the most important thing we can do. No matter what the circumstances may be, prayer puts us into contact with God, especially in our time of need. Hebrews 4:16 says, 'Let us then approach the throne of grace with confidence, so that we may receive mercy, and find grace to help us in our time of need.'

The Bible does not offer a simple answer to the problem of suffering. It does, however, tell us that God is ready to help us whatever the trial may be (Heb. 4:16). God knows every detail of our lives and nothing can touch one of his children without his permission. In the case of Job's suffering, Satan had to receive permission from God before he could carry out his evil plans against Job. This fact can be a source of strength and encouragement for the Christian who comes into a time of severe trial.

Why did God give Satan permission to carry out such wickedness against Job, whom God himself called blameless? God does not owe an explanation to his creatures for anything he does. In the case of Job, God did not offer Job an explanation for his suffering. He simply reminded Job of his own glory and power (Job 38:1–40:2). However, by carefully examining the conversation between Satan and God in the book of Job, we may get some idea of why God allowed Satan to torment Job.

In Job's case, it seems that God decided to prove to the angels that Job did not just love him because he had given him riches, health, and blessings. Through Job's suffering God revealed to the angels that Job loved God for himself. By doing this, God exposed and condemned the lie Satan had spoken before God and the angels (Job 1:6–11), namely: 'Does Job fear God for nothing? Stretch out your hand and strike everything he has, and he will surely curse you to your face' (Job 1:9,11).

Job did not fail this bitterly hard test, even when Satan took the lives of all of Job's children (Job 1:18–19). Job's testimony was, 'The Lord gave, and the Lord has taken away, may the name of the Lord be praised' (Job 1:21). The account goes on to say, 'In all this, Job did not sin by charging God with wrongdoing' (Job 1:22). Job's heart-attitude toward God was revealed in his confession, 'Though he slay me, yet will I hope in him' (Job 13:15). Job also understood God's purpose to purify his life from sin through suffering. In Job 23:10 Job said, 'He knows the way that I take. When he has tested me, I will come forth as gold.' It is therefore clear that God allows suffering for many Christians in order to purify their lives from things which are not pleasing to God (1 Pet. 4:1).

It is also clear that God allows suffering in order to teach his people to rely on his grace and strength and not on their own strength. This is the reason God gave to the Apostle Paul for the suffering in his life (2 Cor. 12:8–10).

The problem with the whole issue of suffering is that we have the idea that we do not deserve to suffer. We easily forget the fact that man is a sinner who rebelled against God right from the beginning.

Adam knew very well what God had told him to do but he willingly chose to rebel against God by eating the fruit which God had forbidden him to eat (Gen. 3:6). Mankind has been rebelling against God ever since. The Bible says, 'There is not a righteous man on earth who does what is right and never sins' (Eccl. 7:20). What then did God mean when he said that Job was blameless (Job 1:8)? In the light of Ecclesiastes 7:20, we must take God's statement about Job to mean that Job was not guilty of a specific sin for which God was punishing him, even though Job had a sinful nature just like all other people.

In ordinary life, when a criminal is caught breaking the law, he is punished by the government. He may complain about his punishment, but the fact is, he deserves his punishment because of his crime. Furthermore, if he is not punished, all the people who know about his crime will be outraged. They will demand that he be punished. This may give us an additional hint as to why God allowed Job to suffer, and why he allows many Christians to suffer.

God is a just and righteous king. Satan and the angels know that all men are sinners who deserve much more suffering than they receive. God could not permit the fallen angels to accuse God of injustice for protecting Job from suffering. In a certain sense, for the sake of maintaining the same standard of justice with every creature in his universe, God was required to answer the charge of Satan against Job by allowing Job to suffer. The Bible says Job himself, 'did not sin by charging God with wrongdoing' (Job 1:22). It was not wrong of God to allow Job to suffer because all men on earth deserve suffering for their sins. However, God does not cause people to suffer as much as they deserve, because he is a God of great mercy. Psalm 86:5 says, 'You are forgiving and good, O Lord, abounding in love to all who call to you.' Psalm 86:15 says, 'You, O Lord are a compassionate and gracious God, slow to anger, abounding in love and faithfulness.'

Psalm 130:3 says, 'If you, O LORD, kept a record of sins, O LORD, who could stand?' Psalm 76:7 says, 'You alone are to be feared. Who can stand before you when you are angry?' The amazing thing is that people do not suffer much more severely for their sins than they do.

This is just what Jesus was teaching when his followers asked why God had allowed some Galileans to be killed by Pontius Pilate (Luke 13:1–2). They also asked why God had allowed a building (the tower of Siloam) to fall on 18 people and kill them (Luke 13:3). In his answer Jesus said, 'Do you think that they were more guilty than all the others living in Jerusalem? I tell you no! But unless you repent, you too will all perish' (Luke 13:5). The truth about God's mercy is stated in Psalm 103:10: 'He does not treat us as our sins deserve, or repay us according to our iniquities' (Psalm 103:10).

The fact that people deserve more suffering than they receive, does not help a person like the young missionary earlier in this chapter. Other questions torment them, such as why one person suffers while another less dedicated Christian escapes suffering. Even more commonly, Christians may ask why do they suffer when evil men, who are not even God's children, escape suffering.

The psalmist Asaph also struggled with this question. He wrote, 'I envied the arrogant when I saw the prosperity of the wicked. They have no struggles; Their bodies are healthy and strong' (Psalm 73:3–4). Finally, Asaph saw the situation from God's perspective. In Psalm 73:16–19 he wrote, 'When I tried to understand all this, it was oppressive to me till I entered the sanctuary of God; then I understood their final destiny. Surely . . . you cast them down to ruin. How suddenly are they destroyed, completely swept away by terrors!' Thus the key to understanding the problem of why the wicked do not always suffer, is to understand what the Bible says about the final judgment of the wicked and the final destiny of the righteous. In the final judgment, God will indeed severely punish the wicked (Matt. 25:41).

Psalm 73 helps us to understand the hard questions of life. We think of our problems and our suffering only from the perspective of our present circumstances. God says that this life and the present situation are only a small part of the whole picture. There is more to the story. There is more to come. One day the wicked will pay in full for their wickedness. One day the righteous will be rewarded for their faithfulness, especially when they have had to suffer for being faithful to Christ. At the end of Job's trials, God rewarded him with double of everything he had in the beginning and gave him ten more children as well (Job 42:10–13).

Paul understood this truth. He could say, 'I consider that our present sufferings are not worth comparing with the glory that will be revealed in us' (Rom. 8:18). In the spirit world, Abraham spoke to the rich man in Luke 16:25 and said, 'Son, remember that in your lifetime you received your good things, while Lazarus received bad things, but now he is comforted here and you are in agony.' The Apostle Peter wrote, 'Praise be to the God and Father of our Lord Jesus Christ! In his great mercy he has given us new birth into a living hope through the resurrection of Jesus Christ from the dead, and into an inheritance that can never perish, spoil or fade – kept in heaven for you . . . In this you greatly rejoice, though now for a little while you may have had to suffer grief in all kinds of trials. These have come so that your faith . . . may be proved genuine and may result in praise, glory and honour when Jesus Christ is revealed' (1 Peter 1:3–7).

God's answer to the hard questions of life is to be patient, the story is not yet finished. When we enter heaven, the answers will be given. The glory and blessing of God's reward will at last be revealed for those who have faithfully lived through hard trials for Christ's sake. Those Christians who have been faithful in their suffering will receive a reward so great that if it were explained to them now they would not understand it. In 1 Corinthians 1:9 we are told, 'No eye has seen, no ear has heard, no mind has conceived, what God has prepared for those who love him.' In Romans 8:28 we read, 'And we know that in all things, God works for the good of those who love him, who have been called according to his purpose.' In heaven, we will understand the reasons for suffering.

B. WHAT ARE THE CAUSES OF SICKNESS?

A Christian man became sick in his village. There was a good church dispensary nearby, and the man's family took him there for treatment. Unfortunately, the man had a history of hepatitis (a disease of the liver), amoebic dysentery and malaria. These illnesses had seriously damaged the man's liver. He was given treatment for the present sickness, but the previous damage to his liver was so bad that he became only more sick. After some days he died. At the man's funeral, the local pastor spoke about the man's life and his relationships to others. He had been a good man and a faithful Christian. Then the pastor made the following statement: 'We have been told by the dispenser that our brother died from damage to his liver. We all know, however, what really happened to him. We know that he was eaten by witches.' Was the pastor right? What are the biblical and scientific facts about sickness?

This true incident draws our attention to the important matter in African life of sickness and its causes. Everyone struggles with the problem of sickness. There are probably very few people in the world who have not been sick at some time in their life. What does the Bible have to say about sickness, the causes of sickness, and the means to cure sickness?

The Bible says that God formed man from the dust of the earth and breathed into his nostrils the breath of life (Gen. 2:7). Since everything which God created was good and perfect (Gen. 1:31, Psalm 18:30), it is safe to say that when God created man, he gave him a body which worked perfectly. Sickness was not part of the original creation. When God told Adam not to eat the fruit of the tree of the knowledge of good and evil, he gave Adam this warning: 'in the day that you eat from it you shall surely die' (Gen. 2:17). Adam disobeyed God and ate the forbidden fruit. We learn from Romans 5:12 that sin and death entered the world as a result of this act of disobedience by Adam.

Death and sickness are related processes. Sickness is the opposite condition of health. Death is often the final result of a serious sickness which cannot be cured. Sickness can lead to death. Healing or wholeness leads to life.

From these verses we can see that the processes of sickness and death came into the world as a result of the disobedience of Adam and

Eve. In a general sense, we can say that sickness occurs because of the fall of man. That is, sickness is in the world because of sin. This is not to say that every sickness is the result of specific sin.

There are some people who think that every sickness is a direct result of a particular sin. The Bible does not teach this. For example, Satan brought physical sickness into Job's life (Job 2:7). This was not related to a specific sin in Job's life, because God himself said that Job was blameless (Job 2:3).

In addition, the Bible does teach that there are some sicknesses which come as a direct result of a particular sin. This is suggested when Jesus healed the man who was sick for 38 years (John 5:5–14). The most obvious examples today of sicknesses directly related to sin, would be the diseases which come from sexual immorality, such as AIDS and syphilis.

In James 5:14–16 Christians who are sick are told to call for the elders of the local church to pray for them. James 5:15 says, 'if he has sinned, he will be forgiven.' There is a clear suggestion in this statement that sickness is sometimes a direct result of specific sin. Because of this, if a Christian does get sick, it is always important for the person to confess and forsake any known sin in his or her life and to ask God for forgiveness. Otherwise the sickness will become worse because of God's judgment against the sin.

Scientists have discovered that many kinds of sicknesses are caused by very small living organisms which can only be seen under a microscope. They are called viruses, bacteria or amoebas. They are popularly called germs. Typhoid fever, malaria and hepatitis are examples of diseases caused by different kinds of germs. Typhoid fever is caused by bacteria, malaria is caused by a blood parasite, and hepatitis is caused by a virus. There are also some types of sickness which are the result of defective genes in the human reproductive cells. Epilepsy and some kinds of cancer are examples of diseases caused by defective genes.

Scientists have also discovered that some sicknesses can be related to the mental and emotional condition of people. Mental health can be closely related to physical health. If a person is very discouraged, very fearful, very angry or in other ways mentally disturbed, it can make a person physically sick.

When a person is exposed to germs, his or her body will develop the particular sickness which the germs cause unless the body has developed the ability to resist or destroy these germs. At any one time our bodies may have many kinds of germs in the blood but we may not feel sick. This is because the body's physical resistance is strong. When the body's physical resistance is strong the germs are not able to make the whole body sick. When the body's physical resistance is weak, the germs may likely cause sickness. The person's resistance may be weak because of poor food, exposure to other germs or because of mental or emotional distress. Mental distress is often caused by a bad relationship with another person.

What about the statement that witches may eat the soul of a person and cause death, as the pastor believed about the man in the story at the beginning of this chapter? It often happens in Africa that a person will become physically sick from his or her great fear of witchcraft. In other words, the person's fear becomes so great that the body becomes too weak to fight against the germs in the blood. It may not be the actual witchcraft, but the fear of witchcraft, which causes the person to become seriously sick and in some cases even to die.

Besides this, many sorcerers and witches do have real demonic power. The power of these sorcerers and witches comes from the demons who work through them. The demons may carry out the curses and spells of such people. When this demonic power is projected on to people through sorcery and witchcraft, the demons can cause physical and mental sickness. In the book of Job, Satan caused Job to be covered with boils (Job 2:6–7). This suggests that Satan or his demons brought Job into contact with the germs that caused his sickness. When King Saul was afflicted with an evil spirit, he went mad and became violent, reflecting the character of the evil spirit (1 Sam. 18:10–11).

We learn from many examples in the four gospels that demons can and do afflict people with various physical and mental problems. It is reasonable to expect that demons will carry out their evil purposes unless they are prevented by God or the holy angels from carrying out such plans. Thus when witches, sorcerers and secret societies claim responsibility for the sickness or death of persons, or for accidents, it may be true because of the power of Satan's demons. Jesus taught us that Satan 'was a murderer from the beginning' (John 8:44).

It is very important for a Christian to remember that he or she has authority over Satan and his demons because the Christian is spiritually joined to Jesus Christ, the King of Kings. A Christian does not need to live in fear of sorcerers, witches and demons. We will see in a moment what a Christian can do about such Satanic powers, curses and spells.

We must be careful not to blame every sickness on witches or demons. It is very likely that the majority of our sicknesses are simply the result of our accidental contact with the germs which cause that sickness.

What are the means to cure sickness? How should a Christian seek healing?

There are some Christians who think that it shows a lack of faith to seek healing by using prescribed medicinal drugs. This idea cannot be supported from the Bible. One of the writers of the four gospels was Luke, a professional doctor (Col. 4:14). The work of doctors is to give the right medicine for a particular sickness. The Apostle Paul suggested a commonly used medicine for stomach trouble to his friend Timothy (1 Tim. 5:23). It only takes a little thought to realize that it was God who gave doctors and scientists the skill and understanding to develop the many kinds of medicine which can cure sickness. What should a Christian do when he becomes sick?

First and most important, a Christian must make sure that there is no open or hidden sin in his life which may bring God's judgment, including sickness, on his or her life. The person should confess and repent of any sin in his or her life. This is especially true concerning the hidden sins of the heart, such as unforgiveness, resentment against others, bitterness over some situation, jealousy, and hatred. A Christian who has a sinful attitude in his or her heart, may continue to remain sick even if he or she takes the prescribed medicine.

Lasting health requires healing of the mind and spirit as well as healing of the body. An interesting verse of Scripture which reveals the relationship between the health of the body and the state of a person's mind says, 'A man's spirit sustains him in sickness, but a crushed spirit who can bear?' (Prov. 18:14). Another verse says, 'A heart at peace gives life to the body' (Prov. 14:30).

Broken relationships among people can crush the human spirit. It is extremely important to restore broken human relationships if a person is to be truly healthy. Jesus reminded his followers that, if they wanted God to answer their prayers (including prayers for healing from sickness), they should forgive anyone against whom they were angry before they prayed to God (Mark 11:25).

If a Christian suspects that a spell or curse has been placed upon him, he can break the spell or curse in the name of Jesus, as described below. In all cases of sickness, a Christian should pray (James 5:13). God usually grants healing, whether it comes through using medicine or without using medicine. If the sickness is very severe, or if there is no medicine available, it would be wise for the person to call for the elders of the local church to come and pray for him or her according to the plan given in James 5:14–16.

A Christian who is sick should seek for the best medical help available. It was mentioned in chapter fourteen under the problem of syncretism that a Christian should be very careful before going to a traditional healer for medicine to cure his sickness. Many of these people are involved with evil spirits through traditional religion. Even when they are not involved with traditional religion, the medicines given by a traditional healer may be unsafe to use. Before using the medicine of a traditional healer, a Christian should carefully investigate how and where the healer got the knowledge of his medicines. A person should also consult the mature Christian elders in the area about the religious beliefs of that healer. Finally, a person should try to discover if others who used the healer's medicine ever had a reoccurrence of the disease or bad side effects.

A Christian's body is the temple of the Holy Spirit (1 Cor. 6:19). He or she should only use those traditional medicines which have been proven to be safe for curing sickness. A medicine can only be considered safe if there is a consistent testimony of success without bad side effects. Medicines from a government or church dispensary have usually been tested for safety by scientists. They are generally safe if they are taken in the right way and in the right amounts.

To summarize the causes of sickness, we can say that sickness is in the world because of sin. Some sicknesses may be directly caused by a particular sin but many sicknesses are not the result of any particular sin in a person's life. Some sicknesses may be caused by the power of demons through sorcery or witchcraft. Some sickness is directly or indirectly related to a person's mental or emotional condition, especially related to human relationships.

Most sickness simply comes from the fact that we have come into contact with the particular germs which cause that sickness. This commonly happens from drinking unsafe water or eating food which has germs. It often happens from failing to wash dirty hands before eating. Our hands touch many things with germs, such as money or the hands of other people. It also happens from being close to people who are sick, and breathing in the germs they have sprayed into the air while coughing or sneezing.

Regardless of the reason for the sickness, God is merciful, and in most situations he grants healing from the sickness in response to prayer and the use of safe medicines. In some cases God grants healing without the use of any medicine. There is really no difference. Healing from God is a gracious gift with or without medicine (Psalm 103:3).

We must also remember that not all healing comes from God. Satan can afflict a person with sickness and then later remove the sickness. By doing this, Satan deceives people and persuades them to believe in the power of witch doctors and other traditional healers instead of trusting in God for healing.

C. HOW CAN A CHRISTIAN DEAL WITH SORCERY, WITCHCRAFT, MAGIC, CURSES AND SPELLS?

Sorcery and witchcraft are found all over the world. These practices are also found in most African cultures. They are the cause of great fear in many African societies, even today. We need to understand sorcery and witchcraft and the power behind them. We need to understand what the Bible says about these things. Most important, we must understand what the Christian can do about this kind of evil.

Some African cultures make a distinction between a sorcerer and a witch. A sorcerer is a person who purposely uses mystical power for or against someone. In sorcery, there is almost always the use of ritual words or ritual practices, such as the use of magic, spells, curses or the use of medicines. In many cases the sorcerer (male) or sorceress (female) will demand a fee for his or her service.

In those cultures which make a distinction between sorcerers and witches, a witch is thought to be a person who compulsively acts with evil supernatural power. According to these cultures, witches act because of an irresistible inner evil power. Sometimes they are believed to act blindly, without knowing what they are doing.

It is thought that witches are either born with these evil powers or get them by becoming part of a community (coven) of witches. The witch is believed to be a prisoner of the evil power within. Thus witches do not need to use ritual words, magic, medicines, spells or curses to perform their evil deeds. Instead, the power to do evil comes out from within.

Witchcraft is thought to be carried out unconsciously by the witch when he or she is asleep. The witch is believed to leave his or her body and fly about at night, seeking to eat human flesh. It is believed that when the witch eats the flesh of a person, the person becomes weak and sick and finally dies. This belief about witches and witchcraft is very strong in many parts of Africa.

For a great many people, including some weak Christians, the fear of witches and witchcraft is the greatest single fear in their lives. As it was pointed out in the section on sickness, the very fear of witchcraft can be so great that a person can develop serious symptoms of physical or mental illness. We must not underestimate the power of fear itself, whether there is actual witchcraft involved or not.

The Bible recognizes sorcery and witchcraft, but it does not make a strong distinction between the two. For example, in Micah 5:12 and Nahum 3:4, the same Hebrew word is translated as sorcery and as witchcraft in different English versions of the Bible. Witchcraft as it is discussed in the Bible has the same intentional character as sorcery. It is often mentioned in relation to casting spells, as in Deuteronomy 18:10–11, Isaiah 47:9,12 and Micah 5:12.

The Bible recognizes that spells and curses and people such as witches and sorcerers do have power. However, their power is nothing in comparison with the power of Almighty God (Isa. 47:9). This gives us a clear hint that the Christian does not need to fear the spells or curses of a sorcerer or a witch, no matter how strongly they are applied. Jesus Christ, who lives in the heart of a Christian, is infinitely more powerful than the power of any sorcerer, witch, evil spirit or evil power in the universe. Indeed, such persons and such powers are terrified in the presence of Christ, who dwells in the heart of a Christian. This was seen in the case of Simon the Samaritan sorcerer, who was humbled in the presence of the apostles Peter and John (Acts 8:9–24). It was seen in the case of the Gerasene demoniac, who was humbled in the presence of Christ (Mark 5:1–8).

Sorcery and witchcraft are described as purposeful (wilful) evil wherever they are mentioned in the Bible. They are severely condemned by God as wickedness, as in Leviticus 19:26 and Deuteronomy 18:10. King Hezekiah's son Manasseh was severely condemned by God for his practices of sorcery and witchcraft (2 Kings 21:6, 2 Chron. 33:6). Since magic is very much a part of the sorcerer's practice, this confirms to us that God condemns all use of magic, whether it is for supposedly good or evil purposes.

Even though the Bible does not speak of witches in the special compulsive way described above, the Bible does speak of people who are demonized. People who are demonized display the unclean and evil character of the demons within them. We learned in chapter eleven that demons carry out many kinds of evil, including torturing people with disease, deformity and death. Thus there is a biblical basis to believe that there are demonized people who have indwelling evil powers who energize them to do evil. Some criminals have testified in court that they felt they were under the control of an inner evil power when they committed their crimes. Many people have testified to hearing inner voices which urged them to do strange and evil things.

Testimonies of this kind reveal the presence and activity of demons in people. Such people are still responsible for what they do, but these testimonies show us that the person's character is being dominated by the demons within. It shows that such people have yielded themselves to sin in such a way that demons have gained a controlling influence over their minds and wills, so that their behaviour becomes the evil desires of the demons within them. This is the meaning of demonization in the Bible. Thus we find the Gerasene demoniac physically cutting and torturing his own body, and wandering among the graves of the dead (Mark 5:5). When King Saul was demonized, he became murderously violent, even to the point of trying to kill his own son, Jonathan (1 Sam. 16:14, 1 Sam. 20:32–33).

In the case of demonized people, we can say that the African idea of witches could be compared with a demonized person. The evil powers within such people are demons. The flying by night and eating of human flesh are issues of traditional belief. The Bible does not address these beliefs.

What we do know from the Bible is that when people are demonized, they display strange, destructive and evil behaviour. Since demons are supernatural beings, people who are demonized may at times be able to perform strange demonic miracles by Satanic power (2 Thess. 2:9).

If an evil person like a witch or a sorcerer places a spell or a curse on someone, it is quite possible that demons will respond to the spell or curse. Unless God prevents them from doing it, the demons may bring sickness or trouble on the person under the spell or curse. God allowed Satan to bring great harm and suffering to Job. The activity of Satan and demons can even cause death. This happened in the case of

Job's children, who were killed by a violent storm which was probably caused by Satan or fallen angels. Demons can also bring about accidents, crime, and other kinds of evil.

Christians can live above the fear of witches and evil spirits because Jesus Christ, the King of Kings, lives within them, and Christ is infinitely more powerful than these spirits (1 John 4:4). God has placed the Christian in Christ, in a position above fallen angels (Eph. 1:20–21, Eph. 2:6). Jesus said he had given authority to his followers to overcome all the power of Satan (Luke 10:17). This is not just a matter of words but of genuine spiritual authority in Christ. The followers of Jesus Christ have authority to cast out demons (Luke 10:17).

People who have demonic power, such as sorcerers and witches, can bring about sickness and can also remove the sickness, giving the illusion of true healing. Evil eye is a demonic power which some traditional people possess. When a person has the power of evil eye, they can stare at people and cause severe physical or mental disorders. A traditional healer may also have demonic powers. It can happen that the traditional healer will be able to remove (appear to heal) the sickness caused by demons through a sorcerer, a witch, or a person with evil eye. In this way, Satan can strengthen both the belief in witchcraft and the belief in traditional healers and witch-doctors at the same time. By doing this, Satan draws people away from trust in God and tempts them to trust in things which God has condemned. As an example of demonic healing consider the following true story:

A child was picked up as a baby by a woman who was known in the village to have the power of the evil eye. That very day, the baby developed severe pain in the abdomen. The pain continued as the baby grew into childhood. The parents took the child to various dispensaries looking for help but the problem continued. The village people strongly urged the parents to seek the help of a witch-doctor. The parents resisted this idea for a long time. As the child's problem continued, however, the parents finally gave in to the urgent demands of their neighbours. They called for a traditional healing woman, who performed a 'spiritual surgery' to remove the cause of the sickness. Not too surprisingly, the pain left the boy immediately and did not return.

Clearly, demons had caused the pain in the first place, and their departure gave the illusion of healing. We cannot help but question why God would allow such parents to be so clearly deceived by demonic power. Why would he even permit the child's sickness in the first place? In order to answer this difficult question, we must remember that trust in God and the promises of his word is a choice which people must consciously make. Just as Eve had to choose between the truth of God and the lies of Satan, so Christians must make the same choices today. Sometimes God does allow Satan or his demons to trouble the people of God, as he did in the case of Job. But God has given us the spiritual weapons through the promises of his word to deal with such attacks of the evil one. The Bible tells us to 'take up the shield of faith, with which you can extinguish all the flaming arrows of the evil one' (Eph. 6:16).

WHAT ARE CHRISTIANS TO DO IF THEY SUSPECT WITCHCRAFT, MAGIC, A SPELL OR A CURSE IS BEING USED AGAINST THEM?

Since witchcraft, magic, spells and curses have power because of the power of Satan and his demons, a Christian who is walking in holiness of life has authority from the Lord to overcome the power of witches and to break the power of such magic, spells and curses in the name of Jesus Christ. The witchcraft or the curse will be broken, because Jesus Christ has power over all evil spirits.

A Christian can say something like this: 'I break this spell (or curse) in the name of Jesus Christ' or, 'I refuse and resist the power of this sorcerer (or witch), and I call on the name of Jesus Christ who is King of Kings and Lord of Lords to crush and disperse these evil powers which have come against me.' By praying this kind of battle prayer of spiritual warfare, a Christian is in good company with the psalmist, who prayed many such prayers against the enemies of God. Read Psalm 35:1–10 and Psalm 83:1–3, 13–18 for examples of such spiritual warfare praying.

In Luke 10:17, Jesus' disciples exclaimed, 'Lord, even the demons submit to us in your name.' Jesus then said to the disciples, 'I have given you authority. . .to overcome all the power of the enemy' (Luke 10:19). A Christian can also pray to the Lord for healing if the witchcraft, magic, spell or curse has caused sickness. When spoken by Christians who are walking close to the Lord, these words are very powerful.

Jesus Christ has power over all creatures in the universe (Eph. 1:20–22). Since Christ lives in the heart of every believer (John 14:23), it is only necessary for a Christian to verbally break the power of demons in the name of Jesus, and that power will be broken by Christ who lives in him. The Bible says, 'You. . .have overcome them, because the one who is in you is greater than the one who is in the world' (1 John 4:4). There is no demon or fallen angel in the universe who can stand against Jesus Christ.

Witchcraft, sorcery, curses and spells are real because of the demons who empower them, but Jesus Christ, the God of heaven and earth, will overcome evil spirits and destroy the power of such witchcraft. The Christian does not need to live in fear, because the Lord is his light and his salvation (Psalm 27:1, 2 Tim. 1:7). God reminds us through Paul, 'Do not be anxious (fearful) about anything, but in everything, by prayer and petition, with thanksgiving, present your requests to God' (Phil. 4:6).

D. HOW SHOULD A CHRISTIAN HANDLE THE PROBLEM OF BRIBERY?

Joshua, a teacher in a Christian school, bought a large piece of land which he wanted to cultivate. The Ministry of Agriculture in his local government had recently bought some tractors. The tractors were available to hire for the work of cultivation. Joshua went to the Ministry of Agriculture before planting time arrived and made arrangements to hire a tractor for plowing his land. He paid the reservation fee and was assigned a day for a tractor.

When the scheduled day came, the tractor driver appeared without the tractor. He said the tractor was being repaired. Joshua contacted the office each day for the next two weeks but he was told the same story each time he came: 'The tractor is still being repaired.' Joshua saw the driver using a Ministry tractor to plow his neighbour's field during the second week. He went to the driver and complained that he had reserved a tractor for that time. Finally the driver told him plainly that Joshua would have to pay a separate (and very expensive) fee to the driver if he wanted to have his plowing done.

Joshua complained angrily that he had paid the required reservation fee but the driver would not cooperate. When Joshua complained to the Ministry official in charge, he was told that it was up to the driver to schedule the time when he could bring the tractor. They could not do anything to help Joshua. Joshua was angry and his land was not plowed. It was obvious that the driver was not going to work without a bribe. Finally Joshua had to hire some men to hoe his land by hand.

What would you have advised Joshua to do? According to the Bible, how is a Christian to handle the problem of bribery?

Just about every country in the world has a problem of bribery. Before a Christian can effectively deal with a specific case of bribery, he should first know what the Bible says about this corrupt practice. It is best to think through matters like this and decide about them ahead of time, before you face a hard decision in real life. When your mind is settled on the matter beforehand, you can resist strong temptations.

WHAT DOES THE BIBLE HAVE TO SAY ABOUT BRIBERY?

Here are some of God's words on the subject of bribery: 'For I know how many are your offenses and how great your sins. You oppress the righteous and take bribes, and you deprive the poor of justice in the courts' (Amos 5:12). In this verse, God says that bribery is a sin, just like depriving the poor of justice in court. In Exodus 23:8 the Lord says, 'Do not accept a bribe, for a bribe blinds those who see and twists the words of the righteous.' If it is wrong to take a bribe because it blinds the minds of those who would otherwise be able to distinguish between right and wrong, then it is also wrong to offer a bribe. Offering a bribe will have the effect of corrupting the person who receives it. To offer a bribe is to put temptation before someone to forsake justice and to break the law.

WHY IS BRIBERY WRONG?

Proverbs 15:27 says that bribery promotes greed. Greed (the love of money) is a great evil and a sin before God. The New Testament teaches us, and human experience shows us, that greed destroys people (1 Tim. 6:9). When people trust in money, they do not trust in God (1 Tim. 6:17). People steal and kill because of greed. Many murders in the world happen every year because of the love of money. Countries go to war because of greed. Judas Iscariot betrayed Jesus Christ for the love of money (Matt. 26:14–15). As a result, Judas lost his soul. Bribery clearly promotes greed, and greed destroys both people and nations.

Proverbs 17:23 and Deuteronomy 16:19 teach that bribery perverts justice. Deuteronomy 16:19 adds that, 'a bribe blinds the eyes of the wise and twists the words of the righteous.' Ecclesiates 7:7 says, 'a bribe corrupts the heart.' Thus bribery contributes to the corruption of society. It makes life hard for everyone.

Consider the problem faced by Joshua in the account above. If he had offered the driver a bribe, he would have encouraged the driver to continue to break the law and to continue to oppress local farmers for his own personal gain. The law in his local government said that when the proper fee was paid to the Ministry of Agriculture, the farmer was entitled to have his land plowed with no further payment.

Joshua refused to pay the bribe, and his land was never plowed with a tractor before that rainy season. Joshua finally had to hire several men to help him hoe the land by hand. Although his decision to do right in the eyes of God was hard and costly, his action was a rebuke from God to the tractor driver. More important, by his example Joshua strengthened the determination of other Christians in his school to resist the temptation to live by bribery. The Lord was faithful and provided Joshua's needs. Most important, Joshua earned a reward in heaven from Jesus for his righteous behaviour.

How else can people be delivered from the evils of bribery if there are no courageous Christians in the society who will refuse to participate in this sinful practice? Many Christians have fallen into bribery because they believe that things cannot be accomplished in any other way. That can only be true if there is no God. As long as there is a God, the Christian can pray and ask the Lord to help him. If God can raise the dead, he can certainly answer such a prayer.

In answering the Christian's prayer, God will usually do more than honour the testimony of the Christian. He may meet the Christian's need in another way. He can use the believer's action to change the hearts of other people. By refusing to participate in bribery, a Christian will reduce corruption in the whole society. If all the Christians in a country were to refuse to practice bribery, it would change the culture of that country.

A Christian who refuses to practice bribery may have to endure suffering or persecution at the hands of evil men, just as Joshua did. The Bible does not promise that we will escape suffering and persecution. But it does promise that God will help his people. The Bible promises that God rewards those who faithfully serve him. In John 12:26 Jesus said, 'My Father will honour the one who serves me.' In Matthew 5:11–12 Jesus said, 'Blessed are you when people insult you, persecute you, and falsely say all kinds of evil against you because of me. Rejoice and be glad, because great is your reward in heaven.' We may not receive our reward for doing what is right until we get to heaven.

If we give a bribe we may get what we want for the moment, but we will be sorry hereafter. If we give bribes, we will also weaken the faith of fellow-Christians. We must trust God to provide for us. We must set a strong example for other Christians. These are the kinds of choices Christians must make when it comes to bribery and other corrupt practices.

SUMMARY

Human suffering has been the experience of mankind from the time of Adam and Eve. The reason for suffering can be traced back to the rebellion of Adam and Eve against the will of God in the garden of Eden. When God placed Adam in the garden, he warned him, 'in the day that you eat from it (the fruit of the forbidden tree) you shall surely die' (Gen. 2:17). Little did Adam, or the rest of mankind, realize how serious the death penalty for sin would be. Suffering, because of the deadly effects of sin, has touched every area of human existence, including nature itself (Rom. 5:12, Rom. 8:20–21). Yet, there is still a great mystery as to why some people suffer more than others, and why some suffering seems so unjust. Many times the innocent suffer at the hands of the wicked, and even the righteous sometimes suffer bitterly, while hardened criminals escape punishment.

The Bible tells us that there will be a final judgment for all human beings, and a final accounting of all human words and deeds (Matt. 12:36, Rev. 20:11–15). In addition, Satan and fallen angels will one day fully pay for the great wickedness they have promoted on earth (Matt. 25:41, Rev. 20:10). For the righteous who have suffered at the hands of evil people or evil angels in this life, there will be an everlasting reward from God, which according to Scripture, will make the sufferings of this life seem small (Matt. 5:11–12, Rom. 8:18).

Sickness is an aspect of suffering in this life which is also related to the sin of mankind. However, it is often difficult to know the reason for a particular sickness. Some sicknesses may be directly caused by a particular sin. Some sicknesses may be caused by the power of demons through sorcery or witchcraft. Some sickness is related to a person's mental or emotional condition. Such emotional problems often come from broken human relationships. Most sickness results from coming into contact with the particular germs which cause that sickness. Whatever the cause, God is merciful, and in most situations he grants healing from sickness in response to prayer and the use of safe medicines. In some cases God grants healing without the use of any medicine.

The Bible recognizes the reality of sorcery, witchcraft, magic, curses, and spells as a part of Satan's work. However, Christians can live above the fear of these evil powers because Jesus is infinitely more powerful than all evil spirits and he lives within every true Christian (1 John 4:4). If a Christian suspects he has been attacked by such demonic powers he can call on Christ to crush and disperse them. It is well to remember that when Jesus confronted a legion of demons in the Gerasene demoniac, the demons were terrified in his presence and begged him not to torture them (Luke 8:26–31)!

Many problems are caused by bribery and corruption. Christians may be tempted to yield to the pressure of giving a bribe in order to get things done. When they yield to such a temptation, they disobey the Lord (Ex. 23:8, Amos 5:12) and set a bad example. In some places Christians say that it is impossible to live without yielding to bribery. That can only be true if there is no God. But there is a God, and the Christian can pray and ask the Lord to help him. As the motto on an African lorry said, 'When God says yes, who will say no?'

DISCUSSION QUESTIONS AND PROJECTS BASED ON CHAPTER SEVENTEEN

1. Let four people in the group tell stories of people they know who have endured seemingly unjust suffering. After each story, discuss how you could have counselled or helped the victims. Find specific verses of Scripture which might be helpful.

2. Let one person explain to the group why God was not doing wrong in allowing Job to suffer as bitterly as he did.

3. Divide into groups of four. Let each group recall cases of illness where the cause of the illness seemed to be related to one of the following situations:
    (a) Specific sin in the sick person's life.
    (b) Witchcraft on the sick person.
    (c) A negligent mistake, such as giving someone dirty (infected) food or water.
    (d) Harmful native medicine from a traditional healer.

   For each of the above situations, let the small groups describe what should be done for the sick person in addition to seeking proper medical attention at a hospital or dispensary.

4. Discuss the African concept of illness and its causes.

5. Let one person explain to the class the two main problems associated with receiving medical treatment from a traditional healer.

6. Let a nurse or trained dispenser come to the class and explain some of the simple practices which can prevent many sicknesses (e.g. washing hands with soap and water before eating).

7. Discuss the African concept of evil and curses.

8. Let three students each tell about an incident when someone suffered after having had a spell or a curse placed on them.

9. What is the real power behind witchcraft, spells and curses? Find a Bible verse to support your answer.

10. Describe what a Christian should do if he suspects that sorcery or witchcraft has been carried out against him or her.

11. Discuss the traditional African view of morality, gifts and bribes.

12. Discuss the nature of corruption in African society and social institutions.

13. Let two people describe real-life situations in which they, or someone they know, bribed another person to get what they needed. Discuss what actions the person could have taken instead of yielding to bribery.

14. Discuss what steps the government could take to reduce the amount of bribery taking place in a country?

SUGGESTED FOR FURTHER READING

Carson, D.A. *How Long, O Lord?* Leicester: InterVarsity Press, 1994.

Krutza, William, ed. *How We Faced Tragedy*. Grand Rapids, Michigan: Baker Book House, 1978.
McGrath, Alistair. *Suffering*. London: Hodder, 1992.
Smith, Anthony M. *Gateway to Life*. Leicester: Intervarsity Press, 1994.
Stott, John. *Issues Facing Christians Today*. Leicester: InterVarsity Press, 2nd edn, 1990.
Werner, David. *Where There Is No Doctor*. Palo Alto, California: The Hesperian Foundation, 1983.

18

The Return of Christ and the End of the Age

Kpaga: 'The world seems to be getting worse and worse. I have a brother who works at the government hospital in the city. He told me that almost every night, now, they bring someone to the hospital who has been beaten or shot by thieves. I wonder if things will ever change for the better again?'

Mungazhi: 'Things were better long ago, in the time of our forefathers. I wish we could go back to those days.'

Kpaga: 'My Christian friend in town told me that the Jesus they preach about is going to return to the world. I even heard a Muslim preaching that Jesus will return to the world. Do you think Jesus will be able to improve things for us?'

Mungazhi: 'I have an uncle who became a Christian. He told me that this Jesus will restore the world when he returns. In fact, he claims that it will be even better than it was at the creation.'

Kpaga: 'How can that be? Things were best at the beginning, in those days of long ago.'

To some people, it may seem that things don't change very much. They think that the world has always been the same. They believe that things will be the same in the future.

However, people who read the newspapers or listen to the radio are aware that something is happening in the world. Crime and violence are increasing. Young people are moving away from the traditions of their people. Inflation in many parts of the world is getting worse almost every day. Families are breaking apart. Great changes are taking place in national governments. Corruption and evil seem to be increasing everywhere. What does it all mean? What does the Bible have to say about the times in which we are living?

Do you know where history is leading? Do you know that there will be an end to this present world? What is the meaning behind the dramatic changes in current events? Most important, what about the promise which Jesus made that he would return to this world (Matt.

24:29–31, John 14:3)? Will such a thing really happen? When Jesus ascended into heaven, 40 days after his resurrection from the dead, an angel told his watching disciples, 'This same Jesus who has been taken from you into heaven will come back in the same way you have seen him go into heaven' (Acts 1:11). When will that happen? How will Christ return to this world? What will take place when he does return?

In this chapter we will see what the Bible says about the return of Christ and the end of this age. We will seek to answer the following questions:

A. Where is history leading?
B. What events will mark the end of the present age?
C. What will the return of Christ be like?
D. When will Christ return?
E. How can a person prepare for the final events of this age and for Christ's return?
F. What are some of the main theories about the order of events at the time of the return of Christ?
G. Why will Christ return?

A. WHERE IS HISTORY LEADING?

People who follow world events are wondering where history is leading. History is changing so fast that even the most influential world leaders cannot predict what will happen next. Does the Bible give us any light on where history is leading? Yes, the Bible tells us what God is doing in the world. The Bible also tells us what Satan is doing to oppose God. When we understand these two things, we will be able to make sense out of some of the changing events of our world.

WHAT IS GOD DOING IN THE WORLD?

To understand what God is doing at the present time, we must understand what he has done in the past and how it relates to what is happening now. The return of Christ is the climax of what God has done in the past and what he is doing today.

Following the creation of a perfect world, sin came into the world through Adam's disobedience to God in the garden of Eden (Gen. 1–3). Through sin, the penalty of death on mankind spread throughout the world (Gen. 3:17, Rom. 5:12). The resulting conditions of corruption and death affected not only mankind, but the rest of creation as well. Romans 8:22 says, 'We know that the whole creation has been groaning, as in the pains of childbirth right up to the present time.'

This terrible situation was brought about by the temptation which Satan brought before Adam and Eve, to rebel against God. Satan himself had rebelled against God long ages before (Gen. 3:1–6, Isa. 14:13–14). By rebelling against God and by taking many of God's angels along with him in his rebellion (Rev. 12:3–4), Satan became the enemy, or adversary, of God. The very name Satan means adversary. From the time of his own rebellion against God, Satan has continued to be the enemy of God and the enemy of all that God does. It is necessary to understand this in order to understand many of the things which are happening in the world today.

God made a promise in the garden of Eden at the time of Adam's sin, that a human being (the offspring of the woman) would finally overcome Satan. Genesis 3:15 gives this promise, and at the same time presents a broad outline of the course of human history. God said, 'I will put enmity between you and the woman, and between your offspring and hers; he will crush your head, and you will strike his heel.' The offspring of the woman who would eventually crush Satan's head was Jesus Christ.

Satan did strike the heel of Christ through the suffering and death of Christ. But God in his sovereignty and love used the apparent defeat of Christ on the cross to bring about the salvation of mankind as well as the defeat of Satan. Colossians 2:13–15 says, 'When you were dead in your sins . . . God made you alive with Christ. He forgave us all our sins, having canceled the written code . . . that was against us; he took it away, nailing it to the cross. And having disarmed the (Satanic) powers and authorities, he made a public spectacle of them, triumphing over them by the cross.'

Right from the time of the temptation of man and woman in the garden of Eden, Satan has actively opposed the work of God all over the world. This is the underlying reason why the world has continued in a turmoil of war, violence, crime and wickedness, right down to the present time.

An example of this invisible satanic opposition to the purposes of God took place when Jesus was born. Wise men came searching for the newborn king to bring him gifts and to worship him (Matt. 2:1–2). King Herod became jealous and angry at the thought that another king might one day challenge his throne. It was then an easy matter for Satan to suggest to King Herod to destroy all the male children in Bethlehem who were two years old and under, in an effort to kill the new king (Matt. 2:7–16). Herod wanted to eliminate a possible competitor to his throne. Satan wanted to destroy God's Messiah.

Much of human history has been like this event. People carry out plans based on their proud and selfish desires. Satan then uses the sinful behaviour of people as a means to carry out his own evil plans of rebellion against God. But in spite of all this evil, God is at work to save people from their bondage to sin and to restore the perfect world he created. God's plan of world redemption began 4000 years ago with one man of faith, named Abraham (Gen. 12:1–3). To this wandering cattle herder, God made an amazing promise. He said, 'I will make your name great, and you will be a blessing . . . and all peoples on earth will be blessed through you' (Gen. 12:2–3). How could all the groups of people on earth be blessed through this one man, Abraham? The answer is, through the salvation of Jesus Christ, the descendant of Abraham (Matt. 1:1–17). Abraham's descendants became the nation of Israel, through Abraham's grandson Jacob. Jacob was renamed Israel by God (Gen. 32:28). Jesus, an Israelite, was born of the tribe of Judah, one of Jacob's sons (Matt. 1:2,24–25).

Through Christ and his followers, the gospel of salvation is being preached throughout the whole world (Matt. 28:19, Mark 16:15). In this way, the blessing of Abraham is being passed on to the whole world. Those who believe in Christ become the spiritual sons of Abraham, because they find the true faith in God which Abraham had. Galatians 3:7–9 says, 'Understand then, that those who believe are children of Abraham. The Scripture . . . announced the gospel in advance to Abraham: "All nations will be blessed through you." So those who have faith are blessed along with Abraham, the man of faith.' As we saw in chapter nine, those who believe in Christ become part of his worldwide extended family, called the church.

In Matthew 16:18 Jesus said, 'I will build my church, and the gates of Hades will not overcome it.' In Matthew 28:19 Jesus gave his Great Commission to his followers. He said, 'Therefore go and make disciples of all nations, baptizing them in the name of the Father, and of the Son, and of the Holy Spirit.' At the first council of the church, the Apostle James summarized what God is doing today with these words: 'Brothers, listen to me. Simon has described to us how God at first showed his concern by taking from the Gentiles (i.e. the non-Jewish nations) a people for himself' (Acts 15:13).

Thus the primary work of God in the world today is to build the church of Jesus Christ. Through the church, all the nations of the earth will hear the gospel of salvation and have the opportunity to receive the blessing promised to Abraham. Jesus is taking from the Gentile nations of the world, 'a people for himself.' According to God's plan, the church is to include people from every tribe and nation on earth. In Revelation 5:9 the Bible says, 'You are worthy to take the scroll and to open its seals, because you were slain, and with your blood you purchased men for God from every tribe and language and people and nation.'

Jesus is building his church as Christians share their faith with other people, and take the good news of his salvation across cultural barriers to every group of people in the world (i.e. to all nations). The church is much closer to this goal today than it was 100 or 500 years ago. There are people who believe that the Great Commission could now be completed in one generation, if the church made an all-out effort to do it.

Although it is true that about half of the world's population still has no church in their midst, yet many new people are professing to follow

Christ every day. Here are some interesting figures. In the year 1000
AD there were perhaps about 220 non-Christians for every one
Christian in the world. In 1950 there were about twenty-one non-
Christians for every one Christian. By 1989, there were only about
seven non-Christians for every one Christian in the world. These
figures refer, of course, to all those who profess to follow Christ. Only
Jesus himself knows which of these people really belong to him and are
born of the Holy Spirit. Nevertheless, these figures still make it clear
that the church is getting closer to completing the task of the Great
Commission.

These facts are related to the return of Jesus Christ to this world.
While speaking about the events which would lead to his return, Jesus
said, 'This gospel of the kingdom will be preached in the whole world
as a testimony to all nations, and then the end will come' (Matt.
24:14). In a similar discussion about the end of the age in the gospel of
Mark, Jesus said, 'The gospel must first be preached to all nations'
(Mark 13:10).

Some people ask, 'Why has Christ not returned already?' The
answer to that question is in the uncompleted task of the Great
Commission. The people who lived in the day of the Apostle Peter
doubted the return of Christ. Peter quoted these people as saying,
'Where is this "coming" he promised' (2 Pet. 3:4)? To this question,
Peter answered, 'The Lord is not slow in keeping his promise, as some
understand slowness. He is patient with you, not wanting anyone to
perish, but everyone to come to repentance' (2 Pet. 3:9).

If the church would take the responsibility of the Great Commission
more seriously and make every effort to reach the remaining unreached
people of the world with the gospel, it would hasten the time of
Christ's return. In the passage quoted above, Peter stated, 'You ought
to live holy and godly lives, as you look forward to the day of God and
speed its coming' (2 Pet. 3:11– 12).

Will the whole world finally believe in Christ before he returns? The
Bible is very clear that the whole world will definitely not turn to
Christ. Jesus said, 'Broad is the road that leads to destruction, and
many enter through it' (Matt. 7:13). Concerning conditions on earth at
the time of his return, Jesus said, 'However, when the Son of Man
comes, will he find faith on the earth' (Luke 18:8)? This statement by
Christ suggests that many will not believe in him at the time of his
return.

WHAT IS SATAN DOING IN THE WORLD?

As Satan sees the gospel reaching more and more groups of people
around the world, he is becoming increasingly angry and violent. He is
angry because people of the human race whom he deceived into
rebelling against God, are now returning to submission to God

through faith in Christ. This makes Satan furious. He does not quietly accept this invasion of what he considers to be his property. Satan also resists the preaching of the gospel because when there are finally believers among all the unreached groups of people, Jesus will return and Satan will be bound (Rev. 5:9–10; Rev. 20:1–3). He knows that the success of the gospel means that his own time is short so he strongly resists the spread of the gospel (Rev. 12:12).

Sometimes Satan fights against the preaching of the gospel and the expansion of the church by stirring up governments or ethnic groups to war and killing. Such conditions will hinder the preaching of the gospel and the growth of local churches. Thus, we are commanded to pray, 'for kings, and all those in authority, that we may live peaceful and quiet lives in all godliness and holiness' (1 Tim. 2:2). In this passage Paul goes on to say, 'This is good, and pleases God our Saviour, who wants all men to be saved and to come to a knowledge of the truth' (1 Tim 2:3). In other words, we are to pray for government officials so that Satan's plans of suggesting violence and war to these leaders will be hindered. When there are conditions of peace, the gospel can be preached and local churches can carry out their activities for the Lord.

At different times in history Satan has fought against the gospel by stirring up non-Christians to persecute Christians. In Revelation 2:10 Jesus warned the believers at Smyrna, 'the devil will put some of you in prison to test you, and you will suffer persecution for ten days. Be faithful even to the point of death, and I will give you the crown of life.' Persecution is a painful discipline, but in times of persecution, the church has become very holy and pure (Heb. 12:5–10).

Satan fights against the gospel by encouraging false religions and cults. When people believe a lie, they will not believe the truth by which they can be saved. At least half of the world's present population is deceived by the teaching of false religions. The Bible says, 'The Spirit explicitly says that in later times, some will fall away from the faith, paying attention to deceitful spirits and doctrines of demons' (1 Tim. 4:1–NASB)

Perhaps the most common way that Satan opposes the work of God is to get people to become totally preoccupied with the things of the present world system, such as making money and satisfying personal ambitions. When people become involved with the love of money and power, they will have no time for God. That is why Jesus said, 'You cannot serve both God and money' (Matt. 6:24).

B. WHAT EVENTS WILL MARK THE END OF THE PRESENT AGE?

The Bible contains many prophecies about what will happen at the close of the present age. Bible prophecy is often very specific about what will take place. However, these prophecies rarely state the time when their predictions will be fulfilled. It is the human tendency to want the specific dates when predictions will be fulfilled. Before Jesus' ascension into heaven, the disciples asked him, 'Lord, are you at this time going to restore the kingdom to Israel' (Acts 1:6)? In his answer to this question, Jesus pointedly told his disciples, 'It is not for you to know the times or dates the Father has set by his own authority' (Acts 1:7).

The same general perspective must be kept in mind concerning the events attending the end of this age and the return of Christ. The Bible has given us considerable detail about some of these events and historical trends, but it has not given us a time schedule (Matt. 24:42–44). Prophetic date-setting and schedule-making are pitfalls into which many well-meaning Christians have fallen throughout church history. Because of it, this book will purposely avoid setting forth a time schedule of end-time prophecies. Instead, the prophesied events will simply be listed along with a brief description of some of the popular interpretations of these events. The reader should bear in mind that some, or perhaps all, of these interpretations may be incorrect. What was meant by each prophecy will become clear to the church only after the prophesied events have taken place.

Before Jesus was born, the Old Testament had given more than 300 specific predictions about the first coming of the Messiah. Every detail of these prophecies was precisely fulfilled in the first coming of Christ. The Jews of Jesus' day knew these prophecies, but unfortunately they did not recognize their fulfilment in their generation (e.g. Matt. 2:5–6; 27:39–44, Luke 4:17–29). Only later did the church correctly understand the fulfilment of these prophecies.

The return of Jesus Christ and the events at the close of this age are described with just as much detail as the prophecies concerning his first coming. There are more than 500 prophecies concerning the second coming of Christ. Since the prophecies of his first coming were fulfilled literally and historically, we can be sure that the prophecies concerning his second coming will also be literally fulfilled. Like the early church, however, we may not immediately recognize their fulfilment at the time they take place.

There are so many prophecies concerning the events near the time of Christ's return that it will only be possible to summarize them in this book. There are other books available which examine these prophecies in more detail. This book will only give a brief description of these prophecies.

PROPHECIES CONCERNING THE NATION OF ISRAEL

1. The Bible says that the Jewish people will be restored to the land of Israel a second time (Isa. 11:11–12, Zech. 10:8–10). The first

restoration of the Israelites to the land of Israel took place after the 70 years of Babylonian captivity (Jer. 29:10).

2. According to Ezekiel 37:1–14,21,25, the restoration of the Jews to the land of Israel takes place in three stages (bones joining, flesh added and life restored). This could include:

    (a) A physical regathering of the Jews. Such a world movement of Jews back to the ancient land of Israel began around 1900 AD and is still going on.

    (b) A political renewal (Amos 9:14–15) and an agricultural renewal of the land (Isa. 35:1–2). Historically, the modern independent state of Israel was born on May 14, 1948 after more than 2300 years without an independent Jewish homeland. Since that time, modern Israelis have made the 'wilderness . . . blossom' (Isa. 35:1–2) through the use of modern agriculture.

    (c) A spiritual rebirth. This may take place at the return of Christ when the unbelieving Jews see him in his glory (Zech. 12:9–14, Rom. 11:23–28).

3. According to Scripture, the city of Jerusalem will be fully restored to the Jews (Isa. 37:31–32, Zech. 12:5–8). This event will take place at the end of 'the times of the Gentiles' (Luke 21:24). Historically, the city of Jerusalem was fully restored to the Jews after 2600 years at the end of the Six Day War with the Arabs in 1967.

4. In the light of Matthew 24:14–15 and 2 Thessalonians 2:4, some Christians believe that the Jewish temple will be rebuilt. Animal sacrifices may be restored in the worship of this restored temple (Dan. 9:27). An article entitled, 'Time For A New Temple?' appeared in *Time Magazine* on October 16,1989. The article states that (a) the Jews are making preparations for a new temple, and (b) they are training priests for restored animal sacrifices in this temple.

PROPHECIES CONCERNING SATAN

1. The Bible speaks of a great increase in the activity of Satan and demons at the end of this age (Rev. 9:1–11; 12:7–12; 16:13–14). This will likely include a great increase in crime, violence and general wickedness (Matt. 24:10–12, Rev. 9:20–21).

2. False prophets and false teachings will abound (Matt. 24:10–11,24, 1 Tim. 4:1).

3. Many Christians believe that Satan will rule the whole world for a short time through a man he controls, known in the Bible as the beast (Rev. 13:1–8), the anti-Christ (1 John 2:18) and the lawless one (2 Thess. 2:8–9). This person will be the last, and perhaps the

worst, of many satanically energized, anti-Christian world rulers in history (1 John 2:18). Other such leaders have included people like the Roman emperor Nero and Adolf Hitler who was responsible for World War II.

The Bible says that the final evil world leader (the beast) will gain control over the world's money system and will require people to take a mark on the hand or forehead in order to buy or sell (Rev. 13:16–17). Through this leader, Satan will stir up a terrible persecution against both Jews (Jer. 30:5–7, Dan. 12:1,7, Rev. 12:13–14) and Christians (Rev. 7:14–17; 12:17; 20:4). Specific details of the time and rule of the beast are found in Daniel 7:8,11,20,25, 2 Thessalonians 2:3–12 and Revelation 13:1–18, and in other places in the Bible. This leader and his assistant, the miracle working 'false prophet,' are cast alive into the lake of fire (hell) at the return of Christ (Rev. 19:20).

4. Satan and his demons will intensify their opposition to God and his people, especially through persecution (Rev. 12:9,17).

Satan has been opposing God in many ways throughout history. As he sees the growth of the church with more and more people turning to Christ, he is intensifying his efforts to oppose God and his work. This can be seen in the very determined efforts to spread non-Christian religions, especially Islam, to many parts of the world. It can be seen in the great increase in murder, crime and violence all over the world. It can be seen in the great increase in pornography, sexual sin, abortion and drug addiction in Europe and North America. It can be seen in the renewed interest in traditional religions in Africa and an increasing interest in occult practices in Europe and North America. It can be seen in severe persecution of Christians in many parts of the world.

The non-Christian people living near the end of this age are described in the following way: 'The rest of mankind . . . still did not repent of the work of their hands; they did not stop worshipping demons, and idols . . . Nor did they repent of their murders, their magic arts, their sexual immorality or their thefts' (Rev. 9:20–21).

PROPHECIES CONCERNING THE CHURCH

1. Christians will be severely persecuted, worse than in any time in past history (Matt. 24:9, Rev. 6:9–10; 17:6; 20:4).

2. Because of persecution and wickedness, many superficially professing Christians will turn away from following Christ (Matt. 24:10,12, 2 Thess. 2:3, 1 Tim. 4:1, 2 Tim. 3:1–5).

3. The true Church (of faithful believers in Christ) will experience revival, in spite of the persecution (Luke 21:12–15, Acts 2:17–21, James 5:7–8).

4. The gospel will be preached to all the ethnic people groups in the world (Matt. 24:14, Rev. 5:9–10). During this time, a great multitude of people from all over the world will come to faith in Christ (Joel 3:14–16, Matt. 24:14, Rev. 7:9–15).

5. From among the unregenerate professing Christians of Christendom, a large politically-oriented world church will be organized. This unfaithful church is described in the Bible as an unfaithful wife, or prostitute (Rev. 17:1–18).

PROPHECIES CONCERNING CONDITIONS IN SOCIETY

1. Society will be characterized by increasing lawlessness and open wickedness, especially rebellion against parents and other authorities (2 Tim. 3:1–4). Brutality, murder, occult practices, stealing and sexual sins will increase greatly (Matt. 24:10,12, Rev. 9:21).

2. The conditions in society will be similar to the conditions before the flood in the time of Noah with respect to selfish living and indifference to God (Matt. 24:37–38, Luke 17:26–27). Conditions will also be like the days of Lot (Luke 17:28–29), which included the homosexual practices of Sodom and Gomorrah (Gen. 19:1–13). Such homosexual practices are becoming common today. Homosexuality and other sexual sins are the main cause of the AIDS epidemic in the world.

3. There will be severe famines in many places (Matt. 24:7, Rev. 6:5–6).

4. There will be severe inflation and a world money crisis (Rev. 6:5–6). Such a money crisis could set up the conditions for the anti-Christ to put his new world order and economic plan into effect (Rev. 13:7,16–17).

5. A confederation of ten European countries will apparently arise in the general geographical area of the old Roman Empire (Dan. 2:40–44). The beast may begin his rise to worldwide political power through this confederation of countries (Dan. 7:7–8,19–25, Rev. 17:12–17).

PROPHECIES CONCERNING THE PHYSICAL WORLD OF NATURE

1. There will be an increasing number of earthquakes around the world (Matt. 24:7). The final earthquake will shake the entire earth (Isa. 24:19–20, Rev. 16:18–20).

2. The earth's air and water will become polluted (Isa. 24:5–6, Rev. 11:18; 16:3–4).

3. The sun's heat will become much more intense, burning trees and grass on earth and drying up rivers (Isa. 30:26, Rev. 8:7; 16:8,12).

4. There will be changes in the earth's winds and weather, with increasingly severe hailstorms (Rev. 7:1; 11:19; 16:21).

5. The sun will be darkened and the moon will turn blood red in colour, just before the return of Christ (Joel 2:30–31, Matt. 24:29, Rev.6:12).

6. There will be a final convulsion and shaking of the earth and the entire universe (Isa. 24:19, Haggai 2:6, Heb. 12:26, Rev. 6:12–14).

C. WHAT WILL THE RETURN OF CHRIST BE LIKE?

The return of Christ will be a real future event in space and time, just as his first coming was a real event 2000 years ago (Matt. 16:27, Acts 1:11). The second coming of Christ must not be confused with meeting Jesus in heaven when we die (2 Cor. 5:6–8). Christians will indeed meet the Lord in heaven when they die, just as Jesus promised the repentant thief on the cross (Luke 23:43), but this is not the second coming of Christ as described in the Bible. When Jesus does return, the Bible says he will bring all the departed saints with him, in order to receive their resurrection bodies (1 Thess. 4:14–16).

The return of Christ will be the greatest event in all of human history. The description of the return of Christ given in the Bible is really beyond human imagination. Nothing which has ever happened in history can be compared to this event.

On that day every human being on earth will be staring at the sky in amazement and fear (Rev. 1:7). And it should be so, for the king of the universe will be returning to the world which he created. He will be returning to receive his eternal bride, the church. He will be returning as the conquering king, to take his throne and his eternal power to rule, as the God of heaven and earth. Jesus said he will return with, 'power and great glory' (Matt. 24:30). He will return visibly, just as he left, in his glorious resurrection body (Acts 1:11). He will be seen by the entire world (Rev. 1:7).

The Bible says he will be, 'revealed from heaven in blazing fire, with his powerful angels' (2 Thess. 1:7). Jesus said he would come, 'in his glory, and all the angels with him' (Matt. 25:31).

Jesus' return means the completion of God's salvation for his people, as we learned in chapter seven. He will return with the sound of a great trumpet (Matt. 24:31, 1 Thess. 4:16). At the moment of his return, the Christians who have died will arise from the dead and be lifted up to join Jesus in the sky. This will happen in the time it takes to blink your eyes (1 Cor. 15:51–52). At that moment Christians will receive resurrection bodies, just like the resurrection body of Christ himself (1 Cor. 15:52). A moment later, the living Christians left on the earth will also be physically transformed into the resurrection image of Christ and will be translated (lifted) into the sky to join Christ and the ones he has just raised from the dead (1 Cor. 15:51–52, 1 Thess. 4:16).

The Bible says, 'Our citizenship is in heaven. And we eagerly await a Saviour from there, the Lord Jesus Christ, who by the power which enables him to bring everything under his control, will transform our lowly bodies so that they will be like his glorious body' (Phil. 3:20–21).

Many other astonishing things will happen at the time of the return of Christ. The Bible says, 'The sky receded like a scroll, rolling up, and every mountain and island was removed from its place' (Rev. 6:14). The Bible speaks of an earthquake so great that, 'No earthquake like it has ever occurred since man has been on earth' (Rev. 16:18)! The Bible speaks of hailstones falling from the sky which weigh 100 pounds each (Rev. 16:21)! The Bible says, 'The sun will be darkened, and the moon will not give its light; the stars will fall from the sky, and the heavenly bodies will be shaken' (Matt. 24:29).

Who can even begin to imagine or describe such an awesome event? How can we picture the millions of angels of God in their brilliance and fire lighting up the entire sky? How can we imagine the millions of Christians suddenly being swept up into the sky from all over the earth in glorious resurrection bodies, to join the Lord and his vast host of mighty angels? How can we imagine the sky itself being rolled up like a scroll?

While this breathtaking scene is taking place in the heavens, the entire earth is being shaken apart by the greatest earthquake in the history of the world (Rev. 16:18). This earthquake is so great that the Bible says, 'every mountain and island was removed from its place' (Rev. 6:14). In another description of this earthquake the Bible says, 'The earth is broken up. The earth is split asunder, the earth is thoroughly shaken' (Isa. 24:19). Speaking of Christ's return in Haggai 2:6, the Lord promises, 'In a little while I will once more shake the heavens and the earth, the sea and the dry land. I will shake all nations, and the desired of all nations will come.'

For the redeemed saints of God, the return of Christ means they will finally be delivered from this evil, corrupt world (Rom. 8:21–23). It means they will be transformed into the glorious image of the Lord Jesus Christ himself (Phil. 3:21–22). For the rest of humanity, the return of Christ will be a terrifying event, which means they will finally be judged for their sinful behaviour. They will finally pay for all their rebellion against God (2 Thess. 1:7–10). The return of Christ is so awesome and fearful to the unsaved that it will make even the most courageous men in the world hide in panic and terror. The Bible says, 'Then the kings of the earth, the princes, the generals, the rich, the mighty, and every slave and every free man hid in caves and among the rocks of the mountains. They called to the mountains and the rocks,

"Fall on us, and hide us from the face of him who sits on the throne, and from the wrath of the Lamb! For the great day of their wrath has come, and who can stand" ' (Rev. 6:15–17)?

D. WHEN WILL CHRIST RETURN?

The Bible makes it clear that no one knows the exact moment of the return of Christ. The Bible does suggest, however, that the last generation of the church will sense that the time of his return is very near. The longest statement by Christ about his return is found in Matthew 24:1–25:46. During this discussion Jesus said, 'Even so, when you see all these things, you know that he is near, right at the door. I tell you the truth, this generation will certainly not pass away until all these things have happened' (Matt. 24:33–34). However, Jesus went on to say, 'No one knows about that day or hour, not even the angels in heaven nor the Son, but only the Father . . . . Therefore keep watch, because you do not know on what day your Lord will come' (Matt. 24:36,42). These two statements suggest that there is both a certainty and an uncertainty, about the time of Christ's return.

In his letter to the Thessalonians, Paul also said something about this certainty and uncertainty concerning the time of the Lord's return. Paul said, 'Now brothers, about times and dates, we do not need to write to you, for you know very well that the day of the Lord will come like a thief in the night . . . But you brothers are not in darkness, so that this day should surprise you like a thief' (1 Thess. 5:1–2,4).

Perhaps the best way to understand the apparent conflict between the certainty and uncertainty of the time of Christ's return is to consider the illustration of childbirth given by Jesus himself. In Matthew 24:7–8, Jesus said, 'Nation will rise against nation and kingdom against kingdom. There will be famines and earthquakes in various places. All these are the beginning of birth pains.'

When a woman begins to have birth pains, she knows that the birth of the baby is very near. However, no doctor in the world can state the precise moment at which the baby's head will appear. Sometimes the birth process takes many, many hours. Sometimes it takes less than one hour. The certainty is that when true birth pains have begun, the birth is not weeks or months away, it is very near.

So it will be with the return of Christ. There will be great birth pains in the world as the time of his return draws near. These birth pains are described in Matthew 24:1–25. Birth pains come closer together and with greater intensity as the final moment of birth approaches. It will likely be that way at the time of Christ's return. The birth pains will be a very difficult time on earth, but this will tell the Lord's people that their Saviour is about to return to take them to heaven forever (Luke 21:28).

E. HOW CAN A PERSON PREPARE FOR THE FINAL EVENTS OF THIS AGE AND FOR CHRIST'S RETURN?

The return of Christ is the blessed hope of the church (Titus 2:13). It is therefore important to study those passages in the Bible which refer to the second coming of Christ. Some of the important passages which do this are Matthew chapter 24–25, Mark 13, Luke 21, 1 Corinthians 15:35–58, 1 Thessalonians 4:13–5:10, 2 Thessalonians 1–2, 2 Peter 3, and Revelation 6–22.

As we saw earlier in this chapter, the end of the present age will be a time of terrible crime, violence, sexual immorality, occult power and persecution of Christians. Christians need to prepare themselves for the last days. They need to:

(a) Be strong in prayer (Eph. 6:18, 1 Pet. 4:7).
(b) Walk in holiness of life (2 Pet. 3:11, 1 John 3:2–3).
(c) Become strong in the Lord and learn to use the weapons of spiritual warfare against Satan (2 Cor.10:3–4, Eph. 6:10–19).
(d) Learn to really love and forgive fellow-Christians (Col. 3:12–14; 1 Pet. 4:8).
(e) Gather together regularly with other believers for encouragement and fellowship (Matt. 18:19–20, Heb. 10:25).
(f) Be ready to witness boldly to others about Jesus, regardless of persecution (Acts 1:8; 1 Pet. 3:14–15).
(g) Become seriously involved in reaching the remaining unreached people groups in the world with the gospel (Matt. 24:14, Matt 28:19–20).

The emphasis on the second coming of Christ in the New Testament is very practical. Without exception, the emphasis is always on present holy living and faithful service for Christ. Nowhere does the Bible encourage us to try to calculate or discover the exact time of Christ's return. Nowhere are we encouraged to make elaborate charts or schemes about the order of events in the last days of this age. Yet many books which deal with the return of Christ mainly try to prove some schedule of events. This is a wrong emphasis. It is a failure to understand the New Testament teaching about the return of Christ.

Jesus showed his disciples that there was something much more important for them than to know the schedule of the final events of history. They were to be his faithful witnesses, even unto death, if necessary (Rev. 2:10). We must faithfully witness to others about Christ since we have the certainty of his return. We must faithfully proclaim his salvation to all who will listen. Jesus said we must do this among our own people, 'in Jerusalem', among other groups of people in our country, 'in all Judea and Samaria', and among people from every country and culture in the world, 'to the ends of the earth', (Acts 1:8).

A local church which does not have a missionary emphasis is not a vital part of God's work in this age. When Jesus returns, he will judge his people as to whether or not they have been faithful. If they have been faithful, they will receive a reward from Christ (1 Cor. 3:14). If they have not been faithful, they will suffer loss (1 Cor. 3:15). The Bible says, 'For we must all appear before the judgment seat of Christ, that each one may receive what is due him for the things done while in the body, whether good or bad' (2 Cor. 5:10). No Christian will escape this judgment on the way he has lived his life as a believer. We are warned to be faithful.

In Jesus' long discussion in Matthew 24:1–25:46 about his return and the events which will accompany his return, he told four stories. The interesting thing is that these four stories teach only two simple lessons, each lesson twice. The lessons are to be ready and to be faithful. These two lessons summarize how the New Testament applies the truth of the second coming of Christ to the daily life of a Christian.

In Matthew 24:37–44, Jesus identified several groups of people who were not prepared for his return and the lesson was, 'So you also must be ready'. In Matthew 24:45–51 he told a story about two faithful slaves and an unfaithful one, whose master had gone away. The lesson was, 'Who then is the faithful and wise servant'. In Matthew 25:1–13 he told a story about ten virgin girls and the lesson was to be ready for the bridegroom's return. In Matthew 25:14–30, he told a story about three men who each received a different amount of money, 'talents', and were told to trade with it. The lesson was, 'Well done, good and faithful servant.'

The most important truth about the return of Christ is that it will definitely take place at God's appointed time. The people of God must be ready. They must be faithful.

What does it mean to be ready? The Apostle Peter explained what it means to be ready when he spoke about the second coming of Christ in 2 Peter 3. In this passage Peter said, 'But the day of the Lord will come like a thief. The heavens will disappear with a roar; the elements will be destroyed by fire, and the earth and everything in it will be laid bare. Since everything will be destroyed in this way, what kind of people ought you to be? You ought to live holy and godly lives as you look forward to the day of God and speed its coming' (2 Pet. 3:10–12).

The Apostle John said something very similar. In 1 John 3:2–3 he said, 'We know that when he appears, we shall be like him, for we shall see him as he is. Everyone who has this hope in him purifies himself, just as he is pure.' With emphasis on the same idea, the Apostle Paul said, 'For the grace of God that brings salvation has appeared to all men. It teaches us to say "No" to ungodliness and worldly passions, and to live self-controlled, upright, and godly lives in this present age, while we wait for the blessed hope – the glorious appearing of our great God and Saviour, Jesus Christ' (Titus 2:11–13).

According to these three apostles of Christ, being ready for Christ's return means living a holy life. This means a life free from lies, free from pride and selfish ambition, free from lust, free from greed, free from tribalism and prejudice, free from bitterness and unforgiveness and free from all the other things which make our lives impure and unholy. If a Christian is not living a holy life, he is not ready for the return of Christ.

F. WHAT ARE SOME OF THE MAIN THEORIES ABOUT THE ORDER OF EVENTS AT THE TIME OF THE RETURN OF CHRIST?

The order of events at the time of the return of Christ has been debated by the church for many centuries. There have been godly and capable scholars on every side of this debate. The surprising thing is that the theories of these scholars are often so different. Why is that? First of all, these events have not yet taken place, so there is a difference of opinion about the meaning of various prophecies. Second, different groups of Christians use different systems of Bible interpretation, hermeneutics, in order to interpret the meaning of prophecy. These different systems of interpretation lead scholars to very different conclusions about the meaning of the same prophetic statements. Third, the order of end-time events is not plainly stated as a schedule in the Bible. If it was presented in that way, there would probably be no disagreement.

One example of these differences of opinion is the statement that the saints, 'came to life and reigned with Christ for a thousand years' (Rev. 20:4–NASB). Revelation 20 is the only passage in the Bible where there is a specific reference to this event, lasting for 1000 years. Many Christians believe this prophecy refers to a literal earthly reign of Christians with Christ for a literal period of 1000 years. They call this period the millennium. Many other Christians do not think this prophecy refers to a literal period of time or to a literal, physical rule with Christ.

Christians who hold the view of a literal 1000 years of rule with Christ believe that Jesus will return just before this period in order to set up an earthly kingdom. Christians with this persuasion are called pre-millennialists. Even among pre-millennialists, there are several different views about what happens just before the millennium.

There is a period of great trouble in the world prophesied to take place just before Christ returns. This period of time is called the great tribulation in Matthew 24:21 and Revelation 7:14. Pre-millennialists ask whether Christ will return for his church before, during, or at the end, of this period of great tribulation. Those who believe he will return before the tribulation are pre-millennial and pre-tribulational. Those who believe he will come in the middle of the tribulation period are pre-millennial and mid-tribulational. Those who believe he will come at the end of the tribulation are pre-millennial and post-tribulational.

Many other Christians do not believe that the reference to 1000 years refers to a literal period of time at all. They point out that the book of Revelation is mainly written in poetic and symbolic language, rather than in literal statements. To them, the prophecy of Revelation 20:4 should be interpreted symbolically. Some would say that the 1000 years simply refers to a long period of time. Others would say that the 1000–year reign refers to a spiritual rather than a physical reign with Christ. Among those who believe that the millennium is a spiritual reign, some believe that it is presently taking place. Since Christians with this viewpoint do not expect a literal period of 1000 years, a millennium, on earth, they are called amillennialists.

Still another group believes that Christ will return to the earth only after the preaching of the gospel has generally christianized the whole world. To them, the millennium is established through the expansion of the church by the increase and promotion of the kingdom of God throughout the world. To this group, the millennium may now be in progress. Christians with this persuasion are called post-millennialists. Concerning the time of the great tribulation, amillennialists and post-millennialists simply recognize that there will be such a time just before the return of Christ.

There are also other opinions about the meaning of Revelation 20:4 and other end-time prophecies, as well as variations of the viewpoints just given. However, for the brief discussion in this book, Christian opinions about the last events of this age are grouped into the pre-millennial, amillennial and post-millennial theological positions.

Each of these groups of Christians are equally committed to the authority and accuracy of the Bible. Each group, however, has a different approach to the interpretation of end-time prophecies. A good rule of fellowship is to agree concerning the major truths that are clearly stated in the Bible and not to argue over details which are uncertain. It is wise to be patient with fellow-Christians who have a different opinion over the details of the final order of events. When the time comes, everyone will discover what each prophecy meant. In reference to the second coming of Christ, clear truth would include the fact that Christ will return to this world physically, visibly, and bodily (Acts 1:11) and that Christians will rise from the dead at his return (1 Cor 15: 50–54).

G. WHY WILL CHRIST RETURN?

The return of Christ is the final event of this age. It is the climax of present history. It is the time when Jesus will complete his great work of salvation for his people which he began with his death, his resurrection and his ascension (Rom. 13:11, 1 Pet. 1:5). There are many things which are not right at the present time which God will set right at the return of Christ. He intends to finish what is unfinished business when Christ returns.

In the present age it often happens that the righteous suffer while the wicked escape suffering. It often happens that Christians are persecuted and harmed, while those who harm them go unpunished. It often happens that evil triumphs instead of good in the affairs of men. Wicked rulers and wicked men revel in their riches and go unpunished. Christians weep in pain, in poverty and in persecution and they die in discouragement. All this is going to be changed by the return of Jesus Christ. What will Christ accomplish by his return?

JESUS WILL GATHER HIS PEOPLE TO HIMSELF (JOHN 14:2–3)

No matter what happens to Christians in this world, they have a certain joyous hope that one day Jesus is going to return and gather his loved ones to be with himself for ever (1 Thess. 4:16–17). In John 14:2–3 Jesus said, 'In my Father's house are many rooms; if it were not so I would have told you. I am going there to prepare a place for you. And if I go and prepare a place for you, I will come back and take you to be with me that you also may be where I am.' According to 1 Thessalonians 4:16–17, Christians are resurrected and translated to be with the Lord at the time of his return. The Bible says, 'For the Lord himself will come down from heaven with a loud command, with the voice of the archangel and with the trumpet call of God, and the dead in Christ will rise first. After that, we who are still alive and are left will be caught up together with them in the clouds to meet the Lord in the air. And so we will be with the Lord for ever' (1 Thess. 4:16–17). What a glorious hope for every Christian to anticipate! It will be the most exciting and joyful day a Christian has ever experienced!

JESUS WILL RAISE ALL THE DEAD (JOHN 5:25–29)

The Old Testament says, 'Multitudes who sleep in the dust of the earth will awake: some to everlasting life, others to shame and everlasting contempt' (Dan. 12:2). Jesus said, 'a time is coming when all who are in their graves will hear his (i.e. Christ's) voice and come out-those who have done good will rise to live, and those who have done evil will rise to be condemned' (John 5:28–29). Christians who have died will be raised from the dead at the moment of Christ's return and receive resurrection bodies just like Christ's body (1 Cor. 15:51–52, Phil. 3:21, 1 Thess. 4:15–17).

Pre-millennialists believe that only the resurrection of Christians takes place at the return of Christ before the millennium. Pre-millennialists believe that the resurrection of non-Christians takes place at the end of a literal 1000–year millennium. Revelation 20:4–6 states, 'I saw the souls of those who had been beheaded because of their testimony for Jesus and because of the word of God . . . . They came to life and reigned with Christ a thousand years. The rest of the dead did not come to life until the thousand years were ended. This is the first resurrection. Blessed and holy are those who have part in the first resurrection. The second death has no power over them, but they will be priests of God and of Christ, and will reign with him for a thousand years.'

Amillennialists and post-millennialists believe that the resurrection of both Christians and non-Christians is part of a single great event at the return of Christ.

JESUS WILL REWARD HIS SERVANTS, THE SAINTS AND THE PROPHETS (REV. 11:18)

There are many Christians who have lived faithfully for the Lord. Jesus knows what they have done and he has not forgotten their works of love for him (Heb. 6:10). Unfortunately, there are other Christians who have lived selfish, useless lives. The Lord knows about them as well. At his return, Jesus is going to hold a judgment for his people (2 Cor. 5:10). Those who have served him faithfully will receive rewards according to their service and faithfulness (Matt. 25:14–30).

There will be great differences between Christians according to what they have done. At this judgment, Jesus will give eternal rewards to those who have been faithful. Those who have been unfaithful will bear the sorrow of losing rewards they could have received from Christ (1 Cor. 3:13–15).

JESUS WILL END THE CONTROL OF SATAN OVER THIS WORLD (REV. 19:20; 20:1–2)

One of the most wonderful things Jesus will do at his return is to overcome the power of Satan in the world, as well as to end the reign of terror of the anti-Christ. He will send an angel to bind Satan with a great chain, and to throw Satan into the abyss (bottomless hole), where he will be imprisoned for 1000 years (Rev. 20:1–3). The beast (the anti-Christ) and his assistant, the false prophet, will be cast directly into the eternal fire of hell at Christ's return to be punished for ever and ever (Rev. 19:20).

The fallen angels will also be imprisoned at the same time as Satan, since Satan is their master (Isa. 24:21–22, Matt. 12:24–26). Referring to that time, the Bible says, 'the LORD will punish the host of heaven, on high, and the kings of the earth, on earth. And they will be gathered together like prisoners in the dungeon, and will be confined in prison; And after many days they will be punished' (Isa. 24:21–22–NASB).

After the 1000 years are finished, Satan will try to carry out one final rebellion against Christ (Rev. 20:7–8). For this final rebellion, he and his demons will be thrown into the eternal fires of hell where they will be tormented and punished for ever and ever (Isa. 24:22, Matt. 25:41, Rev. 20:7–10)

JESUS WILL JUDGE ALL PEOPLE ACCORDING TO THEIR DEEDS (MATT. 25:31–33)

A day of judgment is coming. All those who have ever lived are going to give an account to Jesus Christ for everything they have done or said (Matt. 12:36–37, John 5:22,27, Rom. 14:12). At Christ's coming, the wicked, not the righteous, will suffer. The wicked will pay fully for everything they have done (Psalm 37:12–15).

God will not endure mankind's rebellion for ever. At last his great wrath will be poured out on sinners. The Bible says this is what happened in the flood of Noah's time (Gen. 6:11–13). In the days of Noah people refused to listen to the voice of God's Spirit for 120 years (Gen. 6:3,5,11), so God destroyed them in a judgment of water (Gen. 6:13). The same thing will happen again, except that the final judgment on this world will not be through water, but through terrible fire (2 Peter 3:10).

At the time of Christ's return, Christians will be the first to be called to account for how they have lived (2 Cor. 5:10, 1 Peter 4:17). They will be judged by what they have done for Christ as Christians (1 Cor. 3:10–15). On the basis of this judgment they will either gain or lose eternal rewards (1 Cor. 3:14–15). The judgment of Christians does not have to do with finding or losing salvation, since that was settled when they put their faith in Christ (John 3:16; 5:24). The judgment of Christians is a time of rewarding those who have lived faithfully for Christ (Rev. 11:18).

The non-Christians who are still living on the earth at the time of Christ's return will be judged on the basis of how they treated the people of God (Matt. 25:31–46). Those who mistreated the people of God will be cast into eternal fire (Matt. 25:41–46).

Jesus will also raise all non-Christians from the dead, who died in former times (Dan. 12:2, John 5:28–29). They will stand before the great white throne of God's holy judgment (Rev. 20:11–15). This judgment is so awesome and terrifying that the Bible says, 'Earth and sky fled from his presence, and there was no place for them' (Rev. 20:11). Men and women will be judged for all they have done as non-Christians. The Bible says, 'The dead were judged according to what they had done as recorded in the books. The sea gave up the dead that were in it, and death and Hades gave up the dead that were in them, and each person was judged according to what he had done. Then death and Hades were thrown into the lake of fire. The lake of fire is the second death. If anyone's name was not found written in the book of life, he was thrown into the lake of fire' (Rev. 20:12–14).

JESUS WILL SET UP A RIGHTEOUS GOVERNMENT OVER THIS WORLD (ISAIAH 9:6–7).

Psalm 91:9 says, 'He comes to judge the earth. He will judge the world in righteousness, and the peoples with equity.' This use of the word judgment refers to Christ's rule over the world following his return. In the Psalms, God the Father says to Christ, 'Ask of me, and I make the nations your inheritance, the ends of the earth your possession. You will rule them with an iron scepter; you will dash them to pieces like pottery' (Psalm 2:8). In Revelation 11:17 the elders in heaven cry out, 'We give thanks to you, Lord God Almighty, the One who is and who was, because you have taken your great power and have begun to reign.'

The rule of Christ will be a time of righteousness, peace and indescribable blessing for the world. Christ will put a stop to all wars, crime, evil and violence. Even in the animal world there will be true peace all over the world (Isa. 11:4–9). The Bible says, 'Of the increase of his government and peace, there will be no end' (Isa. 9:7). The Bible says, 'With justice he will give decisions for the poor of the earth . . . with the breath of his lips he will slay the wicked . . . the cow will feed with the bear, their young will lie down together, and the lion will eat straw like the ox. The infant will play near the hole of the cobra. . . . They will neither harm nor destroy on all my holy mountain, for the earth will be full of the knowledge of the Lord, as the waters cover the sea' (Isa. 11:4–9).

JESUS WILL CREATE A NEW HEAVEN AND A NEW EARTH. HE WILL RESTORE ALL OF NATURE TO PERFECTION (ISA. 65:17, REV. 21:1).

The glorious salvation of Christ and his return to this world will affect everything in the world. He will create a new heaven and a new earth which is purged of sin. The Apostle Peter wrote, 'But according to his promise, we are looking for new heavens and a new earth, in which righteousness dwells' (2 Pet. 3:13–NASB). Paul explained, 'We know that the whole creation has been groaning, as in the pains of childbirth, right up to the present time' (Rom. 8:22). But the glorious hope is that, 'the creation itself will be liberated from its bondage to decay, and brought into the glorious freedom of the children of God' (Rom. 8:21).

The beautiful conditions of this new heavens and new earth are described in Isaiah 65:17–25 and Revelation 21:1–5. In both passages, it is stated that there will be no more mourning or crying. Revelation 21:4 adds that there will be no more pain or death, 'for the old order of things has passed away.' In Revelation 21:5 it is stated that God will make everything new. In Isaiah, conditions of peace, harmony, satisfaction and blessing are described. 'The wolf and the lamb will feed together . . . . They will neither harm nor destroy on all my holy mountain, says the LORD' (Isa. 65:25).

The salvation of Jesus Christ means much more than the forgiveness of our sins and the hope of eternal life. It means a complete re-birth of the whole universe into a beautiful and perfect place where sin has been eliminated and where the terrible and painful effects of sin have been put away for ever. Think of what that means! No more sickness, suffering and death. No more tragedy and grief. No more loss of loved ones. No more deformed or retarded children. No more broken homes and broken hearts. No more bitterness, resentment, hatred, greed, anger and abuse. No more crime and violence. No more wars and killing. No more injustice and oppression of the poor and needy.

What a glorious hope for those who have put their faith in the Lord Jesus Christ! The salvation of God is greater than any human being could ever imagine. Paul wrote, 'No eye has seen, no ear has heard, no mind has conceived what God has prepared for those who love him' (1 Cor. 2:9). That is God's promise to those who have received Christ!

SUMMARY

What will be the final outcome of history? The Bible tells us where history is leading and how it will end. The Bible assures us that there will one day be a 'new heaven and a new earth, the home of righteousness' (2 Peter 3:13). But what will happen before that golden age? The Bible predicts many things that will take place as the end of history approaches. These events are related to what God and Satan are doing in the present world.

God is building the church of Jesus Christ with people from every tribe and nation on earth. At the same time Satan is fighting to oppose and delay that work by bringing about evil of many kinds in the world, such as moral corruption, crime, violence, political upheaval, wars, natural disasters and much more. This great spiritual war will finally end with the personal, visible, bodily return of Jesus Christ to this world.

The return of Christ will be the most awesome event ever witnessed in this world. The earth and the heavens will be physically shaken apart when the King of the universe returns with his holy angels. His return will bring unspeakable joy to those who know him and love him, and unspeakable terror to his enemies. But the time of his return remains a secret which no one knows. His people are warned to be ready and to be faithful. To be ready means to be living lives of holiness and commitment to Christ. To be faithful means to serve him with an undivided heart.

When he returns, Jesus will gather his people to himself (John 14:2–3), raise all the dead (John 5:25–29), reward his servants, the saints and the prophets (Rev. 11:18), end the rule of the anti-Christ and end the control of Satan over this world (Rev. 19:20; Rev. 20:1–2), judge all people according to their deeds (Matt. 25:31–33), set up a righteous government over this world, where evil will not be tolerated (Isa. 9:6–7), and create a new heaven and a new earth. He will restore all of nature to perfection (Isa. 65:17, Rev. 21:1). Truly, God will have the last word in history, and no enemy will stand before him. He will reign in glory and majesty for ever and ever, and his people will reign with him.

DISCUSSION QUESTIONS AND PROJECTS BASED ON
CHAPTER EIGHTEEN

1. Most of us feel that things were better in the times long ago, in the days of our forefathers. In what specific ways does the Bible reveal that things will be even better after Jesus returns to the world than they were in the beginning?

2. Statistics prove that crime, violence and evil are increasing in the world today. Let members of the group testify to this fact using incidents they have recently heard of or experienced.

3. Describe seven things which Jesus will accomplish by his return to this world.

4. Divide into small groups of three each. Discuss the matter of what it means to be ready for the return of Christ. Each group should make a list of five to ten specific things which they can do in order to be ready for the return of Christ.

5. Discuss the African concept of time. Then discuss the biblical concept of time and compare these two viewpoints.

6. Divide into small groups of four each. Read Psalm 2:4–12 and Zechariah 14:16–21. Ask each group to make a list of the conditions which will exist when Jesus Christ sets up his government over the world following his return.

7. Read 1 Corinthians 15:35–51 and Luke 24:36–43 aloud as a basis from which to discuss the characteristics of the resurrection body of believers.

8. Discuss the African concept of life after death. Compare this to the Bible's description of conditions when the new heaven and new earth are established, according to Isaiah 65:17–25 and Revelation 21:1–8.

9. Let everyone read Matthew 24:27–31, 1 Corinthians 15:49–53 and 1 Thessalonians 4:14–17. Based on the description given in these passages, ask two people to describe to the group the appearing of Jesus Christ and the resurrection and translation of Christians.

10. What will happen to Satan and his demons at the return of Christ? What will happen to the anti-Christ? Find Bible verses to prove your answer.

SUGGESTED FOR FURTHER READING

Berkouwer, G.C. *The Return of Christ*. Grand Rapids: Eerdmans, 1972.

Cotterell, P. *Dealing with Death*. London: Scripture Union, 1994.

Hoekema, A.A. *The Bible and the Future*. Carlisle: Paternoster Press, 1994.

Pawson, David. *When Jesus Returns*. London: Hodder, reprinted 1995.

Pentecost, J. Dwight. *Things To Come*. Grand Rapids, Michigan: Zondervan, 1990.

Travis, S. *I Believe in the Second Coming of Jesus*. London: Hodder, reprinted 1994.

Index